TEACHING
READING
THINKING
STUDY SKILLS

in Content Classrooms Third Edition

Marian J. Tonjes
Western Washington University

Miles V. Zintz
Late of University of New Mexico

WCB   **Wm. C. Brown Publishers**

Book Team

Editor *Paul L. Tavenner*
Developmental Editor *Sue Pulvermacher-Alt*
Production Coordinator *Carla D. Arnold*

 Wm. C. Brown Publishers

President *G. Franklin Lewis*
Vice President, Publisher *Thomas E. Doran*
Vice President, Operations and Production *Beverly Kolz*
National Sales Manager *Virginia S. Moffat*
Group Sales Manager *Eric Ziegler*
Executive Editor *Edgar J. Laube*
Director of Marketing *Kathy Law Laube*
Marketing Manager *Pamela S. Cooper*
Managing Editor, Production *Colleen A. Yonda*
Manager of Visuals and Design *Faye M. Schilling*
Production Editorial Manager *Julie A. Kennedy*
Production Editorial Manager *Ann Fuerste*
Publishing Services Manager *Karen J. Slaght*

WCB Group

President and Chief Executive Officer *Mark C. Falb*
Chairman of the Board *Wm. C. Brown*

Cover and interior design by Sailer & Cook Creative Services

Copyedited by Kathy Pruno

Printed in the United States of America by Wm. C. Brown Publishers, 2460 Kerper Boulevard, Dubuque, IA 52001

10 9 8 7 6 5 4 3 2 1

Dedicated to
Felicia E. Benton
and Mary Hatley
Zintz, and to the
memory of M.
Warren Benton

In Memoriam

Miles V. Zintz, Professor Emeritus of the University of New Mexico, often referred to as "Mr. Reading of New Mexico," died July 25, 1989, leaving behind a great legacy of life that he devoted to sharing with others through his charismatic teaching, his voluminous writing, and his continuous consulting. We will miss his tremendous enthusiasm and unstinting assistance to people of all cultures. For those of us who knew him, he served as a model of a true educator.

Although critically ill his last summer he managed to tie up loose ends of his many-faceted career, support a former colleague for a national teaching honor, complete other editions of his texts, and perform necessary preliminaries for this third edition, among other things.

Miles Zintz will long be missed. He was irreplaceable as a scholar, humanitarian, model, and beloved friend. Contributions to the Miles V. Zintz Memorial Scholarship Fund may be sent to Dr. Zelda Maggart, CIMTE, University of New Mexico, Albuquerque, New Mexico 87131.

Contents

12 Identifying Writing Patterns and Content-Specific Skills 383

13 Getting It All Together: Reading/Thinking/Study Skills across the Curriculum 407

Appendixes 421

Cognitive Maps and Workshop Activities

Preface

Content teachers usually understand their job as one of guiding students in the learning of a specific subject matter, where the necessary ability to read meaningfully is taken for granted. Although this ability is, in fact, clearly a necessity, it cannot, sadly enough, be taken for granted. Far too many students today are deficient in the basic reading/thinking/study skills deemed necessary to master the content of their texts. Their writing skills could also be improved. And to compound matters, the range of reading levels in any given class widens as students advance through the grades. When improvements in reading occur, the gap tends to widen between the poorest and ablest readers.

Teachers and administrators at all levels have shown increasing concern and interest in finding ways to deal with these problems. At the upper elementary level they are beginning to look more seriously at assisting students in mastery techniques for expository technical writing, not just with the descriptive narrative style found in literature. At the middle and secondary school levels, neither the special reading teachers nor the English department teachers alone can be expected to do the entire job. It takes the concerted effort of each and every content teacher in science, math, foreign language, physical education, vocational education, home economics, English, social studies, and the arts to bridge the gap.

Reading is a major avenue to learning and certainly one of the most efficient. Content teachers are *not* expected to become reading specialists, nor is this necessary in order to incorporate strategies in the class that enhance reading/thinking/study and writing skills. All content teachers will be closer to the goal of student mastery of and positive attitude toward a specific subject area if they assist students to:

1. skim/survey the material to obtain an overview and purpose for reading;
2. systematically develop key vocabulary and concepts;
3. give attention to interpretation of graphics;
4. use study strategies consistently and efficiently;

5. use and coordinate a variety of materials written at appropriate levels;

6. think logically and write thoughts coherently.

Historically, then, in reading practices, teachers have emphasized the "learning to read" skills for stories or children's literature and at the same time have passed lightly over those "reading to learn" skills needed for content reading. There is little assurance in the literature that there is an automatic transfer of learning from one type of writing to the other.

Also, it is still a common practice to select one content text for an entire class and to require everyone to read it for content mastery, regardless of the text's readability level or the class's range of reading ability. No wonder schools are faced with the widespread problem of underachievement and failure!

The concept of developmental reading means that there is a hierarchy of skills and cognition levels that need to be addressed throughout the student's school life in terms of vocabulary development, higher levels of thinking and comprehension, and study skills. Those students who are reading up to or close to their capacity are considered to be developmental readers. One of the strongest reasons why the teaching of reading/thinking/ study skills must continue through the secondary school is that inherent in each subject is the development of many new concepts or meanings. Whereas elementary school children learn to read words that are mostly a part of their listening and speaking vocabulary, older students are continually exposed to newer, unknown technical terms as well as to general or common words that have taken on new or specialized meanings. This emphasis on specialized meanings is quite different from the teaching of vocabulary that commonly occurs in teaching how to read at lower grade levels. For accurate communication, authors and readers must have some common understanding of a concept represented by words or symbols. The teaching of reading/thinking/study skills and the teaching of content are actually quite similar in that each is concerned with concept development.

A school's basic philosophy will determine which of the common elements in the reading act will be emphasized. If the program of the school is content-centered, the emphasis may be on literal comprehension and the recall of facts; if it is process-centered, students will be learning how to learn in such ways that the process will be applicable to their reading and writing for the rest of their lives. In other words, in the process-centered program, the emphasis will be on such things as reading critically, locating and collating information, broadening interests in reading, communicating thoughts clearly through writing, and using higher-order thinking skills.

Special Features of the Third Edition

Important concepts that have been further delineated in this third edition include cooperative learning; writing strategies; unmet needs of our schools today; ethics, values, and our cultural heritage; parents' attitudes toward reading in schools; and censorship concerns.

Additional teaching strategies have been interspersed throughout and references have been updated for each chapter. Chapters 10 and 11 have been carefully reworked for further clarity and timeliness.

Joseph P. McDonald talks about the importance of acknowledging our values, our basic assumptions, when planning for educational change.[1] By writing it down we produce a framework from which to react and expand. Because we believe in practicing what we preach, here is our statement of beliefs, not in any priority order.

WE BELIEVE:

1. in integrating knowledge—blurring borders between subjects, rising above our individual content area ruts, and bringing a fresh perspective to learning.
2. that reading, thinking, writing, and studying are not separate subjects or entities but flow across the entire curriculum.
3. in cooperative teaching and learning, allowing for freedom of choice when feasible.
4. that everyone has the potential for creativity, but that for many it has been downplayed in early years; yet to flourish it must be encouraged and practiced often.
5. in creating a nonthreatening, stimulating classroom environment in which students feel free to risk, experiment, and make mistakes without ridicule.
6. in the innate dignity and worth of every student, no matter what the student's background, culture, or ability.
7. that the process—or keys to opening avenues of learning—is as important or even more so than the product or knowledge gained. When we feel comfortable with how and when to perform the process, we will be more apt to continue learning on our own, and then the knowledge gained will be more personally meaningful.
8. in modeling or practicing what we preach, using exemplars when possible. We should not, for example, just tell our students to summarize, we should first remind or show them how.
9. that because we organize, store, and retrieve knowledge by categorizing data into patterns, we should make it a common practice to construct a cognitive map of our learnings.
10. that teaching is not just telling, nor is it an easy task, if performed properly; that it takes continuous effort, study, and willingness to try the unknown; that it takes a caring heart.

---

[1]Joseph P. McDonald, "When Outsiders Try to Change Schools From the Inside," *Phi Delta Kappan* 71 (November 1989): 206–212.

A Sampling of Content Techniques

Content area teachers may use any of the following techniques without detracting in the long run from time needed for the teaching/learning activities that they have used in the past. As a sample, teachers may:

1. pretest the class for entering knowledge and attitudes (chap. 1);
2. motivate learning and determine interests and needs in a variety of specified ways (chap. 2);
3. evaluate class texts for readability levels (chap. 3);
4. match students to texts by administering their own content informal reading inventory (Content IRI) or, alternatively, a cloze test taken from their text (chap. 4);
5. use walk-through techniques, such as skimming, in previewing as a way to improve effective reading (chap. 5);
6. develop with students key technical vocabulary in preparation for study reading (chap. 6);
7. help students identify types of paragraph organization—expository or narrative—as a comprehension aid (chap. 7);
8. work through with students the SQ3R strategy or its counterpart at periodic intervals to encourage deeper understanding and retention (chap. 8);
9. use grouping techniques to help meet the wide range of reading abilities in each class (chap. 9);
10. teach a content lesson using the format of a directed reading-thinking activity (DRTA) (chap. 9);
11. prepare cognitive maps, structured overviews, or advance organizers for efficient study reading (chap. 10);
12. use collateral reading to enrich and expand the horizons of classroom learning (chap. 11);
13. assist students in identifying writing patterns common to their text (chap. 12).

Who Is the Intended Audience?

This text is intended primarily for college classes in content area reading, grades four through twelve, and/or for middle and secondary school developmental reading courses. It is designed to meet the needs of preservice and inservice teachers in a variety of content areas. Those who have not had a prior course in reading should find sufficient explanation of basic concepts, whereas those students who enter with extensive reading background should find much of direct value in their work with developmental students and in assisting other teachers to implement related strategies in their schools.

Because of its practical emphasis and because each chapter is complete in itself, this text should also prove useful in staff development workshops in local school districts.

This text, although designed primarily to be used in college courses, should prove to be equally effective for inservice workshops. The emphasis is on getting readers to interact with the text. Interspersed throughout the chapters are workshop activities, which should assist the instructor in providing in-class activities to complement lectures. These suggested activities are boxed off from the body of the chapter so as not to interrupt the flow of reading when an activity is to be omitted.

On the page immediately prior to each chapter is a section titled "Anticipatory Questions." Each question is labeled according to the general level of the cognitive domain it addresses. Students should be instructed to use these questions first as purpose-setting guides prior to reading. Questions should then be used as a review following the initial reading. Later, they also may serve as a study guide for test review. Instructors may wish to add, revise, or delete some questions according to their own purposes.

The section immediately adjacent to the questions is titled "Technical Terminology and Concepts." Students should be asked to look over the list prior to reading as another readiness exercise. Terms may be categorized, prioritized, or merely identified in context. All terms listed are explained within the chapter, and many appear in the glossary.

Each chapter also contains a cognitive map—a graphic representation of the central theme or topic. Each map attempts to show interrelationships between and among items and may serve as an overview and a summary review. The cognitive map may also be used as an informal pretest or as a basis for student input about which aspects they wish emphasized. In this case the maps could be considered as structured overviews because of student comment and questions. Development of such a map is a demanding exercise, requiring a holistic grasp of the material. These maps reflect our suppositions and beliefs at the time of writing and are subject to adaptation or change. At times the shapes seem to lend themselves to the topic at hand, which adds a playful aspect.

The chapter on rate is deliberately placed earlier than usual in the sequence of chapters to allow students more practice time to work on their own skills. If this practice is not included as a course requirement, then it may be assigned to be read following the chapter on study skills.

We believe that chapter 11 on collateral reading, by curriculum librarian Enid Haag, is an important contribution to the field, because it is to our knowledge the only one of its kind to appear in a current text on content reading.

For those who wish to use this text in a competency or modular format, a suggested management strategy for conferences and student record-keeping follows.

A Suggested Management Strategy

Depending on class size and instructor time limits, ten- to fifteen-minute conferences may be scheduled three times a term; before or after class, during office hours, or during three class sessions. If held during the regular class time, others may be working on their library or small group assignments as suggested in each chapter. (These assignments are set off typographically under the heading "Workshop Activity.")

As an alternative to individual conferences, meet with students in pairs or triads, which has the advantages of saving time and allowing students to learn from one another. If there is a buddy system, buddies may work cooperatively and attend the conference together, alternating responses.

Students bring to each conference their record sheets, a model of which is shown at the end of this preface. (The tasks are deliberately left blank here for instructor selection.) This record sheet shows completion dates of chapters and tasks, instructors' initials to verify completion, and grades or points with possible comments.

At the end of the term students record the grade expected and instructors write in the final grade during the last conference.

To encourage more creativity, student self-evaluations can be required at midterm and finals time. These may be in the form of a poem, story, cognitive map, or report card and will help students develop their own criteria for evaluating.

Because applied learning is more relevant than passive interpretation, instructors are encouraged to allow their college students to try out material in the schools whenever possible. For example, the chapter on diagnosis describes how to construct a Content Informal Reading Inventory. It will have a more profound effect on college students if they construct such an inventory and find out how it works in a real classroom situation. The same might be done with the DRTA (Directed Reading-Thinking Activity).

All content area teachers, then, have the task of helping their students translate, interpret, analyze, and evaluate the printed page in order to take from it what they need. Only the content teacher—the expert in the field—really knows what is most important to learn in that course. And that is why teaching reading/thinking/study skills belongs in their particular classroom. That is also why they need teaching strategies to promote needed skills and attitudes. It is our hope that this text will start each one on the way. Pleasant journey!

Student Record Sheet

Chapters	Tasks	Completion Due Date	Comments	Grade or Points
Foundations				
1. Mature Reader				
2. Affective Dimensions				
3. Readability				
4. Diagnosis				
	Individual Conference			
Skills				
5. Rate				
6. Vocabulary				
7. Comprehension Theory				
8. Study Skills				
	Individual Conference			
Classroom Applications				
9. Organization				
10. Comprehension Strategies				
11. Collateral Reading				
12. Writing Patterns and Skills				
13. Final Synthesis	*Individual Conference*			

Total: _____

Grade Student Expects: _____

Instructor's Grade: _____

Note: Permission is hereby given to reproduce for class use all student record sheets.

Acknowledgments

The preparation of a text such as this one requires a great deal of planning, reading the research literature, drafting, editing, and finally writing a useful, readable text. For this third edition we tried to bring up-to-date research and references to each topic.

We have also tried to acknowledge the authorities under whose tutelage we have learned, and we hope that our diligent effort at proper footnoting gives evidence of this. And we also acknowledge all the learning, reasoning, and evaluating that we have borrowed from and shared with others who work to improve reading abilities universally.

Many colleagues have shown interest in our work and have given helpful suggestions. Their enthusiasm has spurred us on.

We are especially indebted to Enid Haag who wrote the chapter on "Enriching Content Classrooms Through Collateral Reading." You will find that for this third edition she has again done a superb job of updating references. Mary Hatley Zintz has graciously assisted in proofing, editing, and critiquing.

We also acknowledge the constructive help of our reviewers, both those who reviewed the past editions and those who reviewed the third edition: Richard W. Burnett, University of Missouri–St. Louis; Mark W. F. Condon, University of Louisville; John W. Conner, University of Iowa; Wayne Otto, University of Wisconsin–Madison; Marion Perwin Turkish, William Paterson College of New Jersey; Edna Bridges, University of Mary Hardin Baylor; James Jester, Southwest Missouri State University; and Michael L. Tanner, Northern Arizona University.

Our greatest indebtedness is to the hundreds of teachers who have enrolled in our classes and have responded to and evaluated our ideas so that we could also learn. Surely, they were our best teachers.

Marian J. Tonjes
Miles V. Zintz

Foundations

Figure 1.1
The teacher's role in developing students' reading/thinking/study skills: a cognitive map.

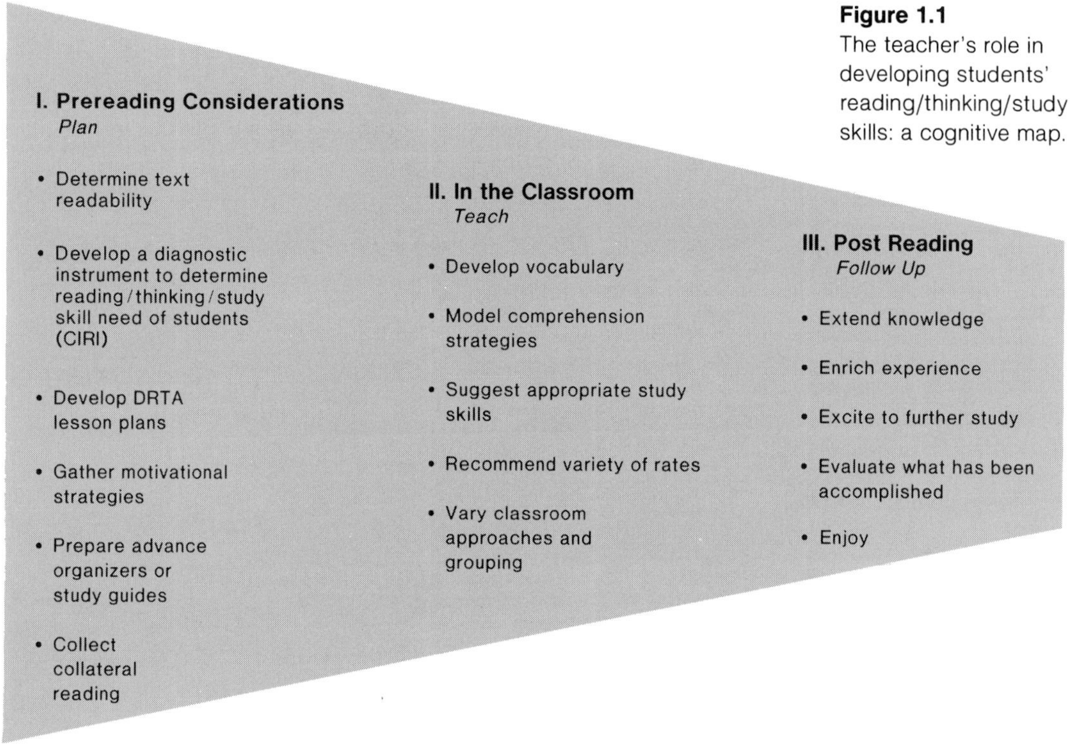

I. Prereading Considerations
Plan

- Determine text readability

- Develop a diagnostic instrument to determine reading/thinking/study skill need of students (CIRI)

- Develop DRTA lesson plans

- Gather motivational strategies

- Prepare advance organizers or study guides

- Collect collateral reading

II. In the Classroom
Teach

- Develop vocabulary

- Model comprehension strategies

- Suggest appropriate study skills

- Recommend variety of rates

- Vary classroom approaches and grouping

III. Post Reading
Follow Up

- Extend knowledge

- Enrich experience

- Excite to further study

- Evaluate what has been accomplished

- Enjoy

Literacy and the Mature Reader

1

Anticipatory Questions

(Literal)
1. What are some general behaviors of mature readers?

(Literal)
2. What is the teacher's role in developing reading, thinking, writing, and study skills?

(Inferential)
3. Compare the pleasures of mature readers with the pains of the functionally illiterate.

(Critical)
4. Evaluate your own level of reading maturity based on the aspects delineated in the Self-assessment Workshop Activity 1.1.

(Critical)
5. React to the stated position on values, ethics, and moral exploration in our schools. Justify your position.

Technical Terminology and Concepts

bottom-up/top-down processing

censorship concerns

criticism and plaudits of today's public schools

defect/deficiency/difference/disruption

functional illiteracy

mature readers

schema/schemata theory

Introduction

Those who have already achieved a high degree of maturity in reading are fortunate indeed for they not only are able to read with efficiency whatever is necessary, but can also find pleasure in reading. One sophisticated skill they have mastered is visualizing through symbolic imagery. For example, from classical antiquity we get the symbols of Cupid's dart or Achilles' heel; from the Bible comes the olive branch; sour grapes from Aesop's fables; and a paper tiger from the Far East. Clichés such as those assist in cutting a long story short without having to spell out descriptions and meaning in lengthy detail. Our language can be enriched as we are able to condense an entire situation into a word or phrase. Think of the political term *quisling,* the scientific term *fall-out,* the business phrase *priming the pump,* or the literary imagery of *the sands running out.*[1] As you read these terms and phrases, they call to mind mental pictures and concepts, which means you are actively involved in communicating with the text, pondering and expanding on the words presented.

Think now of the many times that you, as **mature readers,** have lost yourselves in a good story or have traveled the world over without once leaving your comfortable armchair. Because you enjoy reading you are constantly extending your world, and you have little problem with boredom as long as there is reading material nearby. How fortunate you are!

Survival Literacy

Now, a complete contrast are those who have never attained even a survival level of literacy, those who

> cannot read help-wanted ads;
> cannot fill out forms for Social Security or a driver's license;
> cannot understand the directions on a bottle of medicine;
> cannot read the daily newspaper or a recipe.

Think also of the Minnesota mother, distraught because her little girl had started to bring home books from school, asking her mother to read them to her . . . and she could not do it. Think of the forty-year-old maintenance man who wanted all his life to be a truck driver but could not read road maps or signs. And then, there was the Colorado woman who bought dog food for her family, thinking it was meat![2] See "My Father's Hands" on page 6 for another poignant example. Hägar the Horrible also makes that point in figure 1.2.

These are not just isolated cases. It has been estimated that at least eighteen million adults in our country are functionally illiterate—not having the reading skills necessary for such basic endeavors.[3] This **functional illiteracy** takes a devastating toll and bequeaths a legacy of unemployment, poverty, and alienation.

Figure 1.2
Hägar the Horrible
Reprinted with special permission of King Features Syndicate, Inc.

"My Father's Hands"
A *Reader's Digest* Story
Condensed from *New York Sunday News Magazine,* Nov. 30, 1978. Calvin R. Worthington

His hands were rough and exceedingly strong. He could gently prune a fruit tree or firmly wrestle an ornery mule into harness. He could draw and saw a square with quick accuracy. He had been known to peel his knuckles upside a tough jaw. But what I remember most is the special warmth from those hands soaking through my shirt as he would take me by the shoulder, and, hunkering down beside my ear, point out the glittering swoop of a blue hawk, or a rabbit asleep in its lair. They were good hands that served him well and failed him in only one thing: they never learned to write.

My father was illiterate. The number of illiterates in our country has steadily declined, but if there were only one I would be saddened, remembering my father and the pain he endured because his hands never learned to write.

He started in the first grade, where the remedy for a wrong answer was ten ruler strokes across a stretched palm. For some reason, shapes, figures and recitations just didn't fall into the right pattern inside his six-year-old towhead. Maybe he suffered from some type of learning handicap such as dyslexia. His father took him out of school after several months and set him to a man's job on the farm.

Years later, his wife, with her fourth-grade education, would try to teach him to read. And still later I would grasp his big fist between my small hands and awkwardly help him trace the letters of his name. He submitted to the ordeal, but soon grew restless. Flexing his fingers and kneading his palms, he would declare that he had had enough and depart for a long, solitary walk.

Finally, one night when he thought no one saw, he slipped away with his son's second-grade reader and labored over the words, until they became too difficult. He pressed his forehead into the pages and wept. "Jesus—Jesus—not even a child's book?" Thereafter, no amount of persuading could bring him to sit with pen and paper.

From the farm to road building and later factory work, his hands served him well. His mind was keen, his will to work unsurpassed. During World War II, he was a pipefitter in a shipyard and installed the complicated guts of mighty fighting ships. His enthusiasm and efficiency brought an offer to become line boss—until he was handed the qualification test. His fingers could trace a path across the blueprints while his mind imagined the pipes lacing through the heart of the ship. He could recall every twist and turn of the pipes. But he couldn't read or write.

After the shipyard closed, he went to the cotton mill, where he labored at night, and stole from his sleeping hours the time required to run the farm. When the mill shut down, he went out each morning looking for work—only to return night after night and say to Mother as she fixed his dinner, "They just don't want anybody who can't take their tests."

It had always been hard for him to stand before a man and make an X mark for his name, but the hardest moment of all was when he placed "his mark" by the name someone else had written for him, and saw another man walk away with the deed to his beloved farm. When it was over, he stood before the window and slowly turned the pen he still held in his hands—gazing, unseeing, down the mountainside. I went to the springhouse that afternoon and wept for a long while.

Eventually, he found another cotton-mill job, and we moved into a millhouse village with a hundred look-alike houses. He never quite adjusted to town life. The blue of his eyes faded; the skin across his cheekbones became a little slack. But his hands kept their strength, and their warmth still soaked through when he would sit me on his lap and ask that I read to him from the Bible. He took great pride in my reading and would listen for hours as I struggled through the awkward phrases.

Once he had heard "a radio preacher" relate that the Bible said, "The man that doesn't provide for his family is worse than a thief and an infidel and will never enter the Kingdom of Heaven." Often he would ask me to read that part to him, but I was never able to find it. Other times, he would sit at the kitchen table leafing through the pages as though by a miracle he might be able to read the passage should he turn to the right page. Then he would sit staring at the Book, and I knew he was wondering if God was going to refuse him entry into heaven because his hands couldn't write.

When Mother left once for a weekend to visit her sister, Dad went to the store and returned with food for dinner while I was busy building my latest homemade wagon. After the meal he said he had a surprise for dessert, and went out to the kitchen, where I could hear him opening a can. Then everything was quiet. I went to the doorway, and saw him standing before the sink with an open can in his hand. "The picture looked just like pears," he mumbled. He walked out and sat on the back steps, and I knew he had been embarrassed before his son. The can read "Whole White Potatoes," but the picture on the label did look a great deal like pears.

I went and sat beside him, and asked if he would point out the stars. He knew where the Big Dipper and all the other stars were located, and we talked about how they got there in the first place. He kept that can on a shelf in the woodshed for a long while, and a few times I saw him turning it in his hands as if the touch of the words would teach his hands to write.

Years later, when Mom died, I tried to get him to come live with my family, but he insisted on staying in his small frame house on the edge of town with a few farm animals and a garden plot. His health was failing, and he was in and out of the hospital with several mild heart attacks. Old

Doc Green saw him weekly and gave him medication, including nitroglycerin tablets to put under his tongue should he feel an attack coming on.

My last fond memory of Dad was watching as he walked across the brow of a hillside meadow, with those big, warm hands—now gnarled with age—resting on the shoulders of my two children. He stopped to point out, confidentially, a pond where he and I had swum and fished years before. That night, my family and I flew to a new job and new home, overseas. Three weeks later, he was dead of a heart attack.

I returned alone for the funeral. Doc Green told me how sorry he was. In fact, he was bothered a bit, because he had just written Dad a new nitroglycerin prescription, and the druggist had filled it. Yet the bottle of pills had not been found on Dad's person. Doc Green felt that a pill might have kept him alive long enough to summon help.

An hour before the chapel service, I found myself standing near the edge of Dad's garden, where a neighbor had found him. In grief, I stopped to trace my fingers in the earth where a great man had reached the end of life. My hand came to rest on a half-buried brick, which I aimlessly lifted and tossed aside, before noticing underneath it the twisted and battered, yet unbroken, soft plastic bottle that had been beaten into the soft earth.

As I held the bottle of nitroglycerin pills, the scene of Dad struggling to remove the cap and in desperation trying to break the bottle with the brick flashed painfully before my eyes. With deep anguish I knew why those big warm hands had lost in their struggle with death. For there, imprinted on the bottle cap, were the words, "Child-Proof Cap—Push Down and Twist to Unlock." The druggist later confirmed that he had just started using the new safety bottle.

I knew it was not a purely rational act, but I went right downtown and bought a leather-bound pocket dictionary and a gold pen set. I bade Dad good-by by placing them in those big old hands, once so warm, which had lived so well, but had never learned to write.

Perhaps more devastating, though, is the larger population of literate adults who *can* read and choose not to do so in their daily lives. They, like the functionally illiterate, will generally have tremendous gaps in their store of information. They will be more prone to believe the propagandists, because their access to both sides of any question will be limited.

In editorializing about the historical television series, "The Adams Chronicles," Karl Mayer wrote scathingly in the *Saturday Review:*

> Before discussing the Adams Chronicles, one must take into account a prevailing reality—our appalling ignorance about our national past. . . . A recent Gallup poll found that 28 per cent of the United States public could not specify what important event occurred in 1776. . . . On an average viewing day, one might get the impression that the world began five minutes ago, with John Wayne as the tube's most venerable historic figure.[4]

See appendix 2 for an article by John Micklos, titled "Literacy in the United States: What is the Status? What's Being Done?" for further information.

The cognitive map shown on page 2, in figure 1.1 serves as a general text overview rather than directly addressing the contents of this specific chapter. In this case it depicts the teacher's role in developing students' reading/thinking/study skills through prereading, concurrent, and postreading activities. Many of the stated activities—such as determining readability—are addressed as separate chapters. It is intended that you look back at this cognitive map periodically as you move through the text and course to keep the big picture in mind.

Cognitive Map of the Teacher's Role

Enough commission and task force reports and research studies have appeared since 1983 to constitute a staggering indictment of secondary education in the United States. A few are listed below.

Unmet Needs in Our Schools

1. Richard C. Anderson, et al., *Becoming a Nation of Readers: The Report of the Commission on Reading* (Washington, D.C.: The National Institute of Education, 1985).
2. Ernest L. Boyer, *High School: A Report on Secondary Education in America* (New York: Harper & Row, 1983).
3. College Entrance Examination Board, *Academic Preparation for College: What Students Need to Know and Be Able to Do* (New York: CEEB, 1983).
4. John I. Goodlad, *A Place Called School* (New York: McGraw-Hill Book Co., 1984).
5. National Commission on Excellence in Education, *A Nation at Risk: The Imperative for Educational Reform* (Washington, D.C.: U.S. Government Printing Office, 1983).
6. Theodore Sizer, *Horace's Compromise: The Dilemma of the American High School* (Boston: Houghton Mifflin, 1984).
7. Task Force on Education for Economic Growth, *Action for Excellence: A Comprehensive Plan to Improve our Nation's Schools* (Denver: Education Commission of the States, 1983).
8. Twentieth Century Fund Task Force on Federal Elementary and Secondary Education Policy, *Making the Grade* (New York: Twentieth Century Fund, 1983).

The report, *The Nation at Risk,* released in 1983 brought heavy criticism of the operation of the public schools across the nation. The rising tide of mediocrity, the dangerous results of our misplaced priorities, and other such epithets were intended to shame the profession into doing something about the unacceptable state of affairs in education. The report also contained this statement:

If an unfriendly foreign power had attempted to impose on America the mediocre educational performance that exists today, we might have viewed it as an act of war.[5]

Ethics, Values, and our Cultural Heritage

Francis Schaeffer, a theologian, admonishes us that our culture has accepted two impoverished values to live by: personal peace and affluence. He defines these this way:

> Personal peace means just to be let alone, not to be troubled by the troubles of other people, whether across the world or across the city—to live one's life with minimal possibilities of being personally disturbed. Personal peace means wanting to have my personal life pattern undisturbed in my lifetime, regardless of what the result will be in the lifetimes of my children and grandchildren. Affluence means an overwhelming and ever-increasing prosperity—a life made up of things, things, and more things—a success judged by an ever-higher level of material abundance.[6]

Bellah, et al., in a sociological study called *Habits of the Heart,* critically evaluates values in America today. The study recognizes the drive in middle-class culture for personal peace and affluence; but it also recognizes the unanswered conflict between the fierce individualism and the urgent need for a feeling of community and a commitment to one another.[7]

Perhaps the best word to describe American values today is *confused.* Traditional values were strongly rooted in religion and patriotism, which have been somewhat out of vogue since the "do your own thing" mentality of the 1960s.

> During this time of uncertainty and confusion, schools began to be criticized for representing a single set of religious values. . . . As it was with religious matters, so it became with other matters of deep concern. . . . In response to this turmoil, teachers turned toward 'teaching the facts'. . . . Moral, ethical, aesthetic values were quietly abandoned as integral parts of the curriculum. Thus the gap widened between what we *said* the schools were to foster and what was actually taught.[8]

Many Americans pay lip service to, but do not necessarily practice, the traditional values with which they were reared. Our culture is patterned in conflicts that on the one hand mirror the struggle for the puritan ethic, and on the other hand struggle with the demands of an increasingly materialistic society.

> We say we believe in thrift—but we appear to believe even more strongly in keeping up good appearances.
> We say that success is to be won by hard work—but we emphasize personality and social contacts.
> We laud honesty as a virtue—but acknowledge a need for pragmatic expediency in our "real" life.

See table 1.1 for a comparison of traditional versus current values and classroom results.

Table 1.1

Values

Traditional Values	Current Values	Classroom Results[9]
Honesty	Shrewdness	Fear of "being caught" as a motivator
Hard work	Personality	Excuses
Absolute moral norms	Relative standards of behavior	Docility in conforming to pressure
Loyalty	Looking out for number one	Intragroup aggression
Helping others	Letting "George" do it	Spying; tattling
High regard for formal education	"Do your own thing"	"Get by"
Importance of home and family	Alternate life-styles	Disrespect; apathy

Teachers need to examine values that are being "caught" in their classrooms. To say that moral or ethical instruction is not the function of the public school is simply to condone the status quo.

Much can be done over the short run to improve our schools. We need to clarify goals and functions, develop curricula that reflect a commitment to both academic and ethical development of students. People who cannot communicate are powerless; schools must strive for a high degree of proficiency in the use of language. Schools must promote cultural understanding and diversity. About diversity, Goodlad writes:

> The school fails in its function unless it exists in a state of productive tension with the home: home and family create a press of one ethnic identity, one religion, one social class; the school presses toward a common identification with diversity and a sense of homogeneity which encompasses and integrates diverse elements. Schools created to assure reinforcement of only one set of values or to serve only my race, my neighborhood, and my economic class fail in this function.[10]

About our moral and philosophical legacy, William Pfaff, writing in his *Los Angeles Times* column, which appeared in the *Albuquerque Journal,* states:

> If we do not understand . . . (our) moral and philosophical legacy, its "classics," its history, we are cruelly hampered in managing our lives and society, and in thinking about our future.[11]

This same thought is reflected in a position statement by the National Council for the Social Studies:

> Knowledge about religions is not only a characteristic of an educated person, but is also absolutely necessary for understanding and living in a world of diversity.[12]

United States Supreme Court Justice Tom Clark, writing a majority opinion for the court in Abington v. Schempp (1963) stated:

> It might well be said that one's education is not complete without a study of comparative religion or the history of religion and its relationship to the advancement of civilization.

How are students to understand the Crusades, Joan of Arc, the anti-slavery movement, colonization, World War II kamikaze pilots, or the civil rights movement without a knowledge of the religious principles from which they arose? As textbooks avoid controversial topics, teachers become more and more responsible for adding to the students' understanding. John McDermott states:

> There is evidence that publishers engage in considerable self-censorship and go out of their way to avoid controversial issues that might limit their share of the market.[13]

If thoughtful observers of differing views now agree that religion is inappropriately excluded from the public school curriculum, perhaps the time has come to show how religion in American life permeates much of our behaviors and offer to help textbook writers and curriculum developers represent that knowledge in meaningful and appropriate ways.

Teaching *about* religions in our public schools is legal and educationally sound when it is part of the academic program of the school. Commitment to comprehensive education requires the inclusion of religious studies for *knowledge about* and for *understanding of* religions in the school curriculum.[14]

People who cannot see beyond the confines of their own life experience are ill-equipped to face the future; they need to accept the fact that education is a lifelong process. People must either be able to adapt to change where they are in the workplace or be able to build a better life for themselves and their families by making whatever other adjustments are necessary. People need strong egos, faith in themselves, and dreams, and the school needs to emphasize these values.

Goodlad takes a strong stand against ability grouping and tracking. He writes:

> Since tracking appears to block the poor and disadvantaged from access to knowledge which might serve to advantage them, pressure to abolish it undoubtedly will find its way to the judicial branch of government.[15]

The decision to track is essentially one of giving up on the problem of human variability in learning. It is a retreat rather than a strategy. The self-fulfilling prophecy may be set in motion and low-achievers will remain low-achievers.

A large minority of parents seem to be saying to the school, "Handle it all and don't bother me." But any school's success is dependent on aggressive support by parents, school boards, and community. Without that support, teachers cannot achieve the desired goals of the school curriculum.

Each year Phi Delta Kappa publishes the results of a national poll concerning the public's perception of schools, their level of confidence, and the problems they perceive have not been met.[16] In 1988, 74 percent of parents surveyed—who had students in public schools—reported that schools made a fair to strong effort to attract parents to participate in school affairs. In another poll of parents of elementary children only, these parents recommended that we have more reading in school, smaller reading groups, more skill and oral reading instruction, and less reliance on basal readers and workbooks.

Goodlad suggests that all head teachers can be expected to serve as role models to fellow teachers, provide them with inservice assistance, diagnose knotty learning problems, and serve as heads of teaching teams made up of full- and part-time teachers, preservice teachers in training, and teacher aides.[17]

The present-day youth culture is powerfully preoccupied with itself and made up of individuals much less shaped by home, church, and community than once was the case. Also, the schools have responded much too slowly to the swift advances of technology in virtually all aspects of life. Schools need to direct their thinking toward *mastery learning*—by providing more time for students who take longer to learn, by providing experiential activities designed to overcome difficulties with abstractions, and by providing summaries and reviews of work covered through the use of different media of instruction.

A serious problem in today's educational world is censorship and intellectual freedom. Censors can wield great power as to what publishers dare to print. Censors in America generally look for eight items:

Censorship Concerns[18,19,20]

1. sex (risqúe, filthy, indecent)
2. patriotism (un-American, pro-communism)
3. religion (atheist, irreligious, un-Christian)
4. civil rights (biased)
5. offensive language (profane, unfit for human eyes or ears)
6. secular humanism (nonreligious movement)
7. violence
8. defamation of our historical personalities

The following is a list of books either already censored or liable to be censored soon. Which category do you think these titles fall under?

The Catcher in the Rye
Go Ask Alice
Of Mice and Men
The Grapes of Wrath
Catch-22
Brave New World
Lord of the Flies
To Kill a Mockingbird
Slaughterhouse Five
Forever
My Darling, My Hamburger
Are You There God? It's Me, Margaret
Deenie
Mom, the Wolfman and Me
The American Heritage Dictionary
Romeo and Juliet

One Flew Over the Cuckoo's Nest
The Sun Also Rises
For Whom the Bell Tolls
A Farewell to Arms
The Great Gatsby
1984
Animal Farm
Adventures of Huckleberry Finn
The Outsiders
The Pigman
Othello
Merchant of Venice
Our Town
The Glass Menagerie
Summer and Smoke
Death of a Salesman

. . . and on and on and on.

The Good News   According to recent data from the National Association of Educational Progress (NAEP):[21]

Black and Hispanic nine- and twelve-year-olds have made dramatic progress in the basic skills of reading during the past twenty years;
All students, on average, spell better and write grammatically correct sentences more readily than they could fifteen years ago;
More students *can* read;
More writing is systematically taught and assigned.

Those planning assessments for 1992 are talking more about measuring higher-order skills in all subjects, looking at how "whole language" programs are effecting better reading skills, and studying the impact of more emphasis in the teaching of writing on student compositions.

NAEP results, say Anrig and La Pointe, demonstrate that when goals are clear and the environment supportive our schools *can* deliver and they do. One word of caution: "NAEP is a survey project, not a rigorously controlled research study."[22]

Interrelatedness of Skills   **Reading** is interacting with print. All of us need to acquire competency in the basic communication skills of listening, speaking, writing, and reading. The quality of communication is directly affected by *thinking skills,* such as reasoning, imagining, problem solving, synthesizing, and critically evaluating. Writing about what we have been reading and thinking about is also important. To improve learning and retention, *study skills* are employed. The diagram below shows the interrelatedness of these areas.

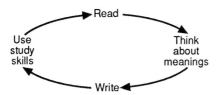

There is a two-pronged aspect to reading that has caused some confusion in the past: (1) the process of *learning to read* (word recognition and comprehension skills), which is diligently taught in the early elementary years, and (2) the process of *reading to learn,* using reading as a vehicle to obtain needed information. This text will be concerned with the second prong, reading to learn. Our general objectives are to demonstrate a variety of ways in which teachers can assist students to improve reading, thinking, writing, and study skills in order to get needed information *and* to help them find some value and joy in the process.

Qualities of a Mature Reader

When the teaching of reading is discontinued formally after sixth grade, it may well be a hit-or-miss proposition whether students fully develop into **mature readers,** those who, having mastered the basic "how to read" skills, develop higher-level skills and attitudes in reading/thinking/study behaviors. Table 1.2 describes general reading factors as they relate to the behavior of mature readers. As you look at this table try to decide how mature a reader you are by personalizing each item. You may use it as a checklist.

Insights in Reading

Research in reading is an expanding phenomenon. In 1980, the International Reading Association published for the first time since 1925 its *Annual Summary of Investigations Relating to Reading* as a separate monograph.[23] The 1980 issue contained over eleven hundred published reports of reading research for the prior year—almost double the entries of the previous year. In 1990 the number of research reports was again expanded. This indicates that we are constantly extending our horizons or adapting ways of looking at commonly accepted concepts.

Examples of recent emphases are the notions of **schemata;** the processing of text through strategies that are "bottom-up," "top-down," or both; and the important role of writing in connection with reading.

Table 1.2

How Mature a Reader Are You?: General Reading Factors as They Relate to the Behavior of Mature Readers

General Factors		Behaviors
A. Interest, Attitude, and Valuing	_____	1. Show enjoyment and appreciation of reading.
	_____	2. Choose to read at times over other pleasant options.
	_____	3. Use reading to satisfy and extend personal interests through a wide variety of topics and materials.
	_____	4. Willingly state a commitment to reading as a lifetime adventure.
B. Purpose	_____	5. Read for specific purposes.
	_____	6. Use a wide range of purposes.
	_____	7. Use their own purposes as well as assigned ones.
	_____	8. Are always ready to change purposes when the need directs.
C. Rate Adaptability	_____	9. Read at rates determined by their purpose and the difficulty of the material.
	_____	10. Have a variety of rates for whole selections or within selections.
D. Study Skills	_____	11. Have mastered locational, reference skills.
	_____	12. Are adept at organizing information through listening, outlining, and note taking.
	_____	13. Interpret graphics of all types.
	_____	14. Apply study-learning strategies for immediate recall and long-term retention.
E. Comprehension	_____	15. Use thinking strategies at the literal, interpretive, and critical/creative levels.
	_____	16. Reflect on ideas presented.
	_____	17. Predict outcomes.
	_____	18. Tap into the writer's organizational plan.
	_____	19. Relate new ideas to old.
	_____	20. Use mental imagery when reading narrative, descriptions, etc.
	_____	21. Perceive paragraph organization.
	_____	22. Read like a writer.
F. Vocabulary	_____	23. Use several strategies for identifying words and establishing meanings, including context, structural analysis, phonics, and/or dictionary.
	_____	24. Consistently enlarge their technical and general vocabulary.
	_____	25. Recognize multiple meanings and connotations in context.
	_____	26. Maintain a positive attitude toward word study.

Foundations

When we perceive an overall structure in a body of concepts and their relationships, this gives us a **schema** of that subject, which in turn facilitates
comprehension. **Schemata** (the plural of schema) can be defined as a series
of ideas or concepts in a structure or framework into which information
can be assimilated or categorized. Once you know the structure, then any
incoming information can readily be organized and stored in memory for
retrieval. Knowledge of this structure is thought to be developmental; that
is, the young child has only a basic structure that becomes more elaborate
over the years.[24]

Take, for example, a short story in literature.

1. Primary children have the schema or structure of beginning,
   middle, and end of story. They use this knowledge to retell the
   story.
2. Intermediate levels will add to this structure. They learn about
   such things as the plot, theme, setting, and characters. Each of
   these is used by students to better assimilate or visualize the
   story and to retell it in greater depth.
3. At the secondary levels even more differentiated structures are
   added, such as symbolism, irony, satire, or flashbacks.[25]

Frank Smith explains a schema in terms of a theory of the world in
our head.[26] We make sense of the world and interpret events based on our
theory. We learn, then, by modifying and elaborating on our theory or
schema.

Theoreticians have examined reading comprehension from the standpoint
of a bottom-up or a top-down processing as two modes for activating appropriate schemata. Frederickson, Rumelhart, Bobrow, and Norman have
said in essence that as we read the text we use either or both processes in
a variety of combinations, depending on our purpose and textual demands.[27,28,29] **Bottom-up,** or data-driven, processing refers to a sequence of
events commencing with the sensation of the print on the retina of the eye;
detecting and combining these sensations into words; organizing words syntactically into phrases and sentences; associating meanings in these sentences through concepts; and, lastly, reasoning and storing meanings. In
other words, this process goes from print to words to sentences, while associating, reasoning, and storing the information.

On the other hand, **top-down,** or conceptually driven processing is a
more sophisticated approach that relies on the three Ps of *purpose, prediction,* and *past knowledge.* In this approach readers use abstract knowledge structures to selectively direct their attention to the print and by doing
so essentially confirm or deny their predictions.

For example, in the sentence, "The skier sped down the s _____ ," you might attack the first part of the sentence in a bottom-up fashion, as described above, and then shift as you progress through the sentence to the final word, which you predict, based on prior knowledge, as "slope." By taking in the initial words, identifying them, and putting them together for meaning, you generate the expectancy that the final word would be a noun and would have the meaning of "hill."

Readers who make good use of the top-down phenomenon are able to assimilate large bodies of print at more rapid rates than those who rely mostly on bottom-up processes.

Referral of Students: The Four Ds

There is a wide range of abilities in any given classroom, but students with severe reading problems should be referred to specialists. An adaptation of the four-D model of Weiner and Cromer—Deficiency, Defect, Disruption, and Difference—helps to identify types of reading/learning difficulties.[30] It is important that you recognize which students need referral and which should remain in the regular classroom.

The first three categories will require help from a reading specialist, counselor, or physician. The fourth category is your responsibility, as the content teacher. For all students who are mismatched as described in number four, instruction may be adjusted with processing strategies developed for handling differences; and/or textbooks may be reorganized, rewritten, or supplemented. This text will assist you in these tasks (see table 1.3).

With this as a background, here are four workshop activities to assess your current attitudes and skills and to alert you to what is to come.

Table 1.3
The Four D's

Referral	1. **Deficiency** in reading means that students are still in the acquisition stage of reading development, unable to pronounce certain words or use other aids to get meanings.
	2. Of those deficient, a small percentage may have physiological **defects,** such as visual or auditory impairment.
	3. Another small percentage may have experienced **disruption,** an emotional or social problem that can interfere with concentration and learning.
Regular Classrooms	4. Most students having difficulty mastering their text fall into this fourth category—there is a **difference** or a mismatch between their reading levels or skills and the readability level or skill demands of the text.

Workshop Activity 1.1
Self-assessment of Reading Maturity

Few of us can claim honestly to be mature readers in *all* aspects. It is actually possible to spend an entire lifetime refining our reading, thinking, writing, and study skills. Attitude about these matters is an important determinant to successful mature reading. The following activities, then, have two main purposes: (1) to give you the opportunity to assess for yourself your specific areas of strengths and weaknesses; and (2) to introduce you to a sampling of the variety and scope of skills to be explored in this text. These exercises should be taken objectively, and any sharing of results in class should be optional.

The following activity is a form of *advance organizer* in that it includes categories of questions representing areas of skills deemed appropriate for a mature reader. Because *no one* is an ideal reader, you should expect to find some areas that are not as strong as others. Again this survey should be considered private information, with sharing on a voluntary basis only.

Quick Survey for Adult Readers: How mature a reader are you?

Directions: Note the organization of this survey. The left-hand side indicates the terminology in the field of reading to which this activity refers; the middle column asks you a question about how you think you function in reading with respect to this category; and a third column is provided for you to write a response to that question. Obviously, this preassessment presupposes no preparation for any given set of answers. Please respond rapidly to the questions. These may be referred to in later class sessions.

Category	Question	Response
1. Motivation	1. List two books you have read lately (*not* work-required or study-related) for pure pleasure, inspiration, or general expansion of your knowledge of the world.	
2. Interests/ Attitudes/Values	2. If you have the choice between reading a story or watching it on television, which would you choose most often?	
	3. How much time each day do you put aside for recreational or pleasure reading?	

Category	Question	Response
3. Variety of Interests	4. Put a "+" by all those read regularly, a "0" by those read occasionally, and a "−" by those read rarely.	

Fiction
1. Romance ___
2. Adventure ___
3. Mystery ___
4. Historical ___
5. Poetry ___
6. Other ___

Nonfiction
7. Autobiography ___
8. Biography ___
9. Political ___
10. Historical ___
11. Other (Specify) ___
   _____

Newspapers
12. Sports ___
13. Front page ___
14. Editorial ___
15. Financial ___
16. Other ___

Magazines
17. Women's/Men's ___
18. News ___
19. Literary ___
20. Sports ___
21. Other ___

5. Look over the above list, would you say that you read widely with a broad range of interests? Circle one of the following:

Very much so   Somewhat
Not as much as I should   Not at all
I'm not sure

---

4. Vocabulary

6. Describe your own system for building up vocabulary. If you have none, leave this blank.

7. List and define three new words that you have encountered through reading in the past three months.
   1. _____ _____
   2. _____ _____
   3. _____ _____

8. Circle strategies you use for identifying unfamiliar words while reading.

   configuration   phonics
   context clues   dictionary
   structural analysis   other: _____

9. List two technical content terms you have learned recently and give exact definitions.
   1. _____ _____
   2. _____ _____

Category	Question	Response
5. Syntax	10. Write the meaning of the italicized nonsense words in the following context: a. Jerry was *glongering* the data. _____ b. The man *galurned* the *troper.* _____ _____	

Category	Question	Response

6. Rate Adaptability	11. At what rate do you read the following?
	
	a. very rapid b. rapid c. average d. slow
	
	1. Novels _____ 4. Magazines _____
	2. Newspapers _____ 5. Textbooks _____
	3. Poetry _____ 6. Other _____
	
	12. Can you skim a text chapter in three minutes and recite the main ideas?
	       (Yes/No/Maybe/Don't Know)
	Do you read everything at the same rate?
	       (Yes/No/Maybe/Don't Know)	

Category	13. How easy is it for you to:	Very Easy	Somewhat Easy	Difficult
7. Getting the Gist of the Topic liberal comprehension)	a. spot the topic sentence in a paragraph?			
	b. read to follow directions?			
	c. identify a pattern or a sequence of ideas?			
	d. relate supporting details to main ideas?			
8. Thinking about What You Read	14. How easy is it for you to:			
	a. spot cause and effect?			
	b. see comparison and contrast?			
	c. identify the mood, time, and place?			
9. Critical/Creative Comprehension	15. How easy is it for you to:			
	a. use what you have learned in new situations?			
	b. combine concepts into new and innovative ideas?			
	c. make judgments about your reading while stating your own criteria for judgment?			

Category	Question	Response			

Category | **Question** | **Response**

10. Study Skills

16. List strategies you use for mastering text reading in content fields.

1. _____
2. _____
3. _____
4. _____

	Very	Average	Not at All	Don't Know
17. How well do you interpret graphics?				
18. How efficient are you in your use of the library to locate hard-to-find materials?				
19. How easily do you identify key points in a lecture from your notes after several months?				
20. How well do you remember material over a period of time?				

11. Self-assessment

Now that you have finished this survey, look back over your responses and identify those categories that you believe need immediate improvement. Set a few goals for yourself for improving at least two or three of these categories by the end of the term. Write here the areas you have selected (e.g., vocabulary):

1. _____
2. _____
3. _____

At the end of the term look back through this self-assessment to reevaluate yourself in terms of how much change, growth, or enjoyment there has been.

I have changed in the area of _____

I have grown most in _____

I enjoy much more than I did _____

Workshop Activity 1.2
Attitudes Toward Teaching Reading in Content Classrooms

1. Using Vaughan's scoring and interpretation on p. 24, first measure your present attitude toward teaching reading in content classrooms.[31] (Save your responses and refer to them at the end of the term to note any changes.)
2. For discussion purposes it is suggested that a group profile be developed from the responses of all classmates. This may serve as a model for processing an attitude survey in a content classroom, e.g., attitudes toward reading in science.
3. When groups of teachers have taken this inventory, there has been a great variety of scores.

Reprinted with permission of Joseph L. Vaughan, Jr., and the International Reading Association.

Directions: Indicate on the left your feeling toward each of the following items using the following scale:

A Scale to Measure Attitudes Toward Teaching Reading in Content Classrooms

7 = strongly agree   3 = tend to disagree
6 = agree   2 = disagree
5 = tend to agree   1 = strongly disagree
4 = neutral

_____ 1. A content area teacher is obliged to help students improve their reading ability.
_____ 2. Technical vocabulary should be introduced to students in content classes before they meet those terms in a reading passage.
_____ 3. The primary responsibility of a content teacher should be to impart subject knowledge.
_____ 4. Few students can learn all they need to know about how to read in six years of schooling.
_____ 5. The sole responsibility for teaching students how to study should be with reading teachers.
_____ 6. Knowing how to teach reading in content areas should be required for secondary teaching certification.
_____ 7. Only English teachers should be responsible for teaching reading in secondary schools.
_____ 8. A teacher who wants to improve students' interest in reading should show them that he or she likes to read.
_____ 9. Content teachers should teach content and leave reading instruction to reading teachers.
_____ 10. A content area teacher should be responsible for helping students think on an interpretive level as well as on a literal level when they read.
_____ 11. Content area teachers should feel a greater responsibility to the content they teach than to any reading instruction they may be able to provide.

_____ 12. Content area teachers should help students learn to set purposes for reading.

_____ 13. All content area teachers should teach students how to read material in their content specialty.

_____ 14. Reading instruction in secondary schools is a waste of time.

_____ 15. Content area teachers should be familiar with theoretical concepts of the reading process.

Nine of the items are positive and six are negative. The negative ones should be scored inversely from the positive ones. The table below is provided to assist the individual scoring process. For example, question 3 is a negative item. If you strongly agree with it, you would give yourself a "1," not a "7."

	Response	Numerical Value
Positive Items	1, 2, 4, 6, 8 10, 12, 13, 15	7, 6, 5, 4, 3, 2, 1 _____
Negative Items	3, 5, 7, 9 11, 14	1, 2, 3, 4, 5, 6, 7 _____

Interpretation of Scores

Score	Attitude
91 or higher	Highly positive
81–90	Above average
71–80	Average
61–70	Below average
60 or lower	Negative

Workshop Activity 1.3
Using the Cloze Procedure

This fascinating tool can be used to determine an approximate readability fit between the reader and text. (_Cloze_ is described in detail in the chapter on informal diagnosis.) When there is little time for developing more complex inventories, cloze may serve as a screening device to alert you to potential problems. It may be helpful to have a practice session with cloze first so that students may become more comfortable with the procedure.

The following selection is taken from a later chapter in this text. Your task is to skim over the following passage and then try to reconstruct the message with as much exactness as possible, filling in what you think is the appropriate word for each blank. Each correct response is worth two points. A score of 44–57 percent correct means that the selection is at your *instructional* reading level, whereas a score above 57 percent means that it is at your *independent* reading level. A score below 44 percent can be interpreted as *frustrational* level.

(See page 261 for the completed section)   **Testing**

Testing in some form is generally a part of classroom learning. Students are rarely ecstatic _____ this state of affairs; _____ , there can be significant _____ for students as well _____ for teachers. Good teachers _____ to find out which _____ have learned what and to discover how well _____ have taught. For the _____ of tests to be _____ true reflection of what _____ has occurred, students should _____ been shown how to _____ as well as how _____ prepare for and take a _____ . It is remarkable how _____ students have learned this _____ by a process of _____ and error. The greatest _____ to students is that, _____ to review and reorganize _____ they might never have _____ at again, they are _____ to remember the ideas _____ a long term.

Assuming _____ your students have been _____ to the study skills _____ discussed and that they _____ learned how to organize _____ time, listen or read _____ , take good notes, _____ a study strategy to _____ concentration and memory, and _____ review their readings and _____ , it is now time _____ help them study for _____ test. Remind students that _____ ideal time to organize _____ consolidate learnings is several _____ prior to taking the _____ . This means that all _____ should have been read, _____ notes are in order, _____ other assignments are completed _____ turned in a clearing _____ the deck, so to _____ .

They must synthesize, find _____ organizing principles, and see _____ in order to successfully _____ large bodies of material. _____ they have not been _____ the material periodically, they will be forced to "cram," which will work only if they are able to select the vital information.

Workshop Activity 1.4
Listening and Note Taking

This activity examines the variety of ways in which people may take down information and shows one possible model for notes. The following excerpt should be read aloud slowly only once at a normal lecture rate by the instructor. You, the reader, should not look at the content, because the purpose of this activity is to compare your notes with a model found immediately following.

Instructors read orally:

Valuing Reading

One reason that many students do not learn to value reading is that they have not learned reading-thinking strategies that help them to extract ideas from print with an economy of effort and with an appreciation for both the quality of the ideas and the craft of the author. They begin reading the selection with no particular purpose. They never pause to reflect upon what they are reading and to put the author's ideas into their own personal language. They are largely unaware of the precise vocabulary, careful organization, and perhaps beautiful figures of speech or creative analogies employed by skillful authors. When they finish the selection, their eyes have been more active with the material than their minds. Consequently, they do not give reading the value it deserves.[32]

Modified Cornell Model for Notes on "Valuing Reading"

Valuing Reading	Students need to learn reading/thinking strategies to extract ideas efficiently from print and to appreciate quality and author's craft.
Aspects Hindering Valuing	1. Read with no purpose
	2. Do not pause to reflect
	3. Do not put ideas into own words
	4. Unaware of: precise vocabulary
	organization
	figures of speech
	creative analogies
	5. Moved eyes, did not use brain

The key words in the left column would be added immediately following the mini-lecture, not during it. There is more than one way to take notes effectively; this is only an example of one way.

Summary

There is a continuum in difficulty levels of reading, thinking, writing, and study skills. In this chapter a comparison has been made between the pleasure of mature readers and the pain of functional illiterates who do not have the necessary survival skills for our culture. Recent national reports were examined briefly from the standpoint of not only what is wrong with our schools but also what is right. After considering the relationship among reading, thinking, writing, and study skills with a special caution to content teachers, qualities of a mature reader were delineated and some insights from recent research were introduced. Exercises for self-assessment of personal skills, habits, and attitudes were also given.

1. E. B. Gombrich, "The Visual Image," *Scientific American* 227 (September 1972): 93–94.
2. Carl T. Rowan and David M. Mazie, "Johnny's Parents Can't Read Either," *Reader's Digest* 110 (January 1977): 153–54.
3. Faite Royjier-Poncefont Mack, "The Illiteracy Concept: Defining the Critical Level," *Reading Horizons* 19 (Fall 1978): 53–60.
4. Karl E. Mayer, "Television Page: A Pride of Adamses," *Saturday Review* 24 (January 1976): 43.
5. National Commission on Excellence in Education, *A Nation at Risk: The Imperative for Educational Reform* (Washington, D.C.: U.S. Government Printing Office, 1983).
6. Francis A. Schaeffer, *How Should We Then Live: The Rise and Decline of Western Thought and Culture* (Westchester, Ill.: Crossway Books, 1976), p. 205.
7. Robert N. Bellah et al., *Habits of the Heart* (New York: Perennial Library, Harper & Row, 1986).
8. Louis E. Raths, Merrill Harmin, and Sidney B. Simon, *Values and Teaching* (Columbus: Charles E. Merrill Publishing Company, 1978), p. 19.
9. Regardless of the teacher's commitment to traditional values or acceptance of current values, the sociostructure of the school classroom tends to impose its own values.
10. John I. Goodlad, *A Place Called School* (New York: McGraw-Hill Book Co., 1984), p. 273.
11. William Pfaff, "Americans Know Little About Western, Other Civilizations," *Albuquerque Journal,* 14 Feb. 1989, commentary section.
12. National Council for the Social Studies, 1985 position statement.
13. John W. McDermott, Jr., "Defining the Role of Religion in the American Classroom," *Religion and Public Education* (April 1987).
14. The subject of teaching about religion has been concisely discussed in the pamphlet, "Religion in the Public School Curriculum: Questions and Answers." This material has been reproduced in the appendix of this book and is highly recommended.
15. Goodlad, *School,* p. 295.
16. Timothy V. Rasinski, "What do Parents Think About Reading in the Schools?" *Reading Teacher* 43 (December 1989): 262–63.
17. Goodlad, *School,* p. 302.
18. Eli M. Oboler, ed. *Censorship and Education* (Bronx, N.Y.: H. W. Wilson, 1981).
19. Ben Brodinsky, "The New Right: The Movement and Its Impact," *Phi Delta Kappan* 64 (October 1982): 87–94.
20. Susan B. Neuman, "Rethinking the Censorship Issue," *The English Journal* 75 (September 1986): 46–50.
21. Gregory R. Anrig and Archie E. La Pointe, "What We Know About What Students Don't Know," *Educational Leadership* 47 (November 1989): 4–9.
22. Ibid., p. 5.
23. Samuel Weintraub et al., eds., *Annual Summary of Investigations Relating to Reading,* 1 July 1978 to 30 June 1979 (Newark, Del.: International Reading Association, 1980).
24. Richard C. Anderson, "Concretization and Sentence Learning," in *Theoretical Models and Processes of Reading,* ed. H. Singer and R. B. Ruddell (Newark, Del.: International Reading Association, 1976).

25. David E. Rumelhart, "Understanding and Summarizing Brief Stories," in *Basic Processes in Reading: Perception and Comprehension,* ed. D. LaBerge and S. J. Samuels (Hillsdale, N.J.: Erlbaum, 1977).

26. Frank Smith, *Reading without Nonsense* (New York: Teachers College Press, 1978), p. 79.

27. Carl H. Frederickson, "Discourse Comprehension and Early Reading," in Pittsburgh Conference on Reading, 12–14 May 1976.

28. David E. Rumelhart, *Toward an Interactive Model of Reading* (San Diego, Calif.: University of California–San Diego, Center for Human Information Processing, 1976).

29. D. G. Bobrow and D. A. Norman, "Some Principles of Memory Schemata," in *Representation and Understanding: Studies in Cognitive Science,* ed. D. G. Bobrow and A. M. Collins (New York: Academic Press, 1975).

30. M. Weiner and Ward Cromer, "Reading and Reading Difficulty: A Conceptual Analysis," *Harvard Educational Review* 37 (1967): 620–43.

31. Joseph L. Vaughan, Jr., "A Scale to Measure Attitudes Toward Teaching Reading in Content Classrooms," *Journal of Reading* 20 (April 1977): 605–9.

32. Richard J. Smith, Wayne Otto, and Lee Hansen, *The School Reading Program* (Boston: Houghton Mifflin Co., 1978), p. 76.

Recommended Readings

Aaron, Ira E.; Chall, Jeanne S.; Durkin, Dolores; Goodman, Kenneth; and Strickland, Dorothy S. "The Past, Present, and Future of Literacy Education: Educators." Parts I and II. *The Reading Teacher* 43 (January 1990): 302–11 and (February 1990): 370–81.

Adler, Mortimer J., and Van Doren, Charles. *How to Read a Book: The Classic Guide to Intelligent Reading.* New York: Simon and Schuster, 1972.

Anderson, Richard C.; Hielbert, Elfrieda H.; Scott, Judith A.; and Wilkinson, Ian A. G. *Becoming a Nation of Readers: The Report of the Commission on Reading.* The National Academy of Education, The National Institute of Education, The Center for the Study of Reading, 1985.

Applebee, Arthur N.; Langer, Judith A.; and Mullis, Ina V. S. *Learning to be Literate in America.* Princeton, N.J.: National Assessment of Educational Progress, 1987.

Cardenas, Jose A. "The Role of Native Language Instruction in Bilingual Education." *Phi Delta Kappan* 67 (January 1986): 359–63.

Cummins, Jim. "Empowering Minority Students: A Framework for Intervention." *Harvard Educational Review* 56 (February 1986): 18–36.

Elley, Warwick B., and Mangubhai, Francis. "The Impact of Reading on Second Language Learning." *Reading Research Quarterly* 19 (Fall 1983): 53–67.

Fox, Barbara J. "Teaching Reading in the 1990s: The Strengthened Focus on Accountability." *Journal of Reading* 33 (February 1990): 336–39.

McDermott, John W., Jr., "Defining the Role of Religion in the American Classroom." *Religion and Public Education* (April 1987).

Ohlhausen, Marilyn M., and Roller, Cathy M. "The Operation of Text Structure and Content Schemata in Isolation and in Interaction." *Reading Research Quarterly* 23 (Winter 1988): 70–88.

Paul, Michael. "Reading After Survival Literacy: Language Immersion and an Idea from Confucious." *Journal of Reading* 29 (February 1986): 428–27.

Pugh, Sharon L. and Garcia, Jesus. "Portraits in Black: Establishing African American Identity Through Non-Fiction Books." *Journal of Reading* 34 (September 1990): 20–25.

Raths, Louis E.; Harmin, Merrill; and Simon, Sidney B. *Values and Teaching.* Columbus: Charles E. Merrill Publishing Company, 1978.

Resnick, Daniel, and Resnick, Lauren. "The Nature of Literacy: An Historical Explanation." *Harvard Educational Review* 47 (August 1977): 370–85.

Rumelhart, David E. "Towards an Interactive Model of Reading." In *Theoretical Models and Processes of Reading,* Harry Singer and Robert Ruddell, eds. 3d. ed. Newark, Del.: International Reading Association, 1985, pp. 722–50.

Taylor, Denny. "Towards a Unified Theory of Literacy Learning and Instructional Practices." *Phi Delta Kappan* 71 (November 1989): 184–93.

Tierney, Robert et al. "The Effects of Reading and Writing Upon Thinking Critically." *Reading Research Quarterly* 24 (Spring 1989): 134–73.

Tonjes, Marian J. "Reading and Thinking Skills Required in the Subject Classroom." In *The Language of School Subjects,* Bruce Gillham, ed. London: Heinemann Educational Books, Ltd, 1986, pp. 68–75.

Figure 2.1
Promoting affective
dimensions in content
reading: a cognitive
map.

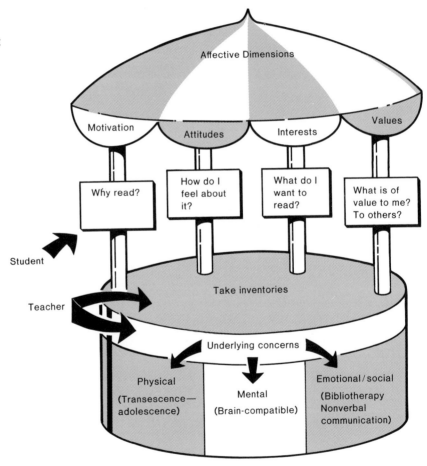

Promoting Affective Dimensions in Content Reading

2

Anticipatory Questions

(Literal)
1. What is meant by levels of the affective domain as described by Krathwohl and others?

(Literal)
2. Describe Maslow's hierarchy of needs.

(Inferential)
3. Why do people read?

(Interpretive)
4. Summarize into one brief paragraph the discussion on limited English proficiency.

(Applied)
5. Select from the general discussion of physical, mental, and emotional/social concerns three ideas that you deem to be most crucial for effective teaching and learning in your content class. Explain your reasons for selection.

Technical Terminology and Concepts

affective dimensions

bibliotherapy

brain-compatible teaching/learning

extrinsic/intrinsic motivation

growth spurts

limited English proficiency (LEP)

motivation

neutral clarifying responses

nonverbal communication

proxemics

transescence/adolescence

values clarification

Students will study what they learn to like, and yet schools too often give only lip service to affective concerns, concentrating instead on cognitive or thinking dimensions. **Affective dimensions** as used here include concern for student motivation, attitudes, interests, and values.

The cognitive map (fig. 2.1) shows the umbrella effect of these four dimensions. The overriding theme of this chapter might well be associated with positive feelings toward learning. For that reason the map takes the general shape of a carousel. Underlying teacher concerns for their students in the physical, mental, emotional, and social stages are reviewed as the underpinnings that affect positive classroom learnings and attitudes.

Affective Dimensions

David Krathwohl and others developed a taxonomy of the affective domain that can be used by content teachers to help elevate students' motivation and involvement.[1] The five levels include receiving, responding, valuing, organizing, and characterizing. A brief description of each level follows.

1. *Receiving.* When students are not receiving information or formulating ideas in whatever form, they are not affectively involved, even at the lowest level. The daydreamer is one example. Those students who dutifully sit in class and pay attention to what is going on are said to be receiving. These are the passive learners. (Range of responses might include: "Tell me about it; I'll listen and think about it.")
2. *Responding.* Students may acquiesce (respond when called upon), volunteer to respond, or show satisfaction in responding voluntarily. (Range of responses here might include: "I'll answer if called upon; I want to answer; I'm glad I answered.")
3. *Valuing.* At a higher level students show that they value reading and learning and, if they read consistently in depth and show their dependence on reading, they have shown a value commitment. Generally, this is the highest level reached in a classroom. ("I value this activity and information; it's important to me; I'll continue to do it and tell others of my interest.")
4. *Organizing.* This is the level where there is some consistency in the value system over a period of time. The value is conceptualized and placed into a niche within the total framework of a student's total value system. ("This is part of my total philosophy.")
5. *Characterizing.* This highest level denotes a total commitment to the value that has been internalized. ("I am willing to state a total commitment to this.")

Lou Burmeister states it well when she says of students: "If they do not receive, they should be elsewhere; if they do not react, they are robots. If they do not value, they do not enjoy, they do not continue to grow and prosper, they do not love: they are devoted to nothing."[2] Thus, teachers need to observe the intensity of interest that students display toward course work and make provisions to intensify that interest.

As they progress through the grades, why is it that many students appear to be less and less interested in school learning? What is it they *do not* want to learn? What is it they *do* want to learn? Could it be that what interests them and what the curriculum provides do not correspond? We *all* want to learn *something*. But when we perceive that the learning expected of us is not meaningful, our reaction is boredom. But no one really wants to be bored either. Content teachers who pay attention to these concerns can do much to alleviate the problem.

Marilyn Van Derbur's questions below may remind us of the need at times to raise rather than lower our expectations of students.[3]

> If you knew about a boy who had twenty-four brothers and sisters, lived in poverty, shuttled from one foster home to another, and dropped out of school at age sixteen, would you expect him to be a success in life or a failure? Should he have set for himself a very high level of aspiration? If you knew that this boy was Flip Wilson, would you say that he was only a rare exception? Flip Wilson said, "I'll never forget one of my teachers. I was always more than a half grade behind because I had been kicked around so much. But she told me I was a bright boy, and she put me at the front of the class with the kids my own age. I did everything to prove to her that I was bright, and I stayed at the head of the class."[4]

Willingness and enthusiasm go hand in hand with attention and involvement. Attentive, involved students will learn more, remember longer, and usually make better use of their learning. They are also less likely to be discipline problems in the classroom.

Many factors influence the inclination to act. Maslow attempted to delineate them in a hierarchical fashion, meaning that lower levels must be satisfied first before achieving higher levels. As shown in figure 2.2, the highest level is the need to know and understand.[5] Those students who still have severe problems in any of the lower levels will not be easily motivated to learn a specified content. As can be seen, prior needs include the physiological, safety, loving and belonging, feelings of self-esteem, and self-actualization.

Figure 2.3 shows growth in acquiring the desire to learn, moving from **extrinsic motivation,** where students need immediate external gratification such as points or prizes, to **intrinsic motivation,** which includes an internal

Motivation

Unmotivated
Students

What Motivated
Flip Wilson?

Bases for Motivation

Motivation and
Maslow's Hierarchy
of Needs

Figure 2.2

Hierarchy and prepotency of needs.

From Herbert J. Klausmeier and William Goodwin, *Learning and Human Abilities: Educational Psychology.* 4th ed. (New York: Harper & Row, 1975), p. 227. Copyright 1975 by Herbert J. Klausmeier and William Goodwin. By permission of the publisher. Drawing based on Maslow.

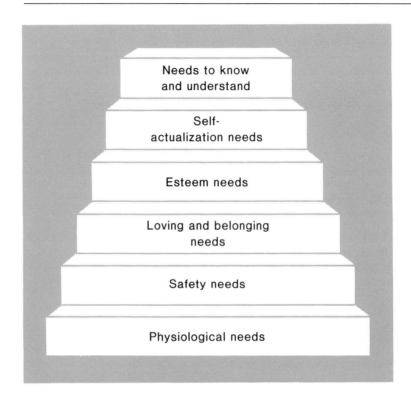

desire for excellence and a natural curiosity. Teachers hope to move students along the continuum to becoming intrinsically motivated to learn their subject.

Motivation and Reading

The focus here is on the role of motivation in reading, especially in reading to master content. As David Ausubel states:

> Even though particular instances of learning may be largely unmotivated, it is undoubtedly true that the subject matter in question must be related to felt needs if significant, *long-term* meaningful learning is to occur. . . . Learners who have little need to know and understand, quite naturally expend relatively little learning effort. . . . It is unrealistic to expect that school subjects can be effectively learned and retained until pupils develop a felt need to acquire knowledge as an end in itself—since much school knowledge can never be rationalized as necessary for meeting the demands of daily living.[6]

Figure 2.3
Growth in intrinsic motivations; acquiring the desire to learn.

From Zintz/Maggart, *The Reading Process,* 5th ed. (Dubuque, Ia.: Wm. C. Brown Publishers, 1989), p. 44. Used with permission.

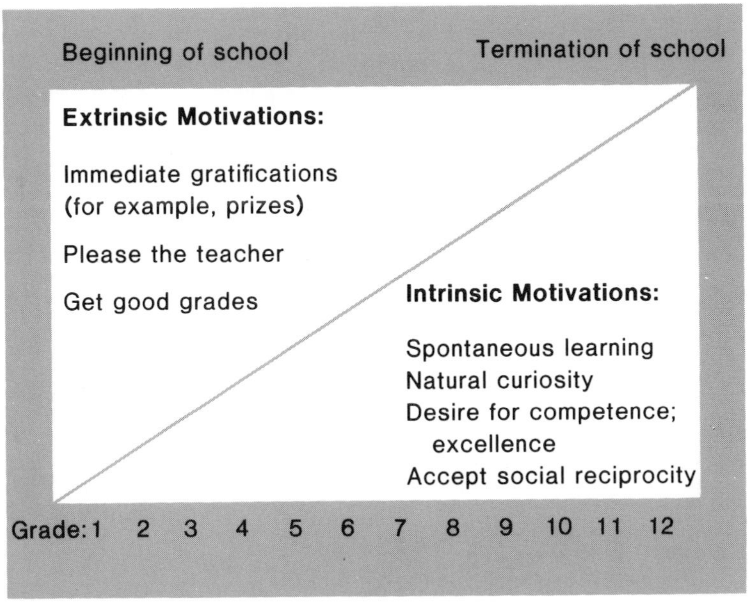

Beginning of school   Termination of school

Extrinsic Motivations:

Immediate gratifications
(for example, prizes)

Please the teacher

Get good grades

Intrinsic Motivations:

Spontaneous learning
Natural curiosity
Desire for competence;
  excellence
Accept social reciprocity

Grade: 1   2   3   4   5   6   7   8   9   10   11   12

Workshop Activity 2.1
Brainstorming: Why Do People Read?

Why do people, students in particular, *choose* to read instead of engaging in other activities? We could easily give you a list here of five or more main points to memorize for a quiz. Instead, we believe you will better remember this if you contribute personally. (Some suggested responses are shown on page 59.)

Initially, some content teachers may find it difficult to see the reasons why they need to motivate students to read more widely for appreciation and pleasure. "That's the job for the English teacher or the reading specialist," they firmly believe. The following three major arguments should help to convince them otherwise.

Why Motivate
Students to Read
for Pleasure?

1. A particular content area, such as science, may be the only one in which a group of students is really interested at the time.

Having collateral reading materials readily available, such as science fiction, should spur them on to reading for pleasure and at the same time reinforce or expand on their knowledge of content concepts.

2. On the other hand, those students who are "turned off" to a subject such as history may develop more positive attitudes toward it when they encounter light fiction set in the same setting and in the same time period. This helps them with their visual imagery of the historical facts and may flesh out important concepts.

3. Some content teachers serve as role models for particular students. They have built up a sense of trust and rapport. Those teachers may be the only ones in the position to convince reluctant readers to try reading for pleasure. For example, physical education teachers can urge reading of sports stories in fiction or biographies of successful athletes.

Enthusiastic content teachers who provide access to an interesting variety of materials, alert their students to what is readily available, and then allow time *in class* for sustained silent reading (self-selected and uninterrupted reading) are helping to create lifelong readers (see also chapter 11).

How to Increase Content Classroom Motivation for Reading

Some guidelines for teachers are included below:

1. Because motivation is as much an effect as a cause of learning, we should not wait for motivation to develop in students before engaging in classroom learning activities.

2. Make the objective of the reading assignment explicit to the students, because when they do not readily see it as being practical, they will need to see a relationship to other kinds of knowledge and abilities.

3. Make use of their existing interests and motivations.

4. Use attention-attracting materials to arouse intellectual curiosity.

5. Assign reading tasks according to each student's ability level to help forestall frustration and failure.

6. Help students set realistic goals and practice self-evaluation of progress toward these goals by giving prompt, informative feedback and providing tasks that test the limits of their abilities.

7. Avoid excessive use of *extrinsic motivation* ("m and m's" or "carrots"), as well as aversive (punitive) motivation that operates on the fear principle ("Do this for a test on Friday").

8. Look for changes in individual needs, differences, and developmental patterns.

Workshop Activity 2.2
Motivating Techniques

Place a plus mark by those items you do or plan to do on a regular, frequent basis with your students. Place a question mark if you are not certain and a minus mark if you think it is completely unnecessary. Use this as the basis for small group discussions with the goal of trying to reach consensus or an agreement to disagree. An alternative would be to rank order the items.

_____ 1. Set aside a regular block of time each week for self-selected, content-oriented, uninterrupted reading.
_____ 2. Provide a wide variety of collateral reading materials in the classroom from newspapers and magazines to serious reference books.
_____ 3. Use a general interest or activity inventory to identify students' areas of interest.
_____ 4. Use a general reading interest inventory to find out how students rate different types of reading from the newspaper (news items, sports articles, editorials, cartoons, comic strips, advice columns, etc.); from magazines (sports, movie, science, mechanical, homemaking, etc.); from books (biographies, short stories, essays, poems, plays, how-to books, etc.).
_____ 5. Use a content interest inventory specifically designed for your course. For example, Walter Lamberg and Charles Lamb describe a sample inventory for a math unit. A portion is included below:

Read through the list of materials and check two you would like to read during our two-week unit on measurement.   Measurement

_____ 1. Short pieces on cultures help to develop measurement ideas (such as foot, inch and mile).
_____ 2. Articles from journals which are in favor of adoption of the metric system.
_____ 3. The history of metrication in the U.S.
_____ 4. Materials on Olympic contests involving metric measurement.
_____ 5. How-to books involving problems in measurement, such as making kites.[7]

Dorothy Rathbun uses an intriguing title for an article on motivation: "How to Get Middle Schoolers to Read When They're Not Too Thrilled about the Idea and You're Not Too Sure about What to Do Anyway."[8] She has several apt statements.

"Paperbacks _look_ easier to read and can be stuffed into pockets or purses."

"Kids _do_ judge books by their covers, and so should you."

"Kids don't set out to steal the books; they're just careless and forgetful."

"*Your* living example is important."

"You *do* need common sense and a lot of time and patience."

"There's really no way to avoid the nasty word 'motivation'—that will always remain largely in the hands of the individual teacher."

> If you walked into a room all sweaty from gym class and so hungry you think you might die before lunch and then some big shot told you to read pages 97 to 108 on the Industrial Revolution and write out good answers to questions 1 through 6 at the top of page 109 and also said, "Don't ask why, just do it because I said so"—well, how anxious would you be to read?[9]

Attitudes

Social Changes Affecting Attitudes

The Jules Feiffer cartoon presented in figure 2.4 clearly demonstrates the serious conflict that exists between many parents and their children. For the great majority of today's parents, they recall that the positive virtues of George Washington were always extolled in school in such a way as to suggest that he had no negative ones. For example, slaves living on plantations were always shown in somewhat obscure pictures as having a jolly time dancing around bonfires. Because textbooks were published to maximize national appeal to increase sales, no negative features were presented that could be offensive.[10] The trails to the West Coast, the severe hardships of the women, the loss of life, and the lack of life's necessities as they traveled led students to see that the European immigrants were the ones who suffered in satisfying their great personal drive to move all the way to the Pacific Coast. To this day, as Kirkness testifies, children are apt to learn, from whatever source, to apply descriptive terms to ethnic groups: "devoted Christians, great Jews, hardworking immigrants, infidel Moslems, primitive Negroes, and savage Indians."[11] And they will probably be able to testify that their generation was, by some subtle means, led to believe that if we had to fight in a war, God would be on *our* side. Textbooks did not change in this respect until about twenty years ago.

This half of the cartoon must be contrasted with the serious effort of the total society (of which *one* agent is the school) to offer people the *truth* as it is now believed of these historical events. In recent times, over three hundred Indian tribes have been empowered to sue the American government for taking possession of their land, and many have won their suits. The nationally televised showing of *Roots*[12] as well as its sequel dispelled for all time the nature of the family life of slaves prior to 1865 and of blacks for decades after. No one wants to deny heroes such as George Washington the heritage that they deserve. However, Washington and others did own slaves—that fact is a part of his life story.

Historians are free now to write about Thomas Jefferson's personal life, facts that have long been omitted from textbooks. Because so many noble achievements are credited to him, it was not until 1975 that *Ebony* magazine provided general reading that Jefferson fathered five mulatto children with the "slave" woman who traveled to France with his family to care for his daughters.[13]

Figure 2.4
Values are changing during the present generation.

These are, for some people, radical changes in textbook writing. Parents need opportunities to discuss with teachers reasons why today's students are expected to understand both sides of an issue and to develop the ability to openly discuss controversial problems.

Kenneth Dulin has described five practical ways in which content teachers may enhance attitudes toward reading.[14] These include (1) identification, (2) rewards, (3) successful experiences, (4) adapting to students' individual reading needs, and (5) building the habit of reading.

Building Positive Attitudes Toward Reading

1. Identification means building strong, positive attitudes by showing our own enthusiasm and respect for reading. This can be accomplished by sharing our own reading experiences with students and encouraging them to share with us and each other; and by creating a classroom atmosphere showing that reading is important and useful. Such teachers as the coach, the music director, or the shop instructor may be a potent model to students in this area.
2. Rewards include grades, social approval, and concrete reinforcement which may be used effectively at the start until intrinsic rewards follow. Reading assignments should *never* be used as punishment.

3. Successful experiences in reading breed positive attitudes. This means providing more opportunities to read materials that are easily comprehended.
4. Adapting to students' individual needs requires that teachers become aware of their interests and reading ability levels as well as the readability levels of the text materials.
5. Building the habit of reading is accomplished through some allowance during class time for some regularly scheduled reading practice, such as sustained silent reading.

Interests

In chapter 4 on informal diagnosis, there is a discussion of assessing student interests through the administration of either a general interest inventory or a content-specific one. In chapter 1, you had the opportunity to ascertain some of your own variety of reading interests, from magazine or newspaper sections to novels, poetry, and plays. This could also be adapted for use with your own students.

Depending on the age group you teach, there are specific problems and interests for each level. After age ten and up to adulthood there appear to be three overriding themes; the search for self-identity, how they relate to others, and the process of becoming an adult.

G. R. Carlsen in 1975 noted a shift of interest from "doing your own thing" to "getting it all together."[15] Teenagers seem to prefer books that deal with worthwhile heroes and values and that offer some sense of hope. Interests of early to late adolescents were grouped in three age levels: early (ages 11–14), middle (ages 15–16), and late (ages 16–18). See table 2.1 for specific interests for each level. Some interests at lower age levels extend on through adulthood.

Table 2.1
Reading Interests of Adolescents

Early Ages 11–14	Middle Ages 15–16	Late Ages 16–18
Animal stories	Nonfiction adventure stories and accounts	Search for personal values, identity
Adventure		
Mystery	War stories	Social significance
Supernatural tales	Historical novels	Strange, unique human experiences
Sports	Mystical romance	
Growing up around the world	Contemporary stories of adolescent life	Transition into adulthood
Slapstick comedy		

Values clarification is a technique used to help people identify their values, think about them, and clarify their position. This necessitates thinking about what is really important and acting on these beliefs when appropriate to do so. In identifying one's own values and clarifying adherence to them, there are three facets: (1) prizing, (2) choosing from alternatives, and (3) acting on those beliefs.[16]

Values

Values Clarification

Values clarification techniques help students answer their own questions and define their own values. There have always been teachers who have tried to help young people think through and find *their own* answers to issues and questions. The term *values clarification* is an attempt to systematize a technique that can be easily understood and incorporated with the content. In values clarification, the process requires that you know *why* you prize certain things, why you consistently choose those things over others, and why you are willing to stand up for and act in accordance with your beliefs.

Teachers can challenge students to think about what they value. Most students in your classes will have already internalized a set of values or habits and practices acquired from their extended family, community, and private world. Teachers need to provide a psychologically safe climate for students to be secure and to express their feelings without being "judged."

Teaching Values Clarification

A helpful tool to have at your command is a few neutral clarifying responses that will help students choose and deepen their commitment to their values. A few neutral statements are:[17]

Neutral Clarifying Responses

> Is this very important to you?
> Was it something you really wanted to do?
> Did you have to do it that way, or did you have a free choice?
> Should everyone think like that?
> How did you feel when that happened?
> Did you *do* anything about that idea?
> Have you felt this way for a long time?

Clarifying values is a process then of guiding students to

1. choose from the available possibilities;
2. prize the choice accepted and be willing to declare it as their choice;
3. consistently act on the choice.

Criteria for valuing are based on self-directed behavior. Values clarification does *not* teach or impose values; it leads to discovery of what we *do* value.

Merrill Harmin gives us some suggestions for helping students clarify values.[18]

1. *Model desirable behavior.* There will be students in all classrooms who are immature in some respects: those whose beliefs of right and wrong are narrow and inflexible; those without a set of working values; those who have never established habits valued in schools, such as punctuality, neatness, finishing assignments, cooperation, or helpfulness. As models, if we talk about tolerance, we must not show annoyance easily. If we ask students to stop complaining, we must show them how to deal with troublesome episodes.

2. *Help students feel that they matter.* Interacting on an open, friendly level and accepting them as responsible people is of primary importance. When responding to students, reflect their feelings and refer to specific examples; "You seem to be saying . . . When you mention. . . ." Use their answer in a questioning situation to constructively expand interaction. Aspy and others suggest that you request students to extend, clarify, justify, or support their answer, redirect their responses to include a prior student's response, and/or incorporate their responses as a basis for elicitation from the next student.[19]

3. *Help students feel capable and appreciated.* Everyone is capable of some contribution to the class. If we emphasize the positive and diminish or eliminate the negative when possible, the emotional climate will improve.

4. *Accept confusion with empathy.* Value confusions can fall into several categories. Examples include the social feeling of "I *don't want* to go along with the crowd"; or the moral dilemma posed by the question "Should Nazis be allowed to march in Skokie, Illinois, where many of the survivors of Auschwitz live?" even if the ACLU says "Yes, they have the *right* to do so"; or the practical dilemma "I'm going to drop out of school to work and save money so I can come back to school." It is helpful here to encourage students to think about alternatives, although still empathizing with the problem. In the latter example, you might ask if there could be another possible solution they could think of.

5. *Encourage the sharing of confusions.* Sometimes we get upset with others, when we are actually upset with ourselves. When students overreact you may ask, "Why are you upset?" or "Why are you upset *with me*?" Thus an effort is made to listen and accept, to relax anxieties through reassurance, and to look for rational answers to problems. The question is "What is the right thing *for me* to do?"

6. *Make learning a living process.* Learning about our values is an active process. Making choices from alternatives, sifting pressures to achieve greater working comfort, and then making commitments to a selected way of behaving is a demanding but rewarding process. There are times when it is appropriate to accept some ambivalence in feelings as a viable alternative.

7. *Introduce neglected issues for deliberation.* Such as, "When, if ever, is a good time to lie or cheat? There are many social injustices that we just have to live with. Do you agree or not? Why?"

8. *Encourage students to include prizing, choosing, and acting in their deliberations.* This will provide students with the opportunity to move from one alternative to the *next* to arrive at a mature conclusion. Give them a choice from alternatives, noting the consequences and encouraging them in prizing, affirming, acting, and building new patterns of behavior.

9. *Expand awareness of consequences.* Students may progress through a series of steps: (a) being unaware; (b) taking punishment; (c) listening to appeal to self-interest; (d) seeking approval of others; (e) stabilizing and structuring.

10. *Be forthright about your own values but do not impose them.* Teachers should be natural—not manipulative—in presenting their own views. For example, "I'd do it this way, but there are other acceptable ways."

11. *Communicate hope and trust.* There were problems in the "good old days," too! If you can look objectively at your surroundings, you are sure to accept the notion that we really are evolving better practices through time.

The human ego is strange and curious—it expresses the frailty of human nature in so many ways. We each have a desperate need to protect our inner being from insult and injury, and we do this in curious ways. Often we fail to accept, or see, or understand those qualities of personality that others exhibit even though we may, to a greater degree, exhibit the same behavior. Being able to identify easily the *mote* in the eye of another, and not recognizing the *beam* in our own, leads to such logic as the following:

I am firm.
You are obstinate.
He is a pig-headed fool.

I am righteously indignant.
You are annoyed.
He is making a fuss about nothing.

I am beautiful.
You have quite good features.
She isn't bad looking, if you like that type.

These patterns of thought may be why values clarification must take a significant place in guidance given to students if they are to take their place in the adult world with greater assurance about who they are, why they are here, and where they are going.

Workshop Activity 2.3

Three Motivating Values Exercises (This first exercise can be done with an entire class or individually.)

1) Twenty Things I Like to Do

Learning about what we really value as it relates to school can be a strong incentive to trying to become a better student, because it is more powerful for students to discover for themselves rather than listen to a lecture on "oughts" and "shoulds." This activity is motivating and can be illuminating. Take a sheet of paper and number 1–20 down the middle. Quickly write down the 20 things you most like to do in this world, knowing you will not be required to share your responses.

Now, go back over your list and do some categorizing with symbols. Put a $ sign by all items that would cost you at least $5 every time you do it. Put an "S" by all items that could easily and appropriately be done in school. Put an "A" by all those items you usually do alone. Other possibilities include:

R—for risktaking
M—for Mother did it at my age
F—for Father did it at my age

Those who wish may share one thing they learned from this exercise.

From Simon, Sidney, L. Home and H. Kirschenbaum, *Values Clarification: Handbook of Practical Suggestions for Teachers and Students,* New York: Hart Publishing Co., 1972.

2) Rank Order

You are shipwrecked alone on a desert island and can have only one of the following. Rank them according to 1–most desired to 3–least desired.

_____ 1. Complete works of Shakespeare
_____ 2. The Bible
_____ 3. Encyclopaedia Britannica

Voluntarily defend your choice with reasons why. (This should provide a dynamic discussion, even with the most reticent class.)

3) Understanding Self and Others

Answer yes or no in column A, fold back, and exchange papers with a partner. The partner answers in column B how he or she thought you answered. You do the same with the partner's paper. When finished, open up and discuss the items that were different. Then find another partner for column C. Do as many times as feasible.

ARE YOU SOMEONE WHO USUALLY:

(These items can be adapted to particular subject areas if desired. For example, select Shakespeare's writings over World History.)

Self			Others			
A	B	C	D	E	F	
						1. Likes to get the highest grade on an exam?
						2. Likes to stay up most of the night talking when friends visit?
						3. Will stop the car anywhere convenient to look at a sunset?
						4. Puts things off until the last minute.
						5. Prefers reading to sports activities?
						6. Will do it yourself when you feel something needs doing?
						7. Will order a new dish in a restaurant?
						8. Will publicly show affection for another person?
						9. Could be satisfied without a college degree?
						10. Could be part of a mercy killing?
						11. Is afraid alone in the dark in a strange place?
						12. Is eager to participate in class discussions?
						13. Eats when worried or upset?
						14. Can receive a gift easily?

Self		Others				(These items can be adapted to particular subject areas if desired. For example, select Shakespeare's writings over World History.)
A	B	C	D	E	F	
						15. Would steal apples from a remote orchard?
						16. Is apt to judge someone initially by physical appearance alone?
						17. Sees life as an exciting adventure?
						18. Watches television soap operas whenever possible?
						19. Could kill in self-defense?
						20. Needs to be alone a great deal?
						21. Prefers reading to watching television?

Limited English Proficiency (LEP)

A few years ago on national television a teenage boy who was an immigrant from the Far East and who had arrived in this country only four years earlier knowing no English delivered the Valedictory address in excellent English for his large high school graduating class. This boy's success is *not* typical. Millions of youngsters have problems today trying to master both our language and an ability to study in that language. The 1980 census showed that 10 percent of school-age children in the United States have varying degrees of limited English proficiency (LEP).[20]

Methods for teaching English as a second language (ESL) have changed in the last thirty years. In the 1960s it was heavily slanted toward adult students, using pattern practice, mim-mem, audio-lingual methodology. Young children, however, did not generally master English by using these pattern drills because it was boring to teachers and students alike.[21] Creative teachers were quick to try something else, thus adding folk songs, verses, rhymes, singing games, and headphones for listening to cassettes, all of which helped with pitch, intonation, and the rhythm of the language.

In the mid-1970s the National Approach to Language Learning came into being.[22] This approach emphasizes a low-anxiety, risk-taking environment; material comprehensible to the learner; and a different viewpoint about how language is acquired. Focus is on the message itself more than the structure of the language. When we start with the students finding out what content is important, interesting, or necessary to them and encourage them to talk freely about it, they will talk because they want to talk. Thus they are negotiating their own language.

James Asher and B. Price developed what has been called the Total Physical Response.[23] In the beginning all new language should be learning to understand spoken commands and to exercise these commands without requiring speaking in any language. If the teacher says "Stand up and turn around twice," everyone in the group does just this. There is no pressure at this point to speak.

A model of bilingualism that Jim Cummins supported is called Common Underlying Proficiency.[24] The cognitive/academic proficiency gained in the first language is equally useful in the second if learners know the labels in both languages so they can associate. The new language learner must develop basic interpersonal communicative skills (BICS), which include all language needed for daily interpersonal communication plus another facet of language to insure success in content areas—cognitive/academic language proficiency (CALP). This includes such things as time, measurement, and distance concepts in mathematics; metaphor, simile, and idiom in English literature; latitude, altitude, equator, and earth life tones in geography.

Further suggestions for all content teachers can be found within the following annotated list:

1. Philip C. Gonzales, "How to Begin Language Instruction for Non-English-Speaking Students," *Language Arts* 58 (February 1981): 175–180. Gives specific suggestions for teaching English to non-English-speaking youngsters.
2. Estolia Perez, "Oral Language Competence Improves Reading Skills of Mexican-American Third Graders," *The Reading Teacher* 35 (October 1981): 24–27. Reports on a small study that improved the competence of Mexican-Americans.
3. Mavis Martin and Miles V. Zintz, "Concerns About Comprehension of Children with Limited English Proficiency," *The New Mexico Journal of Reading* 5 (Fall 1984): 6–11. Illustrates how teachers can use the schema concept through webbing to show language learners multiple meanings and interrelationships among many common words.
4. Don Holdaway, *Foundations of Literacy* (Sydney, Australia: Ashton Scholastic, 1979). Describes the shared book experience as an informal method that works.
5. Warwick B. Elley and Francis Mangabhai, "The Impact of Reading on Second Language Learning," *Reading Research Quarterly* 19 (Fall 1983): 53–67. Describes a second-language program in Fiji Island, South Pacific, where generally very few books were available for student selection. Using a sustained

silent reading program or a shared book experience approach the study strongly supported and provided a wide range of suitable, well-illustrated, high-interest material for LEP students.

Physical Stages of Student Development

Physical stages of growth and development for students in content classrooms include *transescence* and *adolescence.*

Transescence

The years referred to as "preadolescent" and the time following that referred to as "early adolescence" constitute a troublesome time for many students. Donald Eichhorn, who coined the term *transescence,* defined it as the stage in the young person's life that begins prior to the onset of puberty and extends through the early stages of adolescence.[25]

Transescence transfers into adolescence when most of the students have entered puberty and have passed what may have been the anxious or apprehensive period of growing up.

> Transescent preoccupation with the personal and social events surrounding puberty are vividly portrayed in the novels of Judy Blume, such as *Are You There, God? It's Me, Margaret.* Indeed, the phenomenal popularity of her books stems largely from her sensitivity to the concerns of young people in this period of life.[26]

The concept of transescence is useful for upper elementary and middle school teachers and counselors in studying the problems of youngsters in these turbulent years and in meeting with and assisting these students in dealing with their personal and social problems.

The impact of puberty changes is extensive—physically, emotionally, socially, and culturally. Anxiety and emotional stress directly affect learning. Such forces as family stability, family mobility, peer group demands, and the suddenly changing interests of individual students cannot be overlooked by teachers.

> The hidden curriculum today, or what the school teaches by implication, is vastly more complex than the hidden curriculum of earlier decades when there was more likely to be substantial agreement on moral truisms to buttress the schools' efforts.[27]

Concerned teachers may wish to pursue this topic further. (See recommended readings at the end of the chapter.)

Adolescence

Adolescence, which comes from the Latin verb *adolescere,* means the state or process of growing up—that period of life from puberty to maturity that terminates legally at the age of majority.

Understanding the problems of the adolescent has been a major concern of educators since the publication of the monumental work of G. Stanley Hall in 1904.[28] His "evolutionary theory," his "ontogeny recapitulates phylogeny," and his inclusion of moral judgments are aspects of his writing that are seldom talked about today. He discussed the conflicts faced in growing up and becoming "adult," and his personal prestige gave great weight to his teaching and writing at the time.

August Hollinghead, another noted authority, describes adolescence as

. . . the period of life of a person when the society in which he functions ceases to regard him/her as a child and does not accord to him/her full adult status roles, and functions. . . . It is defined by the roles the person is expected to play, is allowed to play, is forced to play, or prohibited from playing by virtue of his/her status in society.[29]

After studying the psychological problems of growing up—from infancy to adolescence—Robert Havighurst identified what he called *developmental tasks*.[30] Some of those tasks of growing up that are related to the preadolescent years are: learning appropriate sex roles; developing concepts for everyday living; developing conscience, morality, and values; and developing social skills of interaction. Some of the tasks related more specifically to adolescence are: accepting their own bodies, developing emotional independence, and becoming socially responsible. Students acquire the skills of growing up in society at very different rates and times. Maturing is an ongoing process that is continued all the way through life. One of the classroom teacher's concerns is that students respond to and meet their daily needs for recognition, acceptance, and status in acceptable ways rather than in unacceptable ways promoted at times by peer groups.

Mental Considerations

Brain-Compatible Teaching and Learning

Characteristic **brain growth spurts** suggest that the period from ages ten to twelve is one of rapid growth and opportunity for innovative learning and that a final stage between ages fourteen to sixteen is one of rapid growth. However, the stage from ages twelve to fourteen when students are normally in grades seven and eight, can be a plateau period in development. Teachers of students in middle school should rely on the possibilities in these findings, realizing the importance of consolidation and review for students of this age.

Leslie Hart defines learning as "the accommodation of facts to what is already known."[31] All learning, he says, is built on previous learning. And because no two individuals have had the same experiences, no two have the same background of knowledge on which to build. Herman Epstein, whose work generally complements that of Hart, identifies growth spurts in brain development.[32] They have identified brain growth spurts at the following age intervals: three to ten months, two to four years, six to eight years, ten to twelve years, and fourteen to sixteen years. These relate well to the growth and development patterns described by Piaget except that Piaget had no counterpart for the fourteen to sixteen age growth spurt.[33]

It is interesting to recall that John Dewey had identified intellectual growth patterns as early as 1938, before such knowledge was available from a research point of view. Dewey wrote that we "must survey the capacities and needs of the particular set of individuals with whom we are dealing and must, at the same time, arrange the conditions which provide the subject matter or content for experience that satisfy these needs and develop these capacities.[34]

And Alfred North Whitehead referred to the idea of intellectual stages as early as 1929, when he wrote:

> "The pupil's progress is often conceived as a uniform steady advance undifferentiated by changes of type or alteration in pace. . . . I hold that this conception of education is based on a false psychology of the process of mental development which has gravely hindered the effectiveness of our methods. Life is essentially periodic. . . . There are . . . periods of mental growth, with their cyclic recurrences. . . . Lack of attention to the rhythm and character of mental growth is a main source of wooden futility in education"[35]

Hart believes that "program structure" is what holds the brain together and the brain is capable of carrying on a huge amount of program structuring simultaneously. Much of the program structuring that gets us through our daily routine is unconscious—no conscious thought need be directed to putting on a shirt or taking off a sock, for example. As long as the brain functions, new program structures are being acquired.[36]

Fox has illustrated how the word *red* carries with it, in our brains, interrelationships of words and events that constitute many program structures (see figure 2.5).[37]

As mentioned earlier, research is suggesting that students in the period of low brain growth (ages twelve and thirteen) may have difficulty initiating new cognitive skills and will thus achieve more when their time is spent consolidating those cognitive skills acquired in the preceding period of greater brain growth (ages ten and eleven).

Herman Epstein and Conrad Toepfer reiterate this thought as they emphasize the difficulty of presenting complex thinking processes to these transescent students:

> With virtually no increase of brain size and mass in the large majority of twelve- to fourteen-year-olds, there is no growth in the capacity of the brain to handle more complex thinking processes usually introduced in grades seven and eight. This continued demand for the youngster's brain to handle increasingly complex input, which he or she cannot comprehend during this period, may result in rejection of these inputs and the possible development of negative neural networks to dissipate the energy of the input. Thus, it is

Figure 2.5
One program structure for the word *red*.

Reprinted with permission of Patricia L. Fox and the International Reading Association. "Reading as a Whole Brain Function." *The Reading Teacher* 33: page 13, Oct. 1979.

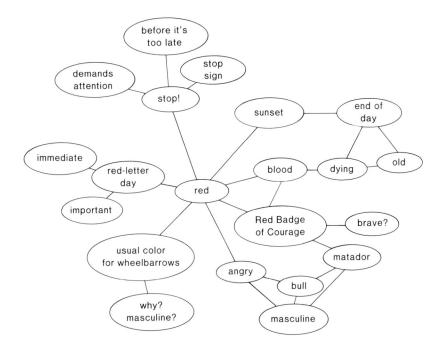

possible that even when the subsequent growth of the brain between ages fourteen and sixteen could support the development of more complex cognitive skills, the untold numbers of individuals who have developed such negative networks have been so "turned off" that they literally can no longer develop novel cognitive skills.[38]

Hart suggests that the process of learning today's lesson depends little on how you present it and much on the total previously stored experiences in the student's brain. He believes that the traditional teaching in schools is grossly brain incompatible. Teaching that *is* brain compatible recognizes that[39]

1. each brain is aggressive, unique in its seeking out, demanding, and accepting only what it needs *now* to make sense out of the reality of the environment;
2. students must *talk* to learn well because much of the brain is devoted to language activity;
3. students have a need to be free to move around, talk to people, explore possibilities, work on real projects;

4. the brain is an elaborate complex of innumerable "programs" that will admit only what it decides to—and each brain processes what it does admit in different ways;
5. the neocortex (the newest part of the brain and five/sixths of the whole brain in humans) does not function well under threat or pressure (think of the implications of that!);
6. the brain has little use for step-by-step logic—it is a computer operating by programs or schemata (established sequences); not by precision, but by great, vague approximations.

Thus, learning means active participation—not being talked at, explained to, prodded to give correct answers, or being constantly corrected or given low grades.

A Call to
Restructure Schools

In 1989 Hart talked about the atrocity of the four-walled classroom box where failure techniques are built into the structure of schooling: lecturing and telling; questioning for "right" answers; using mock discussion techniques; emphasizing recall of facts; relying on textbooks and teacher's manuals; and employing junk seatwork, esteem-shattering grading, and the punishment of "classroom management."[40] He calls our system a factory approach and suggests six specific changes that will be brain compatible.

1. *Work from theory*—not trial and error—which empowers teachers to find instructional directions that regularly help students learn.
2. *Do not teach content in bits*—but integrate, emphasizing patterns of how parts interrelate and also emphasizing programs that ask students to perform tasks in realistic situations.
3. *Do not teach in isolated, lockstep blocks of time*—because learning advances as a flow of experience, exploration, and integration.
4. *Gradually dump unproductive practices*—such as the failure techniques mentioned above.
5. *Shift to activities that promote learning*—such as creating a nonthreatening learning environment, allowing for cooperative learning, and moving away from just correcting the wrong to coaching with encouragement.
6. *Do not isolate teachers*—but encourage collegial team teaching by teacher choice and support conference attendance and teachers' professional organizations.

Another call to restructure schools was made by Theodore Sizer at a lecture to local Albuquerque educators. Sizer said that America should dump its century-old, highly structured public high school system and instead create schools that force students to think. He believes that today's high school curriculum is too fractionalized and relies too much on lecturing. He suggests that high schools begin concentrating on doing fewer things well, do away with grouping students solely on age, and keep teachers' loads to no more than eighty students a day so that they can better know the thinking processes of each student.[41]

Perhaps we will actually begin to apply these learnings when we have reaccepted Dewey's principle of "learning by doing," and when we have listened to Hart's concerns about *how* students learn, to Epstein's concerns about *when* students learn, and to Piaget's concern about *what* they learn. Students and schools can then become more brain compatible.

Social/Emotional Dimensions

Bibliotherapy

Therapy through books (bibliotherapy) is a process in which readers identify with a character or situation and connect it with their own problem. According to Tews, **bibliotherapy** is a program of selected activity involving reading material that is planned, conducted, and controlled as treatment under the guidance of a physician treating emotional and other problems.[42]

The message in print material has different values for different people. If the right book is selected at the right time, books may provide the language and ideas to resolve personal problems. Bibliotherapy is concerned with the personality mechanisms of: (1) identification, (2) catharsis, and (3) insight. Each must be present for a dynamic interaction to occur between reader and text.

1. *Identification* means that readers must identify with character elements of the story; they must share some characteristics such as age, sex, hopes, fears, problems. If readers can identify with and admire the character, they may be able to build self-image or increase feelings of belonging. Sometimes when this personal identification is not possible, these positive effects can occur through hero worship of a character. Identification, then, is the recognition of some commonalities between reader and character.
2. *Catharsis* is the sharing of motivations, conflicts, and emotions of a character in a book. It is an active release of emotions, experienced either firsthand or vicariously. It goes beyond the simple recognition of commonalities and involves empathy (feeling as the character does). Readers relive their own past experience. Generating empathy is basic to catharsis.
3. *Insight* requires that after picturing ourselves in the behavior patterns of a particular character in a book, we build an awareness of our own motivations, needs, or problems. We need to be able to see similarities and differences between the self and the fictional character. At this point readers consider a course of action to try to overcome problems. This step requires taking some action so as to meet a specific need.

Personality changes occur through responses to emotional experiences, not merely through teaching and learning. Intellect is not a key factor in the therapeutic process. The personality change in bibliotherapy requires the three processes of identification, catharsis, and insight. We overcome feelings of guilt, inadequacy, or inferiority by identifying these in a character; generalizing or seeing these traits as universals in human behavior; and then being able to express "bad" feelings while understanding them as a catharsis. With adults this is achieved usually through talking, with children through action (e.g., play therapy).

Bibliotherapy is a powerful tool. If teachers recommend books to their students for therapeutic purposes, they should abide by these cautions:

1. Students *must* have freedom of choice in what they read.
2. There is *no* pressure to show results in terms of book reports or discussions.
3. When in doubt, proceed with caution!

Nonverbal Communication

Nonverbal communication includes all those ways by which we send messages other than by use of words. We actually say more to the students in nonverbal ways than verbal. Generally speaking, students are in need of adult support and are apt to feel defensive when they have done something wrong, made a mistake, or felt inadequate in required tasks. Recognizing these conditions makes it easy to understand the importance of a smile or the withholding of a smile, a pleasant tone of voice or a stern, unfriendly tone, a friendly proximity to the class or a distant, standoffish posture behind the desk. Even eye behavior in our culture requires that the interested person look directly into your eyes to communicate.

Charles Galloway reminds us that

> Nonverbal communication is present in every face-to-face conversation. A person instinctively watches those he talks with to determine whether they are interested in and understand the spoken words. Routinely he glances into the other person's face at the end of the statement. While talking, he notices the other person's posture, body movements, and gestures as additional indicators of interest and understanding. The listener is "hearing" not only the words chosen by the speaker but also the inflections in his voice, the movement of his eyes, and his stance. If their exchange goes well, a rhythmic balance of give and take occurs.[43]

The institutional greens or mud-colored walls of school buildings, the outmoded picture frames that display portraits of Washington and Lincoln, the bolted-down desks and chairs in inflexible rows, the loud jangling of bells at precise times regardless of thinking needs; hair grooming, the mode of dress, the presence or absence of perfume, even the contrast of stiff or relaxed posture of teacher and students—all of these things are communicating messages all day long. The great variety of ways in which approval or disapproval may be expressed include giving simple personal recognition, giving special attention, standing close by, gesturing, smiling, or frowning.[44]

People use nonverbal cues to serve several different functions within the communication process. Six are listed here:

Functions of Nonverbal Behavior

1. *Redundancy* here means responding in more than one way to convey the same message. If you say, "I live over there," and, at the same time, you point with one index finger in the direction of your house, you have conveyed the same message twice. Thus, one response is redundant.
2. A second nonverbal function is *accentuation.* The highlighting or emphasizing of a verbal message with gestures is an example. If the teacher says angrily to the class, "This time no papers will be accepted until they are done correctly," and then hits the desk vigorously with a fist, the nonverbal message emphasizes the verbal one.
3. Sometimes we *substitute* the nonverbal message for the verbal one. If students are severely reprimanded, they may not respond verbally, but as soon as the teacher's back is turned, they may make a gesture or smile knowingly to other students.
4. We have many ways of *regulating* the flow of verbal behavior. Avoiding eye contact in close proximity, giving someone "the cold shoulder," or pretending to be too busy to notice the other person are ways of preventing communication.
5. *Complementary* nonverbal behavior expands and adds emphasis to the verbal behavior. Placing a hand on a student's shoulder when you say, "I liked the way you did that," complements the verbal behavior.
6. Finally, the nonverbal behavior may be clear *contradiction* of the verbal behavior. If the teacher says sweetly, "I'm sure you did the best you could," but has a cold, rejecting manner, then the body language will speak louder than the words, and the student has little trouble reading the real meaning.

Freud wrote:

> He that has eyes to see and ears to hear may convince himself that no mortal can keep a secret. If his lips are silent, he chatters with his fingertips; betrayal oozes out of him at every pore. And thus the task of making conscious the most hidden recesses of the mind is one which it is quite possible to accomplish.[45]

Estimates show that in the normal interpersonal conversation, the verbal aspects carry less than 35 percent of the social meaning and more than 65 percent is transmitted by nonverbal components.[46]

Workshop Activity 2.4
Nonverbal Cues

Using the list of six nonverbal cues as a guide, in triads take turns demonstrating each in mixed order. The others must guess which one is being demonstrated. Students may then make up their own cues. The best ones should be shared later with the entire class.

Observations of Teacher Behavior

Teachers use nonverbal cues frequently in class. If the teachers want students to become quiet, they can simply raise their hand to "shut off" flow of speech. The nonverbal cue clearly contradicts the speaker who says, "I'm *not* angry," in a loud voice with a flushed face and clenched fist. The nonverbal aspects will be read more clearly than the verbal and will be interpreted as the correct message. Thus we can observe posture, voice, and movements as indicators of true feelings.

Proxemics (space) is the way individuals use the personal territory around them. Proxemics is clearly determined by the culture in which we live. Some teachers are bothered if students crowd closely around their desks; others do not seem to mind. Some individuals approach too closely for comfort when they confer with teachers; others prefer maintaining a certain distance.

Proxemics measures social status, too. Who has the largest office? Whose office is nearest the principal's? Which teachers have the newest, most modern desks? Knowledge of nonverbal communication, then, is an essential part of affective concerns.

Developmental Stages of Reader Response

Following a reading assignment, students appreciate having the opportunity at times to select the questions to which they wish to respond. Lamberg and Lamb have described the earlier work of Dwight Burton and Margaret Early, who offered a scheme of developmental stages toward becoming sophisticated or mature readers.[47,48,49] The three general stages described are

1. unconscious enjoyment or imaginative entry into the work;
2. self-conscious appreciation or perception of meaning and central purpose;
3. conscious delight or perception of artistic unity and purpose.

Unconscious Enjoyment

1. At the first stage students are uncritical and subjective readers, able to relate easily to the writing but not ready to examine why they liked or disliked it. They are able to respond to literal

factual questions concerning what the section or chapter or article or story was about—what happened, to whom, when it happened, and in what sequence.

2. At the self-conscious appreciation stage students begin to become objective of the work and their responses to it, comparing their own knowledge, experiences, and values to what they are reading. They begin to read between the lines and describe their evaluative response. Examples of questions at this level include:

Self-conscious Appreciation

Why did the events occur as they did?
Compare yourself to the main character. How are you alike?
Why do you suppose the author wrote this?
What did you find particularly interesting?
Could a particular character have behaved differently? Explain.

3. At the higher stage, conscious delight, students critically examine and reflect on their responses following their reading. Types of questions teachers might ask at this level include:

Conscious Delight

What is the significance of this section in terms of what we have just studied?
What is distinctive about the author's style?
How does the setting contribute to the overall effect of the work?
What is your position on this controversial issue? Describe.
Do you agree with the authors? Why or why not? Defend your choice.
How is this similar to other works of this type?

Workshop Activity 2.5
Responding Affectively

Read the following selection and respond to selected questions at each level. (See the previous section on developmental stages for examples of questions: unconscious, self conscious, conscious delight.)

The crowd in the cavern assembly chamber radiated that pack feeling Jessica had sensed the day Paul killed Janis. There was murmuring nervousness in the voices. Little cliques gathered like knots among the robes.

Jessica tucked a message cylinder beneath her robe as she emerged to the ledge from Paul's private quarters. She felt rested after the long journey up from the south, but still rankled that Paul would not permit them to use the captured ornithopters.

"We do not have full control of the air," he had said. "And we must not become dependent upon offworld fuel. Both fuel and aircraft must be gathered and saved for the day of maximum effort."

Paul stood with a group of the younger men near the ledge. The pale light of glow globes gave the scene a tinge of unreality. It was like a tableau, but with the added dimension of warren smells, the whispers, the sounds of shuffling feet.

She studied her son, wondering why he had not yet trotted out his surprise—Gurney Halleck. Thought of Gurney disturbed her with its memories of an easier past—days of love and beauty with Paul's father.

Stilgar waited with a small group of his own at the other end of the ledge. There was a feeling of inevitable dignity about him, the way he stood without talking.

We must not lose that man, Jessica thought. *Paul's plan must work. Anything else would be highest tragedy.*

She strode down the ledge, passing Stilgar without a glance, stepped down into the crowd. A way was made for her as she headed toward Paul. And silence followed her.

She knew the meaning of the silence—the unspoken questions of people, awe of the Reverend Mother.

The young men drew back from Paul as she came up to him, and she found herself momentarily dismayed by the new deference they paid him. *"All men beneath your position covet your station,"* went the Bene Gesserit axiom. But she found no covetousness in these faces. They were held at a distance by the religious ferment around Paul's leadership. And she recalled another Bene Gesserit saying: *"Prophets have a way of dying by violence."*

Paul looked at her.

"It's time," she said, and passed the message cylinder to him.[50]

Summary

Promoting the affective dimensions of motivation, attitudes, interests, and values of all students is a critical concern for teachers if relevant learning is to take place. The term *affective domain* is based on a taxonomy developed by Krathwohl and others, consisting of receiving, responding, valuing, organizing, and characterizing. We must consider carefully how to motivate students to read, how to build more positive attitudes toward reading, and how to determine students' interests and ways to assist them in clarifying their own values. As we learn more about our students, we will take into consideration the problems of those with limited English proficiency; what is involved in students' physical stages of development—including transescence to adolescence; mental considerations—including brain-compatible teaching and learning; and social and emotional needs. Successful teachers always take heed of their students' affective state.

Possible Responses to Workshop Activity 2.1 Why Do People Read?

People read to learn something new, to help them solve a problem, to construct something, to complete assigned tasks or take a test, to help them look good to significant others, to verify or reinforce an attitude they already have, to obtain vicarious experiences, to escape, to find pleasure, to temporarily avoid some pain or sorrow by losing themselves in the text material, or to savor the beauty of the language.

References

1. David Krathwohl, Benjamin Bloom, and Bertram Masia, *Taxonomy of Educational Objectives: Handbook II, Affective Domain* (New York: David McKay, 1964).
2. Lou Burmeister, *Reading Strategies for Secondary School Teachers* (Reading, Mass.: Addison Wesley, 1978), p. 68.
3. Marilyn Van Derbur, "Motivating Students," *Today's Education* 63 (September–October 1974): 68–70.
4. Ibid., p. 68.
5. Herbert J. Klausmeier and William Goodwin, *Learning and Human Abilities: Educational Psychology,* 4th ed. (New York: Harper & Row, 1975), p. 227.
6. David P. Ausubel, *Educational Psychology: A Cognitive View* (New York: Holt, Rinehart & Winston, 1968).
7. Walter J. Lamberg and Charles E. Lamb, *Reading Instruction in the Content Areas* (Chicago: Rand McNally, 1980), p. 346.
8. Dorothy Rathbun, "How to Get Middle Schoolers to Read When They're Not Too Thrilled about the Idea and You're Not Too Sure about What to Do Anyway," *Learning* 6: 132–36.
9. Ibid., p. 136.
10. Frances Fitzgerald, *America Revised: History Schoolbooks in the Twentieth Century* (Boston: Little, Brown and Company, 1979).
11. Verna Kirkness, "Prejudice about Indians in Textbooks," *Journal of Reading* 20 (April 1977): 595–600.
12. Alex Haley, *Roots* (New York: Doubleday, 1976).
13. C. C. Douglas, "Dilemma of Thomas Jefferson," *Ebony* 30 (August 1975): 64.
14. Kenneth L. Dulin, "Reading and the Affective Domain," in *Aspects of Reading Education,* ed. Susanna Pflaum-Connor (Berkeley, Calif.: McCutchan Publishing Co., 1978), pp. 106–25.
15. G. R. Carlsen, "Big Change in Adolescent Reading," *Intellect* 104 (July/August 1975).
16. Merrill Harmin, *What I've Learned about Values Education,* The Phi Delta Kappa Foundation, Fastback No. 91 (Bloomington, Ind., 1977).

17. Louis Raths, Merrill Harmin, and Sidney Simon, *Values and Teaching* (Columbus: Charles E. Merrill, 1966).

18. Harmin, *Values Education.*

19. D. N. Aspy et al., *Interpersonal Skills for Teachers,* National Institutes for Health, Interim Report #2, NIMH Grant No. 5 PO 1 MH 19871 (Monroe, La: Northeast Louisiana University, 1974), p. 144.

20. "Portrait of America," *Newsweek,* 17 Jan. 1983.

21. Sabine Ulibarri, "Children and a Second Language," *New Mexico School Review* 40 (October 1960): 22–23.

22. Stephen D. Kashen and Tracy D. Terrell, *The National Approach: Language Acquisition in the Classroom* (San Francisco: Alchemy Books, 1983).

23. James J. Asher and B. Price, "The Learning Strategy of the Total Physical Response: Some Age Differences," *Child Development* 38 (1967): 1219–27.

24. Jim Cummins, *Bilingualism and Minority Children,* Language and Literacy Series (Ontario, Canada: The Ontario Institute for Studies in Education, 1981), pp. 27–32.

25. Donald H. Eichhorn, *The Middle School* (New York: Center for Applied Research in Education, 1966), p. 3.

26. Gordon F. Vars, "Chapter I: Prologue," in *Toward Adolescence: The Middle School Years,* ed. Mauritz Johnson (Chicago: University of Chicago Press, 1980), p. 2.

27. Donald H. Eichhorn, "The School," in *Toward Adolescence: The Middle School Years,* chapter IV, ed. Mauritz Johnson (Chicago: University of Chicago Press, 1980), p. 65.

28. G. Stanley Hall, *Adolescence, Its Psychology and Its Relation to Physiology, Anthropology, Sociology, Sex, Crime, Religion, and Education,* two volumes (New York: D. Appleton Century, 1904).

29. August B. Hollinghead, *Elmtown's Youth, The Impact of Social Classes on Adolescents* (New York: John Wiley and Sons, 1949), pp. 6–7.

30. Robert Havighurst, *Developmental Tasks and Education* (Chicago: University of Chicago Press, 1948), pp. 30–45.

31. Leslie Hart, *How the Brain Works* (New York: Basic Books, 1975), p. 185.

32. Herman T. Epstein, "Growth Spurts during Brain Development: Implications for Educational Policy and Practice," *Education and the Brain,* National Society for the Study of Education, the 77th Yearbook, Part II, eds. Jeanne Chall and Allan Mirsky (Chicago: University of Chicago Press, 1978).

33. Ibid., p. 344.

34. John Dewey, *Experience and Education* (New York: Crowell, Collier and Macmillan, Inc., 1938), p. 58.

35. Alfred North Whitehead, *The Aims of Education* (New York: Manor Books, 1929), cited by Epstein, *Growth Spurts during Brain Development,* pp. 345–46.

36. Leslie Hart, "The New Brain Concept of Learning," *Phi Delta Kappan* 59, No. 6 (February 1978): 393–96.

37. Patricia L. Fox, "Reading as a Whole Brain Function," *The Reading Teacher* 33 (October 1979): 7–14.

38. Herman T. Epstein and Conrad F. Toepfer, Jr., "A Neuroscience Basis for Reorganizing Middle Grade Education," *Educational Leadership* 35 (May 1978): 658.

39. Leslie Hart, *New Brain Concept of Learning,* p. 396.
40. Leslie A. Hart, "The Horse Is Dead," *Phi Delta Kappan* (November 1989): 237–42.
41. Christopher Miller, "New High School System Needed, Educator Says," *Albuquerque Journal,* 16 Mar. 1989, sec. D2.
42. R. M. Tews, "Introduction," *Library Trends II* (October 1962): 97–105.
43. Charles Galloway, *Silent Language in the Classroom,* The Phi Delta Kappa Foundation, Fastback No. 86 (Bloomington, Ind.: 1976), p. 8.
44. Benjamin S. Bloom, *Human Characteristics and Human Learning* (New York: McGraw-Hill, 1976), p. 119.
45. Sigmund Freud, "Fragment of an Analysis of a Case of Hysteria," *Complete Works of Freud,* vol. 7 (1905), p. 77.
46. J. Dan Rothwell and James I. Costigan, *Interpersonal Communication: Influences and Alternatives* (Columbus, Ohio: Charles E. Merrill, 1975), p. 127.
47. Lamberg and Lamb, *Reading Instruction,* pp. 343–45.
48. Dwight L. Burton, *Perspectives in Reading: Reading Instruction in Secondary Schools* (Newark, Del.: International Reading Association, 1964).
49. Margaret Early, "Stages of Growth in Literary Appreciation," *English Journal* 49 (March 1960): 161–67.
50. Frank Herbert, *Dune* (New York: Berkley Publishing, 1965), pp. 424–25.

Recommended Readings

Bereiter, Carl. "Toward a Solution of the Learning Paradox." *Review of Educational Research* 55 (Summer 1985): (Page 210 deals with why affect is important in learning.)

Cardenas, José A. "The Role of Native Language Instruction in Bilingual Education." *Phi Delta Kappan* 67 (January 1986): 359–63.

Clary, Linda Mixon. "Getting Adolescents to Read." *Journal of Reading* 34 (February 1991): 340–45.

Cooler, Robert B., Jr., and Griffith, Robert. "Thematic Units for Middle School: An Honorable Seduction." *Journal of Reading* 32 (May 1989): 676–81.

Cummins, Jim. "The Entry-Exit Fallacy in Bilingual Education." *NABE* Journal 4 (Spring 1980): 25–59.

Davis, Flora. *Inside Intuition: What We Know about Nonverbal Communication.* New York: McGraw-Hill, 1973.

Donelson, Kenneth L., and Nilsen, Alleen Pace. *Literature for Today's Young Adults,* 3d ed. Glenview, Ill.: Scott, Foresman, 1989.

Dumont, Robert V., Jr. "Learning English and How to Be Silent; Studies in Sioux and Cherokee Classrooms." In *Functions of Language in the Classroom,* Courtney Cazden, Vera P. John, and Dell Hymes, eds. New York: Teachers College Press, 1972, pp. 344–69.

Epstein, Ira D. "What Happened the Day You Were Born?" *Journal of Reading* 20 (February 1977): 400–402.

Frymier, Jack. *Motivation and Learning in School.* Bloomington, Ind.: Phi Delta Kappa, 1974.

Gentile, Lance M., and McMillan, Merna M. "Why Won't Teenagers Read?" *Journal of Reading* 20 (May 1977): 649–53. First, reasons why teenagers reject reading; then suggested materials for overcoming their reluctance.

Goldbecker, Sheralyn S. *Values Teaching, What Research Says to the Teacher.* Washington, D.C.: National Education Association, 1976.

Harmin, Merrill; Kirschenbaum, Howard; and Simon, Sidney. *Clarifying Values through Subject Matter, Applications in the Classroom.* Minneapolis: Winston Press, Inc., 1973.

Harris, Stephen G. "More Haste Less Speed: Time and Timing for Language Problems in Northern Territory Aboriginal Bilingual Children." *The Aboriginal Child at School* 8 (August–September 1980): 37.

Hart, Leslie. *Human Brain and Human Learning.* Longman, 1983. (Reviewed in *Journal of Reading,* January 1984.)

Hart, Leslie A. "The Horse Is Dead." *Phi Delta Kappan* (November 1989): 237–42.

Johnson, Daniel P. "The Bumpy Road from Dependence to Discovery. *Middle School Journal* (February 1984).

Johnson, Mauritz, ed. *Toward Adolescence: The Middle School Years.* National Society for the Study of Education Yearbook, 1980. Chicago: University of Chicago Press, 1980.

Manning, Diane Thompson, and Manning, Bernard. "Bibliotherapy for Children of Alcoholics." *Journal of Reading* 27 (May 1984): 720–25.

Mason, George E., and Mize, John M. "Twenty-two Sets of Methods and Materials for Stimulating Teenage Reading." *Journal of Reading* 21 (May 1978): 735–41.

Mathison, Carla. "Activating Student Interest in Content Area Reading." *Journal of Reading* 33 (December 1989): 170–77.

Matthewson, Grover C. "Toward a Comprehensive Model of Affect in the Reading Process." In *Theoretical Models and Processes of Reading,* Harry Singer and Robert Ruddell, eds. 3d ed. Newark, Del.: International Reading Association, 1985, pp. 841–55.

McWhiter, Anna M. "Whole Language in the Middle School." *Reading Teacher* 43 (April 1990): 562–67.

Moody, Mildred T., ed. *Bibliotherapy.* Chicago: American Library Association, 1971.

Nell, Victor. "The Psychology of Reading for Pleasure Needs and Gratifications." *Reading Research Quarterly* 23 (Winter 1988): 6–50.

Neva, Charmaine Della. "Brain-Compatible Learning Succeeds." *Educational Leadership* (October 1985): 83–85.

Noland, Ronald, and Craft, Lynda. "Fifteen Approaches to Motivate the Reluctant Reader." *Journal of Reading* 19 (February 1976): 387–91.

Ovando, Carlos J. "Bilingual/Bicultural Education: Its Legacy and Its Future." *Phi Delta Kappa* 64 (April 1983): 566.

Pantoja, Antonia; Blourock, Barbara; and Bowman, James. *Badges and Indicia of Slavery: Cultural Pluralism Redefined.* Lincoln, Neb.: University of Nebraska Printing and Dupl. Serv., 1975, pp. 2–24.

Russell, David, and Shrodes, Caroline. "Contributions of Research in Bibliotherapy to the Language Arts Program." *The School Review* (September 1950).

Shrodes, Caroline. "The Dynamics of Reading: Implications for Bibliotherapy." *Etc.: A Review of General Semantics* 18 (April 1961): 21–33.

Simon, Sidney; Howe, L.; and Kirschenbaum, H. *Values Clarification: Handbook of Practical Suggestions for Teachers and Students.* New York: Hart Publishing Co., 1972.

Stipek, Deborah J. *Motivation to Learn: From Theory to Practice.* Englewood Cliffs, N.J.: Prentice-Hall, 1988.

Stone, Nancy R. "Accentuate the Positive: Motivation and Reading for Secondary Students." *Journal of Reading* 27 (May 1984): 684–90.

Sutton, Christine. "Helping the Nonnative English Speaker with Reading." *The Reading Teacher* 24 (May 1989): 684–89.

Tillman, Chester E. "Bibliotherapy for Adolescents: An Annotated Research Review." *Journal of Reading* 27 (May 1984): 713–19.

Winfield, Evelyn T. "Relevant Reading for Adolescents: Literature on Divorce." *Journal of Reading* 26 (February 1983): 408–11.

Young, Robert. *The Navajo Yearbook: Report Number Eight.* Navajo Agency, Window Rock, Ariz., 1961, p. 476.

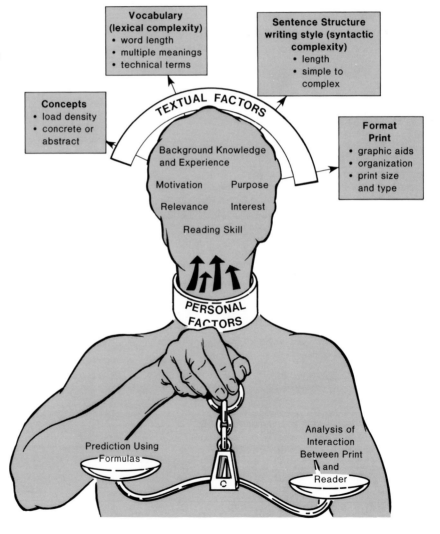

Figure 3.1
Determining
readability, or how
readable is the text?:
a cognitive map.

**Vocabulary
(lexical complexity)**
• word length
• multiple meanings
• technical terms

**Sentence Structure
writing style (syntactic
complexity)**
• length
• simple to
  complex

Concepts
• load density
• concrete or
  abstract

**Format
Print**
• graphic aids
• organization
• print size
  and type

TEXTUAL FACTORS

Background Knowledge
and Experience

Motivation   Purpose

Relevance   Interest

Reading Skill

PERSONAL
FACTORS

Prediction Using
Formulas

Analysis of
Interaction
Between Print
and
Reader

Matching Print with Reader, Part I: Determining Readability of Instructional Materials

3

Anticipatory Questions

(Literal)

1. What factors affect the difficulty level of print for a reader?

(Literal)

2. How have American and English novels changed stylistically over time?

(Inferential)

3. Compare the importance of personal versus textual factors in determining readability levels.

(Applied)

4. Describe the effect your knowledge of readability (personal and textual) factors will have on your classroom practices.

Technical Terminology and Concepts

concept load or density

format/print factor

Fry readability graph

lexical/syntactic complexity

Marshall's readability checklist

personal/textual factors

readability of text

reader performance criteria/reader ratings

reader/print interaction

SMOG formula

stylistic age of novels

Introduction   The ease and success with which readers can handle their reading assignments is of vital concern to most teachers. A practical tool for the content teacher is a readability formula that estimates quickly and with sufficient accuracy the approximate difficulty level of print materials.

In this chapter factors affecting difficulty levels of reading material and ways of measuring those levels through either prediction or analysis will be presented. It is well to remember that formulas may yield some useful information but they are only tools. It is the teachers who must judge among the many factors affecting their own students' comprehension.

Workshop Activity 3.1

Reader Speculation of Difficulty Factors and of Reading and Writing Levels

A. Before reading any further, what factors do *you* believe contribute to the ease or difficulty with which you read something? Think of texts, novels, or magazines that you have enjoyed or disliked. With a partner or alone, list below as many factors as you can think of that have affected your ability to comprehend.

1.   5.

2.   6.

3.   7.

4.   8.

B. Take an educated guess as to the overall average *readability* levels (reading grade levels) of any of the following. (A readability level is an arbitrary assignment based on what an average student should be able to read at each grade or the lowest grade level at which at least half the students can read and understand 75 percent of the material.)

1. *Silas Marner*   _____

2. *Shōgun*   _____

3. *Time Magazine*   _____

4. *Reader's Digest*   _____

5. *Psychology Today*   _____

6. *Popular Mechanics*   _____

7. A big city newspaper   _____

8. A small town newspaper _____

C. Which section in a newspaper generally has the highest readability level?
1. Front page _____ 2. Sports page _____ 3. Financial _____
4. Comics _____ 5. Editorial _____

D. At which level do you think you write
   1. a letter to a friend? _____
   2. a term paper? _____
   3. a study guide for your students? _____
Answers to sections B and C are at the end of the chapter.

The term *readability* then refers to the difficulty or ease with which material is read. Selections that are difficult to read are considered to have a high readability level, those that are easy a low readability level.

It is unfortunate that even today many content texts from fourth grade through high school are written at higher levels than the reading ability levels of many of the students expected to read them. Also it is not uncommon to find a text with such a wide variability of readability levels within the one volume that it can bewilder or frustrate the reader.

Factors Affecting and Determining Print Difficulty

There are two major factors that make printed material easy or difficult to comprehend: personal factors inherent in the reader, and textual factors inherent in the print. Figure 3.1 depicts many of these factors. You may compare it with the list you made for part A in workshop activity 3.1.

Personal Factors

Take any text as an example. Look at it first from your own personal viewpoint. (Figure 3.1 shows personal factors as represented by the head and shoulders of a person.)

   1. Is the topic of particular interest to you?
   2. Are you motivated to read it with gusto?
   3. Do you have a compelling purpose for reading it?
   4. Are the topics relevant to your life?
   5. Do you have the necessary background experiences or prerequisites in the subject matter?
   6. Are your reading skills adequate for the task at hand?
      A "no" response to any of these personal questions will tend to hamper the ease with which you interact with the written ideas.

Textual Factors

On the other hand, **textual considerations** in readability are also crucial factors in mastering the message. (In figure 3.1 these radiate out of the personal factors.)

   1. First, the **concepts** of your content area must be examined. Are the number of major ideas presented in quick succession without adequate explanation, repetition, or examples (load density)?

Are the concepts fairly concrete (visible, tangible) such as lab equipment care, triangles and rectangles, breadmaking? Or are they more abstract, as for example with the concepts of democracy, illusion, or an algebraic equation?

2. Second, *vocabulary level,* or **lexical complexity,** plays a key role. Longer, multisyllabic words are generally considered to be more difficult than shorter words. Words so often have multiple meanings, which can be especially confusing if you already know one general meaning and then see the word in an entirely different context; for example, the student who knows 'root' as in the plant root but now finds it used as square root or root of the problem. Also, most content fields have their own body of technical terminology that may not be immediately familiar to the reader.

3. *Sentence structure,* or writing style, is another factor, often referred to as **syntactic complexity.** A lengthy sentence will often be more difficult to comprehend than a short one, especially for a slow reader. A sentence's complexity can also be determined by the distance between words or phrases and their modifiers. Edward Fry's Kernel Distance Theory defines a sentence kernel as noun, verb, and sometimes object.[1] The distance (number of words) between the nouns and verb makes the sentence harder than distance outside the kernel. For example, "No conclusion, if we carefully consider all the arguments on both sides, can be reached quickly," is more difficult than "No conclusion can be reached quickly if we carefully consider all the arguments on both sides."

4. The final textual factor considered here is the **format/print factor.** Graphic aids (pictures, maps, graphs, charts), when appropriately used, can enhance readability considerably. The way the text is organized in terms of format, subheadings, and other organizing features can ease the path to the separation or delineation of major ideas from supporting ones. Finally, the size of print used and the style of type may influence legibility and, therefore, reading ease.

Two major ways to determine the difficulty level of print is either through prediction, using a readability formula, or through analysis, examining the interaction between the reader and the text. (In figure 3.1 these are represented as scales for weighing.)

Prediction Using Formulas

Various formulas have been developed to measure the difficulty level of printed materials. Most of those in common use today measure only two language elements—vocabulary and sentence difficulty. Vocabulary measures can be: word length in letters or number of syllables, word familiarity, or word difficulty. Sentence difficulty is usually determined by its length. No matter which formula is used, you will need to remember that the results are only an approximation of difficulty. Your experience and professional judgment as to the concepts, purpose, and student interest are also critical factors to be considered.

The concepts of readability have been around for many years. Table 3.1 shows in chronological order the formal beginnings of readability considerations and selected formulas developed since 1852.

Historical Perspective

If you become familiar with at least one readability formula, you will find it to be a useful tool for checking approximate difficulty levels of your classroom materials.

Table 3.1

Selected Readability Formulas in a Nutshell

Date	Formula	Factors Measured			
		Sentence Length	Vocabulary		Other
			Word Length	Familiarity	
1852	Spencer "Philosophy of Style"[2]				
1921	Thorndike's list of most frequently used words[3]				
1923	Lively and Pressey, formal beginnings[4]				
1935	Gray and Leary[5]				
1939	Lorge[6]				
1943	Flesch Reading Ease[7]	X	X		
1948	Dale-Chall[8]	X		X	
1948	Flesch's Human Interest Scale[9]	(number of personal pronouns and personal references in 100 words)			
1952	FOG (Gunning)[10]	X	X		
1953	Spache[11]	X		X	
1953	Cloze (Taylor)[12]				X
1968	Fry's Graph (made assessment easily available)[13]	X	syllables		
1969	SMOG (McLaughlin)[14]	X	syllables		X
1975	SEER (Singer)[15]				X
1978	Rauding (Carver)[16]				X
1979	Raygor Readability Estimate[17]	X	count letters		

Until Fry's graph appeared in 1968, two of the best known readability formulas were the Dale-Chall and Spache. These were used mainly by researchers and publishers because of their complexity and time-consuming demands.

The formulas we will be looking at in this chapter are neither complicated nor time consuming; yet they are considered to give accurate enough estimates, correlating highly with more complex formulas.

The Fry Readability Graph

One of the most popular measures, validated on all levels of material, grades one through seventeen, is **Fry's graph,** which has undergone several changes since its first publication.[18] The extended graph and extended directions are shown in figure 3.2.

McLaughlin's SMOG Formula

McLaughlin's SMOG formula[19] is

$$\text{SMOG} = 3 + \sqrt{\begin{array}{l}\text{number of words with three}\\\text{or more syllables in thirty sentences}\end{array}}$$

This simple formula is based on the interrelationship of sentence length and number of polysyllabic words. Words with more syllables are considered to be more difficult than shorter words. The number of polysyllabic words in three ten-sentence samples are determined first. Because short sentences will have less opportunity to include many large words, the difficulty level may be determined by the number of polysyllabic words in three ten-sentence samples.

The steps to the SMOG formula are as follows:

1. Count *ten consecutive sentences* near the beginning of the text, ten near the middle, and ten toward the end.
2. Taking the total of thirty sentences, count every word of *three or more* syllables when they are read aloud (e.g., "graphed" is only counted as one syllable because you do not hear the "ed" ending). Count words of three or more syllables, even when they are repeated.
3. Estimate to the nearest perfect square—the square root of the total number of polysyllabic words. (If your total was twenty-four, the nearest perfect square would be twenty-five, and the square root of twenty-five is five. If the total number of polysyllabic words falls exactly between two perfect squares, take the lower of the two.)

Figure 3.2

Edward B. Fry's graph for estimating readability—extended.

From ''Fry's Readability Graph: Clarification, Validity, and Extensions to Level 17,'' by Edward B. Fry, *Journal of Reading,* December 1977, p. 249.

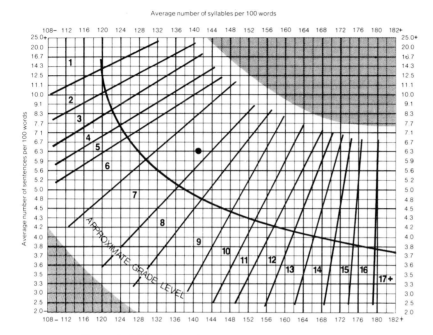

Expanded Directions for Working Readability Graph

1. Randomly select three (3) sample passages and count out exactly 100 words each, beginning with the beginning of a sentence. Do count proper nouns, initializations, and numerals.
2. Count the number of sentences in the hundred words, estimating length of the fraction of the last sentence to the nearest one-tenth.
3. Count the total number of syllables in the 100-word passage. If you don't have a hand counter available, an easy way is to simply put a mark above every syllable over one in each word, then when you get to the end of the passage, count the number of marks and add 100. Small calculators can also be used as counters by pushing numeral 1, then push the + sign for each word or syllable when counting.
4. Enter graph with *average* sentence length and *average* number of syllables; plot dot where the two lines intersect. Area where dot is plotted will give you the approximate grade level.
5. If a great deal of variability is found in syllable count or sentence count, putting more samples into the average is desirable.
6. A word is defined as a group of symbols with a space on either side; thus, *Joe, IRA, 1945,* and *&* are each one word.
7. A syllable is defined as a phonetic syllable. Generally, there are as many syllables as vowel sounds. For example, *stopped* is one syllable and *wanted* is two syllables. When counting syllables for numerals and initializations, count one syllable for each symbol. For example, *1945* is four syllables, *IRA* is three syllables, and *&* is one syllable.

4. Add three to the estimated square root to determine the reading level. (When the square root is five, add three and the readability will be eight.)
5. When samples of the three ten-sentence selections vary considerably (for example, seventeen, five, ten) further samples should be selected for greater accuracy.
6. Note that by adding "three" to the score it will not be usable for primary materials.

Fry versus SMOG

Research has shown that Fry and SMOG, although both considered accurate, do not always agree as to readability level. If you use both, it is important to understand how to interpret this difference. Fry's graph estimates the reading ability needed to comprehend with 50 to 75 percent accuracy, or somewhere between frustrational and instructional reading levels; whereas SMOG predicts reading ability required by 90 to 100 percent understanding, or the independent level. (However, because Fry changed in 1977 to counting proper nouns, these variances may be less notable.) A Fry score of eight means that the true range is one above and one below or a range of seven to nine. Students reading at an eight-grade level can handle this material if you give them some instructional aid. A SMOG score of eight means that students reading at an eighth-grade level could handle the material independently, as homework.

Workshop activity 3.2 will give you an opportunity to practice using both the Fry and SMOG formulas on the same passage for comparative purposes. Because there is less than the required number of sentences for running a SMOG, you will need to multiply the multisyllabic word count by six.

Workshop Activity 3.2
Practice with Two Readability Formulas: Fry and SMOG

First, try the Fry formula. When counting syllables, remember that each syllable has one vowel sound. For example, *bi-cy-cle* has three sounds and three syllables. It is what you *hear* rather than what you *see*. *Counted* has two syllables but *skipped* has only one, because you do not hear the "ed." How many syllables are there in *readability*? If you have trouble determining the number, pound out the sounds on a table: *read-a-bil-i-ty* (five!).

Because it is easy to become distracted or interrupted, it is suggested that you use the following format when counting, keeping track at the end of each line, and then adding the numbers for a total score.

The omelet was tasty. Note that omelet may be pronounced *om-let* as well as *om-e-let,* and thus it has two or three syllables. This dialectical difference will not change or affect the final results significantly, as you will be using three samples. Now try this example.

"The foregoing extensive discussion of generalizations is predicated on the author's assumption that prepositional knowledge is the single most essential product of any science, including social studies in secondary schools. As has been pointed out, generalizations or propositions between properties of nature are more or less general, ranging from the nomological universal sort to the prevalent type. Generalizations must be stated in the present tense if they are to serve those holding them most effectively. Present-tense generalizations are timeless in the sense that they refer to the past as well as to the present and future. Present-tense generalizations. . . ."[20]	<u> 18 </u> ____ ____ ____ ____ ____ ____ ____ ____ ____ ____ TOTAL: _____	*Teaching for Explanation and Prediction by Richard Phillips*

Now, let us suppose that you have already run a Fry readability on two other sections of the Phillips book. These scores are already filled in on the following chart. Add your findings on the above selection and calculate the readability level and range of this social studies text. (The range will be one year above and one year below the level you found.)

Book Title/Author _____ Formula: <u>Fry</u>

100 word selections	Number of sentences	Number of syllables
1. "Thinking skills," p. 149	3.7	171
2. "Advantages of matching," p. 310	5.4	179
3. "Teaching for explanation and prediction," p. 134	+ _____	+ _____
TOTAL	3) _____	3) _____
Average (divide total by 3)		

Fry Readability   _____
True Range   _____

Now try SMOG on the same passage and multiply the multisyllabic word count by six.

SMOG Readability

1. Total number of 3-or-more syllable words _____ .
2. Nearest perfect square in the total = _____ .
3. Estimated square root of perfect square = _____ .
4. Estimated square root plus 3 = _____ readability level.

Check your findings with the answers found at the end of the chapter.

Table 3.2

Evaluating Reading Difficulty of Short Selections

Number of Words in Selection (Less than 100)	Multiply by
30	3.3
40	2.5
50	2.0
60	1.67
70	1.43
80	1.25
90	1.1

From Harry Forgan and Charles Mangrum II, *Teaching Content Area Reading* (Columbus, Ohio: Charles E. Merrill Publishing Co., 1981). Used with permission.

Evaluating Shorter Passages

It is often important to be able to determine the difficulty level of passages shorter than 100 words, such as those found in math texts, directions, or essay questions. Harry Forgan and Charles Mangrum have outlined procedures for doing this using the Fry graph:[21]

1. Count the total number of words in the passage. For example, the total might be sixty-nine words.
2. Round *down* to the nearest ten. In this case you would round down the sixty-nine words to sixty.
3. Use this number (in this case sixty) when counting the number of sentences and syllables.
4. Multiply the number of sentences and the number of syllables by the corresponding number found in the conversion chart above (see table 3.2). With our example of a sixty-nine word passage, rounded *down* to sixty, you would multiply the number of sentences by 1.67 and then the number of syllables by 1.67.
5. Use these numbers to enter Fry's graph to find your readability estimate.

This knowledge may be useful when you are writing test questions, study guides, directions, or explanations for students.

Edward Fry developed a new readability formula designed to work on passages of forty to ninety-nine words, as long as a passage contains at least three sentences.[22] His formula leans heavily on the research of Edgar Dale and Joseph O'Rourke published in *The Living Word Dictionary,* Elgin, Ill.: Dome, 1976. (This book is out of print but can be found in many libraries. World Book is considering a new edition.)

After selecting a passage of at least three sentences and forty words, select at least three key words necessary to understand the passage. Look up the grade level with the same meaning of each key word in *The Living Word Dictionary.* Average the grade level of the three hardest key words to get the word difficulty. Count the number of words in each sentence,

Foundations

Table 3.3
Sentence Length (Difficulty) Chart

Words per Sentence	Grade Level Estimate
6.6 or below	1
8.6	2
10.8	3
12.5	4
14.2	5
15.8	6
18.2	7
20.4	8
22.2	9
23.2	10
23.8	11
24.3	12
25.0	13
25.6	14
26.3	15
27.0	16
above 27	17

giving each sentence a grade level by using the sentence length chart as shown in table 3.3. Average the grade level of all sentences to get sentence difficulty. The final step to get the readability estimate is to average the sentence difficulty and the word difficulty. The formula is

$$\text{Readability} = \frac{\text{Word difficulty} + \text{Sentence difficulty}}{2}$$

Workshop Activity 3.3
Measuring Your Own Writing Level

Take a sample of forty to ninety words of your own expository writing. This might be a portion of a term paper or an explanation to a class. Using the new Fry chart or the adaptation for smaller samples above, run a readability estimate on your own writing. Do the same with a personal letter. What did you learn about yourself? Would your students benefit from running readabilities on their own writing? Might this improve some aspects of writing? Which is more accurate or more useful for you—the new Fry chart or the adaptation in table 3.2?

Another interesting option is to take the Fry graph and write your sample two grades higher and then two grades lower. Which was more difficult? Why?

Sticht's FORCAST

Thomas Sticht reported on a quick estimate of readability called "FOR-CAST" that can be readily applied to materials at fifth-grade level or above.[23] Although he cautions that ten samples must be used for accuracy, the authors have applied the formula only to the three passages used with Fry, necessarily adding fifty words each time. This has proven in practice to be a fairly accurate quick check of the Fry score. The formula is

$$20 - \left\{ \frac{\text{Number of one-syllable words in 150 words}}{10} \right.$$

The important thing to remember with this formula is that you do the work of counting the words first, moving the decimal over one place to the left (dividing by ten), and then subtracting the result from twenty for the readability level.

Raygor's Readability Estimator

Alton Raygor's estimator is more recent and is an easy and speedy indicator of readability level that purports to give an approximate grade placement, accurate within one grade level.[24] Its ease and speed are due to the fact that there is no need to count syllables or determine the complexity of words. Instead it relies on counting the number of sentences in three one-hundred-word passages and counting the number of words of more than six letters appearing in those passages. This estimator requires the use of a slide rule indicator.

Rewriting or Writing Materials for Clarity

Even though it is not always practical to rewrite large segments of textual material, it is still useful to be aware of how it can be done using a readability aid such as Fry's graph. It is suggested that you practice on one short selection, writing it at both a lower level and a higher one. If, for example, your selection is at a college level, you should decide to rewrite it at a targeted readability level of seventh grade or twelfth grade. The example in figure 3.3 was taken from a sociology text written at a high college level.

Along with learning to write text segments at different readability levels, you may wish to tailor your own writing for students. The following guidelines for clear (not literary) writing have been suggested by Lawrence Hafner.[25]

1. Write from an organized plan.
2. State ideas clearly and succinctly by eliminating needless words or negative statements and by amplifying or using more concrete examples for concepts.
3. Use more short sentences than long ones.
4. Be specific and concrete.
5. Have specific facts for your generalizations.
6. Emphasize verbs and nouns, as these are the main message-bearing units.

Figure 3.3
Rewriting materials for clarity.

College Text Material		Rewritten at Easier Levels	

College Text Material

Despite their large size, the great complexity of their organizational structures, and the indirectness of the ties between members, societies nevertheless meet our broad definition of a group as "a number of individuals who interact recurrently according to some pattern of social organization." Like a community, a society is an integrative system that coordinates and binds together the great many smaller groups of which it is composed. It is the largest group with which most people can feel a sense of personal identity, and in some ways it is the most important in its effects on the life of the individual.

A society is the only group, for example, that can legitimately claim the power of life and death over its members. It also plays a very significant role in determining the kinds of interaction that take place within its constituent groups and in shaping their norms, roles, sanctions, and ranking. A society, in short, can be analyzed as an enormously complex pattern of social organization that interrelates its members in patterns of mutual dependency and provides them with guidelines for all areas of social behavior.

Count Sentences and Syllables ____ ____
Find grade level ____

Counts: 7, 12, 10, 9, 11

Rewritten at Easier Levels

Societies are large in size and need a lot of organized ways of doing things. Many of the people in a society do not know each other and are bound together by their work, their interests, and their ways of behaving. There are certain rules for behaving that all people are expected to follow. A society is like a community. Many different small groups live in it and get along well with each other. Each person can enjoy his or her personal rights. But individuals cannot take away from the freedom of other people to enjoy their rights. The group needs to have ways to make all of the people get along well together.

Count Sentences and Syllables ____
Find grade level ____

Societies may be thought of as being large in size, very complex in organization, and having only loose, or indirect, ties between the people in them. A society is a number of people who interact with each other according to the usual behavior of that group. It is like a community. It holds together the many small groups within it so they get along well with each other. People in a given society have enough in common so that each person can express an individual personality. The group has very important effects on each one of the people who live in it.

Count Sentences and Syllables ____ ____
Find grade level ____

Counts: 9, 11, 9, 11, 8

7. Use organizational devices such as summaries, headings, and enumeration or listings.
8. Use direct rather than colorful language, such as "feeling bad" rather than "under the weather" or "aching heart."

In education we seem to think that the use of such tools is solely the domain of teachers. But students as well as teachers can benefit from learning how to use a formula to determine readability level. For example, an English teacher had a problem with showing some of her students how to upgrade their writing. When these tenth-grade students were taught to apply a readability formula to their own writing, their shock was apparent. Some discovered they were writing below a third-grade level. Suddenly there was a great demand from the students themselves to find ways to improve. Using a readability formula on their own had given them a built-in motivator.

Other Options for Measurement

Marshall's Readability Checklist for Comprehensibility

Because readability formulas do not measure meaning per se, and because our goal is that students comprehend the text, Nancy Marshall has suggested that educators examine their texts using a checklist to determine comprehensibility.[26] Her questions in table 3.4 may be used as a tool for examining the various elements in a text and can be a valuable addition to readability formulas.

Table 3.4
Marshall's Readability Checklist for Comprehensibility

		Well Done + Average 0 Poor −
Main ideas	1. a. Are major points clearly stated?	_____
	b. Are chapter titles and headings meaningful?	_____
	c. Do titles clearly outline major points?	_____
Vocabulary	2. a. Are key vocabulary terms clearly defined when the subject is new?	_____
	b. Are these terms used in a variety of contexts meaningful to the reader?	_____
Concepts	3. a. Are new concepts introduced in the context of familiar concepts?	_____
	b. Are they well-defined in the text?	_____
Related ideas	4. a. Are ideas clearly related to each other?	_____
	b. Will the reader be able to understand relationships among ideas?	_____
	c. Could the reader illustrate these graphically?	_____
Referents	5. a. Are pronouns used unambiguously?	_____
	b. Do they usually refer to referents no more than one sentence away?	_____
Audience	6. Has the author addressed the audience intended?	_____

From Nancy Marshall, "Readability and Comprehensibility," *Journal of Reading* 22 (March 1979): 542–544. Used with permission.

Walter Hill discusses three other general approaches to assessing read-ability that do not use formulas.[27] These are:

1. *Reader ratings.* Students are asked to react subjectively to the materials, often using a checklist or other classification system to rank them.
2. *Reader performance criteria.* Here the student's performance on the materials is measured directly by means of an objective test that generally has a minimum standard of 75 percent accuracy in comprehension; a cloze test (discussed in detail in chapter 7) with 44 to 57 percent accuracy for instructional level; a reading efficiency or rate of reading test; or having students mark the words that they do not recognize or for which they do not know the meaning.
3. *Performance on criterion materials.* Finally, another approach involves a combination of the first two: reader ratings and reader performance criteria. First, reading testing is used to establish a criterion set of reading selections at successive readability levels. Second, readability of other materials is determined by comparing them with the criterion selections. Carver's *Rauding Scale of Prose Difficulty* may serve this purpose, as also may the McCall-Crabbs *Standard Test Lessons in Reading,* and basal reader material.[28] McCall-Crabbs was never initially intended to be used as a criterion model.[29]

Because of the time efficiency factor, it is usually better to use read-ability formulas when screening and purchasing instructional materials, and then use the other approaches when grouping students or individualizing their assignments.

Workshop Activity 3.4
Estimate the Difficulty Level

Using Carver's *Rauding Scale of Prose Difficulty,* here are four examples that not only have been verified by seven different formulas including the Dale-Chall, Fry, Flesch, SMOG, and cloze, but also are purported to take into consideration concept load.[30]

Now that you have had some practice in determining readabilities with two or more formulas, see if you can estimate, without using a formula, within one to two years the levels of the following. Groups of six to eight may want to pool their information to try to reach a consensus. Answers will be found at the end of the chapter.

From J. R. Bormuth, Development of readability analyses. U.S. Office of Education Final Report, Proj. no. 7-052, Contract no. OEC-3-7-0 70052-0326, University of Chicago, March 1969.

1. Italians

Gregariousness, curiosity, and a fondness for communicating make Italians a universal people, the most universal in Europe. The provincial peasant with whom you share a railroad compartment is completely at home in your company. The peasant may be part of a delegation traveling to a papal audience, and it may be a first trip to Rome, but the peasant is nonetheless a citizen of the world. At noontime the peasant will offer you a chunk of bread with slices of salami and a handful of shiny black olives. The peasant will hand you a Chianti bottle with the crumbs from the bread still clinging to it.

GRADE _____

2. Tadpole

To a young tadpole the world is an amazing place. The waters all about it are filled with tangled forests of bright green weeds all dripping with moss, which wave back and forth with every passing current. From these forests tower great trees, up and up and up until they reach the surface. Some flatten out into huge umbrella-like tops. These are the lily pads. Others go right through and out into the world beyond. These are the cattails and the pickerel weed. In and out of the murky depths of the green forest swim a constant stream of strange and unbelievable things.

GRADE _____

3. Sternglass

Yet it would, I suggest, be both unfortunate and inaccurate to depict Sternglass simply as either an irresponsible scientific maverick or as a victim of bureaucratic self-interest. For the question that Sternglass addresses is not a "scientific" one in the rigorous sense of that term. The question "Should the U.S. continue atmospheric testing of nuclear weapons?" is, rather, a question that attempts to mediate between historical circumstance where the available evidence is necessarily incomplete and the need for action rests on future contingencies. The question dealt with by Sternglass is, in short, an essentially rhetorical proposition. And the disagreement between Sternglass and the governmentally linked scientific establishment is just another example of the classic "type error"; a dispute arising from alternative interpretation of the same proposition.

GRADE _____

4. Trading

Trading things without the use of money is called barter.

Did you ever trade toys or cards with friends? If you did, then you, too, were using barter. Such barter has been going on for thousands of years. It is an old, old way of doing business.

At one time, barter was done at big trading centers. People came from miles away to trade things. They brought animals, or grain, or blankets, or straw baskets. Then they traded what they had for something that they needed.

GRADE _____

Our English language is constantly changing. Wayne Danielson and Dominic Lasorsa conducted a study of 240 years of English and American novels.[31] They found that marked stylistic changes over time can be used to date novelistic prose with some accuracy. Sentence length has declined at the rate of ten words per century. Writers started to use fewer long words and fewer types of punctuation marks. Today we have a more informal, speech-like style with more contracted words and frequent direct quotations. Thus, four predictors of novels over time are sentence length, word length, rare punctuation marks, and word shortening or more informal speech.

Readability of English and American Novels: Stylistic Age

Factors affecting readability fall into one of two categories, personal or textual. Most of these are not easily measured. Readability formulas then give us an important predictive tool for quickly and objectively finding out the difficulty level of print materials in terms of lexical and syntactic complexity of style. When combined with teacher judgment, expertise in subject matter, and knowledge of student capabilities, print and readers can be matched with surprising accuracy. Another way to get a match is to use analysis of reader/print interaction using reader ratings or performance criteria. The important thing is to find the right match.

Summary

Answers to Workshop Activity 3.1

Part B: 1. ninth, 2. eighth, 3. ninth, 4. eighth to twelfth, 5. tenth,
6. twelfth, 7. tenth, 8. eighth.
Part C: 2. sports page.

Answers to Workshop Activity 3.2

Syllable total counts for each line are: 18, 17, 17, 16, 16, 16, 18, 17, 15, 16, 16, 6. The total number of syllables in the first hundred words was 188. There were four sentences and two additional words in the first 100 words making approximately 4.1 sentences. By averaging 4.1 sentences and 188 syllables with the other two sets of figures, the average is 4.4 sentences and 179 syllables. The readability is then 16 with a true range of 15 to 17.

It is understood that the passage is much too short to estimate the readability on the SMOG, but as an exercise the student may multiply the twenty-three polysyllabic words by 7½ to compensate for only four sentences when the minimum need is thirty. The product is 172 and this is the nearest perfect square of 169 or 13. Then, 13 + 3 equals 16 as an estimated readability level.

1. eleventh, 2, fifth, 3. seventeenth, 4. second (2.8).

References

1. Edward B. Fry, "A Kernel Distance Theory for Readability," in *Reading: Convention and Inquiry,* ed. George McNinch and Wallace D. Miller, National Reading Conference, 24th Yearbook (Clemson, S.C.: Clemson University, 1975).
2. Herbert Spencer, *Philosophy of Style, An Essay* (New York: Appleton-Century-Crofts, 1924).
3. Edward L. Thorndike, *The Teacher's Word Book* (New York: Columbia University, Bureau of Publications, Teachers College, 1921).
4. Bertha A. Lively and S. L. Pressey, "A Method for Measuring the Vocabulary Burden of Textbooks," *Educational Administration and Supervision* 9 (October 1923): 389–98.
5. William S. Gray and B. Leary, *What Makes a Book Readable?* (Chicago: University of Chicago Press, 1935).
6. Irving I. Lorge, *The Lorge Formula for Estimating Difficulty of Reading Materials* (New York: Columbia University, Bureau of Publications, Teachers College, 1939).
7. Rudolph Flesch, "A New Readability Yardstick," *Journal of Applied Psychology* 32 (June 1948): 221–33.
8. Edgar Dale and Jeanne Chall, "A Formula for Predicting Readability," *Educational Research Bulletin* 27 (January 1948): 11–20.
9. Flesch, *Readability Yardstick.*
10. R. Gunning, *The Technique of Clear Writing* (New York: McGraw-Hill, 1952).
11. George Spache, "A New Readability Formula for Primary Grades Reading Materials," *Elementary English* 53 (March 1953): 410–13.
12. Wilson Taylor, "Cloze Procedures: A New Tool for Measuring Readability," *Journalism Quarterly* 30 (1953): 414–38.
13. Edward Fry, "A Readability Formula That Saves Time," *Journal of Reading* 11 (April 1968): 513–16, 575–78.
14. G. H. McLaughlin, "SMOG Grading—A New Readability Formula," *Journal of Reading* 12 (May 1969): 639–46.
15. Harry Singer, "The SEER Technique: A Non-Computational Procedure for Quickly Estimating Readability Level," *Journal of Reading Behavior* 7 (1975): 255–67.
16. Ron Carver, "Measuring Prose Difficulty: The Rauding Scale," *Reading Research Quarterly* 11 (1975–1976): 660–85.
17. Alton L. Raygor, "The Raygor Readability Estimate: A Quick and Easy Way to Determine Difficulty," in *Reading: Theory, Research and Practice,* ed. P. David Pearson, pp. 259–63, National Reading Conference, Twenty-sixth Yearbook (Clemson, S.C.: National Reading Conference, Inc., 1977).
18. Edward Fry, "Fry's Readability Graph: Clarification, Validity, and Extensions to Level 17," *Journal of Reading* 21 (December 1977): 242–53.
19. McLaughlin, *SMOG Grading.*
20. Richard Phillips, *Teaching for Thinking in High School Social Studies* (Reading, Mass.: Addison-Wesley, 1974), p. 134.

21. Harry Forgan and Charles Mangrum II, *Teaching Content Area Reading,* 2d ed. (Columbus, Ohio: Charles E. Merrill Publishing Co., 1981).
22. Edward Fry, "A Readability Formula for Short Passages," *Journal of Reading* 33 (May 1990), 594–97.
23. Thomas Sticht, ed., *Reading for Working,* Human Resources Research Organization (Alexandria, W. Va.: 1975), pp. 15–32.
24. Alton C. Raygor, "Raygor Readability Estimator" (Rehoboth, Mass.: Twin Oaks Publishing Inc., 1979).
25. Lawrence Hafner, "Critical Problems in Improving Readability of Materials at the Secondary Level," in *Vistas of Reading,* ed. J. A. Figurel (Newark, Del.: International Reading Association, 1967), pp. 116–19.
26. Nancy Marshall, "Readability and Comprehensibility," *Journal of Reading* 22 (March 1979), 542–44.
27. Walter Hill, *Secondary School Reading: Progress, Program and Procedure* (Boston: Allyn & Bacon, 1979), p. 192.
28. Carver, *Measuring Prose Difficulty.*
29. Gisela G. Fitzgerald, "Reliability of the Fry Sampling Procedure," *Reading Research Quarterly* 15 (1980): 489–503.
30. Carver, *Measuring Prose Difficulty,* p. 683.
31. Wayne A. Danielson and Dominic L. LaSorsa, "A New Readability Formula Based on the Stylistic Age of Novels," *Journal of Reading* 33 (December 1989): 194–97.

Recommended Readings

Anderson, Jonathon. "Lix and Rix: Variations on a Little Known Readability Index." *Journal of Reading* 26 (March 1983): 490–96.

Baldwin, R. Scott. "A Concurrent Validity Study of The Raygor Readability Estimate." *Journal of Reading* 23 (November 1979): 148–53.

Bormuth, John R. *Development of Readability Analysis.* Final Report, Project No. 7–0052, Bureau of Research, U.S. Office of Education, 1969.

———. "Readability: A New Approach." *Reading Research Quarterly* 1966: 79–132.

Cullinan, B., and Fitzgerald, S. "IRA, NCTE Take Stand on Readability Formula." *Reading Today,* International Reading Association, 1984–85 vol. 2, No. 1.

Danielson, Wayne A., and LaSorsa, Dominic L. "A New Readability Formula Based on the Stylistic Age of Novels." *Journal of Reading* 33 (December 1989): 194–97.

Dreyer, Lois Goodman, "Readability and Responsibility." *Journal of Reading* 27 (January 1984): 334–38.

Duffelmeyer, Frederick A. "Estimating Readability with a Computer: Beware the Aura of Precision." *Reading Teacher* 38 (January 1985): 392–94.

Fitzgerald, Gisela G. "Reliability of the Fry Sampling Procedure." *Reading Research Quarterly* 15 (1980): 489–503.

Fry, Edward. "Fry's Readability Graph: Clarifications, Validity, and Extensions to Level 17." *Journal of Reading* 21 (December 1977): 242–53.

FuSaro, Joseph A. "Applying Statistical Rigor to a Validation Study of the Fry Readability Graph." *Reading Research and Instruction* 28 (Fall 1988): 44–48.

Gross, Phillip P., and Sadowski, Karen. "FOG INDEX—A Readability Formula Program for Microcomputers." *Journal of Reading* 28 (April 1985): 614–618.

Harrison, Colin. "Readability in the United Kingdom." *Journal of Reading* 29 (March 1986): 521–29.

Hittleman, Daniel R. "Readability, Readability Formulas, and Cloze: Selecting Instructional Materials." *Journal of Reading* 22 (November 1978): 117–22.

Kintsch, W.; Kozininsky E.; Streby, W. J.; McKoos, G.; and Keem, J. M. "Comprehension and Recall of Text as a Function of Content Variables." *Journal of Verbal Learning and Verbal Behavior* 14 (1975): 196–214.

Klare, George R. "Assessing Readability." *Reading Research Quarterly* 10 (1974–75): 62–103.

———. *The Measurement of Readability.* Ames, Iowa: Iowa State University Press, 1963.

Maxwell, Martha. "Readability: Have We Gone Too Far?" *Journal of Reading* 21 (March 1978): 525–31.

Nelson, Joan. "Readability: Some Cautions for the Content Area Teacher." *Journal of Reading* 21 (April 1978): 620–25.

Smith, Ron F., and Smith, Kay L. "A Comparison of Readability Formulae as Applied to Newspaper Stories." *Journal of Reading* 28 (October 1984): 20–23.

Spiegel, Dixie Lee, and Wright, Jill D. "Biology Teachers Use of Readability Concepts When Selecting Texts for Students." *Journal of Reading* 27 (October 1983): 28–34.

Strahan, David B., and Herligy, John G. "A Model for Analyzing Textbook Content." *Journal of Reading* 28 (February 1985): 438–43.

Zakuluk, Beverly L., and Samuels, S. Jay. *Readability: Its Past, Present and Future.* Newark, Del.: International Reading Association, 1988.

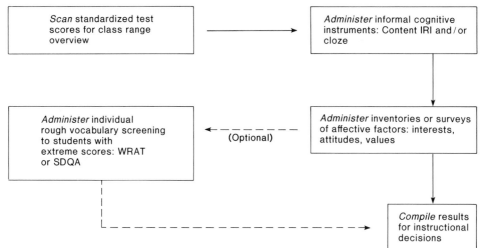

Figure 4.1
Diagnosing students'
levels, needs, and
interests: a cognitive
map.

Matching Print with Reader, Part II: Diagnosing Students' Levels, Needs, and Interests

4

Anticipatory Questions

(Literal)

1. What procedural steps will *you* take in diagnosing your students' reading levels, needs, and interests?

(Literal)

2. Discuss uses and abuses of standardized test scores.

(Critical)

3. Select three skill areas you would use in a Content IRI and discuss why they are most relevant to your content area.

(Critical)

4. Evaluate benefits and problems between using the Content IRI and the cloze procedure for diagnosis, using your own stated criteria.

Technical Terminology and Concepts

Attitude and Interest Assessment

cloze procedure

Content IRI (CIRI)

grade equivalent scores/percentile scores/stanines

informal diagnosis/standardized tests

norm-referenced/criterion-referenced tests

test reliability/validity

WRAT/San Diego Quick Assessment Test

Introduction

Determining the readability of a content text is only an initial step in matching print with reader. It is also necessary to identify those students who can handle the reading assignments, those who need either direct assistance or alternative materials, and those who would most benefit from being exposed to more challenging intellectual discourse. Such instructional decisions can best be made following an **informal diagnosis** of students in each content classroom. The initial diagnosis need not be a time-consuming process; in most cases it can be accomplished in one fifty-minute class session.

Prior to this initial informal diagnosis performed by the content teacher in the classroom, some attention should be paid to interpreting students' standardized test scores. The cognitive map (fig. 4.1) on page 86 gives you an overview of content teachers' tasks in diagnosis.

Standardized Test Scores

A **standardized test** is one in which there is rigid adherence to procedures for administering and scoring. It has been given to representative groups of individuals to establish norms, which are the average scores made by the representative groups. A **norm-referenced test** score tells how well any student performed as compared with a specified norm population. Often this population does not represent all grade level scores appearing on the test, but instead some are interpolated and/or extrapolated.

Standardized test scores generally found in students' record folders are survey or achievement test scores. These group-administered tests measure several reading skills but yield only one or two overall general scores representing performance in vocabulary, comprehension, and, occasionally, rate. Some examples are the *Gates-MacGinitie* test, the *Sequential Test of Educational Progress* (STEP), and the *Iowa Silent Reading Tests.*[1,2,3]

Reliability and Validity

Standardized tests are said to be *reliable* if the scores are consistent over time and are *valid* if they measure what they purport to measure. For example, if you complete a test of comprehension today and then at a later time retake the same test (or equivalent form) and earn approximately the same score, the test is said to be reliable. It is valid if it really does measure your comprehension and not some other factor such as your prior knowledge of the topic.

As mentioned earlier, norm-referenced scores give a basis for comparing students' performance with the performance of a specified norm group. The use of norms puts test scores into proper perspective. For example, three students' test scores are compared in table 4.1. John earned a grade placement score of 8.5, which ranked him at the fiftieth percentile and at the fifth stanine. Because John is in the eighth grade, this test result indicates that he is performing normally in the "middle" of the distribution

Table 4.1

Representative Standardized Scores

Student	Raw Score	Grade Equivalent	Percentile	Stanine
John	42	8.5	50	5
Bill	72	11.9	97	9
Tom	21	4.2	07	2

for his class. Bill, with a grade placement score of 11.9, performs much better than the average of his class, and Tom is achieving much below the class average.

The raw score alone is meaningless; it has to be interpolated into at least one of the other scores—*grade equivalent, percentile,* or *stanine*—to be informative.

Grade equivalent scores encompass the school grade range from 1.0 to 12.9 and, as such, indicate the grade level at which the average student in a norm group had a given number correct. A major limitation of this range of scores is that the teacher needs to understand that the *sizes* of units of learning representing what constitutes grade one, four, seven, or eleven are not necessarily equal units. It is difficult to say, for example, whether growth from 7.1 to 8.1 in reading is equivalent to all the rapid growth a student may make in reading from 2.1 to 3.1. Also, a common misconception occurs when we look at students' scores that are above their grade level. Take Nina, for example. Nina is a seventh grader, with a score of 11.4. This means that she is doing extremely well for a seventh grader but does not mean that she should be doing eleventh grade level work or promoted to a higher grade. She is only being compared with other seventh graders. Because of common misinterpretations of grade equivalent scores, test publishers are being urged to use percentile scores instead.

Grade Equivalent Scores

A **percentile score** is a point on a distribution that shows the relative position of one student to the total group. Expressed in terms of percents, it is easily understood. For example, a percentile rank of fifty-eight means that 42 percent of all those tested performed better and 58 percent performed less well. Students who rank at the seventy-fifth percentile or above have done well, exceeding the performances of at least 75 percent of their peers. Students who rank at the tenth percentile performed better than only 10 percent of their norm group.

Because percentiles are easy to compute, interpret, and understand, they are frequently used for local norms in a school district. Publishers

Percentile Scores

almost always provide percentile norms with their test data. However, percentile norms are meaningful only in terms of a specific test administered to a particular group at a given time. And local percentile norms may be different from the national norms.

Percentiles are not based on a scale of equal units of difference. For example, the raw score difference between the ninetieth and ninety-fifth percentiles may not be the same number of raw score points between the forty-fifth and fiftieth percentiles. Raw scores tend to cluster around the mean of the distribution so that many scores will be the same or nearly the same at the middle, or fiftieth percentile.

Stanines

The **stanine** is a norming term expressed in the numbers one to nine. The distribution of raw scores is divided into nine parts. The fifth stanine accounts for all the students whose raw scores cluster at the middle of the distribution. A stanine of nine is the highest level and a stanine of one the lowest. Stanines also are not of equal value: the fifth stanine represents the performance of the large group in the middle (20 percent of the total population). The fourth and sixth stanines are those below and above average (each stanine accommodates 17 percent of the total population). Stanines three and seven include those students farther above and farther below average. The lowest achievers are in stanines one and two and the highest achievers are in eight and nine. Distribution of the percentages of the norm group is shown below:

Percent of cases:	4%	7%	12%	17%	20%	17%	12%	7%	4%
Stanines:	1	2	3	4	5	6	7	8	9

If you keep in mind that 54 percent of a distribution falls in stanines four, five, and six, you will know that stanines one, two, and three account for the bottom 23 percent of the distribution and stanines seven, eight, and nine account for the 23 percent at the top of the distribution.

Norms, then, give us a consistent way of interpreting achievement scores. As grade equivalents, they express average performance of students at various grade levels. As percentiles, they describe a student's place in a distribution in terms of the percent of the students who scored lower and higher. Stanines indicate how far above or below the average a given student is in the norming group.

Possible Uses of Scores in Content Classrooms

1. Students can be rank ordered from most proficient to least proficient for flexible grouping purposes.
2. Some very general areas of strengths and weaknesses for a class can be noted.
3. Scores can be tallied to assess group gains for the year.
4. One school program can be compared with another.

The reading grade level scores may inflate the actual reading level by as much as two years. The score may represent the student's actual frustration level. In other words, a student with a reading level score of ninth grade might actually be able to handle only seventh-grade material.

On the other hand, group administration of the test may work against some individuals. Students with the flu or who are emotionally upset about a recent event will probably not do as well as they could. Their scores may be invalid.

By the very nature of the concept of test norms, there will always be some students with scores falling below as well as above the average scores.

Historically, test scores have too often been used to label students as slow learners or remedial readers when such may not be the case. Making such inaccurate judgments can be detrimental to self-concepts.

Workshop Activity 4.1
Standardized Reading Tests

To get a better perspective of what is generally measured in a standardized reading test, several of these tests should be examined.

1. Divide into small groups of three to four each. You may wish to group according to interest or teaching levels.
2. Each group examines a different test, such as *The Gates-MacGinitie Reading Test, The Iowa Silent Reading Test,* or *The Sequential Test of Educational Progress.*
3. Timing themselves, individuals take the test and respond to the questions. It is best to agree on a working time, for example, thirty minutes.
4. The group then checks with each other first as to correct responses and then is given an answer key.
5. Each group, with one member acting as recorder, compiles a list of perceived strengths and weaknesses of the test.
6. One member prepares to report the group's conclusions to the class.

Because standardized reading test scores are not very helpful for making instructional decisions, criterion-referenced tests have been suggested as an alternative. A **criterion-reference** interprets a student's score "by comparing it to some absolute standard, usually some specified behavioral criterion of performance; the focus is on what the student can do." For example, the criterion for mastery may be set at 80 percent or above for a particular

Criterion-referenced Testing

skill, without comparing it with anyone else's score. This kind of test measures achievement of specific behaviors and may be either constructed by the classroom teacher or commercially produced.[4]

Individual Quick Screening

Sometimes it is helpful for a content teacher to get a rough estimate of the reading level of one or more individual students. This can be accomplished in approximately five minutes for each individual, using one of the following word-calling devices: *The Wide Range Achievement Test* (WRAT) or the *San Diego Quick Assessment*.[5,6]

The Wide Range Achievement Test: Reading

This widely used one-page word test is divided into two parts. Part I is normed for students under twelve years of age and Part II for anyone twelve or over. The student reads aloud to the teacher individual words across the page until twelve consecutive words are missed. At that point the student stops and, with the aid of the numbers at the end of each line, the teacher obtains an immediate raw score. This is then converted into a reading grade level by referring to the box in the center of the page.

Several cautions should be given: (1) When administering this to older students, it is wise to warn them that the words rapidly accelerate in difficulty from first-grade to nineteenth-grade level, so they are not expected to complete the test; (2) the WRAT does not measure comprehension or knowledge of definitions; (3) because it is a widely known standardized test, at no point should the words be explained or pronounced for the students.

The San Diego Quick Assessment Test

Similar to the WRAT, this easy-to-administer word list can also be completed in about five minutes. It has been carefully prepared and has been found useful and reliable by many teachers at all grade levels. Like the WRAT the *San Diego Quick Assessment Test* provides a rough estimation of a student's reading level. The directions for administering it and the list of words needed by the teachers are as follows (the test is presented in table 4.2).

1. Have the individual student read the lists until the student misses three words in one list.
2. The list in which the student misses no more than one of the ten words is the level at which the student can read independently. Two errors indicate instructional level. Three or more errors identify the level at which reading material will be too difficult.

Administration

1. Type each list of ten words on index cards, one list to a card. If available, type the first three or four lists with larger type.
2. Begin with a card that is at least two years below the class grade level of the student.

Table 4.2

San Diego Quick Assessment

pp	Primer	1	2
see	you	road	our
play	come	live	please
me	not	thank	myself
at	with	when	town
run	jump	bigger	early
go	help	how	send
and	is	always	wide
look	work	night	believe
can	are	spring	quietly
here	this	today	carefully
3	**4**	**5**	**6**
city	decided	scanty	bridge
middle	served	certainly	commercial
moment	amazed	develop	abolish
frightened	silent	considered	trucker
exclaimed	wrecked	discussed	apparatus
several	improved	behaved	elementary
lonely	certainly	splendid	comment
drew	entered	acquainted	necessity
since	realized	escaped	gallery
straight	interrupted	grim	relativity
7	**8**	**9**	**10**
amber	capacious	conscientious	zany
dominion	limitation	isolation	jerkin
sundry	pretext	molecule	nausea
capillary	intrigue	ritual	gratuitous
impetuous	delusion	momentous	linear
blight	immaculate	vulnerable	inept
wrest	ascent	kinship	legality
enumerate	acrid	conservatism	aspen
daunted	binocular	jaunty	amnesty
condescend	embankment	inventive	barometer
11			
galore	exonerate		
rotunda	superannuate		
capitalism	luxuriate		
prevaricate	piebald		
risible	crunch		

From Margaret La Pray and Ramon Ross, "The Graded Word List: Quick Gauge of Reading Ability," *Journal of Reading*, 12: 305–307, Jan., 1969. Reprinted with permission of the authors and the International Reading Association.

3. Do not put the reading level on the cards where the students can read it. Do your coding on the back of the card.

4. Ask each student to read the words aloud to you. If they misread any words on the list, drop to easier lists until there are no errors. This indicates the base level.

5. Keep reading the lists until three words on any one list are missed or all lists are exhausted.[7]

Need for Informal Diagnosis	Because standardized tests are not the best way to determine students' abilities to handle content materials, two important tools that should be considered for development are the Content Informal Reading Inventory (**Content IRI or CIRI**) and the **cloze** procedure. The advantage of either of these is that they are used with the teacher's own actual content materials. One or both may be used as a diagnostic tool as well as an interest inventory and/or attitude survey.

The Content IRI

The **Content IRI,** sometimes referred to as a Group IRI or CIRI, is a powerful tool in a content teacher's repertoire. It should not be confused with the IRI (Informal Reading Inventory) used widely by elementary teachers and reading specialists.

The Content IRI versus the IRI	The original concept of an informal reading inventory was that an individual student read aloud (and sometimes silently) a series of brief graded paragraphs, while the teacher duly noted the number and types of word recognition errors made. After each selection the student was asked to respond orally to a series of comprehension questions based on the reading. Armed with this information of miscues made and questions missed, the teacher could determine the student's instructional reading level as well as frustration and independent levels. Administering this type of IRI takes time and practice.

On the other hand, a Content IRI is prepared by each content teacher using the text for that class. It is administered to an entire class simultaneously during one period and reflects directly the area being studied and the types of questions the teacher considers to be important. The purpose of the Content IRI is to ascertain how well individuals in a particular class will be able to handle that text and what skills still need to be worked on.

Constructing a Content IRI	The following steps should help you to build your own diagnostic tool:

1. Select from near the beginning of the text a *representative* sample of approximately 250 to 400 words, depending on grade level of the class.
2. The selection may be typed or printed, or students can be asked to read it directly from the text.
3. Compose an introductory motivation paragraph that includes a general statement about the topic to be read—a frame of

reference statement and a sentence telling the reader the purpose for reading it. For example, the following was used with a fifth grade social studies text.

Preparation/Motivation:
Rice is something that you have probably eaten because it is used in many kinds of foods, such as breakfast cereals, chocolate bars, and Chinese food. Read this story to find out where rice comes from and how it is grown.

4. Prepare ten or more comprehension questions that include several vocabulary definitions, stated facts (literal), and inferential questions, asking the reader to go beyond what is directly stated. Vocabulary terms should always be used in context, not isolated. Some examples from the same fifth grade Content IRI follow. Each type of question can be readily identified by the letters V, F, or I, standing for vocabulary, fact, or inference, appearing before the question.

   (V) 1. Because the paddy must be flooded, its surface must be *level*.
   "Level" here means _____

   (F) 2. Name three things that rice plants need in order to grow.

   _____   _____   _____

   (I) 3. Why do you suppose we do not grow rice crops on the farms around our town?

   _____

   _____

5. When you complete the rough draft of your questions (at *least* three in each category), evaluate each according to the following:
   Vocabulary—Did you select key terms important for your students to know? Did you use them in context?
   Fact—Were the details you asked them to recall clearly stated in the selection?
   Inference—Did these questions relate the topic to their background experience? Did they go beyond stated information? Did you use words like "do you think" or "suppose?"

You have now completed a description of Part I of your Content IRI, which will determine the suitability or the fit between your students and their text. This first part should not take your students longer than twenty minutes to complete.

Part II consists of a needs assessment of selected skills. You are the best judge of those skills your students need to master to achieve success in your class.

1. As you read this list below, check three skill areas you think are important for you to assess.

    Skill Areas

    _____ a. *Use parts of texts*—Are they efficient in locating and using textbook aids, such as the table of contents, index, appendices, glossary, references?

    _____ b. *Locate reference materials*—Can they locate and use information in encyclopedias, almanacs, reader's guides, and other reference materials?

    _____ c. *Outline and take notes*—Are they able to outline information and take notes from reading reference material or from listening to lectures?

    _____ d. *Interpret graphics*—Do they know how to interpret maps, charts, diagrams, tables, graphs, and cartoons?

    _____ e. *Follow directions*—Are they able to follow directions correctly and exactly?

    _____ f. *Translate symbols or formulas*—Do they know the meaning of specific symbols or formulas needed for your subject?

    _____ g. *Define content-specific vocabulary*—Do they recognize and understand the special vocabulary of your area?

    _____ h. *Display comprehension skills*—Are they able to note main ideas, supporting details, sequence of events, conclusions, effect and cause?

    _____ i. *Use study strategies*—Do they know and use appropriate study skills and strategies?

    _____ j. *Adapt rate*—Do they adapt their rate to the purpose and difficulty of the material?

Having selected three areas considered important, you have completed the first step in Part II.

2. Prepare your test questions based on the text and other class materials you use. An example of each is shown below.

    a. *Parts of text*—On what pages will you find information about _____ ? (Table of Contents)

    When was the text written? (Copyright)

    How do these authors define _____ ? (Glossary)

    On what page will you find a table or figure on the topic of _____ ? (List of Tables)

    What use might you have for the information in the appendix?

b. *Reference materials*—Where would be the first place you would look for information about _____ ?

What kinds of information would you find in an almanac?

c. *Outline and take notes*—Ask students to outline a passage in the text, or dictate a short passage and ask them to take notes.

d. *Graphics*—Use the textbook or duplicate a map, diagram, or chart and ask questions such as:

What is the topic of this diagram?

What does the symbol _____ mean here?

What are the vertical headings?

What is one conclusion you can draw from this chart?

How many miles are there between _____ and _____ ?

e. *Follow directions*—Select a segment of reading or test material you use, and ask students to follow the directions as written. Also, you might ask them to write their names on the upper left corner or mark true or false, using the symbols T and F.

f. *Symbols and formulas*—What do the following symbols mean?

$$=, <, II, \neq, \therefore$$

What is meant by the formula $A = \frac{1}{2}$ bh?

Solve for x in the equation $2x$ is $3 = 7$.

g. *Content-specific vocabulary*—Match the words with the definitions by writing the correct letter from the column on the right next to the number on the left. Always have more choices in the right-hand column to avoid choosing correct responses by a process of elimination.

1. _____ oxymoron
2. _____ simile
3. _____ metaphor

a. two unlike things are compared using the words "like" or "as"
b. words of opposite meaning are used together
c. a direct comparison between two things
d. a pleasant term for something considered unpleasant
e. repetition of the beginning consonant

Concisely define the following terms in the subject area of science:

protein   RNA
endoplasmic reticulum   energy
ribosomes

Cross out any unrelated terms in the above list and explain the relationship of the remaining words. These terms might well be presented in phrases to show context.

h. *Comprehension skills*— What is the main idea of this section? What conclusion can you draw from this statement? Determine which was the effect and which the cause. List the events in the order in which they occurred. What three CIRI facts support the main idea of this passage?

i. *Study strategies*—Administer a study habits survey asking students how often they do such things as the following:

survey the chapter first
ask questions as they are reading
check their answers as they read
review immediately after reading
schedule their time for study

j. *Adaptable rate*—Short paragraphs may be typed and students asked to read each for a different purpose. They mark whether they intend to read it very rapidly, very slowly, or somewhere in between.

Administering and Scoring the Content IRI

The Content IRI should be administered to a total class at the beginning of the term. It should not take longer than one fifty-minute class period to administer. In elementary grades, teachers may wish to break up the inventory into sections, giving one part each day for two or more days. When introducing it to a class, the teacher should mention that this is an *inventory* of their strengths and needs, not a *test*. This inventory will help determine what they need.

To score the inventory, you should follow your own criteria. For example, in one area you may decide that it is necessary to get three out of five items correct to show skill competency. In another area, 95 percent correct might be deemed necessary. Regardless of the criteria, you will benefit from constructing and filling out a class chart showing general areas of the class's strengths and needs as well as individual student scores. An example of a class profile is shown in table 4.3. Be sure to include a key that will state your criteria or cut-off points and whether a check mark means "strength" or "needs improvement."

Table 4.3
Content IRI Class Profile (Sample)

Name of Student	Part I			Part II			Overall Individual Needs
	Vocabulary (3 out of 3)	Fact (3 out of 4)	Inference (4 out of 5)	Parts of Text	Graphics	Study Strategies	
1. Margaret Jones	✓					✓	some
2. Sue Jaramillo					✓		yes
3. John Johnson	✓				✓		yes
4. Kevin Riley	✓	✓			✓	✓	some
5. Arthur Chin	✓		✓	✓	✓	✓	no
6. Janice King	✓	✓				✓	some
7. Loretta Lorrenzo					✓		yes
8. Jacob Kruger	✓	✓	✓	✓	✓	✓	no
Class Skill Need	no	yes	yes	yes	no	some	

This profile may be used to determine classroom groupings. Skill centers may also be set up around the classroom for students to work individually on specific needs.

Key: ✓ means skill mastery

The Cloze Procedure

The evident simplicity and relative accuracy of the cloze procedure makes it a potentially potent tool for content teachers. Students may initially find cloze tests to be a frustrating experience. Some practice time is therefore strongly recommended. It may be used in lieu of or along with a more elaborate Content IRI to get a general sense of student ability to handle a specific text.

Background

The idea behind the cloze procedure was conceived in the early 1950s by Wilson Taylor, and much research has been done on it during the intervening years.[8] It stands today as a viable diagnostic instrument.

The term **cloze** comes from the Gestalt psychological term *closure* and means the tendency of a thinking individual to anticipate the completion of a not quite finished pattern. With a natural tendency to perceive things as wholes, the reader, listener, or viewer determines what is missing based on what is already there. For example, if someone said to you "Merry Christmas and Happy New ＿＿＿," you would automatically supply the word "Year"; or if you viewed an incomplete portrait with one eye still missing, you would mentally fill the gap by picturing the other eye. To complete a cloze, readers must know the meanings of the words, their form or function (e.g., noun, adjective), as well as the combined meanings or how the words make sense together.

Constructing a Cloze

Strict guidelines must be adhered to when using cloze as a test of readability.

1. Select a representative passage from the text of approximately 300 words that the students have not seen before.
2. Leave the first and last sentences intact.
3. Starting with the second sentence, delete every fifth word, substituting a standard length blank of twelve spaces, until fifty words are deleted. It has been suggested that science material may require every seventh word deletion.
4. Do not number the blanks or give answer sheets, or you will invalidate the results.

Administering and Scoring the Cloze

1. Explain to the students that the purpose of this exercise is to determine the ease with which they can handle the text. Tell them that only one word has been deleted from each blank and that you will not count off for misspellings. Suggest that they look over the entire passage before commencing to fill in the blanks. They are to try to determine the exact word the writer used in each case.
2. Allow unlimited time for each student to complete the typed passage.
3. When scoring, allow only the exact word replacement. Each blank is worth two points. Table 4.4 shows how to interpret the scores. Scores falling within the instructional level are said to be equivalent to approximately a 75 percent score on a multiple choice test on the same material.

John Bormuth's research has shown that overall relative ranking changes very little, regardless of whether synonyms are counted as correct or incorrect.[9] When synonyms are allowed, the tests are much more difficult and time consuming to score—an important consideration for any teacher.

Advantages, then, to using the cloze procedure are that they are easy for teachers to construct, that no questions need to be developed (and possibly misunderstood), and that no special expertise is required in test development.

Foundations

Table 4.4

Reading Level Based on Cloze Scores

Score	Level
58–100	independent
44–57	instructional
0–43	frustration

A second use of cloze is to measure general reading comprehension. Marian Tonjes found that using lexical deletions of every fifth noun or verb and allowing for synonyms was a valid way to measure factual comprehension of an entire story.[10] Wesley Schneyer also found the cloze to have adequate validity for evaluating general reading comprehension.[11]

Other Uses of Cloze

A third use of cloze is as a teaching instrument, which can provide students with practice in reading to note significant details, find main ideas, and make inferences from text. When cloze is used as a teaching instrument, all sorts of variations may be applied:

1. Synonyms are encouraged.
2. Deletions may vary according to purpose from every tenth to seventh to fifth word or every fifth noun or verb; or all adjectives or adverbs.
3. Clues may be given such as the first letter of each deleted word, or an indication of length by the size of the line, or the number of letters by using dashes for each in lieu of the line.

(See the chapter on teaching strategies for further examples of adaptations of cloze for the classroom.)

Workshop Activity 4.2

Developing a Content IRI and a Cloze

After completing this chapter, your task is to construct a Content IRI and a cloze using a text from your content area at the grade level you teach or propose to teach. Rough drafts should be shared with your group for further refinement.

When your instructor is satisfied with the rough draft, it should be typed and administered to a class or a group of students. The results should be written in chart form, as shown in table 4.3, and a written discussion included.

Taxonomy of the Affective Domain

Determining attitudes, interests, and values in connection with your content area is also an important diagnostic consideration. The most neglected area in education and one of the most important is the affective or emotional side of learning. As mentioned in chapter 2, Krathwohl's levels of the affective domain are reviewed here, moving from lowest to highest.[12]

1. *Receiving.* The passive, taking in, listening but not responding (anything lower than this would mean no affective involvement at all). Students may be ranged from being merely aware of what is happening to willingly receiving ideas, to exhibiting controlled attention. Some students have become quite adept at fooling the instructor as to their actual involvement.
2. *Responding.* At this level students progress from acquiescing in responding ("Okay, if you call on me, I'll answer") to those willing to respond ("I really need the grade, so I'll volunteer to answer") to those who show satisfaction in responding ("Hey, I like this, I'll gladly volunteer an answer!").
3. *Valuing.* All content teachers hope that their students will value their subject matter. At the lower level of valuing, students accept and approve of what they are learning. Next, they show a preference for this learning over something else. Finally, they are committed to the value. They show this by consistently reading in depth as well as being willing to state their interest and belief in its worth. Most classes rarely proceed beyond this level.
4. *Organizing.* At this level the student conceptualizes the value and organizes it into life goals.
5. *Characterizing.* Here is where every action shows commitment to the value. At this level the student *becomes* a scientist or a lover of poetry, for example.

Workshop Activity 4.3
Brainstorming Unique Values of Reading

This activity may be used successfully not only in the university classroom but also in classrooms at all levels.

The task is to ask the students to brainstorm, answering the question, "What are the unique values of reading (in competition with television, games, etc.)?" Students should be told or reminded of the following basic ground rules of brainstorming.

1. All ideas are accepted; no negative comments are allowed.
2. Ideas should be called out as rapidly as possible.

3. The instructor will write these on the board without editing.
4. Periods of silence for thinking are often necessary.
5. If students start getting far off the track, the instructor may repeat the original statement or question.

After the brainstorming phase, an optional follow-up activity would be to categorize and label the entries. Students will enjoy comparing their responses with the following list from "experts."

1. readily accessible when needed
2. can react individually
3. time for reflection, rereading
4. information is easily rechecked
5. memories are renewed
6. can select segments, ignoring others
7. sources can be readily compared
8. can skim a wide range of materials
9. can check author's credentials
10. provides contexts for concept development and vocabulary study
11. provides an easy escape

Assessing Attitudes and Interests

Lou Burmeister suggests that teachers concerned about student attitudes might make a chart for each unit with the affective levels across the top, and students' names listed on the left.[13] By observing behaviors in class on various units, teachers may be able to determine what aspects best motivate students. Questions Burmeister suggests that teachers might ask themselves when they see less involvement than they wish are:

Attitudes

1. Why isn't interest growing?
2. Are my materials appropriate to the variety of reading levels of my students?
3. Is there enough diversity of materials?
4. Am I doing an adequate job of building the skills necessary for concept development?
5. Are my approaches to teaching varied enough?
6. Do I provide material and time for free reading on unit-related topics?
7. Are students given adequate opportunity to share ideas with each other?

Interests

When students are asked to complete an interest inventory such as that shown in figure 4.2 (Tonjes Interest Inventory), teachers may then try to tie content to those interests. In an English class that could mean developing a short story unit, where students read different stories of their own

Figure 4.2

Tonjes Interest Inventory (TII).

Name _____ Date _____

A. Circle each activity that you enjoy.

1. football	27. sailing	53. auto remodeling
2. baseball/softball	28. canoeing	54. motorcycling
3. basketball	29. power boating	55. disco dancing
4. soccer	30. fishing	56. square dancing
5. hockey	31. hunting	57. card games
6. la crosse	32. bicycling	58. packaged games e.g.
7. volleyball	33. backpacking	(Trivial Pursuit)
8. tennis	34. archery	59. chess
9. badminton	35. gymnastics	60. parties
10. racketball	36. reading newspapers	61. picnics
11. handball	37. reading magazines	62. singing
12. golf	38. reading novels	63. playing a musical instrument
13. track	39. reading nonfiction	64. listening to music
14. wrestling	40. ping pong	65. raising animals
15. jogging	41. pool, billiards	66. gardening
16. surfing	42. bowling	67. jigsaw puzzles
17. skin diving, scuba	43. movies	68. crossword puzzles
18. water skiing	44. watching television	69. drawing, painting
19. swimming	45. acting in plays	70. attending plays
20. diving	46. attending museums	71. sculpturing
21. roller skating	47. concerts	72. writing
22. ice skating	48. ballet	73. composing
23. down-hill skiing	49. cooking	74. photography
24. cross-country skiing	50. sewing	75. videogames
25. horseback riding	51. ham radio	76. other: _____
26. mountain climbing	52. carpentry	

B. List any other recreational activities not on this list you have engaged in during the past year and enjoyed.

77. _____   79. _____

78. _____   80. _____

C. Look over the activities you have selected and decide which three you most prefer. List in order of preference.

1. _____

2. _____

3. _____

D. Add up the number of activities you enjoy. _____

What is one thing you learned about yourself from taking this interest inventory? I learned that _____

What will you do with this information now, to enhance learning? Explain _____

_____

_____

choices or from a list, and then share common characteristics. In a history class current popular music could be shown as reflecting the spirit of the times. Students interested in that music might research the type of music played in the era they are studying and compare and contrast it to the music of today.

Summary

Matching print with reader at the onset necessitates some type of informal diagnosis of students' reading levels and abilities based on (1) the results of scanning standardized test scores for the overall range within a class; (2) the general comprehension of text based on a cloze exercise, (3) the specific skill needs as shown by a group Content IRI; and (4) the individual rough reading levels for extreme scores using a word list. The teacher is then in an excellent position to make curricular decisions that will serve to meet individual learning needs of all students. Taking into consideration interests and attitudes will make the course content more relevant and will better serve their affective needs.

References

1. A. I. Gates and W. MacGinitie, *Gates-MacGinitie Reading Tests* (New York: Teachers College Press, 1965, rev. 1970).
2. *Sequential Tests of Educational Progress-Reading,* rev. (Princeton, N.J.: Educational Testing Service, 1972).
3. Roger Farr et al., *The 1973 Iowa Silent Reading Tests* (New York: Harcourt Brace Jovanovich, 1973).
4. J. R. Jastak and Sidney Bijou, *Wide Range Achievement Test: Reading* (WRAT), rev. (Wilmington, Del.: Guidance Associates, 1975).
5. Margaret La Pray and Ramon Ross, "The Graded Word List: Quick Gauge of Reading Ability," *Journal of Reading* (January 1969): 305–7.
6. Kenneth Kavale, "Selecting and Evaluating Reading Tests," in *Reading Tests and Teachers: A Practical Guide,* ed. Robert Schreiner (Newark, Del.: International Reading Association, 1979), pp. 9–34.
7. La Pray and Ross, *Graded Word List.*
8. Wilson Taylor, "Cloze Procedure: A New Tool for Measuring Readability," *Journalism Quarterly* 30 (Fall 1953): 415–533.
9. John Bormuth, "The Cloze Readability Procedure," *Elementary English* 45 (April 1968): 429–36.
10. Marian J. Tonjes, "Evaluation of Comprehension and Vocabulary Gains of Tenth Grade Students Enrolled in a Developmental Reading Program" (M.A. thesis, The Graduate School, The University of New Mexico, Albuquerque, 1969), pp. 67–69.
11. Wesley J. Schneyer, "Use of the Cloze Procedure for Improving Reading Comprehension," *The Reading Teacher* 19 (December 1965): 174–80.
12. David R. Krathwohl, Benjamin Bloom, and Bertram Masia, *Taxonomy of Educational Objectives—Handbook II: Affective Domain* (New York: David McKay, 1964), pp. 176–85.
13. Lou E. Burmeister, *Reading Strategies for Middle and Secondary School Teachers,* 2d ed. (Reading, Mass.: Addison-Wesley, 1978).

**Recommended
Readings**

Ashby-Davis, Claire. "Cloze and Comprehension: A Qualitative Analysis and Critique." *Journal of Reading* 28 (April 1985): 585–89.

Athey, Irene. "Reading Research in the Affective Domain." In *Theoretical Models and the Processes of Reading,* H. Singer and R. Ruddell, eds. Newark, Del.: International Reading Association, 1976.

Blanton, William E.; Farr, Roger; and Tuinman, J. J., eds. *Measuring Reading Performance,* 2d ed. Newark, Del.: International Reading Association, 1986.

Buros, O. K. *Reading Tests and Reviews II.* Highland Park, N.J.: Gryphon Press, 1975.

DeSanti, Roger J. "Concurrent and Predictive Validity of a Semantically and Syntactically Sensitive Cloze-Scoring System." *Reading Research and Instruction* 28 (Winter 1989): 19–40.

Glazer, Susan M.; Searfoss, L. W.; and Gentile, Lance M., eds. *Reexamining Reading Diagnosis: New Trends and Procedures.* Newark, Del.: International Reading Association, 1988.

Jacobson, Jeanne M. "Group vs. Individual Completion of a Cloze Passage." *Journal of Reading* 33 (January 1990): 244–51.

Johns, Jerry. "A List of Basic Sight Words for Older Disabled Readers." *English Journal* 61 (October 1972): 1057–59.

Lewandowski, Lawrence J., and Martens, Brian K. "Selecting and Evaluating Standardized Reading Tests." *Journal of Reading* 33 (February 1990): 384–88.

McKenna, Michael C., and Robinson, Richard D. *An Introduction to the Cloze Procedure: An Annotated Bibliography.* Newark, Del.: International Reading Association, 1980.

O'Reilly, Robert P., and Streeter, Ronald E. "Report on the Development and Validation of a System for Measuring Literal Comprehension in a Multiple-Choice Cloze Format." *Journal of Reading Behavior* 9 (Spring 1977): 45–69.

Readence, John E., and Moore, David W. "Why Questions? A Historical Perspective on Standardized Reading Comprehension Tests." *Journal of Reading* 26 (January 1983): 306–13.

Schmitt, Maribeth Cassidy. "A Questionnaire to Measure Children's Awareness of Strategic Reading Processes." *The Reading Teacher* 43 (March 1990): 454–63.

Schreiner, Robert, ed. *Reading Tests and Teachers: A Practical Guide.* Newark, Del.: International Reading Association, 1979.

Sternberg, Robert J. "Are We Reading Too Much Into Reading Comprehension Tests?" *Journal of Reading* 34 (April 1991): 540–47.

Webb, Melvin W. "A Scale for Evaluating Standardized Reading Tests, With Results for Nelson-Denny, Iowa, and Stanford." *Journal of Reading* 26 (February 1983): 424–29.

Skills

2

Figure 5.1
Adapting rate for efficient comprehension: a cognitive map.

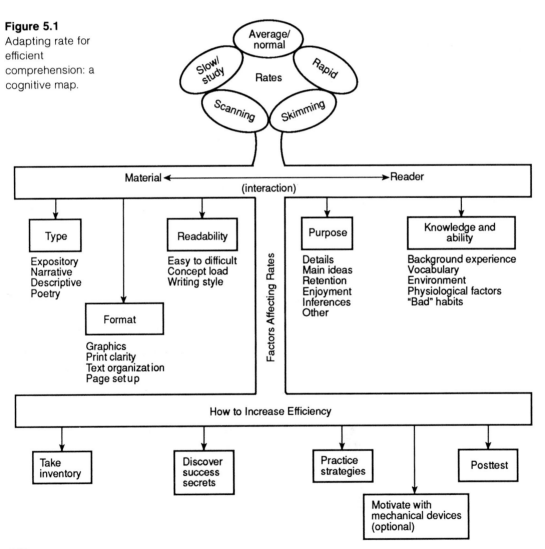

Adapting Rate for Effective Comprehension

5

Anticipatory Questions

(Literal)

1. List three reasons why rate adaptability is considered to be important.

(Literal and applied)

2. Discuss factors affecting rate and ways to improve effectiveness. How does this tie in with the chapter on readability?

(Applied)

3. Predict your own reading rates for expository, narrative, and poetic materials when your purposes are content mastery, appreciation of the beauty of the language, or escape. After determining these rates, evaluate your adaptability.

(Critical)

4. Rank order the various factors affecting rate and justify your choices.

Technical Terminology and Concepts

adaptability index

concept load or density

cue reduction

directional words or signposts

fixations

mechanical devices

rate adaptability

scanning/skimming rates

subvocalizing/inner speech

reading in thought units

WPM rate/effective rate

Introduction

No matter how well you read at the present moment, the chances are great that you are not reading up to your potential. While studying this chapter you not only will learn about **rate adaptability** as it applies to your students, but also may discover and experience for yourself your own most efficient reading rates. The term *adaptability* is used in lieu of the more commonly used term *flexibility* throughout this chapter because its meaning is more closely allied to the concept we wish to develop. *Adaptable* means adjusting your rate so it is suitable to a new or special situation and effective for your purpose.

Immediately following this introduction are three short selections, which may be read in class and timed by your instructor or timed at home using a stopwatch or a second hand. In any case, they are to be completed before reading the remainder of the chapter.

The first selection is of average difficulty and should be read at your normal rate, as it will give you a baseline for comparing future readings. Timing can be done with any watch or clock with a second hand. The number of words in the article is given after each selection, along with the formula for finding the base rate in words per minute (WPM). This is later used in combination with the comprehension percentage to obtain the **effective rate.** Without looking back, answer the ten comprehension questions. The answers to these questions will be found at the end of this chapter. Each question is worth ten points; thus it is a simple matter to figure the comprehension percentage score.

The **WPM rate** is figured by dividing the number of words in the article by the number of seconds it took you to read the selection, then multiplying by sixty to convert seconds into minutes.

$$\frac{\text{number of words}}{\text{number of seconds}} \times 60 = \text{WPM}$$

Because rate alone is meaningless without comprehension, it is necessary to go one step further and find the effective rate. This is accomplished simply by multiplying the WPM by the comprehension percentage. The result is a rough estimate of efficiency or effective rate.

$$\text{WPM} \times \text{Comprehension percentage} = \text{Effective rate}$$

For example: suppose you read a 540-word article in one minute and thirty seconds. One minute and thirty seconds = ninety seconds.

$$\left(\frac{540 \text{ words}}{90 \text{ seconds}} \times 60\right) = 90 \overline{)540} \quad 6 \times 60 = 360 \text{ WPM}$$

Suppose you get a score of 80 percent comprehension.

$$360 \text{ (WPM)} \times .80 \text{ (comprehension)} = 288 \text{ effective rate}$$

$$\begin{array}{r} 360 \\ \times\ .80 \\ \hline 288.00 \end{array}$$

Thus, although your speed was 360 WPM, the fact that you missed two questions means that your effective rate was actually only 288.

Your goal over the weeks ahead is not only to vary and increase your rate when it is called for, but also to bring your WPM and your effective rate as close together as possible.

Read the second selection, which is more difficult, for full comprehension with the major aim of getting 90 to 100 percent on the comprehension questions. Time yourself and figure your rates. You will expect that your WPM will be much slower than the first selection.

The third selection should be read or skimmed at the fastest speed possible in order to grasp just the main idea of each paragraph.

After completing all three selections you can find your *adaptability index* by simply subtracting your slowest effective rate from your fastest. The difference between these two rates gives you some idea of the range of rates you have at your command at present. For example, if you read the second selection at 180 WPM, the third selection at 288 WPM, and the first selection at 210 WPM, your adaptability index is 108. The larger the number the more adaptable you are.

$$\begin{array}{r} 288 \text{ Fastest effective rate} \\ -180 \text{ Slowest effective rate} \\ \hline 108 \text{ Adaptability index} \end{array}$$

During this term you should devote *at least* three sessions a week of approximately twenty minutes each to a rate improvement practice. The Reading Rate Progress Record (table 5.1) may be duplicated for multiple use.

Table 5.1
Reading Rate Progress Record

#1. Date _____

Type of Material*	Your Purpose**	Intended Rate***
Readability Level	Your Level of Interest	Your Familiarity with the Topic

Title: _____

Author: _____

Reading Rate (WPM) _____ × Comprehension % = Effective Rate _____

#2. Date _____

Type of Material*	Your Purpose**	Intended Rate***
Readability Level	Your Level of Interest	Your Familiarity with the Topic

Title: _____

Author: _____

Reading Rate (WPM) _____ × Comprehension % = Effective Rate _____

*Type of Material	**Purpose	***Intended Rate
1. Expository/text	1. Locate specific times	1. Slow/study
2. Narrative	2. Germane ideas	2. Average normal
3. Descriptive	3. Study for retention	3. Rapid reading
4. Poetry	4. Enjoy beauty of language	4. Skimming
5. Other _____	5. Recreation/escape	5. Scanning
	6. Other _____	6. Other _____

Workshop Activity 5.1
Three Rate Exercises

**Rate Exercise 1
Read at your
normal rate.
(1310 words)**

(This article was written in 1966.)

*The Computer: Its
Promise for the Future*

In our increasingly complex world, information is becoming the basic building block of society. However, at a time when the acquisition of new scientific information alone is approaching a rate of 250 million pages annually, the tide of knowledge is overwhelming the human capability for dealing with it. So we must turn to a machine if we hope to contain the tide and channel it to beneficial ends.

The electronic computer, handling millions of facts with the swiftness of light, has given contemporary meaning to Aristotle's vision of the liberating possibilities of machines: "When looms weave by themselves, man's slavery will end." By transforming the way in which he gathers, stores, retrieves, and uses information, this versatile instrument is helping man to overcome his mental and physical limitations. It is vastly widening his intellectual horizon, enabling him better to comprehend his universe, and providing the means to master that portion of it lying within his reach.

Although we are only in the second decade of electronic data processing, the outlines of its influence on our culture are beginning to emerge. Far from depersonalizing the individual and dehumanizing his society, the computer promises a degree of personalized service never before available to mankind.

By the end of the century, for the equivalent of a few dollars a month, the individual will have a vast complex of computer services at his command. Information utilities will make computing power available, like electricity, to thousands of users simultaneously. The computer in the home will be joined to a national and global computer system that provides services ranging from banking and travel facilities to library research and medical care. High-speed communications devices, linked to satellites in space, will transmit data to and from virtually any point on earth with the ease of a dial system. Students, businesspeople, scientists, government officials, and housewives will converse with computers as readily as they now talk by telephone.

In the health field, computers will be employed to maintain a complete medical profile on every person in the country from the hour of birth. The record will be constantly updated by a regional computer for immediate access by doctors or hospital personnel. The computer also will maintain files on every known ailment, its symptoms, diagnosis, and treatment. A doctor will communicate a patient's symptoms to the computer center and within seconds receive suggestions for treatment based on the symptoms and the patient's history.

Computers will handle the nation's fiscal transactions from a central credit information exchange, to which all banks, business enterprises, and individuals will be connected. Purchases will be made, funds invested, and loans issued by transfers of credit within the computer without a dollar or penny physically exchanging hands. Even the soil will be computerized. The long-range outlook for agriculture includes new sensing devices that will be placed on larger farms, feeding information to the computer on soil moisture, temperature, weather outlook, and other details. The computer will calculate the best crops to plant, the best seeding times, the amount of fertilizer, and even the correct harvesting time for maximum yield.

Some of the most profound changes wrought by the computer will be in education. Here, the machine will do more than assist students to solve problems and to locate up-to-date information: It will fundamentally improve and enrich the entire learning process. The student's educational experience will be analyzed by the computer from the primary grades through university. Computer-based teaching machines, programmed and operated by teachers thoroughly trained in electronic data processing techniques, will instruct students at the rate best suited to each individual. The concept of mass education will give way to the concept of personal tutoring, with the teacher and the computer working as a team. Computers will bring many new learning dimensions to the classroom. For example, they will simulate nuclear reactors and other complex or remote systems, enabling students to learn through a form of experience what could formerly be taught only in theory.

The computer's participation in the field of learning will continue long after the end of formal education. The government estimates that 50 percent of the jobs to be held ten years from now do not even exist today. With this tremendous rate of occupational obsolescence, future generations of Americans may pursue two or three careers during their lifetimes. The home computer will aid in developing career mobility by providing continuing self-instruction.

Just as it is recasting the educational process, the computer is also fundamentally changing the production and distribution of the printed word. Five centuries ago, Gutenberg broke words into individual letters. Electronic composition now breaks the letters into tiny patterns of dots that are stored in the computer's memory. Any character can be called up by the computer, written on the face of a cathode ray tube, and reproduced on film or paper in thousandths of a second. Nothing moves except the electrons.

When the electronic computer first appeared in composition rooms and printing shops several years ago, its job was to hyphenate words and justify text. But the computer, working at speeds of thousands of words a minute, was driving mechanical typesetting devices capable of setting only a few words per minute. Now the development of computerized composition makes it possible to set text at hundreds of lines per minute. Photographs and drawings will be set the same way. Since the printed picture is itself a dot structure, the computer can electronically scan any photograph or drawing, reduce it to dots and store it, then retrieve it and beam it on a cathode ray tube for immediate reproduction.

In the future, electronics will develop processes that will make it possible to go from final copy and illustrations to printing in one integrated electronic process. One result will be that newspapers, in the foreseeable future, will no longer be printed in a single location. Instead, they will be transmitted through computers in complete page form to regional electronic printing centers that will turn out special editions for the areas they govern. Local news and advertising will be inserted on the spot. Eventually, the newspaper can be reproduced in the home through a small copying device functioning as part of a home communications center.

Basic changes also will come to other areas of the printed word. For example, of the more than one billion books published every year, almost half are textbooks. The growth of knowledge and the factor of obsolescence mean that these texts must be supplemented by a professor's mimeographed notes. Today, these notes have a small distribution of only a few hundred copies. Computers will make it possible to catalogue this information and thus broaden its availability.

Some of these developments are probabilities, some of them are certainties, and all of them are or soon will be within the capabilities of the computer art.

Nevertheless, for all its potential to stretch the mind a thousandfold, it is perhaps necessary to point out that the computer is still a thing—that it cannot see, feel or act unless first acted upon. Its value depends upon human ability to use it with purpose and intelligence. If our postulates are wrong, the computerized future can only be a massive enlargement of human error.

Ramsay MacDonald once warned against "an attempt to clothe unreality in the garb of mathematical reality." Computers echo this warning. For they cannot usurp the unique human ability to blend intuition with fact, to feel as well as to think. In the end, this remains the basis of human progress.

The task ahead will be to assign to the machine those things which it can best do, and reserve for people those things which they must provide and control. It is my conviction that society will adjust itself to the computer and work in harmony with it for the genuine betterment of life.[1]

Comprehension Check

In the article that you just read the author made certain predictions and statements. Select the group of words that best completes each question or statement below in terms of what the author said. Write the letter preceding that group in the space provided for it at the left of the statement. Do not look back at the article before answering.

_____ 1. The computer promises to (a) depersonalize the individual, (b) dehumanize society, (c) mechanize human beings, (d) provide a degree of personalized service not before available.

_____ 2. The computer in the home will be joined to (a) the church and school, (b) the U.S. Office of Education and the U.S. House of Representatives, (c) the local hospital and the fire department, (d) a national and global computer system.

_____ 3. Computers will be employed to keep a complete medical file of (a) every baby, (b) every person, (c) every married woman, (d) every old person.

_____ 4. No money will physically change hands because the nation's physical transactions will be handled by (a) a national financial center, (b) a central credit information exchange, (c) a local bank, (d) a state bank.

_____ 5. The concept of mass education will give way to the concept of personal tutoring with (a) the computer doing all of the teaching, (b) the student teaching himself independently, (c) the teacher doing all the teaching, (d) the teacher and computer working as a team.

_____ 6. A computer can call up a character, write it on the face of a cathode ray tube, and reproduce it on film or paper in (a) a second, (b) a thousandth of a second, (c) thousandths of a minute, (d) half a minute.

_____ 7. The computer can electronically scan, store, and retrieve pictures because the printed picture itself is (a) a line structure, (b) a dot structure, (c) a mathematical structure, (d) a proportioned figure.

       8. The development of computerized composition makes it possible to set text at (a) twenty lines per minute, (b) fifty lines per minute, (c) hundreds of lines per minute, (d) thousands of lines per minute.

       9. In the future, newspapers will be transmitted through computers to be printed in (a) large publishing houses, (b) city electronic printing presses, (c) copy devices in stores, (d) regional electronic printing centers.

     10. The computer is still considered a thing because (a) many people have never seen one, (b) it is in the experimental stage, (c) it cannot see, feel, or act unless acted upon, (d) it is not widely used.

Comprehension score: _____

WPM: _____

Effective rate: _____

Answers will be found at the end of the chapter.

Rate Exercise 2
Read this more
difficult selection
at your normal
rate. (1251 words)

(This article was written in 1966.)

Diversity

We develop some things well and other things not at all. We send men into orbit and we can fly faster than sound, but our clothes are inferior to those of a bird in many ways. The technical design of clothes is still prehistoric, in spite of synthetic fibers and sewing machines. The fibers must still be drawn out like animal or plant fibers, then spun, then woven or knitted, and then cut and sewn more or less to fit, just as fibers and cloth have been spun and sewn for thousands of years. And then these threads do not protect us against rain or cold, or ventilate or shade us in the hot sun, unless we put on and take off many layers which we must carry around in a suitcase. Why should someone not make us a single suit that would shed rain and that we could ruffle up for comfort in any weather, as a bird ruffles its feathers? A bird needs no suitcase. The reason is that no one—not even the Army, which might be expected to have the greatest interest in it—has put a task force on the problem of designing clothing material of variable pores and variable heat conductivity that could be molded to the body. Not everybody would want a single universal suit, but it would be nice to have the option. It might not even be very hard to invent. But we still have prehistoric patterns of thought in what touches us most closely. Helicopters, *sí;* clothes, no.

Adapted from J. R. Platt, "Diversity," *Science* 154: 1132–1139, 2 December 1966. Used with permission.

It is the same story with shoes, which are still sewn of pieces of leather or plastic. And again with housing, which lags far behind automobiles in technology and still has piece-by-piece assembly and leaking roofs and windows and no standard modular connection to the needed city services.

It is as though we had collective taboos against certain types of development, like the taboo against work or the refusal to consider or finance Buckminster Fuller's geodesic dome buildings until the Army used the principle for radomes, or the reluctance of psychologists and physiologists to study sleep before the work of Nathaniel Kleitman and his coworkers made it respectable. Scientists are not really innovators, and neither are industrial companies and government agencies and their research-and-development teams. They all shrink, like other men, from unheard-of-projects for which there is no precedent, even obvious and important projects, because they are afraid they will be cut off from support.

I think we neglect many important alternatives in our patterns of housing and living. We have automobiles in plenty—and I am no longer one of those who complain about their design; they are remarkably functional and economical and satisfying, and some day they may even be safe! But why should not our magnificent economic and social system be able to give us a similar level of technological skill and competitive cost in the construction of our houses? And why should we not be able to have more diversity and choice in our patterns of houses and lots? Again, there is a coupling of money to conventional patterns of tradition and taboo. If we were to put our houses at the edge of the streets, facing inward on the block, the houses could all look onto a sizable little park in the middle of the block, with trees and a fountain and swings and a place for oldsters to sit and for children to play safely away from the street. Given the pleasure of facing your very own park, who would prefer all these separate private lots with their wasteful driveways and unused areas? Very few, perhaps; but most of us will never know, because our system is focused on a different image and it is not flexible enough to give us the option.

It would also be useful to try animal-copying with the nucleus taken from one species and the egg in which it was implanted taken from another. Donkey and horse can be mated; will a donkey nucleus in a horse egg cell give a donkey—or something more like a mule? This might teach us something about the developmental embryonic differences between species. If it would work, we might be able to save some vanishing species by transplanting their cell nuclei into the egg cells of present related species. Is the DNA that carries heredity destroyed immediately when an animal dies? If the meat of woolly mammoths locked for thousands of years in the Arctic ice is still edible, perhaps their DNA is still viable and might be injected, say, into elephant egg cells to give baby mammoths again. By some such methods, perhaps we might achieve "paleo-reconstruction" of the ancient Mexican corn, or of "mummy wheat," or even of the flies that are sometimes found preserved in amber. One man has devoted his life to reconstructing creatures like the ancient aurochs, by backcrossing modern cattle. May not these other genetic methods of paleostudy also be worth trying? Success is uncertain, but the rewards would be great.

There must be dozens of other areas of study that contain such families of unconventional experiments just waiting to be tried. In biological technology alone there are the experiments required for the selective breeding and herding of sea animals and "farming the oceans"; experiments on animal development, in which our new knowledge of embryonic growth would be used in attempts to develop larger brains or stronger muscles; experiments on the closer shaping of animal behavior, not just to make trick animals for the movies, but to make more versatile pets or better dogs for the blind; and experiments on electronic transducers to bring animal sounds into our range of hearing and our sounds into their range of hearing, so as to learn whether dolphins or chimpanzees or Siamese cats might learn to use signals and symbols more as we do if we made it easier for them. This might give us a better understanding of the origins of our own communication and linguistic development over the last few hundred thousand years.

Finally there is an important set of experiments and developments needed for devising more sophisticated machines that would serve biological functions. Not just artificial kidneys, and pacemakers, and artificial hearts, which are all now under study, but things like balancing machines, to help the paralyzed to walk, with motors as compact and powerful and fast as our own muscles, and with feedback circuits as clever as our own balancing. Should these be so hard to devise, for those whose electronic circuits have flown past Mars transmitting pictures? Perhaps not; but the amount of scientific and engineering effort devoted by the nation to such problems is probably less than a ten-thousandth of the space effort.

The balancing problem is part of the interesting problem of making self-guiding automata with pattern-perceiving sensory systems, communication systems, and control programs, and with self-contained power sources and motor motions. Such devices will be needed for exploring the hostile surface of the moon and Mars and sending back data, but they would also be useful for exploring sea bottoms and volcanoes and for fire-fighting and other dangerous operations. We are on the edge of understanding how to make such automata, but the problem is still being studied at only a half-dozen centers, and still does not enlist the hundreds of trained and inventive minds that will be needed to make such devices work cheaply and well.

It is time for more scientific diversity. The question to be asked is no longer, what does physics have the apparatus and the equations for? It is, rather, what are the curious things in the world? And what are the needs of human beings?[2]

Comprehension Check

The author of this article expressed his personal opinion. Possibly you will disagree with some of his ideas. Perhaps in your judgment some of the choices in the statements other than what the author said are the correct ones. But remember this is not a check of your personal opinion. It is a check of how well you grasped what the author said in the content of his article. Although in this chapter and throughout the text, your opinion will have high priority, in this exercise, choose the group of words that best completes the statement under consideration in terms of what the *author* has said. Write the letter of that group of words in the space provided for it at the left of the number.

_____ 1. The technical design of our clothes is (a) futuristic, (b) of universal convenience, (c) prehistoric, (d) in keeping with present technological developments.

_____ 2. Automobiles are (a) safe and pollution free, (b) difficult to operate and extravagant, (c) dangerous and distributors of pollutants, (d) functional and economic.

_____ 3. Houses should be built (a) at the edge of the street facing the street, (b) at the edge of the street facing each other, (c) at the back edge of the lot facing the street, (d) at the edge of the street facing inward on the block.

_____ 4. We might be able to save some vanishing species by (a) placing their cell nuclei into incubators, (b) reviving their remains, (c) transplanting their cell nuclei into the egg cells of present related species, (d) mating them with other animals.

_____ 5. Experiments are required in biological technology such as (a) making better space craft, (b) improving computers, (c) devising plans for making better shoes, (d) selective breeding and herding of sea animals.

_____ 6. Experiments in shaping animal behavior are needed to make them (a) perform tricks for movies and amusement of children, (b) more versatile pets or better dogs for the blind, (c) better protectors of people and property, (d) larger and stronger.

_____ 7. Experiments into animal ranges of hearing might enable us to learn whether dolphins, chimpanzees, or Siamese cats might learn to (a) talk with people, (b) write messages to us, (c) use signals and symbols as we do, (d) use a code language.

_____ 8. More sophisticated machines should be developed to serve biological purposes such as (a) artificial hearts, (b) machines for detecting contagious diseases, (c) mechanical breathing apparatus, (d) balancing machines to help the paralyzed to walk.

_____ 9. Self-guiding automata will be needed in exploring Mars and also in (a) helping doctors to perform operations, (b) exploring sea bottoms and volcanoes, (c) helping an author write a book, (d) playing a difficult musical composition.

_____ 10. It is time for more scientific diversity. The questions to be asked are (a) Does physics have the apparatus and equations? (b) Do we have enough money and other resources for experimentation? (c) Do modern scientists possess the necessary knowledge and skill? (d) What are the curious things in the world and what are the needs of human beings?

Comprehension score: _____
WPM: _____
Effective rate: _____

Answers will be found at the end of the chapter.

**Rate Exercise 3
(1225 words)**

The Unsolved Mystery of the Mayas

One of the most interesting of all available studies of human behavior waits, barely sampled, just beyond our own back yard in what anthropologists call Middle America: the region extending from Central Mexico to southern Honduras and El Salvador. The southerly part of this area was occupied by the Mayas, who developed the highest civilization native to the New World.

The Mayas appear to us as an intriguing, puzzling people. Of metals they knew only gold, silver, and copper, all of which they used for jewelry, not for tools, yet they carved beautifully in wood and stone. They also painted on walls and on paper, modeled plaster, and drew with brushes, like Orientals, their best work showing rapid, strong, sensitive lines. They knew nothing of the wheel, hence did not use pulleys, yet they erected pyramids of great size, temples, "palaces," and such structures, and moved large altars and steles from the quarries to the place where they wanted them.

Without metals, but with infinite patience, they carved jade. Their ceramics, fine art, and architecture are comparable to the Greek only in a few instances, but they compare favorably to the Hindu and South Asiatic.

They had a true system of writing. To our knowledge, they indulged in the learned arts of mathematics, astronomy, and history; there are hints of others, yet to be made known. We may note that the Mayas knew how to inlay teeth and trepan skulls. Judging by what some of their descendants wrote shortly after the Spanish conquest, they had a poetic, vigorous literature. We know very little about their religion, and are still in the stage of denoting certain figures as "God A" or "God G."

They seem—again we are unsure—to have been organized into something on the order of city states, ruled, probably somewhat tyrannically, by priest-nobles. We used to believe that at their height the Mayas were innocent of warfare and human sacrifice; the evidence is that this ingratiating picture is too good to be true. But in their heyday they held interstate conferences of learned men and unified their calculations, astronomy, and written forms across hundreds of miles of territory. When they were going full blast, they abandoned the whole central part of their territory—mounds, terraces, pyramids, buildings by the hundreds, monuments, and all—and their culture petered out rapidly, leaving us with a puzzle.

To form a just idea of the importance of this change, let us turn from Maya research per se and consider it in relation to world archaeology and the study of human beings.

Archaeology is a humane science, a branch of anthropology dedicated to uncovering the story of the human race—the culture, advances, retrogressions—over long periods of time. Its potential contribution, both theoretical and practical, is great; modern thinking about humankind's course is already importantly influenced by it. In this contribution New World archaeology has a special part, and within that field Middle American studies occupy a place of unusual interest.

Adapted from an article by Oliver La Farge. Copyright © 1958, by The Atlantic Monthly Company, Boston, Mass. Reprinted with permission.

I have already sketched the highlights of the Mayas' "Stone Age" culture. In a general conversation, at this point, someone will insist that such advancement must mean that the Mayas were influenced from the Old World. Then the Maya scholar comes back with his crusher—and it is not only a crusher, but the final evidence of the height of the Mayan achievement. The Hindus may have conceived of zero as early as 300 A.D., but not until 700 A.D. did they produce a symbol for it and thus make possible the place system of numbers we call "Arabic." We have clear examples of large numbers written in a place system with the use of zero in Middle America from just before the time of Christ, if not several centuries earlier. The important mathematical discovery involved must have been made, according to available evidence, not later than 600 B.C., and probably earlier.

The mere desertion of the central region is a teasing puzzle. We speak of the great sites therein as "cities," but there is a question whether they were. They are imposing concentrations of pyramids, temples, assorted monuments, and buildings that may have been palaces, convents, or dormitories, but it is not at all certain that they were centers of any great concentrations of population. Is it possible that in Middle America civilization developed without cities, urbanity without urban life? If so, we must rewrite considerable portions of modern social science.

There is another great question asking for an answer. The excavations reaching furthest into the past, the stratifications most thoroughly worked out, such as those of the Carnegie Institution at Uaxactún in the Petén forest, present us with a well-advanced culture—civilized or at least semicivilized people, artists, builders of pyramids—at the earliest level. About 10,000 B.C., hunters roamed Mexico. About 2000 B.C., corn was domesticated and primitive farming communities developed. From then we take a long leap to proto-Maya centers. This is unreasonable.

What is very important is the appearance that civilization developed in a classically tropical area of drenching rainy seasons. A large part of the area is underlain by a limestone formation that lets the water drain through, so that supplies of drinking water today will barely enable a sizable archaeological expedition to last through a dry season; and the whole terrain is covered by the stupendous rain forests commonly but inaccurately called "jungles." That is no setting for the development of simple cultures into high ones. It is a hostile region even with today's equipment, a region in which one would look for primitive hunting tribes or peoples practicing rather precarious farming in clearings made and kept open only by great effort.

We expect early farming and village life to develop in fairly open, wooded country where ground can easily be cleared and worked with digging sticks and other such tools. Heavy bush or strong prairie sod defeats the primitive gardener. Felling mahogany trees twenty feet in diameter with stone tools, even with jade, seems excessive.

These paradoxes are plainly apparent. They may or may not be real; part of our trouble is that the Middle American forests are as inhospitable to archaeologists as they are to farmers. In order to determine the width of a terrace, I have had to guide myself by compass while I paced it off; I could not see the score or so meters from one side to the other. An archaeologist could perfectly well spend several seasons doing a thorough job on what he/she believed to be the center of a ruin, when in fact the greatest part stood a couple of hundred yards from him.

For about seventy-five years we have been seriously at work mapping the problem of Middle America, stopping now and again for a little digging. In the last thirty years, study has broadened out from the Maya zone to the whole area, and we begin to have hints of how the Maya can be reasonably related with the rest. We need more geology, a lot more climatology; the crucial question of what the now forbidding forest areas were like two and three thousand years ago awaits a final answer. We are on the threshold of the knowledge that will turn a lot of bits and pieces into a strange and wonderful story.[3]

Comprehension Check

Check the correct answer to each statement. You may find more than one answer to some of the questions. You are to select one, *best* answer in terms of the information that is given in the selection. The correct answers should be reached in class by consensus.

_____ 1. The Mayas developed their civilization in the (a) southern part of North America, (b) southern part of South America, (c) northern part of Mexico, (d) southern part of Middle America.

_____ 2. These ancient people erected pyramids and moved altars with the use of (a) wheels, (b) pulleys, (c) metal tools, (d) none of these.

_____ 3. We know very little about their (a) art, (b) religion, (c) pyramids, (d) calculations.

_____ 4. Archaeology is a branch of anthropology dedicated to finding information about (a) the human physical organism, (b) early human's relationship to other species, (c) cultural advances and regressions over a long period of time, (d) the possible evolution of human beings from their earliest form of life.

_____ 5. Evidence that the Mayas' advanced civilization was not influenced by the Old World is found in the fact that (a) they drew with brushes like the Orientals, (b) their fine arts were comparable to those of the Greeks in a few instances, (c) their general achievements were comparable to those of the Hindus and the South Asiatics, (d) they conceived the zero before the Hindus did.

_____ 6. What is the most fundamental question about the urban life of the Mayas? It is whether (a) their cities were concentrations of buildings, (b) they were centers of art, (c) they were industrial centers, (d) the Mayas had urbanity without urban life.

_____ 7. Which of the following facts, revealed by present-day archaeologists, suggests the existence of a problem concerning the drinking water of these ancient civilizations? (a) all water in the rain forest is contaminated, (b) all the water drains off, (c) the supply of water will barely last an archaeological expedition through the dry season, (d) no ancient drinking cups have been found.

_____ 8. Which of the following is a *very* important question yet to be answered? (a) How did the Mayas raise crops without the use of metals? (b) How did they cut down trees twenty feet in diameter? (c) How did they develop a high civilization in a rain forest? (d) How did they raise crops without domestic animals?

_____ 9. A part of the trouble which has prevented solving puzzling questions about the Mayas is the (a) hostility of the present natives, (b) inability of archaeologists to decipher Mayan writing, (c) lack of interest in the Mayas, (d) forests that offer difficulties to archaeological expeditions.

_____ 10. In which one of the following areas do we need a lot more information about the Mayan civilization? (a) their means of constructing temples, pyramids, and palaces, (b) their work with gold, silver, and copper, (c) their contributions to astronomy and history, (d) the geology of their country, and its climatology.

Comprehension score: _____
WPM: _____
Effective rate: _____

Use the scores from the preassessment inventory as baseline data for your personal improvement program. At the conclusion of the rate practice sessions, look over your record and state in writing at least three conclusions or observations concerning it.

Having completed the first step in increasing your reading rate efficiency by taking this inventory, study the cognitive map in figure 5.1. This will give you a type of *advance organizer* of the topic "Rate Adaptability."

Reading Rates

What Are the Rates?

The various rates of reading can be arbitrarily broken down into five types. Actual rates are approximate only.

1. slow/study .... 50 – 250
2. average/normal .... 250 – 350
3. rapid reading .... 350 – 800
4. skimming .... 800 – up
5. scanning .... 1,000 – up

What Is a Normal Rate?

What is a normal rate? The answer to this question naturally depends on a number of factors, but students reading average secondary material of medium difficulty can normally read at a rate between 250 and 280 words per minute, whereas upper elementary children may still be reading more slowly. However, effective readers will vary their rate depending on their background knowledge, interest, and purpose. According to Albert Harris, a superior adult reader reading light fiction for pleasure and nonretention should be able to read at least 400 words per minute.[4] A normal reading rate for more careful reading might be only two-thirds as fast as the most rapid rate, and at times it is desirable to slow down to less than one-third of the rapid rate.

Because reading rate is related to thinking rate, trying to read faster than ideas can be assimilated is not helpful. When asked how fast one should read, the answer usually is "faster than you read now, except for very difficult material."

Why Increase Rate?

With the wealth of reading material in existence today, being able to read faster when we choose, or slower when it is appropriate, is an important skill to have. Here are a few of the reasons why adaptability is so important.

1. *Saves time.* If students who read two hours a day increase their speed by just 25 percent, it will give each of them three extra hours of free time a week. This is an excellent motivator.
2. *Helps in remembering.* Readers who are bogged down in word-by-word reading may, with long sentences and paragraphs, take so long to reach the end they forget what was said at the beginning.
3. *Improves comprehension.* This comes with continual practice with a variety of material. The very slow reader is often the one who opts not to read for pleasure because of the time and effort it takes, and thus gets little practice.
4. *Cuts down interference.* Choosing an inappropriate reading rate can interfere with comprehension. Children taught to read through elementary grades using only light fiction or the literature approach may become rapid, fluent readers with that material. Later, when they are expected to read difficult, expository text materials, their rapid, superficial style of reading may fail them. On the other hand, those who are carefully drilled to be accurate, slow readers will easily note details but may have problems finding main ideas or the gist of a selection. Too often readers have not been taught to be adaptable.

Principles of Rate Assessment

A review of research by Phyllis Miller makes the following major points concerning rate assessment for adaptable, efficient reading.[5]

1. There is more than one aspect of rate to be measured. Rather than having only one base rate, a reader should develop a variety of rates. Adaptability means that the reader will change

strategies and/or rate, depending on the purpose, the difficulty, or type of material and familiarity with the topic. P. L. Nacke has suggested that the flexibility (adaptability, or shifting 'gears') concept is based on the assumption that a reader has the capability to use a range of rates from slow to rapid and that a fluent reader also uses a variety of strategies.[6] There should be some relationship then between rate and strategy.

2. S. J. Samuels and P. R. Dahl found that when students were given different instructions regarding their purpose for reading, they read materials of the same difficulty levels at significantly different rates.[7] For example, readers slowed down considerably when their purpose was to get details from unfamiliar content.

3. Any valid test of rate must not only consider the reader's purpose and the textual factor, but also control for topic familiarity. Some studies have reported that more highly skilled readers vary their rate more often for purpose, whereas less skilled readers vary their rate more often for the difficulty of the material. In other words, better readers seem to have in mind what they are looking for while reading, and the less skilled readers seem to spend more time and energy just coping with the words on the page.

Instructing Students in Rate Adaptability

Content teachers can help students become aware that when they are reading technical material, they may improve their comprehension by having a purpose clearly in mind and deciding on the time it will take and the strategies that will be needed. It is often more practical to estimate the amount of time it takes to read one page or a thirty-page chapter than figuring words per minute. Any rate adaptability practice in content classrooms should use the actual text material in present use.

Until students become adept enough to do it for themselves automatically, they should be reminded about purposes, rates, and possible strategies when assigned a particular chapter. For example, it might be suggested that the purpose of the first section of the chapter is to find three main points of information, and they should be encouraged to use a skimming strategy to locate those three points. One main point might be given as an example for them to follow. Also, students may be given sample questions on a section and told to read quickly to find the answers. They might try key word skimming, looking at only the content-bearing words (mostly nouns and verbs), or they might preview by reading rapidly the introduction, summary, and first sentence of each paragraph. It is also helpful to differentiate among the text variations of content style and patterns; narrative material often proceeds in a different manner than expository material. Themes in literature may be subtle, whereas in expository writing a thesis will usually be stated explicitly. Any of these points should be pointed out to the students in the context in which they appear.

Major Factors Affecting Rate   Two major factors controlling how rapidly or slowly a person reads are the material being read and the reader.

The Reading Material   Reading material may be expository (textlike), narrative/descriptive, or poetical. Each of these types has a variety of readability levels depending on (1) **concept depth and load,** or how many ideas are packed into a short space (2) sentence length, and (3) vocabulary difficulty. Other factors affecting how rapidly the material is comprehended include: (4) the author's writing style, (5) the use of graphics and their placement, (6) the clarity of the print in terms of size, style, and density, (7) the general organization of the material, and (8) the format of each page.

Workshop Activity 5.2
Adapting Rate to Purpose and Difficulty

Read the following excerpts and jot down the type of writing (expository, narrative, descriptive, poetic) and the factors for each that might inhibit or enhance your effective rate.

1. Writing for Teenagers

   There are special joys in writing for teenagers. One is that it allows us to relive our youth and express at this later point in our lives the truths that we see in retrospect but could not then put into words. There is also the satisfaction that comes with planting seeds in fertile soil. Whether we are imparting information, planting values, or simply trying to instill a love of reading, we have a power when writing for the young that we do not have when writing for older, more blasé readers.[8] _____

2. Empiricism and Racism

   He [Bracken] has argued that the relation between empiricism and racism is historical, not in that there is a logical connection, but in that empiricism facilitated the expression of the racist ideology that came naturally enough to philosophers who were involved in their professional lives in the creation of the colonial system.[9] _____

3. From the Old Legends

   Now the Three Kindreds of the Eldar were gathered at last in Valinor, and Melkor was chained. This was the Noon-tide of the Blessed Realm, the fullness of its glory and its bliss, long in tale of years, but in memory too brief. In those days the Eldar became full grown in stature of body and of mind, the Noldor advanced ever in skill and Knowledge; and the long years were filled with their joyful labours, in which many new things fair and wonderful were devised.[10] _____

_____

4. *Our Fight for Freedom*

The arbitrary ruling
        Of a monarch overseas,
Was chief among the causes
        Of war that made us free.
A sovereign extremely jealous
        of ''rights'' he thought were his,
Especially the ''right'' to tax
        His foreign colonies.
                        ***

Thus with momentous problems
        And countless questions due
For prompt consideration
        By Number Thirty-Two,
We're leaving him to carry on
        The onerous tasks begun
With Faith each battle for the right
        Will finally be won.
For ''Truth proclaims this motto
        In letters of living light,
No question is ever settled
        Until it is settled right.''[11]

5. Buttons and Bones

    . . . So suddenly I flung the door wide on him.
    A moment he stood balancing with emotion
    And all but lost himself. (A tongue of fire
    flashed out and licked along his upper teeth.
    Smoke rolled inside the sockets of his eyes.)
    Then he came at me with one hand outstretched,
    The way he did in life once; but this time
    I struck the hand off brittle on the floor,
    And fell back from him on the floor myself.
    The finger-pieces slide in all directions
    (where did I see one of those pieces lately?
    Hand me my button box—it must be there.) . . .[12]

6. The Welcoming Sentinel

When Pentaquad steered toward the eastern river he was confronted by the tree-covered island he had seen from a distance, for it dominated the entrance. Poised between two headlands, one reaching down from the north, the other up from the south, it served as a welcoming sentinel and seemed to proclaim: All who enter this river find joy.[13]

7. Bernoulli's Treatment of the Brachistochrome Problem

The early method developed for the brachistochrome problem by Jacob
Bernoulli can be understood with comparatively little technical knowledge.

A _____
  _____
  _____
  _____
  _____
  _____
  _____
  _____
                      P

We start with the fact . . . that a mass point falling down from rest at A along
any curve C will have at any point P a velocity proportional to $\sqrt{h}$ where h is the
vertical distance from A to P; that is $V = C\sqrt{h}$ where C is a constant. . . . Now
we dissect the space into many thin horizontal slabs, each of thickness d and
assume for the moment that the velocity of the moving particle changes . . . in
little jumps from slab to slab so that in the first slab adjacent to A the velocity is
$C\sqrt{d}$ in the second $C\sqrt{2d}$, and in the nth slab $C\sqrt{nd} = C\sqrt{h}$ . . .[14]

The Reader

With this variety of material in mind, let us look now at readers themselves.
As mentioned earlier, a major factor determining appropriate rate will
depend on the reader's purpose for reading the material. If the need is to
locate specific items, a scanning rate may be used; if the purpose is to get
the gist or pick up the main ideas, a skimming rate would be appropriate.
Studying a chapter in a text for complete retention would usually require
a slow, careful study rate; and someone reading poetry or a lyrical descriptive passage, wishing to savor the beauty of the language, lingering over
particular words or phrases, would use a slow rate. Recreational or escape-
type reading might take a rapid rate or a relaxed average rate. Readers
must decide which rate is appropriate to their purpose with each set of
materials.

When learning a skill, students must be able to perform the parts correctly and smoothly before attempting to increase the rate at which the
parts are performed. The pianist must practice an arpeggio over and over
until the sequence of notes and the fingering are mastered before attempting to play it at tempo. The tennis coach works patiently on perfecting
students' easy and smooth strokes before allowing them to try the overhand
smash. It is much the same in reading. Until students have mastered the
basic skills of learning how to read, little attention should be placed on
increasing their rate. A sensible rule of thumb is that little concern should
be shown for rate until students, regardless of age, are reading at or above
a fourth-grade level and are reading fluently.

Some habits that students may have acquired or sustained unnecessarily over the years may interfere with their reading fluency. In some cases these habits are no longer needed as reading aids; at other times, however, they may serve as a vital crutch for getting at the comprehension of text.

Pointing with a finger. This may still be an aid to those who tend to lose their place or reverse letters. The act of pointing itself does not interfere with their rate of comprehension, but it may indicate that the person is a word-by-word reader, possibly bogged down in word analysis. Placing a card under the line of print or holding the book with both hands may be helpful to many.

Moving the head. Moving the head from side to side is another unnecessary habit for most people but not a harmful one either. Unless readers have a problem in binocular coordination, there is little advantage in moving the head, because the eyes can move more rapidly. One suggestion for breaking this habit is to cup the chin in one hand during reading.

Moving the lips. Learning to read generally means associating the printed symbols with the known sounds they represent. To get at the meaning the beginning reader first reads the words carefully. Gradually this reading aloud is reduced to mumbling and then to silently moving the lips. Skilled readers who as a rule do not move their lips can be observed reverting to this practice when given reading material written at a difficult or frustration level. As long as readers need to form each word with their lips they will not be able to read any faster than they can speak (generally, less than 200 words per minute). As long as lip movements are not needed for comprehension, an easy way to break the habit is to actively chew gum during reading.

Subvocalizing. Students with strong auditory imagery will "hear" an inner voice saying each word to them while reading. In silent reading most people go through the motions of speaking the words but without readily observable movement or sound. This is accompanied by **subvocal reading** or **inner speech** where the words are heard inside the head as though someone were speaking.[15]

Silent reading comes gradually by a process described as **cue reduction,** where the readers recognize most words instantaneously, take in phrases at a glance, and focus on key words; this allows for rates up to three times their oral reading rate.

To find out how much movement of throat muscles is necessary for comprehending a particular piece of writing, instruct students to place one hand at the throat with thumb and middle finger just below the jawbone. Then have them place a pen or pencil between the teeth so that the tongue and lips do not touch it at any time. After reading a page or two this way students must be able to explain what they have just read. To discover the need for inner speech, have them try to read for comprehension while continuously making the sound z-z-z-z.

The best way to help students become efficient silent readers is to allow them ample exposure and time to practice with provocative materials written at readability levels that match the students' ability levels. (This practice will more often be in the domain of reading and English teachers.)

Other Factors
Affecting Rate

It is then the reader's purposes and habits that affect reading rate. Other factors that should be considered include the following.

1. *General reading ability.* The more skilled readers are able to read more rapidly for effective comprehension.
2. *Background experience.* The more knowledge a reader has about the topic in general, the more rapidly the new material can be assimilated.
3. *Physiological factors.* Such factors as vision and hearing problems, poor health, or fatigue can impede rate effectiveness.
4. *Physical environment.* The location for reading may enhance or detract from rate efficiency: a noisy, busy classroom may interfere with rapid comprehension, whereas a quiet corner of the library may be conducive to thoughtful study.
5. *Eye movements or mechanics.* Eye movement cameras show us the number of fixations (rests) made per line, the length of the fixation, how frequently we regress (return to previously covered material to reread it), and our ability to make the return sweep smoothly from the end of one line to the beginning of the next. However, these pictures only tell us what readers *do*, not *why* they do it. Miles Tinker, after more than thirty years of studying eye-movement training, stated that there was no evidence to support the idea that eye movement determines proficiency in reading, nor did he find that faulty eye-movement habits were very prevalent.[16]

**How to Increase
Effectiveness**

Take Inventory

The first step in increasing students' effective reading rates is to have them take an inventory of present rates. (This was modeled at the beginning of the chapter so that you, the reader, could take your own inventory before reading on.)

Push Yourself
and Practice

Much of what is covered in expensive speed reading courses can be accomplished at home or in class by motivated students. Consistent practice is the key. Thus, the first step is to push consistently to get students out of that comfortable rut that they may not even be aware exists.

An amusing story was recounted by Nila Banton Smith concerning Puccini, the great Italian composer.[17] One day, when late for an appointment, Puccini dashed up a street near his flat in Milan and met an organ grinder slowly cranking out one of the composer's arias from *Madame Butterfly*. Puccini was so annoyed by the agonizingly slow tempo that he cried out to him, "Faster, faster." As Puccini continued to run he tried to show the organ grinder the proper tempo by waving his hand back and forth rapidly. The next week he met the same organ grinder playing the same aria at the rapid, sprightly tempo he had indicated to him More surprising, though, was the sign around the organ grinder's neck: "Pupil of Puccini."

Thus, "faster, faster" means consciously racing across the lines as rapidly as possible to extract from the page the ideas needed.

Word-by-word readers are those who are often mired in the mechanics of identifying words rather than in grasping meanings. Imagine what can happen to the comprehension of a lengthy sentence with word-by-word readers—by the time they reach the end of the sentence they have forgotten the message from the first part.

Read in Thought Units

1. *Word-by-word:* is/in/the/habit/of/taking/in/just/one/word/at/a/time/.
2. *Thought units:* The student should/get in the habit of taking in/ large groups of words/ in one glance./ (The slashes mark possible thought units.)

Developing adaptable rates includes practice in skimming and scanning. **Skimming** can be generally thought of as a rapid search for the overall picture or gist, whereas **scanning** is a rapid search for specific detail, such as a telephone number. Skimming requires the reader to skip over large segments of material to extract the kernel of what has been written. It is most helpful as a preview before reading or as a quick review following the reading. Martha Maxwell found that, although skimming was not very helpful in identifying the main idea of one paragraph or identifying more than one idea in a series of paragraphs, it did prove helpful when the content of the material was familiar.[18]

Skim and Scan

Skimming to preview a chapter means that the eyes sweep fleetingly over the material, taking in the title, subtitles, topic sentences (at times), graphic aids, and the summary statement. A newspaper article may be skimmed to discover who did what, when, where it happened, how, and why. When skimming to review something just read, concentration is on seeing the relationships among major ideas. Subtitles and their organization may be helpful here.

Scanning, on the other hand, is the fastest rate for getting prespecified facts or items. If scanning for a term, date, or fact, the eyes move very rapidly until the item is found, then the rate is reduced, and the sentence or surrounding sentences are reread to verify the findings. Scanning is useful when trying to find something in a text to answer a specific question; when locating a phone number; or when reading transportation schedules, newspaper ads, the card catalog, guide words, or references.

Practice with students on actual content material with such instructions as: "See how quickly you can find the part of the text that describes _____ ," "Which ad presents the best buy, pricewise?" "What is the main theme in part II?"

<table>
<tr><td>Signposts</td><td>Directional words or signposts direct readers to slow down or speed up. They increase reading efficiency by alerting them to what will happen. There are two general categories of direction words: the "go-ahead" words, and the "turnabout" words. Go-ahead words signal that more ideas will be added to the main thought. The most common of these is the word and. Others conveying the same message are:</td></tr>
</table>

more	likewise
moreover	furthermore
also	too

Some go-ahead words carry a slightly different, but still forward-moving message. They signal that a deeper thought or a summary statement is coming; that is, "it is time to slow down and pay closer attention to what follows."

thus	consequently
therefore	accordingly

The most decisive group of go-ahead words are those that signal that the end is near, words and phrases such as:

finally	concluding
as a result	in conclusion

The second category of direction words, the turnabout words, negate preceding statements and prepare the reader for an abrupt change. When a turnabout word appears in reading, it means to stop going ahead along the same line of thought and instead turn abruptly in another direction. Examples are:

but	in spite of
yet	not
nevertheless	on the contrary
otherwise	however
although	not withstanding
despite	rather

The study technique of previewing has been described earlier in the chapter under the skimming section and also in the study skills chapter in the section on SQ3R. (Survey and preview are used here synonymously.) Once you have instructed students a few times in the art of previewing before reading for retention, they will begin to see for themselves how this can significantly improve their reading rate and at the same time increase their comprehension.

Previewing

In any discussion of rate adaptability, the importance of vocabulary needs to be mentioned. Knowing the appropriate meaning in the context of a multitude of words will greatly increase effective comprehension rate. Strategies for developing word power will be found in the chapter on vocabulary.

Vocabulary

What do readers generally do when they are reading along at a rapid rate and they encounter an unknown word? Skip it? Stop and ponder? Reach for a dictionary? Usually the best thing to do is to skip over the word for the time being and to pick up its general sense in context. A light pencil mark in the margin will mark its place. Then later the reader may return to it and look up its precise meaning in the dictionary or glossary.

Skipping for Context

A variety of ideas are presented here for your selection and use, either personally or with your students. For further ideas, refer to the list of workbooks and references at the end of the chapter.

Practice Strategies

Florence Sherbourne suggests the following type of practice to help increase eye span and smooth out eye movements.[19] (Some authorities disagree on whether this really does help with rate improvement.)

Key Word Skimming

You .... remem
ber .... we
said .... that,
in .... order
to .... read
rap .... idly,
you .... must
learn .... to
read .... whole
phrases .... at
once ....

The lengths of the gaps are longer to assist in breaking old habits. Another type of key word skimming is similar to composing a telegram. Only key words are noted, the others ignored. "The lengths of the gaps are longer" would be read as "lengths-gaps-longer."[20]

Skimming Practice (for English and Reading Classes)

Take materials of high interest but easy readability levels and place in separate packets, setting up a practice center in the classroom. Students select a packet and are instructed to read rapidly or skim the article to answer questions drawn from a box. They should record the time it took to complete the tasks. Questions for an English class could include:

1. How would this story be changed if the main character were male?
2. What part would *you* have played in this story?
3. How is the title related to what happened in the story?
4. Describe the incident that was most intriguing to you, explaining your reasons.

"Beat the Clock"

To increase students' rate and text comprehension without pressure, choose an important but brief text selection and have students read it silently. Make no reference to rate except to tell them that you will keep track of their time in general terms. Ask them to describe what they read and continue asking questions until comprehension is satisfactory for all. Then have students reread at a faster pace except this time tell them that you will time them to see how rapidly they can read it. Have them read it a third time and time them again. Because they have already mastered the content there is no pressure. This third reading should be much faster than the second one, and because they have read the material three times, it should be remembered more easily at a later date.[21]

Workshop Activity 5.3
Which Rate?

At what rate would you read the following paragraphs? Number each from fastest to slowest (1) skim, (2) scan, (3) rapid, (4) average, (5) slow. Compare with your group and discuss differences.

_____ 1. *Purpose:* Discover main idea
             Topic: Description of football strategies
_____ 2. *Purpose:* Use details
             Topic: Explanation of mathematical function

3. *Purpose:* Make inferences
   Topic: Poem, Frost's "The Road Not Taken" (or a portion of it)
4. *Purpose:* Integrate or synthesize with two other sources for a report
   Topic: Nutrition and vitamin therapy
5. *Purpose:* Kill time in the dentist's waiting room
   Topic: Boy meets girl in New York City
6. *Purpose:* Find number among others
   Topic: Used-car deal in newspaper

Hill has suggested a strategy that demonstrates the value of using different rates for different purposes.[22]

Valuing Rate Adaptability

Divide the class into three groups. Give the same four- to five-page content selection to each person to read but give each group a different set of directions for reading and corresponding questions.

Group 1. Scan to find specific facts, terms.
Group 2. Skim to find the main idea and the topic sentence for each paragraph.
Group 3. Read rapidly to answer ten general questions over the content.

All record their own time to complete the tasks, and the group leader averages those times. These three averages are placed on the board. Students will probably observe that one group had an easier task than another. When the rapid reading group decides its group has comprehended more, it is time to pull out a set of "twenty questions" that require higher-level thinking, such as making inferences and analyzing writer technique or arguments. Each group must attempt to answer the same questions without looking back at the material. In most cases the rapid reading group's score will be better than the others' score but certainly not perfect. If no student suggests that rereading the material would improve scores, then tell them to read the material and discuss improvements noted in the scores. The concluding discussion should center on how the different modes of reading relate to purpose and rates as well as the usefulness of rereading.

Although this strategy was originally suggested for use in a reading class, it can be extremely helpful with important content material that you wish to reinforce with your students.

Even for content areas, no chapter on rate would be complete without mention of mechanical devices or pacers. This has been reserved until the very last because of our belief that expensive mechanical devices serve best only as initial motivating devices and that a school's reading budget is far better

Motivate with Mechanical Devices

served by the purchase of a multitude of paperback books. Content teachers who serve on advisory committees for materials acquisition need to be aware of some of the concerns regarding cost effectiveness of this hardware. Some considerations include:

1. Although reading rate may be increased, gains are not necessarily lasting.
2. An increased rate using a machine does not automatically transfer to regular print material.
3. Motivated reading with a clear purpose in mind can improve rate as much as any mechanical devices.

Mechanical devices for promoting rate can be categorized under two main types: those that pace the reader's rate by pushing (pacers) and those that control the perception span by purporting to reduce the number of eye fixations and regressions while increasing the number of words read during one fixation (controlled readers). As far back as 1958, Robert Karlin concluded in reviewing the research that, although gains can be achieved using machines, instruction that does not favor them has shown even better results.[23]

Accelerating devices such as the Controlled Reader, the Craig Reader, Shadowscope, and Rateometer attempt to reduce fixations and regressions and force better attention and concentration. The Controlled Reader (Educational Development Laboratories) presents material from left to right at a predetermined rate, accomplished by a slot moving across the screen uncovering a portion of a line at one time. The rate can be adjusted to the student.

Tachistoscopes are special devices that present a word or phrase for a fraction of a second. The Flash X is an inexpensive hand model that can be used on an individual basis. For a more detailed account of mechanical devices, see Burmeister's chapter on speed.[24]

Workshop Activity 5.4

Rate Posttest (for end-of-term use)

Skim this article first in thirty seconds and then try to answer the ten questions without looking back, marking responses in the first column. Now, time yourself reading at your most rapid rate with the purpose of finding the main ideas only. After noting your time, mark your answers to the same questions in column two. Check your answers against those at the bottom of the next page, comparing your first "guestimate" with the second response. How close are they? How much did the skimming help your effective rate? How much information did you pick up during the thirty seconds of skimming? Have you become more adaptable?

Terror struck at the hearts of hundreds of thousands of persons in the length and breadth of the United States last night as crisp words of what they believed to be a news broadcast leaped from their radio sets—telling of catastrophe from the skies visited on this country.

Out of the heavens, they learned, objects at first believed to be meteors crashed down near Trenton, killing many.

Then out of the "meteors" came monsters, spreading destruction with torch and poison gas.

It was all just a radio dramatization, but the result, in all actuality, was nationwide hysteria.

In Philadelphia, women and children ran from their homes, screaming. In Newark, New Jersey, ambulances rushed to one neighborhood to protect residents against a gas attack. In the deep South men and women knelt in groups in the streets and prayed for deliverance.

In reality there was no danger. The broadcast was merely a Halloween program in which Orson Welles, actor-director of the Mercury Theater on the Air, related, as though he were one of the few human survivors of the catastrophe, an adaptation of H. G. Wells' *The War of the Worlds*.

In that piece of fiction men from Mars, in meteorlike space ships, come to make conquest of earth. The circumstances of the story were unbelievable enough, but the manner of its presentation was apparently convincing to hundreds of thousands of persons—despite the fact that the program was interrupted thrice for an announcement that it was fiction, and fiction only.

For the fanciful tale was broadcast casually, for all the world like a news broadcast, opening up serenely enough with a weather report.

The realism of the broadcast, especially for those who had tuned in after it had started, brought effects which none—not the directors of the Federal Radio Theater Project, which sponsored it, nor the Columbia Broadcasting Company, which carried it over a coast-to-coast chain of 151 stations, nor Station WCAU, which broadcast it locally—could foresee.

Within a few minutes newspaper offices, radio stations, and police departments everywhere were flooded with anxious telephone calls. Sobbing women sought advice on what to do; broken-voiced men wished to know where to take their families.

Station WCAU received more than four thousand calls and eventually interrupted a later program to make an elaborate explanation that death had not actually descended on New Jersey, and that monsters were not actually invading the world.

But calm did not come readily to the frightened radio listeners of the country.

The hysteria reached such proportions that the New York City Department of Health called up a newspaper and wanted advice on offering its facilities for the protection of the populace. Nurses and physicians were among the telephone callers everywhere. They were ready to offer assistance to the injured or maimed.

Hundreds of motorists touring through New Jersey heard the broadcast over their radios and detoured to avoid the area upon which the holocaust was focused—the area in the vicinity of Trenton and Princeton.

In scores of New Jersey towns women in their homes fainted as the horror of the broadcast fell on their ears. In Palmyra some residents packed up their worldly goods and prepared to move across the river into Philadelphia.

A white-faced man raced into the Hillside, New Jersey, police station and asked for a gas mask. Police said he panted out a tale of "terrible people spraying liquid gas all over Jersey meadows."

A weeping lady stopped Motorcycle Patrolman Lawrence Treger and asked where she should go to escape the "attack."

A terrified motorist asked the patrolman the way to Route 24. "All creation's busted loose. I'm getting out of Jersey," he screamed.

"Grover's Mill, New Jersey," was mentioned as a scene of destruction. In Stockton more than a half-hundred persons abandoned Colligan's Inn after hearing the broadcast and journeyed to Groveville to view the incredible "damage." They had misheard the name of the hypothetical town of "Grover's Mill," and believed it to be Groveville.

At Princeton University, women members of the geology faculty, equipped with flashlights and hammers started for Grover's Corners. Dozens of cars were driven to the hamlet by curious motorists. A score of university students were phoned by their parents and told to come home.

An anonymous and somewhat hysterical girl phoned the Princeton Press Club from Grover's Corners and said: "You can't imagine the horror of it! It's hell!"

A man came into the club and said he saw the meteor strike the earth and witnessed animals jumping from the alien body.

The Trenton police and fire telephone board bore the brunt of the nation's calls, because of its geographical location close to the presumed scene of catastrophe. On that board were received calls from Wilmington, Washington, Philadelphia, Jersey City, and Newark.

North of Trenton most of New Jersey was in the midst of a bad scare.

A report spread through Newark that the city was to be the target of a "gas-bomb attack." Police headquarters were notified there was a serious gas accident in the Clinton Hills section of that city. They sent squad cars and ambulances.

They found only householders, with possessions hastily bundled, leaving their homes. The householders returned to their homes only after emphatic explanations by police.

Fifteen persons were treated for shock in one Newark hospital.

In Jersey City one resident demanded a gas mask of police. Another telephoned to ask whether he ought to flee the area or merely keep his windows closed and hope for the best.

Many New Yorkers seized personal effects and raced out of their apartments, some jumping into their automobiles and heading for the wide-open spaces.

Samuel Tishman, a Riverside Drive resident, declared he and hundreds of others evacuated their homes, fearing "the city was being bombed."

He told of going home and receiving a frantic telephone call from a nephew.

Tishman denounced the program as "the most asinine stunt I ever heard of" and as "a pretty crummy thing to do."

The panic it caused gripped Harlemites, and one man ran into the street declaring it was the President's voice they heard, advising: "Pack up and go North, the machines are coming from Mars."

Police in the vicinity at first regarded the excitement as a joke, but they were soon hard pressed in controlling the swarms in the streets.

Reactions as strange, or stranger, occurred in other parts of the country. In San Francisco, a citizen called the police, crying:

"My Gosh, where can I volunteer my services? We've got to stop this awful thing."

In Indianapolis, Indiana, a woman ran screaming into a church.

"New York is destroyed; it's the end of the world," she cried. "You might as well go home to die."

At Brevard College, North Carolina, five boys in dormitories fainted on hearing the broadcast. In Birmingham, Alabama, men and women gathered in groups and prayed. Women wept and prayed in Memphis, Tennessee.

Throughout Atlanta was a wide-spread belief that a "planet" had struck New Jersey, killing from forty to seventy thousand persons.

At Pittsburgh one man telephoned a newspaper that he had returned to his home in the middle of the broadcast and found his wife in the bathroom clutching a bottle of poison.

"I'd rather die this way than like that," she screamed before he was able to calm her.

Two heart attacks were reported by Kansas City hospitals, and the Associated Press Bureau there received calls from Los Angeles, Salt Lake City, Beaumont, Texas, and St. Joseph, Missouri.

Minneapolis and St. Paul police switchboards were deluged with calls from frightened people.

Weeping and hysterical women in Providence, Rhode Island, cried out for officials of the electric company there to "turn off the lights so that the city will be safe from the enemy."

In some places mass hysteria grew so great that witnesses to the "invasion" could be found.

A Boston woman telephoned a newspaper to say she could "see the fire" from her window, and that she and her neighbors were "getting out of here."

The broadcast began at eight P.M. Within a few minutes after that time it had brought such a serious reaction that New Jersey state police sent out a teletype message to its various stations and barracks, containing explanations and instructions to police officers on how to handle the hysteria.

These and other police everywhere had problems on their hands as the broadcast moved on, telling of a "bulletin from the Intercontinental Radio News Bureau" saying there had been a gas explosion in New Jersey.

"Bulletins" that came in rapidly after that told of "meteors," then corrected that statement and described the Mars monsters.

The march of the Martians was disastrous. For a while they swept everything before them according to the pseudo-bulletins. Mere armies and navies were being wiped out in a trice.

Actually, outside the radio stations, the Martians were doing a pretty good job on the Halloween imaginations of the citizenry. The radio stations and the Columbia Broadcasting Company spent much of the remainder of the evening clearing up the situation. Again and again they explained the whole thing was nothing more than a dramatization.

In the long run, however, calm was restored in the myriad American homes which had been momentarily threatened by interplanetary invasion. Fear of the monsters from Mars eventually subsided.

There was no reason for being afraid of them, anyway. Even the bulletins of the radio broadcast explained they all soon died. They couldn't stand the earth's atmosphere and perished of pneumonia.[25]

Reprinted by permission of *The Philadelphia Inquirer,* November 1, 1938.

Checking Comprehension

Write the letter of the answer that is correct in the space at the left of each numbered statement.

_____ _____ 1. According to the radio dramatization, it was believed that the first objects to crash down from the heavens were (a) balloons, (b) meteors, (c) rockets, (d) flying saucers.

_____ _____ 2. Then out of these objects came (a) human beings, (b) torches, (c) reptiles, (d) monsters.

_____ _____ 3. According to the radio fiction, men from Mars had come to (a) make friends, (b) learn our language, (c) make conquest of the earth, (d) learn our military secrets.

_____ _____ 4. The broadcast opened by (a) announcing that something dreadful was going to happen, (b) announcing that a fanciful play would be enacted, (c) announcing that the stock market fell, (d) giving a weather report.

_____ _____ 5. The program was (a) at no time interrupted to say that it was fiction, (b) interrupted frequently to say that it was fiction, (c) interrupted three times to say that it was fiction, (d) interrupted once to say that it was fiction.

_____ _____ 6. The effect of the broadcast had been foreseen by how many of the three radio companies that were involved in sponsoring, carrying, and broadcasting it? (a) three, (b) two, (c) one, (d) none.

_____ _____ 7. The destruction was supposed to be centered in (a) New York, (b) West Virginia, (c) North Carolina, (d) New Jersey.

_____ _____ 8. The broadcast began at (a) six P.M., (b) eight P.M., (c) ten P.M., (d) three P.M.

_____ _____ 9. What did the bulletins mentioned in the broadcast say were being wiped out in a trice? (a) whole cities, (b) armies and navies, (c) radio and TV stations, (d) airports and railway stations.

_____ _____ 10. After they had caused all of this havoc, how did Columbia Broadcasting Company spend much of the remaining evening? (a) repeating the same show, (b) giving similar dramatizations based on outer space topics, (c) issuing pseudo-bulletins, (d) clearing up the situation.

Comprehension score: _____
WPM: _____
Effective rate: _____

Answers to Workshop Activity 5.1

Rate Exercise 1. Computer
1. d   2. d   3. b   4. b   5. d   6. b   7. b   8. c   9. d   10. c
Rate Exercise 2. Diversity
1. c   2. d   3. d   4. c   5. d   6. b   7. c   8. d   9. b   10. d
Rate Exercise 3. Mayas
No answers are given because it has been found to be more beneficial for students to call out their choices and argue about their conclusions, returning to the reading itself for verification.

Answers to Workshop Activity 5.4

Mars
1. b   2. d   3. c   4. d   5. c   6. d   7. d   8. b   9. b   10. d

Summary

Refer back to the cognitive map in figure 5.1 (p. 108) for a summary of rate adaptability.

Please note that the first three references are reading rate exercises. Other early dates are excerpts used in workshop activities.

References

1. "The Computer: Its Promise for the Future." Copyright © 1966 by *Saturday Review.* All rights reserved. Reprinted with permission. Adapted as a reading exercise by Nila Banton Smith, *Be A Better Reader,* Book VI (New York: Prentice-Hall, 1973), pp. 7–9.
2. J. R. Platt, "Diversity," *Science* 154 (December 1966): 1132–1139. Used with permission. Adapted as a reading exercise by Nila Banton Smith, *Be A Better Reader,* Book VI (New York: Prentice-Hall, 1973), pp. 18–20.
3. Oliver La Farge, "The Unsolved Mystery of the Mayas." Copyright © 1958 by The Atlantic Monthly Company, Boston, Mass. Reprinted with permission. Adapted as a reading exercise by Nila Banton Smith, *Be A Better Reader Series,* Book IV, 2d ed. (New York: Prentice-Hall, 1972), pp. 6–7.

4. Albert J. Harris and Edward R. Sipay, *How to Increase Reading Ability,* 6th ed. (New York: David McKay Co., 1975), p. 549.

5. Phyllis A. Miller, "Considering Flexibility of Reading Rate for Assessment and Development of Efficient Reading Behavior," in *What Research Has to Say about Reading Instruction,* ed. Jay Samuels (Newark, Del.: International Reading Association, 1978), pp. 72–84.

6. P. L. Nacke, "Assessment of Flexible Efficient Reading," in *Reading: The Right to Participate,* ed. F. P. Greene, Twentieth Yearbook, National Reading Conference (1971), pp. 256–265.

7. S. J. Samuels and P. R. Dahl, "Establishing Appropriate Purpose for Reading and Its Effect on Flexibility of Reading Rate," *Journal of Educational Psychology* 67 (1975): 38–43.

8. Lois Duncan, *"How to Write and Sell Your Personal Experiences* (Cincinnati: Writer's Digest Books, 1979), p. 182.

9. Noam Chomsky, *Reflections on Language* (New York: Pantheon Books, 1975), p. 130.

10. J. R. R. Tolkien, *The Silmarillion* (Boston: Houghton Mifflin, 1977), p. 63.

11. Sarah E. Benton Richardson, *Our Fight for Freedom.* Unpublished manuscript (Montclair, New Jersey: 1948), pp. 1, 255.

12. Robert Frost, *The Poetry of Robert Frost,* ed. Edward Connery Lathen (New York: Holt, Rinehart & Winston, 1969), pp. 79, 80.

13. James A. Michener, *Chesapeake* (New York: Random House, 1978), p. 10.

14. Richard Courant and Herbert Robbins, *What Is Mathematics? An Elementary Approach to Ideas and Methods* (New York: Oxford University Press, 1941), p. 383.

15. Harris and Sipay, *Reading Ability,* p. 558.

16. Miles Tinker, *Bases for Effective Reading* (Minneapolis: University of Minnesota Press, 1965).

17. Nila Banton Smith, *Speed Reading Made Easy* (New York: Popular Library, 1963).

18. Martha Maxwell, "Skimming and Scanning Improvement: The Needs, the Assumptions and the Knowledge Base," *Journal of Reading Behavior* (1972–73), pp. 54–55.

19. Florence Sherbourne, *Toward Reading Comprehension,* 2d ed. (Lexington, Mass.: D. C. Heath, 1977).

20. Mark Aulls, *Developmental and Remedial Reading in Middle Grades,* abridged ed. (Boston: Allyn & Bacon, 1978).

21. W. Graham Mallett, " 'Joining the Race' is Open to Suggestion," *Journal of Reading* (November 1978): 103–104.

22. Walter Hill, *Secondary School Reading: Progress, Program and Procedure* (Boston: Allyn & Bacon, 1979), p. 334.

23. Robert Karlin, "Machines and Reading: A Review of Research," *The Clearing House* (February 1958): 349–352.

24. Lou Burmeister, *Reading Strategies for Middle and Secondary School Teachers,* rev. ed. (Reading, Mass.: Addison-Wesley, 1978), pp. 305–314.

25. George Mawhinney, "Invasion from Planet Mars." Reprinted by permission of The Philadelphia Inquirer November 1, 1938. Adapted as a reading exercise by Nila Banton Smith, *Be A Better Reader,* Book V (New York: Prentice-Hall, 1972), pp. 3–5.

Carver, Ronald P. "Is Reading Rate Constant or Flexible?" *Reading Research Quarterly* 18 (Winter 1983): 190–215.

Carver, Ronald P. "How Good Are the World's Best Readers?" *Reading Research Quarterly* 20 (1985): 389–417.

Carver, Ronald P. "Silent Reading Rates in Grade Equivalents." *Journal of Reading Behavior* 21, no. 2 (1989): 155–166.

Chabot, Robert J., and others. "The Speed of Word Recognition Subprocesses and Reading Achievement in College Students." *Reading Research Quarterly* (Winter 1984): 147–161.

Hoffman, James. "The Relationship between Rate and Reading Flexibility." *Reading World* (May 1978): 325–328.

Jensen, Paul Erik. "Theories of Reading Speed and Comprehension." *Journal of Reading* 21 (April 1978): 593–600.

McCracken, Robert A. "Internal versus External Flexibility of Reading Rate." *Journal of Reading* 8 (1965): 208–209.

Miller, Phyllis A. "Considering Flexibility of Reading Rate for Assessment and Development of Efficient Reading Behavior." In *What Research Has to Say about Reading Instruction,* Jay Samuels, ed. Newark, Del.: International Reading Association, 1978, pp. 72–84.

Samuels, S. J., and Dahl, P. R. "Establishing Appropriate Purpose for Reading and Its Effect on Flexibility of Reading Rate." *Journal of Educational Psychology* 67 (1975): 39–43.

Smith, Helen K. "The Development of Effective, Flexible Readers," *Proceedings of the Annual Reading Conference.* Chicago: University of Chicago Press, 1965, pp. 159–168.

Tonjes, Marian J. "Adaptable Rates and Strategies for Efficient Comprehension: The Effective Reader." In *The Reading Connection,* Gwen Bray and Anthony Pugh, eds. United Kingdom Reading Association. London: Ward Lock Educational, 1980, pp. 144–153.

Recommended Readings

Figure 6.1
Enhancing vocabulary
development: a
cognitive map.

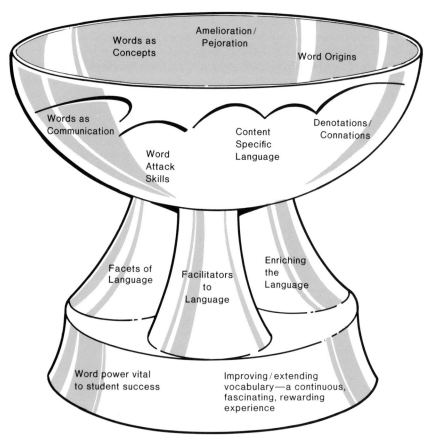

Amelioration/
Pejoration

Words as
Concepts

Word Origins

Words as
Communication

Content
Specific
Language

Denotations/
Connations

Word
Attack
Skills

Facets of
Language

Facilitators
to
Language

Enriching
the
Language

Word power vital
to student success

Improving/extending
vocabulary—a continuous,
fascinating, rewarding
experience

Enhancing Vocabulary Development

6

Anticipatory Questions

(Literal)

1. List types of problems that content area students may have with the vocabulary they encounter.

(Literal)

2. What are the three levels of knowing a word? Describe each level.

(Applied)

3. Select three strategies that you believe will be most useful in enhancing technical vocabulary in your classes. Explain why you selected each one.

(Applied)

4. Take one of the three strategies you selected in question 2 and develop a content lesson activity in your area.

(Critical)

5. Synthesize into one page or less the major facets of language development as they connect to vocabulary.

Technical Terminology and Concepts

accent clues

acronyms

amelioration/pejoration

context clues

CSSD

denotations/ connotations

etymology or roots

euphemisms

oxymorons

phonics

pivotal words

receptive/expressive vocabulary

similes/metaphors

structural analysis

thesaurus/dictionary

VCCV/VCV

Introduction

Two basic beliefs underlining this chapter are: (1) word power is vital to effective comprehension of written discourse; and (2) the process of improving and extending vocabulary can be a continuous, fascinating, and rewarding adventure.

The following exercises are intended (if needed) to nudge you out of any lethargy you might feel toward vocabulary development per se. If you do well on any of them, you may consider yourself to be in the top 2 percent of preservice and inservice teachers, both elementary and secondary. You might then consider offering your services to the workshop instructor as a cofacilitator or group leader.

Preassessment Workshop Activity 6.1
How Is Your General Vocabulary?

Activity: How Is Your Verbal Speed?

Two examples taken from Funk and Lewis are included here.[1]

A. Verbal Speed (easy—60 seconds)

In this warm-up exercise, allow only one minute to write in each blank space a word beginning with "S" that has the opposite meaning to the given word. For example: fast—slow, sweet—sour, buy—sell.

1. tall _____
2. north _____
3. happy _____
4. different _____
5. dangerous _____
6. big _____
7. dull _____
8. noisy _____
9. sit _____
10. receive _____

B. Verbal Speed (Advanced—90 seconds)

Do the same in 1½ minutes for this exercise.

1. generous _____
2. meaningless _____
3. believing _____

4. complicated   _____

5. doubtful   _____

6. careful   _____

7. wakefulness   _____

8. rough   _____

9. objective   _____

10. laugh   _____

Adequate scores: Ninety percent on the easy test and seventy percent or more on the advanced one.

A. Assuming that you know the terms indigenous to your own content field, this pretest is concerned with the technical vocabulary of language and word recognition. These are terms that will appear in this chapter. It is suggested that you attempt to define these words now in pencil and revise where necessary as you encounter each one within the chapter.

How Is Your Technical Vocabulary?

	Before Reading	*After Reading*
synonym	_____	_____
antonym	_____	_____
homonym	_____	_____
simile	_____	_____
metaphor	_____	_____
amelioration	_____	_____
pejoration	_____	_____
affixes	_____	_____
phoneme	_____	_____
morpheme	_____	_____
grapheme	_____	_____
syllable	_____	_____
context clue	_____	_____
structural analysis	_____	_____
denotation	_____	_____
connotation	_____	_____
acronym	_____	_____
phonics	_____	_____

B. What is your definition of the term *radical*? _____
What content area are you concentrating on at the moment?

_____

Now, please note the general meanings of *radical* compared with the technical meaning of that term.

General: fundamental, basic, or extreme
Math: the root of a quantity as indicated by the radical sign
Social Studies: a revolutionary
Botany: growing from the root
Chemistry: an atom or group of atoms with at least one unpaired electron

---

If you were ever confused about which ending to use, the cartoon strip in figure 6.2, a graphic worth one thousand words, should help clarify.

Background and Purpose

A major responsibility of content teachers is to assist students in mastering key terminology of that field. By building that vocabulary, they are actually clarifying concepts connected to their subject.

However, a problem arises all too often when teachers use a standard, hackneyed technique to teach these words. Where have you heard this before? "Look at this list of fifty words that I have compiled for you. Your assignment is to look them up and then use each one in a sentence." This single, all-too-common practice could easily account for the large number of students whose attitude toward vocabulary development is at best apathetic and often downright hostile. Meaning is not inherent in words themselves; the reader supplies meaning based on past experience.

Figure 6.2
A graphic worth one-thousand words.
An Ed Leek illustration, University of New Mexico Alumnus.

A Latin Lesson for Alumni

| **alumnus** | **alumna** | **alumni** | **alumnae** | **alumni** |

The relationship between reading and vocabulary development is two-fold: (1) when the meanings of words in context are clear, the reader is able to effectively comprehend connected discourse; (2) through the act of reading, new words are acquired and shades of meaning are expanded and refined. These are mutually reinforcing, and readers constantly switch back and forth between the two.

With this as a brief background, then, the purpose of this chapter is threefold: (1) to show the breadth of the multiple approaches to vocabulary development; (2) to specify a variety of teaching strategies from which content teachers may select the most appropriate ones; (3) and last, but of utmost importance, to demonstrate to the reader that vocabulary development can be useful, enjoyable, and profitable.

"The refractory attitude would militate against a palliation of the opprobrium directed toward the clerical lugubrious termagant."[2] Do you agree or disagree? Explain! _____

Stumbling Blocks

How do you feel when confronted with this type of reading? Probably much as a number of your present or future students feel when faced with a text that is loaded with technical terminology or difficult general vocabulary. Poor readers, handed a two-pound book with over six hundred pages of this kind of writing, think seriously of dropping out.

Some problems with vocabulary include:

1. *Obsolete words*—such as hooch, arctics, and nosegay.
2. *Colloquial words*—often found in English literature and used to give flavor to the story; may be unknown in other regions.
3. *Scientific, technical, and specific words*—explained in the light of meaning for that particular context. Scientific terms such as *hydrogen* have very specific definitions. Such terms as *root* or *hedge* mean different things in science or math or economics.

Kenneth Goodman and Olive Niles state that

Every time learners push into a new field or into a new subject area within an old one, they encounter new vocabulary or new uses for old terms. . . . The vocabulary is unfamiliar because the ideas and concepts it expresses are unfamiliar. Like new concepts, new vocabulary learned in relationship to the new knowledge must be built on the base of pre-existing vocabulary. If the new vocabulary is more effective in manipulating the new ideas it will be absorbed, and the old language may be modified or set aside. *Vocabulary development outside of the context of new ideas of pre-existing language is not possible.*[3]

What we think of as a vocabulary problem is not just putting a label on an object. A variety of problems for students include: (1) the word is not recognized in their listening vocabulary; (2) the form is not familiar but they know the concept if this new word is associated with the old; (3) they do not recognize the printed form or the concept (concept development is then often necessary first); (4) a written form is familiar and they have heard it before but have no meaning for it—in oral reading they read it correctly; (5) more mature readers encounter printed forms never heard in speech. We do not always need to pronounce a word correctly in order to understand its meaning. Just think of the word *synecdoche*. If you have encountered it in reading but never heard it pronounced, you might well know what it means but be hearing it as *sin-ek-dosh*, rather than its correct pronunciation of *sin-ĕk-do-key*.

Facets of Language

Words as Communication

Words are a communication device. We have developed over time a pre-scribed code of words for communication with others and for exploring our own thoughts. Carl Smith warns us, however, that definitions are not enough in interpreting meaning.[4] Whereas words imply meaning and meaning is the heart of language, that meaning does not reside in definitions. Meanings occur in people's minds in response to certain words with the association they arouse. In understanding, we create our own meaning from what we already know and feel. It is within this largely personal framework that we interpret language. Thus, when readers have little background for new words, they will have difficulty associating them to anything meaningful.

Words as Concepts

Words stand for concepts, which grow as we do. We acquire new vocabulary only as we can grasp the concepts denoted, which in turn depend on our experiences and general development. Finer conceptualizing of anything—e.g., colors, feelings—depends on experiences in that subject area. As an example, your concept for the word *snow* may be very limited—dry, wet, powder—but Eskimos will distinguish many different types of snow because of their vast experiential background with it.

Vocabularies

Edgar Dale, Arnold Burron and Amos Claybaugh, and others have sug-gested general classifications of words.[5][6] Roughly, these categories include: (1) a general category of both basic and supporting words, which includes all words not specific to one field or area; (2) technical words dealing with specific fields (such as scientific or political terms); (3) proper nouns (names of people or places); (4) flagging (directional) and joining words such as *in retrospect, and, therefore, but*.

Another way to look at vocabularies is to consider the four major communication channels: listening, speaking, reading, and writing. These can be classified into two major categories as shown below.

Receptive Vocabulary	*Expressive Vocabulary*
1. listen	3. speak
2. read	4. write

Young children's listening and speaking vocabularies are much greater than their reading or writing ones, whereas adults tend to know more words through listening and reading. Until reading is a strong habit most people learn new words orally through conversation, television, radio, and movies.

Numerous studies have attempted to determine the vocabulary size of different ages and sociological groups, with the results varying widely, depending on whether the figures refer to speaking, listening, writing, or reading vocabulary.

Problems with Estimating Vocabulary Size

Another discrepancy in total figures may be due in part to the confusion about what is considered to be a word. If *run* is a word, is *ran* another one? *Go, going, gone*—three words or one? *Run* and *go* are part of our *basic* vocabulary. Total vocabulary, then, would include all derivatives such as *going-gone* and compounds such as *runaway.* An abridged dictionary may have as few as 80,000 words because it does not include all the derivatives. Edgar Dale and M. K. Smith have given estimates of sizes of vocabularies (see table 6.1).

No matter who is closer to the mark, developing vocabulary should be a continuing process throughout life.

Other considerations that should be mentioned are:

1. Do we really *know* a word if we do not know all of its literal (denotative) meanings? Take a collegiate dictionary and look up the word *run.* How many meanings can you find? There are at least 130 definitions!
2. Do we really know a word if we do not know its connotation? Yellow is a color, but its connotation is *a coward.*

Table 6.1
Sizes of Vocabulary

	Dale[7]	Smith[8]
First grade	3,000	17,000
Sixth grade	8,000	32,000
Twelfth grade	15,000	47,000

With over a million words in the English language, approximately half belong to special fields, leaving around 500,000 that appear in an unabridged dictionary.

A few years ago a computer analysis was made by Henry Kucera and W. Nelson Francis on a collection of texts using a total of over one million words.[9] This corpus was divided into samples representing fifteen types of subject matter and prose styles, with the exception of poetry and drama. The content ranged from the sports page to the scientific journal and from romantic fiction to deep philosophical discussion. Analysis showed that over fifty thousand different words appeared, and of these the most frequent were words such as *the, of, and, to, is.* This was not surprising, but what was of interest was the finding relating to style. For example, *of* appears more often in informative writing, whereas *and* and *to* appear more often in imaginative prose.

Funk and Lewis speak of forty-three words that make up one-half of the words listed in daily speech—words similar to the ones in the computer study, including such words as *you, me.*[10]

In a study of 100,000 running words, Mario Pei reported that 3,000 words used over and over accounted for 95 percent of the total.[11] That suggests a limited basic vocabulary. However, the illiterate or semiliterate may have a total vocabulary not exceeding 500 words.

Enriching the Language

Word Origins (Etymology of Roots)

The oldest recorded languages of the Indo-European family are Sanskrit (2000 B.C.), Greek (1400 B.C.), and Latin (500 B.C.) in that order. Approximately one-half of the population on earth speaks some derivative of Indo-European language, and most English vocabulary can be traced back to that.

According to Pei, only a few words in our modern language can be traced directly back to preclassical tongues of antiquity.[12] Among them are:

1. wine (Latin *vinum*) comes from Etruscan
2. mules (Sumerian *mulus*), meaning house slippers
3. gum (Greek *kommi*) from ancient Egyptian *qmit*
4. *eeny, meeny, miney, mo*—numerals used by ancient Welsh tribes
5. ten (Indo-European), a compound of *two* and *hand* and *five-finger*
6. school (Greek), leisure—having time to think and learn
7. reading—to guess, to riddle

The term *etymology* comes from the Greek, with *etymon* meaning true or original meaning, and the *ology* coming from *logia,* meaning science or study. This study of the true or original meaning of words can be compared to a tree where the roots are the origins, the branches are the word families stemming out of them, and the leaves are the words themselves and their meanings. Each word originally had only one meaning, but with use it sprouted green shoots of new meaning. For example, with the word *run* some common uses are:

The boy will *run* a race.

The disease has *run* its course.

The fence *runs* east and west.

The man *runs* a garage.

The boy has *run* a splinter in his finger.

She will *run* out of money.

He will *run* up a hill.

She may have *run* across an old friend.

He can knock a home *run.*

There was a *run* on the bank.

She's not the common *run* of persons.

The radishes have *run* to seed.

The splinter made a *run* in her stocking.

Tracing a word back to its origins can give concreteness to a concept in that often a mental picture is associated with the words. The following examples are related to different content areas.

Calculate: Ancient Romans had an instrument called a hodometer or road measurer, which was quite like our taxi meters. Imagine a tin can with a revolving cover holding a quantity of pebbles. Each time the wheel of the carriage turned, the metal cover revolved and a pebble dropped through the hole into the can. At the destination the driver then counted the number of pebbles and "calculated" the bill. (The Latin word for 'pebble' was *calculus!*)[13] *Math*

When studying military battles and men, can you guess where or how we got the terms *lieutenant, captain,* and *colonel? Lieutenant* comes from the French words *lieu* (in place of) and *tenir* (to hold). A lieutenant, then, is one who takes the place of the captain when the captain is not around. *Captain* comes from the Latin *caput,* or head. *Colonel* comes from *columna* (Latin for *column*), so this name is derived from the column being led. *Social Studies*

Conspirator: In the light of recent politics and government, this is an interesting word taken from Latin *spirare*—'to breathe'—prefix *con*—'together'. Truly, conspirators breathe together. (Sometimes they "sing" together, too!)

Capital punishment: Originally from death by one means only: severing the head from the body. The Latin word for head, *caput,* is the base for this term. Today, of course, the meaning has been broadened to include execution by any means.

Mnemonic: Achilles (the man with a vulnerable heel) had another problem too—that of remembering things. He solved this by keeping Mnemon near him as a companion to remember things for him. The name Mnemon means 'mind' or 'memory'; thus a mnemonic device such as a string on your finger aids memory.

Curfew: This comes from the French *couvrir* (cover) and *feu* (fire). In olden days the curfew bell meant 'put out or cover up the fire and go to bed'.

Did you know also that

1. The American slang word *guy* is from Guy Fawkes, the historic British conspirator who tried to blow up the House of Lords?
2. *Bonfire* was once a *bonefire,* often made of bones of heretics in the Middle Ages?
3. *Amnesty* (which we now think of as a pardon for offense) actually came from a Greek word meaning 'loss of memory'? When amnesty is asked for, we are actually asking the judge to have amnesia—to forget it.
4. *Senate* literally means 'a group of old men': Latin, *senex,* an old man?
5. *Tammany* Hall was actually named after an Indian saint of the seventeenth century, Chief Tammany?

For these and other examples, see Funk's *Word Origins and Their Romantic Stories,* especially the two chapters on political and war words.[14]

English

The branches of word study can be found in the Latin word *spectare* (to look). More than 240 words have sprouted from this base, words such as *spectator, spectacle, inspect, introspection.* How many others can you think of offhand? List them below. Compare with classmates.

_____	_____	_____
_____	_____	_____
_____	_____	_____

Home Economics

The blanks below have been filled in with the nationality of the people who originated the following foods, or the country from which they came.

1. *Tortilla* is a (*Mexican*) word for 'pancake'.
2. *Macaroons* were first baked by (*Italians*).
3. Twice-baked bread, called *Zwieback,* got its name in (*Germany*).
4. The *meringue* of whipped egg whites is a (*French*) word.
5. *Chocolate* is a (*Spanish*) word that comes from the Nahuatl Indian language.
6. The (*Hungarians*) gave us *goulash.*
7. *Minestrone* is a thick (*Italian*) vegetable soup.
8. *Sukiyaki* is a (*Japanese*) dish.
9. *Poi* comes from the (*Hawaiians*).
10. *Oatmeal* originated in (*Scotland*).[15]

Did you realize that we actually control our own language? We have invented over 600,000 usable English words, with the others taken directly from foreign languages, such as *bouquet* from French. We ourselves have devised the queer spellings and pronunciations of our English language. Some of our spellings are due to errors made by ignorant typesetters centuries ago. We have actually honored their misspellings by continuing to use them!

How the English Language was Created

This year, as every year, about 5,000 new words will enter the English language.[16] Scholars do not sit around inventing them—usually the words just appear and are used. Much of our language today was yesterday's slang, usually cropping up in slum areas. Purists and highbrows, although protesting, have eventually had to give in and agree to include these words in the dictionary.

Two hundred thirty years ago slang words included *bubble, sham, bully, hips*. Other past slang included *gin, boycott, cab, greenhorn*, and *hoax*.

When these words are included in the dictionary, their definitions actually come from the sentences or context in which the new word appeared.

Denotations of words refer to the literal or scientific meanings of words. Most technical terms, especially in science or mathematics, have very precise definitions; there is no ambiguity about which meaning they portray.

Denotations and Connotations

Connotation refers to the interpretive or emotional meanings of words. What does yellow mean to you? Your definition will depend on your point of view or the context. Do you have a green thumb? Am I referring to the color of your thumb or your ability to grow plants? If the latter, that is the connotation. Figures of speech most commonly found in literature include *similes, metaphors*, and *oxymorons*, among others. Examples of these will be given later.

It has been said that Sir Christopher Wren, the great architect of St. Paul's Cathedral in London, was told by King George I that Wren's work was "amusing, awful, and artificial." Wren was delighted with this royal compliment because three hundred years ago *amusing* meant 'amazing', *awful* meant 'awe-inspiring', and *artificial* meant 'artistic'! This shows us how meanings of words can change drastically over time.

Amelioration and Pejoration

Amelioration (the up-elevator) and **pejoration** (basement bound) are terms concerned with the changes in meaning up and down the social scale over a period of time. Some examples of amelioration, where the connotation of the word has been elevated today, are:

minister once meant 'servant'
lord once meant 'breadgiver'
govern once meant 'steer a ship'
nice once meant 'ignorant'

Pejoration, on the other hand, is concerned with words that now have a negative connotation:

silly once meant 'blessed'
propaganda once meant 'spreading of ideas or faith'
lewd once meant 'unlearned'
lust once meant 'joy and pleasure'
stupid once meant 'amazed'
hussy once meant 'housewife'

Similes and Metaphors

As most of you will recall, a **simile** is an analogy where two unlike things are compared and are preceded by the words *like* or *as*. Perhaps you did not know that the word simile comes from the Latin *similia* meaning "like": "He fought like a tiger."

Cliché similes using *as:*

		Answers
as easy as	_____	*pie*
as sure as	_____	*shootin'*
as quick as a	_____	*wink*
as slow as	_____	*molasses in January*
as smart as a	_____	*whip*
as right as	_____	*rain*
as cute as a	_____	*button*

Metaphor comes from the Greek *metaphora* meaning 'transfer', from *meta* ('over') plus *pherein* ('to carry'). It draws a comparison directly between two things without using *like* or *as*. "All the world's a stage" (Shakespeare). "No man is an island" (Donne).

Metaphor/idioms with body parts:

	Explain what each means
don't split hairs	_____
lend an ear	_____
keep a stiff upper lip	_____
a finger in every pie	_____

Explain what each means

browbeating   _____

nose to the grindstone   _____

without batting an eyelash   _____

giving an arm or a leg   _____

A **euphemism** is a pleasant term for something considered unpleasant. Your students will enjoy adding to this list or creating their own.

Euphemisms

Unpleasant Situation	Euphemism
1. overdrawn bank account	negative saver
2. fired from a job	terminated
3. old people	senior citizens
4. janitor	sanitation maintenance superintendent
5. to die	pass away
6. draft	selective service
7. quiz, test, exam	educational opportunity

An **oxymoron** is a figure of speech where words of almost opposite meaning are used together for effect. Writers will use these for the strong effect that comes from putting together words not in harmony. The word *oxymoron* comes from the Greek *oxys* ('sharp') and *moros* ('foolish'). By combining the opposites of *sharp* or *bright* with *dull* or *foolish,* you get an oxymoron.

Oxymorons

Examples of Oxymorons

broadly ignorant	infinitely small	golden ghetto
gentle strength	honest thief	gigante chiquito
wasteful thrift	dictatorial democracy	icy heat
absolute possibility	bittersweet	jumbo shrimp
restless quiet	sublime folly	organized mess (or
wonderfully stupid	dynamic bore	chaos)
dumb scholar	brilliant failure	favorite enemy
pure evil	elementary calculus	good war

A contest or an "oxymoron for the day" activity in a middle and high school class has proved to be a successful motivator. Finding oxymorons in different content areas is a challenge.

The list below can be used as a quick review of other common terms used
in English classes.

Term	Definition
simile	direct comparison using *like* or *as*
alliteration	repetition of the beginning consonant
assonance	repetition of the same vowel sound
onomatopoeia	words that imitate sounds, setting a mood through sound
hyperbole	exaggeration for effect
metaphor	comparing two things not using *like* or *as*

Coining New Words

Blending the first part of a word with the last part of another is one way
to coin a new word. Two well-known examples are *smoke + fog = smog;
breakfast + lunch = brunch.* Other examples include:

American + Indian = Amerindian

dictation + telephone = dictaphone

grit + slime = grime

squirm + wriggle = squiggle

Europe + Asia = Eurasia

combine + mingle = commingle

From Lewis B. Carroll's *Alice in Wonderland,* we find:

slimy + lithe = slithy

flimsy + miserable = mimsy

chuckle + snort = chortle

Building new words from parts of old words is another way new words
are coined:

astro—astrodome, astrometeorologist

biochemistry—bionic

consort—consortium

metropolitan—megalopolis

panorama—cinerama

medicine—medicare

culture—acculturate

Shakespeare coined over 1,700 words, many of which still survive today.*
For example:

suspicious	monumental
lonely	dwindle
laughable	critical
castigate	leapfrog
bump	barefaced
hurry	

In World War II, British fliers coined *gremlin*—a goblin accused of playing
tricks on planes. Other words to come out of that war were *radar, flak,
gestapo,* and *blitzkreig.*

*(See Edgar Dale and Joseph O'Rourke, *Techniques on Teaching Vocabulary*.)

Acronyms are words that are formed from the first letters of several words. In polite society *SNAFU* stands for "situation normal: all fouled up." Other acronyms include:

MIA	Missing in Action
WIN	Whip Inflation Now
HUD	Housing for Urban Development
SIDS	Sudden Infant Death Syndrome
TOPS	Take Off Pounds Sensibly
POSH	Port Out Starboard Home
RADAR	Radio Detecting and Ranging
NATO	North Atlantic Treaty Organization
LEM	Lunar Excursion Module
WASP	White Anglo-Saxon Protestant
PAL	Police Athletic League
LOX	Liquid Oxygen
NOW	National Organization for Women
TESOL	Teaching English to Speakers of Other Languages
RSVP	Repondez s'il vous plait (please reply)

Before reading this, jog down a word you recently learned.

Language of Content Areas

Levels of Knowing a Word

In a major review of vocabulary research, one overall conclusion was that it is better to focus on a few words in depth, with all the various shades of meaning and uses, than to give long lists of words with single definitions.[17] The general recommendation was that vocabulary development must be intensive, systematic, and regularly conducted by all content teachers.

Harry Forgan and Charles Mangrum have delineated three levels of knowing a word: the specific, functional, and general or conceptual levels.[18] At the lowest level (specific) we have just one definition, idea, or synonym for the word. The second level, where most of the newer words fall, is the functional level. Here we are able to use the word appropriately when speaking or writing; we understand how the word is used. And finally, at the general or conceptual level, we have many ideas about the word and can place it as a part of a larger category and give shades of meaning to it.

Taking the example of Forgan and Mangrum, using the word *vote* (*vote* comes from Latin meaning 'to vow'), we see that at the *specific level* vote means 'something done during elections'; at the *functional level* it is 'a way of getting someone elected'—a vote means 'making a choice'; and at the *general* (*conceptual*) *level* it is just one part of a complex government process called 'democracy'. We would then be able to discuss the place of the word *vote* and its role within the broader framework, giving details.

| Pivotal Words | Prepositions and conjunctions signal directions in reading. The examples in table 6.2 are especially relevant to social studies and English. When students have difficulties comprehending the material, it may help to point out how a particular group of words signal the writer's intention or direction. For example, the word "furthermore" signals readers that more of the same information will be coming and it will be just as important. |

Improving Vocabulary through Word Attack

Context, Structure, Sound, Dictionary, (CSSD)

Strategies that a reader uses to identify and pronounce a word are referred to as *word attack* or *word recognition*. The mature reader quickly uses more than one strategy to unlock an unknown word, whereas poor readers often rely on a single word attack strategy. Thus, they are often frustrated by the inefficiency inherent in being limited to any one method. Four major strategies can be remembered easily by the letters **CSSD,** which stand for context, structure (structural analysis), sound (phonics), and dictionary. Usually the reader first tries to figure out the word in question by looking at it in its context. If the reader can pronounce it and the context explains it, the reader need go no further. If not certain of the meaning, the reader will try structural analysis, or units of meaning, also referred to as morphemes. The root and affixes are located for meanings. If the word does not lend itself to this analysis, it may be broken into syllables, each sounded out. This is phonics, or looking at the sound-symbol relationship. As a last resort, or when verification or clarification of definition is needed, the reader will go to the dictionary or glossary.

Smith states, "Many persons with a well-developed writing style report a period in adolescence when they became outrageously 'sesquipedaelianistic,' seeking the learned or esoteric phrase, often at the expense of meaning."[19]

Workshop Activity 6.2
Pivotal Words

Using table 6.2 on pivotal words, in content area groups of not more than four, write a sentence for each of the thirteen types of words. Each sentence should relate to your content area. You should select only one example word to use. For example, #4. "Alternative" Math: Either you take _____ or _____ . Social Studies: It was neither war nor was it peace.

Skills

Table 6.2

Pivotal Words

Type of Words	Meaning	Examples
1. Additive	More of the same to come and just as important	also, and, besides, further, furthermore, in addition, moreover, too
2. Equivalent	What has been said plus what is to come	as well as, at the same time, likewise, similarly, equally important
3. Amplification	To understand the idea here is a specific instance	for example, for instance, specifically, such as, as, like, (e.g.,)
4. Alternative	Sometimes a choice and sometimes not	either/or, neither/nor, otherwise, other than
5. Repetitive	Said once but will say again	to repeat, in other words, that is (i.e.,)
6. Contrast and Change	Having one side, now look at the other	but, still, yet, regardless, notwithstanding, whereas, though, instead of, rather than, in spite of, conversely, despite, however, nevertheless, on the contrary
7. Cause and Effect	Having happened, now look at why	so, since, thus, therefore, hence, consequently, because, for this reason, accordingly
8. Qualifying	What to expect or conditions to work under	if, unless, although, providing, whenever
9. Concession	Agreeing to this much	of course, granting that, accepting that
10. Emphasizing	Take notice!	more important, above all, indeed
11. Order	Keeping it straight	finally, first, next, then, second, last
12. Time	Who said what and when	afterwards, meanwhile, now, previously, presently, subsequently, later, formerly, ultimately
13. Summarizing	Pulling together what has been said	as has been said, in conclusion, in brief, for these reasons, to sum up, in sum

Looking at the new word *sesquipedalianistic,* how do you go about deriving its meaning? Apply what you just read!

Context: _____

Structure: _____

Sound: _____

Dictionary: _____

Context (The Intelligent Guess)

Here is a most powerful strategy, especially when combined with any of the others. Using **context clues** to figure out the meaning of words in a particular setting is the strategy most often used by mature readers to attack new words. It is often explained as a major reason that avid readers have larger vocabularies than reluctant readers. The exposure to a word in context may well give us a better idea of its meaning than looking it up in the dictionary, where a variety of meanings are listed from which to choose.

Steps in context analysis are as follows:

1. Decide on the *syntax* or function of the unknown word as used in the sentence. Is it a noun, verb, adjective, adverb, etc.? Knowing which part of speech it is will cut down on the possible meanings.
2. Using your knowledge of types of context clues (see the list on page 163), try to decide its meaning from the words around it.
3. Check the *semantics* or meaning by substituting a synonym for the unknown word and see if it makes sense here. Try it with these examples.
   a. The thief made a *surreptitious* movement, stealthily pocketing the money. _____

   b. It was a *maudlin* performance, sentimental to the extreme. _____

   c. Her *sardonic* or bitter expression told the story. _____
   _____

There are many students who rarely use context clues knowingly, because they have learned to rely too heavily on other strategies. The major types of clues included in table 6.3 should be reviewed regularly when students have difficulties.

Table 6.3
Semantic Context Clues

Clue	Example
1. Definition	To expire is to die.
2. Restatement	The *cliché* or stereotyped phrase . . .
3. Example	"It's a great life if you don't weaken" is an example of a cliché.
4. Comparison/Contrast	A harpsichord, like a piano, . . . She was quiet in class, but extremely *loquacious* with her peers.
5. Description	A *ginkgo* is a shade tree found in eastern China that has leaves in the shape of a fan.
6. Synonyms/Antonyms	To vindicate or justify his actions . . .
7. Familiar Expressions or Experience	"The Emancipation Proclamation was . . . ." helps to understand an *emancipated* woman.
8. Association	It was as airy and *buoyant* as a feather.
9. Reflection of Mood	He was *aggravated* by the constant raspy whine and the repetition of complaints.
10. Summary	She was *despondent;* could not sleep or eat, cried much of the time, and could not keep her mind on her work.

Structural Analysis (Meaningful Word Parts)

The **structural analysis** approach to word attack divides a word into its meaning-bearing parts or morphemes, such as root words, prefixes, and suffixes. For example: *underhandedness.* The root is *hand,* the prefix is *under,* and the two suffixes are *ed* and *ness.*

For structural analysis to be a successful strategy, the student must have some knowledge of meanings of common *affixes* (prefixes and suffixes). Because many English root words and affixes are derived from Latin and Greek, reviewing those common to your content area is time well spent.

The precise technical terminology of the sciences lends itself to this strategy. See appendix 5 for a listing of common roots and affixes used in science. Using this list as a reference, students may unlock meanings of long technical scientific terms. One way to become familiar with meanings of word parts such as *bi* or *corpus* is to use them in coining new words. Students must get at the meaning by referring to the list. For example, what is a "*chlor dermato bi capit corpus?*" (It is a coined word for 'green-skinned two-headed body'. *Chlor* means 'green', *dermato* is 'skin', etc.)

Table 6.4 is an activity using knowledge of structural analysis.

Table 6.4
Numerical Word Elements Activity

Can you mathematicians unlock the mysteries of these words?

1. monolithic   _____

2. dichotomy   _____

3. triptych   _____

4. quadrennial   _____

5. quintessence   _____

6. hexagon   _____

7. hebdomadal   _____

8. octavo   _____

9. novena   _____

10. decalogue   _____

Problems with these numerical words? Counting from one to ten in Greek and Latin may help.

	Latin	Greek
1.	unos	mons
2.	duo	dis/dy/di
3.	tres	tri
4.	quattuor	tetra
5.	quinque	penta
6.	sex	hexa
7.	septem	hepta
8.	octo	octo
9.	novem	ennea
10.	decem	deca/deka

Phonics (Sounds, Syllables, and Accents)

Although some people still believe that phonics is *the* panacea for helping poor readers, research such as that done by Robert Mills has shown it to be the least successful approach to teaching word acquisition, and this is especially true of the student with a below-average IQ.[20] With older students, being able merely to decode the words is not enough; they must be cognizant of connotations and special meanings in specific contexts. Decoding the following sentence literally will not help comprehension, and confusion abounds when we already know the word in another context: "He will house the guest" versus "he goes into the house." "The *root* of the problem" versus "the square root." "The culture of the southwest" versus "the test tube culture in the science lab." On the other hand, it cannot be assumed that all phonics skills were taught, much less mastered, in early elementary years. Two higher-level skills not needed by students until they meet multisyllabic words are *syllabication* and *accent generalizations*. Because many technical terms are multisyllabic, a brief discussion of syllabication and accent follows.

For those who wish to review more basic phonic generalizations than are presented here, refer to the word attack references listed at the end of this chapter.

Breaking down a word into its separate syllables, each with one vowel sound, may help readers recognize that term if it is already in their listening or speaking vocabulary. Prerequisite to pronouncing syllables is, of course, some basic knowledge of consonant and vowel sounds and some ability to blend those sounds.

Students need to be reminded that every syllable has one vowel sound; that even though it may have more than one vowel (e.g., *boat*) it will not have more than one vowel sound; a second vowel sound would mean a second syllable. They may also need to review open and closed syllables. An open syllable has one vowel in a final position, e.g., *glo*, and can have long, short or schwa sound (*uh*, ə,) in an unaccented syllable. A closed syllable has a single vowel between two consonants, e.g., *bag, beg, big, bog, bug*, the vowel having the short sound. (The long sound is the same as the name of the letter—e.g., the *i* in *ice*).

Three important syllabication patterns or generalizations will help students unlock many terms. These are: (1) VCV (vowel-consonant-vowel); (2) VCCV (vowel-consonant-consonant-vowel); and (3) -le (consonant plus *le* at the end of a word).

1. *VCV.* When two vowel graphemes are separated by one consonant, the consonant may go with either vowel. It is necessary to try it both ways to determine which sounds right or makes sense. Look at the following words and divide accordingly:
   tiger   lemon   frigid   spider
2. *VCCV.* When two vowel graphemes are separated by two consonants, the division is made between the two consonants. For example, with *subject*, divide between the *b* and the *j*. Do the same for *silver, mascot, dinner.*
3. *-le.* When a word ends in a consonant plus *le* (e.g., maple), divide before the consonant, *ma-ple*. Other examples include *table, obstacle.*

Table 6.5

Marking Accents

Accent on First Syllable (except prefixes)	Beginning Syllable Unaccented	Unaccented Syllable Endings	Shift of Accent Changes Meanings
1. sec' re tary	1. a bout'	1. por' tion	1. pre sent'/ pres'ent
2. . . .	2. . . .	2. . . .	2. . . .
3. . . .	3. . . .	3. . . .	3. . . .

Accent
Generalizations

An aid to pronouncing and recognizing multisyllabic words is the use of accent clues. If you accent the wrong "sy*lah*bul," you might not recognize the term as one you already know. Walter Barbe suggests five clues:

1. The first syllable is usually accented unless it is a prefix (e.g., vólume).
2. The beginning syllables of *de, be, re, in,* and *a* are usually unaccented (e.g., de/sir'/able).
3. Endings that form syllables are usually unaccented (e.g., rún/ing).
4. The shift in placing the accent changes the meaning of some words (e.g., con'/tent or con/tent').
5. At other times, try all the syllables with an equal accent.[21]

An activity that will help students is to give them a list of representative words and have them fill in for each under its appropriate heading and mark the accents (see table 6.5).

The Dictionary: A
Multipurpose Tool

How many uses can you think of for a dictionary? Brainstorming with others, you should be able to come up with a multitude of responses beyond the three obvious ones of meaning, pronunciation, and spelling.

The dictionary has been described as being more an abridged encyclopedia or history book than a law book. It is certainly an important but often misused tool. Acquiring meanings of new words strictly from the dictionary rather than from the context in which they appear is a rote memorization exercise not likely to remain in our long-term memory.

The plethora of definitions for each word may also serve to confuse rather than clarify. It is a misuse to select the first definition, as some students automatically do. Synonyms are not much help to a student when neither word is known, such as the example of "to disparage is to denigrate."

A dictionary is an important tool for vocabulary development, which, unfortunately, many students never master. When uncertain as to your students' skill in this area, it is a simple matter to administer a very brief diagnostic "pretest." The results may surprise you. With a word such as *pentathlon,* examples of pretest questions follow:

1. Look up the word _____ . What are the guide words on that page? (Students may not know what a guide word is.)
2. What does _____ mean? (Students may only give you the first definition.)
3. Where would you find the pronunciation for _____ ?
4. What is a synonym for _____ ?
5. What is an antonym for _____ ?
6. What is the derivation of the word _____ ?
7. What part of speech is the word _____ ?
8. How is _____ spelled phonetically?
9. How many syllables are in the word _____ ?
10. Which syllable in the word _____ receives the primary accent?

The following skills are prerequisites for making efficient use of a dictionary.

1. Knowledge of alphabetical order beyond the first letter of a word.
2. Ability to use the guide words for speedier locating.
3. Ability to locate root words, variants, and derivatives.
4. Ability to interpret accent marks.
5. Ability to use the pronunciation key and interpret phonetic spellings.

Because there is likely to be a very broad range in reading achievement in any one content classroom, it is helpful to have some dictionaries at a variety of levels. Examples of simplified dictionaries follow. Look for the most recent copyright date. Examples of dictionaries available include the following annotated list, not in order of importance.

Marion Sadler, Ed. *Reference Books for Young Readers: Authoritative Evaluations of Encyclopedias, Atlases and Dictionaries.* Bowker Buying Guide Series, R. R. Bowker, New York, 1988.

Grades 3–6	*The American Heritage Children's Dictionary,* Houghton Mifflin, 1986. Solid information in an attractive format that encourages browsing. Will facilitate language acquisition.
Grades 7–10	*The American Heritage Student's Dictionary,* 1986. A well-crafted dictionary, designed to help students understand the more advanced dictionary.

Grades 5–7	*MacMillan School Dictionary,* 1987. Comprehensive for its size and scope, along with conventional definitions it gives 37,000 examples in context, with sentences illustrating how the word is used.
Grades 5–9	*Simon and Schuster's Illustrated Young Reader's Dictionary,* 1984. A convenient handbook for those who wish to know more about words. Heavily emphasizes words related to social and natural sciences. Most appropriate for younger middle school students, younger, gifted or older, slower students.
Grades 3–5, Adults ESL, Adolescent Developmental Readers	*Scott Foresman Beginning Dictionary,* 1988. Part of a series which includes intermediate and advanced. The intent here is to capitalize on children enjoying learning about words and using them in writing and conversation.
Grades 5–8	*Scott Foresman Intermediate Dictionary,* 1988. Comprehensive in terms of textbook language and vocabulary. Students will meet with special features geared to many content areas. The format encourages browsing.
Intermediate and Advanced ESL Students	*Longman Dictionary of American English,* 1983. Designed for use by ESL students with full literacy and comprehension skills. It moves them away from using bilingual dictionaries; shows connotative values, and shows word expression and usage in English.

Dictionary versus Thesaurus

Another handy tool, particularly in the English classroom, is a thesaurus. Whereas a dictionary goes from words to meaning, a thesaurus takes the meanings and gives many words to fit the meaning. A thesaurus is a list of words that are classified according to meaning (see the sample in figure 6.3).[22]

Sight Vocabulary

Those words that a reader recognizes instantaneously without resorting to word recognition techniques are considered to be *sight words.* During early elementary years, much emphasis is placed on instant recognition of such words as *how, when, if, come,* and *go.* For older students in content areas,

---

704. DIFFICULTY.—*N.* difficulty, hardness, impracticability, uphill work, herculean task; dead weight, dead lift.

dilemma, predicament, fix [*colloq.*], quandary, embarrassment, deadlock, perplexity, intricacy, entanglement, knot, Gordian knot, maze, coil, strait, pass, pinch, rub. critical situation, exigency, crisis, trial, emergency, scrape, slough, quagmire, hot water [*colloq.*], pickle, stew, imbroglio, mess, muddle, botch, hitch, stumbling block.

vexed question, poser, puzzle, knotty point, paradox; hard nut to crack, crux.

V. be difficult, go against the grain, try one's patience, go hard with one, pose, perplex, bother, nonplus.

flounder, boggle [*local*], struggle, stick fast; come to a deadlock.

render difficult, enmesh, encumber, embarrass, entangle; spike one's guns.

Adj. difficult, hard, tough [*colloq.*]; troublesome, toilsome, irksome; laborious, onerous, arduous, herculean, formidable.

awkward, unwieldy, unmanageable, intractable, stubborn, perverse, refractory, knotted, knotty, thorny; pathless, trackless, intricate.

embarrassing, perplexing, delicate, ticklish, critical, thorny.

in difficulty, in hot water [*colloq.*], in a fix [*colloq.*], in a scrape, between Scylla and Charybdis; on the horns of a dilemma; on the rocks; reduced to straits; hard-pressed; run hard; pinched, straitened; hard up [*slang*]; puzzled, at a loss, at one's wits' end, at a standstill; nonplused, stranded, aground.

Adv. with much ado; uphill, upstream; in the teeth of; against the grain.

the focus turns to the technical vocabulary important to a particular field, with words such as *photosynthesis* or *impressionism*. For those working with older disabled readers, Jerry L. Johns developed a list of basic sight words.[23]

Dorothy Piercey has created a useful strategy for building word meanings and concepts.[24] Students' success in using this strategy is attributed to three major factors.

Improving Vocabulary through Teaching Strategies

A 'Talk-Through'

1. "Talk-Through" is based on the psychological principle of paired association or connection of new ideas to old.
2. Emphasis is more on student response than teacher talk. The teacher questions the class in an attempt to have them discover meaning (inductive) rather than telling them outright (deductive).
3. "Talk-Through" builds on strengths rather than weaknesses by relating new vocabulary to familiar concepts.

Piercey's example of this strategy is with the term *importation* in social studies. (See her first chapter in *Reading Activities in Content Areas* for use with other content areas.) Steps in this strategy are:

1. Write the word to be discussed in context so that students will see it as well as hear it and will be able to use context clues to get at meaning. "Importation of sugar stopped when Castro took control of the government."
2. The teacher begins asking questions such as "Who has a camera?" "Where was it made?" (You hope someone will say Japan, Germany, etc.) "Who has been to the Imports Limited Shop?" "What is found there?" "What is alike about all these products we've talked about?" (They were made in foreign countries and brought into the United States to sell.)
3. The teacher now writes the word *importation* on the board and then erases *im* and *ation*. To *port* is added *are* or *portare*. The teacher states that this means 'to carry' and that is what their answers implied.
4. Next they are asked what other words have the root *port* (*porter* carries bags, *portable* television, etc.).
5. The students apply this to the original word *importation* for closure.

Word-for-the-Day

Write one significant content word on the board before class and circle it. As students come in and while roll is taken, they can try to decode it and think of all possible meanings. In a sophomore English class with low achieving readers, the word one day was *ambiguous*. No one knew what it meant, then context clues were given and someone asked, "Does it mean 'not clear'?" After discussing the definition and with a sentence as an example, the students' assignment with that word was to use it three times before the next class, both in writing and orally. The next day when the word was reviewed, a student reported that it was a dangerous word. He had told his science teacher that his lecture was ambiguous and incurred the teacher's wrath. Needless to say, the student never forgot that word!

Student Selected Key Words

In a subject such as science or social studies, as a review at the end of the course, ask students to decide the key words to remember. Have them list these first individually, then meet in small groups to compare. Finally each group reports to the total class. Teachers should have their lists ready, too, so that the similarities and differences can be discussed. The important thing to remember is not simply the word itself, but the reason why the students felt it was one to remember. This can be an excellent synthesis activity, because decisions must be made about what is important and why.

Frank Green developed an interesting offshoot to the cloze procedure (where every 7th word is deleted and the exact word must be found to fill in the blank).[25]

OPIN Technique

OPIN, standing for opinion or open vs. closed, combines readers' prior knowledge with textual context clues. OPIN is concerned with *why* we choose a certain word as the best word for that particular context. The only requirement is a rational defense of your choice.

The four steps include:

1. Individually read over the mutilated text to fill in the best word you can think of for each blank.
2. In triads discuss and evaluate each person's inserted word, trying to convince others that your word is best and always using reasons for the choice. If the rest convince the others their word is best, that word is adopted with no loss of face.
3. Each triad meets with another triad to discuss and try to convince the others that its group's word is best.
4. The teacher then asks each group of six to share results with the rest of the class.

The only caution is that this can become quite noisy as students become actively involved in defending their own words.

1. Fill one word in the blank space.
2. Have a reason for your answer.
3. You may change your answer as often as you wish, but you must know why.

Sample OPIN Exercises

Sample #1 (unrelated sentences)
1. Primitive people used musical instruments, not to make music, but to _____ away evil spirits.
2. Sarah is _____ a fine musician, but long years of study lie ahead of her before her skill can be perfected.
3. Anyone living near bodies of water can _____ in fishing, which is one of man's oldest pastimes.

Sample #2 (paragraph) Few animals are more disliked than spiders. Nevertheless, these _____ creatures catch billions of insects that destroy crops. In fact, many scientists believe it would be difficult to _____ insects if there were no spiders.

This is an excellent way to introduce technical terms and concepts, because cognitive maps show key relationships among concepts and words that serve as labels for these concepts. To diagram the map, first the concepts and key

Cognitive Maps

vocabulary are listed. The second step, and the most difficult, is to organize these into a structure that shows their relationships. The cognitive maps developed for this text are examples of a type of advance organizer. Another type is a study guide for students to follow as they read the chapter. These will be discussed more thoroughly in part III.

"Search-Insert-Verify"

To connect past events to the present, use a search-insert-and-verify technique.[26]

> A notable example of obscurantism and its resulting inability to see the interdependence of peoples was shown in the complaints of numerous people during the United States sea-and-air lift of hundreds of thousands of Vietnamese who were subsequently brought to this country. Some people were so compassionless that all they could say was, 'Why did they bring them here? There are not enough jobs to go around the way it is.' That one of the great rescue operations of all times elicited such prosaic and heartless responses is dumbfounding![27]

1. Underline words that could have synonyms.
2. Write one or two synonyms for each, using the dictionary or thesaurus.
3. Discuss the connotations that retain original meaning.
4. Rewrite, giving divergent meanings.

Content "Kwicky Kwiz"

To discover those students who will have difficulty reading your text because they lack proficiency in sight vocabulary, go through your text and select twenty to thirty key terms. List these terms in columns and individually ask a student to merely pronounce them for you, not asking for meanings. They should pronounce one word every two seconds without any hesitations. Examples of terms:

Vocational Education: electronic   synchronize
   fluctuate   mechanize
Social studies: monarchy   diplomacy   constitution   ceremonies
Literature: direful   compassionate   demeanor   concede
Science: translucent   radioactive   homogeneous   accelerated
Math: equidistant   diagonal   perpendicular   congruent

Synonym Clustering

Because we want students to understand key words or concepts with all their shades of meaning, one way to classify a term is to have the students do synonym clustering using a dictionary and a thesaurus. This activity can be done in pairs, as well as singly.

Figure 6.4

Synonym clustering, a way to increase vocabulary and get more in-depth shades of meaning.

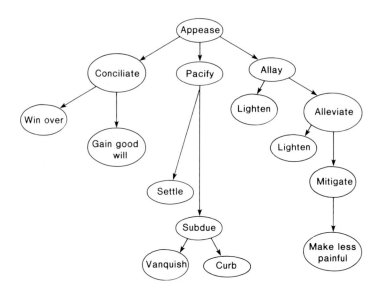

As shown in figure 6.4, the word *appease* was considered important to a social studies class. When looking up *appease* in the dictionary, three synonyms were found, *conciliate, pacify,* and *allay.* As often happens to students, none of these synonyms may help to clarify meaning. So, having duly written these down on the diagram, each is looked up in turn, and the synonyms are noted. One social studies teacher was shaken to discover that, although he had always taught that *appease* had a negative connotation, there are positive aspects to the meaning, as can be seen, for example, under the term *allay.*

With just this one term, *appease,* students might add six new terms to their vocabulary, and they would have the added benefit of being able to picture them all within a larger category.

Or a teacher might take a concept such as *truth.* Three synonyms found in one dictionary are *verisimilitude, verity,* and *veracity.* From *veracity* we get 'factual accuracy and honesty.' From *verity* we get 'enduring and repeatedly demonstrated.' If you continued with *verisimilitude,* you would then have a better "handle" on this complex term.

This exercise is most useful for words with several synonyms listed in the dictionary, not those with only lengthy definitions. Students should make their own clusters and share their findings. It might be taken one step further using antonyms. Synonym clustering can be used also as a creative writing technique starting with a word such as *intrepid* and having students rapidly free associate (five minutes) and then select one cluster as a basis for writing. Again, give them only five to ten minutes to write before voluntarily sharing.

Boners

Substitute the correct word for the following, and be prepared to enjoy these slips.

1. He is not *legible* for the service.
2. He suffers from *allusions* of grandeur.
3. My tire was *punctuated*.
4. My sister has *romantic* fever.
5. He suffers from *indolent* fever.
6. *Respectively* yours.
7. He stepped on the *exhilarator*.
8. We are studying *jubilant* delinquency.

"Innocent Words":
A Social Studies
Activity

Jan Forsman has developed an activity for use in a social studies classroom.

Forsman's Innocent Words

B.S. (Behavioral Stimuli)

1. Before reading the following, the student will use the terms in a given sentence with one hundred percent accuracy.

infamous	high
quartered	redress
inferior	magazines
vested	respecting
domestic	enjoy

2. After reading, the student will define these words as they appeared in context.

1. We the People of the United States, in Order to form a more perfect Union, establish Justice, insure *domestic* Tranquility, provide for the common defence, promote the general Welfare, . . .
2. All legislative Powers herein granted shall be *vested* in a Congress of the United States, which shall consist of a Senate and House of Representatives.
3. The judicial Power of the United States, shall be *vested* in one supreme Court, and in such *inferior* Courts as the Congress may from time to time establish.
4. No Soldier shall, in time of peace be *quartered* [set apart] in any house, without the consent of the Owner, nor in time of war, but in a manner to be prescribed by law.
5. No person shall be held to answer for a capital, or otherwise *infamous* [notorious] crime, unless on a presentment or indictment of a Grand Jury.
6. In all criminal prosecutions the accused shall *enjoy* [to have use of or profit by] the right to a speedy and public trial, by an impartial jury of the State, and district wherein the crime shall have been committed.

7. Congress shall have Power . . . to exercise exclusive legislation in all Cases whatsoever, and to exercise like Authority over all Places purchased by the Consent of the Legislature of the State in which the Same shall be for the Erection of Forts, *magazines* [rifle parts] [Arabis = storehouse—store, stories], arsenals, dock-yards, and other needful Buildings.]

8. Congress shall make no law *respecting* [relating to] an establishment of religion, or prohibiting the free exercise thereof; or abridging the freedom of speech, or of the press; or the right of the people peaceably to assemble, and to petition the Government for a *redress* [reform] of *grievances* [troubles, problems—government has to adjust].

9. The President, Vice-President and all Civic Officers of the United States, shall be removed from Office on Impeachment for, and Conviction of, Treason, Bribery, or other *high* [anything Congress and House of Representatives say it is—Nixon] Crimes and Misdemeanors.

10. The Senate shall *choose* their other Officers, also a President pro tempore in the Absence of the Vice-President, or when he shall *exercise* the Office of President of the United States.[28]

Figure 6.5 is an example of a worksheet that can be used to keep track of new words in any content class. You may either repeat the information on sheets of paper, or it may be printed on the back side of cards. The front side is left blank for the word alone.

Vocabulary Worksheet

The art of obfuscation, gobbledy gook, doubletalk, jargon, euphemisms, circumlocutions—anything goes, "verbalizationwise." *Newsweek* magazine reported on an ingenious way to win at wordmanship.[29] Phillip Broughton, a U.S. Health Service official, had developed a "systematic buzz phrase projector," using a lexicon of thirty carefully selected buzzwords. Call out any combination of the numbers one to three, such as 201. You now have the impressive phrase, "systemized management flexibility."

Winning at Wordmanship

I. (adjective)	II. (adjective)	III. (nouns)
0 integrated	management	options
1 total	organizational	flexibility
2 systematized	monitored	capability

This idea could be adapted to any content field. For example:

Math

0 bimodal	congruent	percent
1 antisymmetric	interaxial	factor

Science

0 biaxial	hypodermic	progenitor
1 ultrasonic	bivalent	spectrum

Figure 6.5
Vocabulary worksheets—all content areas (or use 3-by-5 inch cards).

Word _____ Date _____ Sketch _____

Context _____ _____

_____ _____

Origin _____ Pronunciation _____

Meanings _____

_____

_____

Synonym _____ Illustration _____

Word _____ Date _____ Sketch _____

Context _____ _____

_____ _____

Origin _____ Pronunciation _____

Meanings _____

_____

_____

Synonym _____ Illustration _____

Word _____ Date _____ Sketch _____

Context _____ _____

_____ _____

Origin _____ Pronunciation _____

Meanings _____

_____

_____

Synonym _____ Illustration _____

Skills

First, students assist in compiling the master list. Then a three-digit number is given, such as 101. In science that would be an 'ultrasonic hypodermic spectrum.' An individual student or team must decide what the phrase entails. In some cases they might be asked to illustrate it.

Cover up the right-hand column. The following "nouns of multitude" or "company terms" or "nouns of assemblage" in the left-hand column can be used as incentives for students to sharpen their vocabulary. Try asking a group if they can tell you the name for the following. How many do you know?

"A Parliament of Owls"[30]

What is a Group of?	Collective Noun	What is a Group of?	Collective Noun
1. geese	gaggle	11. walrus	pod
2. leopards	leap	12. seals	trip
3. fish	school	13. wolves	pack
4. crows	murder	14. turtles	glag
5. cats	clowder	15. gorillas	troop
6. lions	pride	16. larks	exaltation
7. donkeys	pace	17. owls	parliament
8. insects	swarm	18. nightingales	watch
9. bears	crowd/sloth	19. bananas	hand
10. beavers	colony	20. bicycles	wobble

Workshop Activity 6.3
"Words Can Make You Rich!"

An exercise used with high school and college students for a number of years with interesting reactions is included here as an additional pre-self-assessment possibility. The tongue-in-cheek idea is that you may determine your salary level based on your age and the number of words you can identify correctly. The terms come from a wide field.

1. Did you see the *clergy*? /funeral/dolphin/churchmen/monastery/bell tower/
2. Fine *louvers*. /doors/radiators/slatted vents/mouldings/bay windows/
3. Like an *ellipse*. /sunspot/oval/satellite/triangle/volume/
4. *Dire* thoughts. /angry/dreadful/blissful/ugly/unclean/
5. It was the *affluence*. /flow rate/pull/wealth/flood/bankruptcy/
6. Discussing the *acme*. /intersection/question/birthmark/perfection/low point/
7. How *odious*. /burdensome/lazy/hateful/attractive/fragrant/
8. This is *finite*. /limited/tiny/precise/endless/difficult/

9. Watch for the *inflection.* /accent/mirror image/swelling/pendulum swing/ violation/
10. The *connubial* state. /marriage/tribal/festive/spinsterly/primitive/
11. See the *nuance.* /contrast/upstart/renewal/delinquent/shading/
12. Where is the *dryad?* /water sprite/fern/dish towel/chord/wood nymph/
13. Will you *garner* it? /dispose of/store/polish/thresh/trim/
14. A sort of *anchorite.* /religious service/hermit/marine deposit/mineral/promoter/
15. *Knurled* edges. /twisted/weather beaten/flattened/ridged/knitted/
16. Is it *bifurcated?* /forked/hairy/two-wheeled/mildewed/joined/
17. Examining the *phthisis.* /cell division/medicine/misstatement/dissertation/ tuberculosis/
18. *Preponderance* of the group. /majority/heaviness/small number/foresight/
19. Ready to *expound.* /pop/confuse/interpret/dig up/imprison/
20. Staring at the *relict.* /trustee/antique table/corpse/widow/excavation/

Now, based on your raw score, find your salary level. (Answers are found at the end of the chapter)

Number Correct

Age 13–16		Age 17–20	
20–12	$50,000 and up	20–15	$50,000 and up
11–10	42,000–$49,999	14–13	42,000–$49,999
9–8	38,000– 41,999	12–11	38,000– 41,999
7–6	35,000– 37,999	10–9	35,000– 37,999
5–4	30,000– 34,999	8–7	30,000– 34,999
3–2	25,000– 29,999	6–3	25,000– 29,999
Below 2	Under 25,000	Below 3	Under 25,000

Age 21–29		Age 30 and up	
20–17	$50,000 and up	20–19	$45,500 and up
16–15	42,000–$49,999	18–17	42,000–$45,499
14–13	38,000– 41,999	16–15	38,000– 41,999
12–11	35,000– 37,999	14–13	35,000– 37,999
10–5	30,000– 34,999	12–11	30,000– 34,999
Below 5	Under 30,000	10–7	25,000– 29,999
		Below 7	Under 25,000

Summary

Vocabulary study is a study of language and concepts and is integral to any content area. All teachers need a variety of strategies to help students build and master their specific technical terminology, eliminating any possible stumbling blocks. Although everyone benefits from a better understanding of language, its facets and enrichment, English teachers especially should take careful note of this area. All content teachers will be able to help students better master their content text when direct teaching of words takes place in the classroom in a variety of ways that motivate students to continue building their vocabulary. A reminder of the four ways to attack a new word may help those students who give up after trying one way only.

A parting question—has your attitude changed about word power since reading this chapter? If so, please discuss why and how with your small group or class.

Answers to Workshop Activity 6.1

Test 1
1. short   2. south   3. sad   4. same, similar   5. safe   6. small
7. smart, sharp, sparkling   8. silent, still   9. stand   10. send
Test 2
1. selfish, stingy   2. sensible, significant   3. skeptical, suspicious
4. simple   5. sure   6. slipshod, slovenly, sloppy   7. sleep, sleepiness, slumber, somnolence   8. smooth   9. subjective   10. sob, scowl

Answers to Workshop Activity 6.3

1. churchmen	6. perfection	11. shading	16. forked
2. slatted vents	7. hateful	12. wood nymph	17. tuberculosis
3. oval	8. limited	13. store	18. majority
4. dreadful	9. accent	14. hermit	19. interpret
5. wealth	10. marriage	15. ridged	20. widow

References

1. Wilfred Funk and Norman Lewis, *Thirty Days to a More Powerful Vocabulary* (New York: Pocket Books, 1975), pp. 7–9.
2. Larry Hafner, *Developmental Reading in Middle and Secondary Schools: Foundation Strategies and Skills for Teaching* (New York: Macmillan, 1977), p. 95.
3. Kenneth S. Goodman and Olive Niles, *Reading: Process and Program* (Urbana, Ill.: National Council of Teachers of English, 1970), p. 25.
4. Carl B. Smith, *Teaching Reading in Secondary School Content Subjects* (New York: Holt, Rinehart & Winston, 1978), p. 187.
5. Edgar Dale, "Vocabulary Development and Reading Instruction," in *Reading in Modern Communication,* vol. I, ed. Bruce Brigham and Marjorie Seddon Johnson (Philadelphia: Proceedings of the Annual Reading Institute, Temple University, 1962), pp. 27–28.
6. Arnold Burron and Amos L. Claybaugh, *Reading in Subject Matter Areas: A Programmed Approach* (Columbus, Ohio: Charles E. Merrill, 1974), pp. 13–14.
7. Edgar Dale, "Vocabulary Measurement: Techniques and Major Findings," *Elementary School Journal* (December 1965): 895–901, 948.
8. M. K. Smith, "Measurement of the Size of the Central English Vocabulary through the Elementary Grades and High School," *General Psychology Monographs* 24 (1941): 313–345.

9. Henry Kucera and W. Nelson Francis, *Computational Analysis of Present-Day American English* (Providence, R.I.: Brown University Press, 1967).

10. Funk and Lewis, *Vocabulary,* p. 219.

11. Mario Pei, *The Story of Language,* rev. ed. (New York: Mentor Books, New American Library, 1965), p. 125.

12. Ibid., p. 29.

13. *Funk and Wagnalls New Standard Dictionary of the English Language* (New York: Funk & Wagnalls Co., 1958), p. 21.

14. W. J. Funk, *Word Origins and Their Romantic Stories* (New York: Funk & Wagnalls Co., 1968).

15. Edgar Dale and Joseph O'Rourke, *Techniques of Teaching Vocabulary* (Palo Alto, Cal.: Field Educational Publications, 1971), p. 292.

16. *Funk and Wagnalls New Standard Dictionary,* p. 119.

17. Anthony Manzo and J. K. Sherk, "Some Generalizations and Strategies for Guiding Vocabulary Learning," *The Journal of Reading Behavior* 4 (1971–1972): 81–82.

18. Harry Forgan and Charles Mangrum II, *Teaching Content Area Reading Skills* (Columbus, Ohio: Charles E. Merrill, 1981), pp. 136–141.

19. Smith, C., *Teaching Reading,* p. 211.

20. Robert E. Mills, "An Evaluation of Techniques for Teaching Word Recognition," *Elementary School Journal* 56 (1956): 221–225.

21. Walter Barbe et al., *Reading Skills Check List and Activities: Advanced Level* (New York: The Center for Applied Research in Education, 1976).

22. C. O. Sylvester Mawson, ed., *Roget's Pocket Thesaurus* (New York: Pocket Books, Inc., 1962), p. 205.

23. Jerry L. Johns, "A Supplement to the Dolch Word Lists," *Reading Improvement* 7 (Winter 1971–1972): 91.

24. Dorothy Piercey, *Reading Activities in Content Areas* (Boston: Allyn & Bacon, 1976).

25. Frank Green, Unpublished presentation given at Western Washington University, Bellingham, Wash., April, 1978.

26. Lawrence Hafner, *Developmental Reading in Middle and Secondary Schools* (New York: Macmillan, 1977), p. 114.

27. Ibid., p. 197.

28. Jan Forsman, unpublished activity, Western Washington University, Bellingham, 1978.

29. Phillip Broughton, "Anything Goes, Verbalizationwise," *Newsweek,* 6 May 1968.

30. James Lipton, *An Exaltation of Larks* (Westford, Mass.: Penguin Books, 1977).

Recommended Readings

Asimov, Isaac. *Words from History.* Boston: Houghton Mifflin Co., 1968.

———. *Words from Myths.* Boston: Houghton Mifflin Co., 1961.

———. *Words of Science and the History Behind Them.* Boston: Houghton Mifflin, 1959.

———. *More Words of Science.* Boston: Houghton Mifflin, 1972.

———. *Words on the Map.* Boston: Houghton Mifflin, 1962.

Bernstein, Theodore. *The Reverse Dictionary.* New York: Quadrangle/New York Times, 1976.

Bierce, Ambrose. *The Devil's Dictionary.* Owing Mills, Md.: Stemmer House, 1978.

Boatner, Maxine T., and Gates, John E. *A Dictionary of American Idioms.* Rev. ed. Edited by Adam Makkai. Woodbury, N.Y.: Barron's Educational Services, Inc., 1975.

Brandreth, Gyles. *The Joy of Lex: How to Have Fun with Words.* New York: William Morrow and Company, Inc., 1980.

Burmeister, Lou E. *Words—From Print to Meaning: Classroom Activities for Building Sight Vocabulary, for Using Context Clues, Morphology and Phonics.* Reading, Mass.: Addison Wesley, 1975.

Carroll, J. B. et al. *American Heritage Word Frequency Book.* Boston: Houghton Mifflin, 1971.

Casale, Ula Price. "Motor Imaging: A Reading-Vocabulary Strategy." *Journal of Reading* 28 (April 1985): 619–621.

Chase, Ann C. and Duffelmeyer, Frederick A. "VOCAB-LIT: Integrating Vocabulary Study and Literature Study." *Journal of Reading* 34 (November 1990): 188–193.

Coley, Joan, and Ganbrell, Linda. *Programmed Reading Vocabulary for Teachers.* Columbus, Ohio: Charles E. Merrill, 1977.

Dale, Edgar, and O'Rourke, Joseph O. *Techniques of Teaching Vocabulary.* Palo Alto, Calif.: Field Educational Publications, 1971.

De Bono, Edward. *Wordpower, An Illustrated Dictionary of Vital Words.* New York: Harper Colophon Books, 1977.

Demetrulias, Diana A. Mayer. "Gags, Giggles, Guffaws: Using Cartoons in the Classroom." *Journal of Reading* 26 (October 1982): 66–68.

Dupuis, Mary M., and Snyder, Sandra L. "Develop Concepts through Vocabulary: A Strategy for Reading Specialists to Use with Content Teachers." *Journal of Reading* 26 (January 1983): 297–305.

Eeds, Maryann, and Cockrum, Ward A. "Teaching Word Meanings by Expanding Schemata vs. Dictionary Work vs. Reading in Context. *Journal of Reading* 28 (March 1985): 492–497.

Espy, Willard R. *An Almanac of Words at Play.* New York: Clarkson N. Potter, Inc., 1975.

———. *O Thou Improper, Thou Uncommon Noun: An Etymology of Words That Once Were Names.* New York: Clarkson N. Potter, Inc., 1978.

Frager, Alan M. "An Intelligence Approach to Vocabulary Teaching." *Journal of Reading* 28 (November 1984): 160–164.

Funk, Charles E. *A Hog on Ice.* New York: Warner Publishing Co., 1948. Reprinted 1985.

Funk, Charles E., and Funk, C. E., Jr. *Horsefeathers.* New York: Harper Paperback Library, 1972.

Funk, W. *Word Origins and Their Romantic Stories.* New York: Funk and Wagnalls, 1968.

Garbe, Douglas G. "Mathematics Vocabulary and the Culturally Different Student." *Arithmetic Teacher* 33 (October 1985): 39–42.

Green, Jonathon. *The Dictionary of Contemporary Slang.* London: Pan Books, Inc., 1984.

Greene, Amsel, *Word Clues.* New York: Harper and Row, 1980.

Hague, Sally A. "Vocabulary Instruction: What L2 Can Learn from L1." *Foreign Language* 20 Annals (May 1987): 217–225.

Johnson, Dale D., and Pearson, P. David. *Teaching Reading Vocabulary.* 2d ed. New York: Holt, Rinehart and Winston, 1984.

Konopak, Bonnie C. "Using Contextual Information for Word Learning." *Journal of Reading* 31 (January 1988): 334–338.

―――. "Effects of Inconsiderate vs. Considerate Text on Secondary Students' Vocabulary Learning." *Journal of Reading Behavior* 20 (November 1988): 25–41.

Kossack, Sharon. "A Proposed Taxonomy of Mathematical Vocabulary." In *Reading Research to Reading Practice: Third Yearbook of the American Reading Forum,* George McNinch, ed., 1983, pp. 60–63.

Lehr, Fran. "Promoting Vocabulary Development." *Journal of Reading* 27 (April 1984): 656–658.

Lewis, Norman. *Word Power Made Easy.* New York: Pocket Books, Inc., 1949.

Lipton, James. *An Exaltation of Larks, or The Venereal Game.* Westford, Mass.: Penguin Books, 1977.

Makkai, Adam, ed. *A Dictionary of American Idioms.* Rev. ed. Woodbury, N.Y.: Barron's Educational Series, Inc., 1975.

Marks, William, and Marks, Mary. *Dictionary of Word and Phrase Origins.* New York: Harper and Row, vol. 1, 1962; vol. 2, 1967; vol. 3, 1971.

Nagy, William E.; Anderson, Richard C.; and Herman, Patricia A. "Learning Word Meanings from Context During Normal Reading." *American Educational Research Journal* 24 (Summer 1987): 334–338.

Nurnberg, Maxwell, and Roseblum, Morris. *How to Build a Better Vocabulary.* New York: Popular Library, 1961.

―――. *All about Words: An Adult Approach to Vocabulary Building.* New York: Mentor Books, 1966.

O'Connor, Johnson. *English Vocabulary Builder.* Vols. I and II. Boston: Human Engineering Lab, 1951.

O'Neill, Mary. *Words Words Words.* New York: Doubleday and Co., 1966.

Pei, Mario. *The Story of Language.* Rev. ed. New York: Mentor Books, 1965.

Pei, Mario, and Romodicio, Salvatore. *Dictionary of Foreign Terms.* New York: Dell, Laurel Edition, 1974.

Piercey, Dorothy. *Reading Activities in Content Areas.* Boston: Allyn & Bacon, 1976.

The Random House Thesaurus: College Edition. New York: Random House, 1984.

Rinsky, Lee Ann. *Teaching Word Attack Skills.* Dubuque, Iowa: Gorsuch Scarisbrick Publishers, 1988.

Roget's Pocket Thesaurus. Special Scholastic Book Services Edition. New York: Pocket Books, Inc., 1946

Ryder, Randall James. "Student Activated Vocabulary Instruction." *Journal of Reading* 29 (December, 1985): 254–259.

Saffire, William. *Saffire's Political Dictionary.* Rev. ed. New York: Random House, 1978.

Schwartz, Robert M. "Learning to Learn Vocabulary in Content Area Textbooks." *Journal of Reading* 32 (November 1988): 108–118.

Smith, Jack. *How to Win a Pullet Surprise: The Pleasures and Pitfalls of Our Language.* New York: Franklin Watts, 1982.

Smith, Robert W. L. *Dictionary of English Word-Roots*. Totowa, N.J.: Littlefield, Adams & Co., 1977.

Special Issue on Vocabulary—Journal of Reading 29 (April 1986). (This entire journal is devoted to articles that discuss theoretical concerns, recommend instructional guidelines, and present specific teaching strategies aimed at stated instructional goals.)

Sperling, Susan Kelz. *Poplollies and Bellibones: A Celebration of Lost Words*. New York: Clarkson N. Potter, Inc., 1977.

Stieglitz, Ezra L., and Stieglitz, V. S. "Savor the Word to Reinforce Vocabulary in the Content Areas." *Journal of Reading* 25 (1981): 46–51.

Thomas, Ellen Lamar, and Robinson, H. Alan. *Improving Reading in Every Class*. 2d ed. Boston: Allyn & Bacon, 1977.

Urdang, Lawrence. *The Basic Book of Synonyms and Antonyms*. New York: Signet Books, 1978.

Williams, Raymond. *Key Words: A Vocabulary of Culture and Society*. London: Oxford University Press, 1976.

Figure 7.1
Comprehending
written discourse—an
interactive process—a
cognitive map.

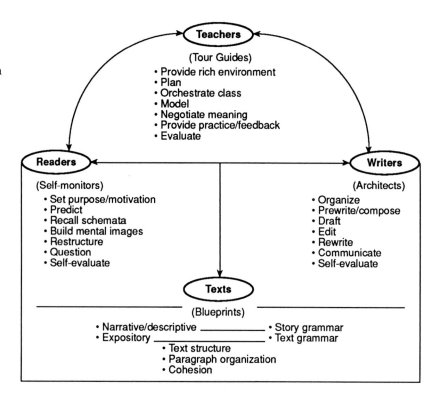

Comprehending Written Discourse: An Interactive Process

7

Anticipatory Questions

(Literal)

1. What are two significant conclusions from recent comprehension research?

(Literal)

2. Describe conditions necessary for comprehension to occur.

(Interpretive)

3. How are the processes of comprehending and writing alike? How different?

(Applied)

4. Give three concrete examples of cohesive ties in your content area. Discuss potential problems if the ties were omitted or were unclear.

(Creative)

5. Looking over subtitles in this chapter, how might you restructure this information? Defend your reasons for changes.

(Creative)

6. Using Shepherd's lists of comprehension difficulties and recommendation guides, decide which ones are most likely to occur in your content classroom and select two remedies for each, not necessarily from this text.

Technical Terminology and Concepts

cohesion/cohesive ties in writing

comprehending process/ comprehension product

knowledge of structure (schemata)

making inferences

metacognition for executive monitoring

modes of writing/ thinking

narrative/descriptive/ expository/ argumentative writing

reading/teacher/text interaction

text structure

your own term (in context): _____

Introduction

In this chapter we are attempting to give you, the reader, a theoretical framework of the complex notion of comprehending written discourse (extended writing). In reality, comprehension infiltrates most of this text in a variety of ways. Because of the complexity of this topic you may well wish to return to this chapter later after further reading. Chapter 10 will give you practical applications tied to this theory. Perhaps the best way for you to deal with this chapter initially is to do the workshops, glance over the questions and key terminology, study the cognitive map, survey or preview, and then read with the purpose of trying to maintain the "big picture." In that way it will serve as a foundation for later learning. This chapter also can be assigned in two parts.

Reading Comprehension

When we speak of reading we automatically assume that there is comprehending, because the act of reading implies that readers understand the message implicitly or explicitly stated in a text. The term *reading* as used in this text also refers to silent reading rather than oral, as it is often the case that when we read aloud we do not focus on meaning. Oral readers may well concentrate on voice pitch, intonation, or dramatic expression rather than the underlying, connected meaning necessary for comprehension to occur.

At one time meaning was thought to be found basically on the printed page in the text itself. Today, however, we look at the process of comprehending as being an interactive one. That is, we see meaning as residing in the readers themselves, who comprehend according to what they already know about the topic as they interact with the text. Their comprehension can be facilitated by teacher intervention when deemed necessary. For example, teachers might build background, clarify concepts, or set purposes. The text itself, the style in which it is written, its level of difficulty, or the way information is organized may also affect comprehension.

Thus in figure 7.1 we see comprehending as a four-pronged process of active readers who tie new information to what they already know, with the metaphors of teachers as tour guides of the terrain in print, and the text itself as a blueprint for meaning. Writers of text could then be considered to be architects. Content teachers who want their students to master knowledge, skills, and strategies in their subject will decide, then, that it is vital to be concerned with helping their students comprehend their text.

Preassessment Devices

In the next few pages you will find five workshop activities that have been included as preassessment devices. A selection may be made from among them by you or your instructor.

Workshop Activity 7.1
Questioning

Read the following excerpt and formulate two questions concerning it. Write each question on a separate slip of paper, initialing each one. Make a copy of each for your records. Place all the questions in a box, to be drawn at random for processing in small groups or with the entire class. These questions may then be used in a variety of ways.

1. Judge the best questions according to some stated criterion, such as "thought-provoking" or "open to a variety of interpretations."
2. Sequence the questions on the chalkboard according to levels, from literal to creative.
3. Hold the questions in abeyance for group processing after reading this chapter.

This way of handling questions may be applied to your content area.

The Relativity of Comprehension
by Frank Smith

Now at last I can say what I mean by 'comprehension'. Prediction is asking questions and comprehension is getting these questions answered. As we read, as we listen to the speaker, as we go through life, we are constantly asking questions, and as long as these questions are answered, as long as we are left with no residual uncertainty, we comprehend. We do not comprehend how to repair a radio if we cannot answer our own question, 'which of these wires goes where?' We do not comprehend speakers of a foreign language if we cannot answer questions like 'what are they trying to tell me?' And we do not comprehend a book or newspaper article if we cannot find answers to our own questions concerning information that we believe resides in the print.

You may observe that such a definition of comprehension is quite different from the way in which the word is used in school. Teachers often regard comprehension as the *result* of learning rather than the basis for making sense of anything. So-called comprehension tests are usually given after a book has been read, and as a consequence are more like tests of long-term memory.[1]

Workshop Activity 7.2
Levels of Comprehension Questions

Do not ponder labels at this point but respond quickly to the questions. After reading the chapter, return to this exercise and determine how you might respond differently. Be ready to discuss how you could apply this activity in your classroom. Were some levels more difficult to answer than others? Explain.

Levels	Before Reading	After Reading
Literal (Details)	1. What are two conditions necessary for comprehension to occur? a. _____ b. _____	
Interpretive/Applied (Anticipate outcomes and transfer information)	2a. How do you think this chapter will address the relationship between reading and writing? ____ 2b. How might you use information about various modes of writing in your classroom? _____	
Evaluative/Critical (Make value judgment)	3. As a content teacher how much time should be devoted in your classes for teaching reading comprehension skills and strategies? Defend your position stating your criteria for making this judgment. _____	
Creative/Personal	4. What are possible consequences for you as a teacher if you decide to devote more time to guiding comprehending and writing processes in your class? _____	

Workshop Activity 7.3
Language Facility and Comprehension Questions

How is your language facility? A number of years ago Kenneth Goodman developed a nonsense passage followed by typical textbook comprehension questions.[2] Read about the "Marlup poving his kump" and write your answers to the four questions. You may look back at the passage as necessary. We predict that most of you will get a score of at least 75 percent "comprehension" on material you know nothing about! What you do know is how to manipulate the language.

Reprinted from *The Psycholinguistic Nature of the Reading Process*, 1968, pp. 23–24, by Kenneth S. Goodman, editor. By permission of the Wayne State University Press.

A marlup was poving his kump. Parmily a narg horped some whev in his kump. "Why did vump horp whev in my frinkle kump?" the marlup juf'd the narg. "Er'm muvvily trungy," the narg grupped. "Er hashed vump norpled whev in your kump. Do vump pove your kump frinkle?"

1. What did the narg horp in the marlup's kump? _____

2. What did the marlup juf the narg? _____

3. Was the narg trungy? _____

4. How does the marlup pove his kump? _____

The first three questions cover lower-level, explicitly stated facts. The fourth is not directly stated and requires you to make an inference, so it probably took you more time to figure out. Allow yourself twenty-five points per correct response, which should be determined by small group consensus. You may want to discuss any strategies you used to make sense out of the nonsense. For example, did you try substituting real nouns or verbs for the nonsense ones? What does this exercise tell you about comprehension questions?

Workshop Activity 7.4
Importance of Background Knowledge: What Is the Topic?

These passages should be read carefully with an analytical mind. For each one you should be ready to tell what the topic is and be able to explain the sequence of events. Depending on your own background of experiences, one passage may be much more comprehensible than the other. How many times did you have to read each passage to get the answer?

Passage A

The procedure is actually quite simple. First you arrange things into different groups, depending on their makeup. Of course, one pile may be sufficient depending on how much there is to do. If you have to go somewhere else due to lack of facilities, that is the next step; otherwise you are pretty well set. It is important not to overdo things. It is better to do too few things at once than too many. This may not seem important, but complications can arise. A mistake can be expensive. At first the whole procedure will seem complicated. Soon, however, it will become just another fact of life. It is difficult to foresee any end to the necessity for this task in the immediate future, but then one never can tell.[3]

(The answers appear at the end of the chapter.)

Topic? _____

Sequence? _____

J. D. Bransford and M. K. Johnson, "Contextual Prerequisites for Understanding: Some Investigations of Comprehension and Recall," *Journal of Verbal Learning and Verbal Behavior*, 11: 717; 726, 1972. Used with permission.

Passage B

A newspaper is better than a magazine/ A seashore is a better place than the street/ At first it is better to run than to walk/ You may have to try several times. It takes some skill but it's easy to learn/ Even young children can enjoy it/ Once successful, complications are minimal/ Birds seldom get too close/ Rain, however, soaks in very fast/ Too many people doing the same thing can also cause problems/ One needs lots of room/ If there are no complications, it can be very peaceful/ A rock will serve as an anchor/ If things break loose from it, however, you will not get a second chance/[4]

Topic? _____

Sequence? _____

Workshop Activity 7.5
Classifying Terminology

This readiness activity may be completed first by you alone and then compared with your partner or small group for clarification, consensus, or recognition of confusion. Working out the categorizing may help you in seeing how parts fit together. The following alphabetized list contains some key terminology to be encountered in this chapter. Categorize these terms by some similar attribute, placing them in lists under appropriate labels: for example, *modes* might have under it *inventive, personal,* etc. After reading the chapter, meet again in your small group and revise categories as necessary. Be prepared to share pertinent insights with the total class. The number of separate categories will vary depending on the unifying reasons given. Some may find it easier to write each term on a separate small card and then simply manipulate the cards. Add any significant terms not included. This activity may also be carried out using the board. Having groups compare their final products on the board may show great diversity.

1. Background knowledge
2. Cohesion of cohesive ties
3. Comprehending process
4. Comprehension levels
5. Comprehension product
6. Descriptive writing
7. Discourse or extended writing
8. Expository or explanatory writing
9. Inferencing
10. Interactive model or process
11. Metacognition or metacognitive behaviors
12. Modes of discourse
13. Narrative writing
14. Patterns of organization
15. Personal mode
16. Projective mode
17. Reflective mode
18. Relational mode
19. Schemata or knowledge structures
20. Text structure
21. Types of paragraphs
22. Visual imagery while reading
23. Word calling in oral reading
24. Writing types

Those who are effective readers monitor their own comprehension by making decisions at all stages of their reading. They understand the processes needed for comprehending in order to reach a particular comprehension goal. Metacognitive readers not only monitor their own reading, but also regulate it when necessary and orchestrate needed strategies based on their specific goal or goals.[5]

For example, good readers may sail through a chapter, readily picking up major points and supporting arguments or may visualize a particular scene described in literature. When they stop to reflect, tie to background knowledge, decide what more is needed (i.e., what strategy), they are practicing metacognition. Good readers almost unconsciously take stock often and make wise decisions as to how best to proceed. They have alternatives, not just one way of approaching the task. Teachers can model this process so that poor readers can practice better approaches. This may be accomplished by reading aloud a portion of text and verbalizing thought processes as they occur, including those unclear aspects. For example, the teacher might say, "Hm-m, this term is rather familiar but perhaps I better verify its meaning in the glossary before going on." Or "I don't seem to be putting these facts together. I forgot to preview first by skimming over key points. That should help me get the big picture so that these facts can be categorized."

Poor readers, on the other hand, tend *not* to

1. form good hypotheses;
2. make predictions about meaning;
3. form mental images while reading;
4. use prior knowledge effectively;
5. monitor understanding as they read;
6. fix a difficulty when it occurs;
7. realize the variety of strategies they can try to use.

The process of **comprehending** refers to how—not what—we comprehend. It is what we actually do to get at needed meaning.

For example, some processes would include:

Comprehending

1. focusing attention on the topic;
2. connecting meanings to what we already know about the topic (our internal map or schema to which new meanings can be added);
3. deciding what strategies or skills will be called on (metacognition or executive monitoring);
4. making inferences (tying the new meanings to what we already know);
5. predicting what will come;
6. revising predictions when necessary;
7. evaluating the worth of the message.

Thus, comprehending is a complex interactive process that involves building a bridge between what is being read and what we already know in the real world; predicting, interpreting, relating ideas into some sort of organizational pattern; deciding what strategies or skills are needed for a given purpose; revising when necessary; and finally evaluating the worth of the message.

Readers move back and forth between concentrating on the message in the print and deciding on the processes needed to meet their purpose.

Comprehension

On the other hand, instead of a process, the term **comprehension** refers to facts, meanings, or knowledge gained from reading, regardless of how this was gained. Comprehension is the end product of what is understood, remembered, or used, whereas comprehending is the process of getting there. Dolores Durkin helped us to recognize this difference.[6] She showed clearly that by our questions we have been testing students' comprehension as a product of their reading, rather than directly teaching them the process of comprehending. For example, when teachers merely ask students to summarize or find the main idea or discuss the effect and cause, they are testing students' ability to do this. If, on the other hand, teachers spend time explaining or reminding students of how to summarize or how to locate the main idea, etc., they are teaching the comprehending process.

> Teacher A asks, "What is the sequence of events in this chapter?"
> Teacher B says, "Remember when we are trying to put events into their proper sequential order we must. . . . Now, what is the sequence here?"

Teacher A is of course testing. Teacher B is teaching because Teacher B is explaining or reminding how to do something before asking students for an answer.

Recent Research in Reading Comprehension

In recent years, research has made great strides in changing the focus of reading instruction from an overemphasis on decoding individual words (sometimes out of context) and the basic "learning how to read" skills, to looking more at the overall process of comprehending, where the act of reading has as its purposes reading to learn and enjoy. With this change in emphasis, content teachers can no longer say that they are not concerned with the process of comprehending text. It also means that teachers of reading must ensure that children from early on have exposure to many types of writing and thinking, not just the fiction found predominantly in elementary reading materials.

Some significant conclusions discussed by P. David Pearson from recent comprehension research findings are concerned with a variation in focus when reading, involving both process and knowledge structures (schemata) when comprehending.[7] Readers are said to vary their focus from concentrating on the writer's message to predicting what that message ought to be. This variation in focus is determined by:

What is to be done with the information
How much is already known about the topic
How much interest and motivation already exists for the topic
How familiar readers are with the conventions of this type of
  discourse (the style of writing)

Knowledge structures, or schemata, refer to what is already in our long-term memory and how that information is organized. For example, when reading in Social Studies about the Middle East, and Jordan in particular, readers may trigger prior knowledge of a topic by picturing a geographical map of the area; recalling biblical stories of Moses and the Dead Sea; reviewing friends' descriptions of their travels to "the rose red city of Petra, half as old as time" and Amman the "humming" capital; remembering their experiences when crossing the Allenby Bridge from an Arab State into Israel with machine guns on them; or visually recalling pictures in the *National Geographic* portraying this part of the world. In other words, the more readers know about a topic in a variety of ways, the more able they will be to call on appropriate knowledge structures in which to tie the new information. They will be able to comprehend, integrate, and recall the necessary information when needed.[8]

Knowledge of the overall text structure is also important. One such structure would be story structure, referring to knowledge of plot, characters, problem, resolution, and the like. There are also differences to be pointed out among the structures of a novel, short story, poem, or play.

Expository (explanatory) writing found in texts has a much different overall structure from the literary. Open any Science, History, Vocational, Education, or similar text and the actual format, the way the information is presented, contrasts markedly with the novel or anthology. This will be discussed in more detail later in this chapter when we describe types of writing, reading like a writer, and the role of writing in content learning. Hopefully then, you will be able to see similarities and differences in the process between comprehending and composing (writing).

Thoughts to Ponder

1. What we do or think about when reading the text can be more important than what actually exists on the page.
2. What we bring to the print has more effect on comprehension than the facts, action, or description on the page.
3. Meaning resides essentially in the reader, rather than in the text.

Ponder the truth or implications of these statements and decide whether you agree. Be ready to justify your responses.

Reader-Teacher-Writer-Text Interaction

As mentioned earlier, the cognitive map (figure 7.1) at the beginning of the chapter shows the comprehending process as involving interaction among key aspects: active readers; teachers as guides; writers as architects; and text as blueprint to meaning. All of these are connected to a particular situation and setting.

Reader's Role

The reader's role is one of an active learner, using schemata (background, organized knowledge already known) and metacognition (executive self-monitoring of task, needs, and process).

When comprehending, readers are building mental models in which to store bits of information in an organized fashion for easy retrieval. They often use visual imagery to personalize and clarify the message being read. They predict what is to come and modify those predictions or restructure as needed, while constantly and simultaneously inferring and monitoring as they read. They should be progressively more metacognitively aware of what it is they need to do to master the material.

Teacher's Role

The teacher's role is like that of a tour guide, helping students negotiate meaning by using sensitive intervention, providing focus and structure to the reading when needed. Teachers have a handle on where readers should be going, how best to get them there, and how each will know when they have arrived. Teachers act as diagnosticians. Their tasks are to guide readers as needed before, during, and after their reading. In the first stage, *Orienting,* or *Prereading,* teachers will have done careful preliminary planning where they have defined the problem in their own minds; delineated necessary activities and strategies based on their students' known levels of functioning; modeled or "walked-through" processes or strategies with the class; and prepared students for vocabulary, concepts, and problems to be encountered. They have then set the stage for the comprehension product to come and will have motivated students to want to read the material. At a more advanced level they will have also worked on helping students become more *metacognitively aware* of their own needs and choices of strategies so that students are able to become more independent learners.

During directed silent reading, occuring while students are reading, teachers may give practice using worksheets, study guides, note facilitators, inserted questions, or glosses (see the chapter on strategies for descriptions of these teaching strategies).

In Postreading or *processing,* teachers offer feedback, help draw threads together or summarize, ensure that knowledge and comprehension of the content has taken place, and extend or enrich when appropriate (see table 7.1 for examples of strategies for each stage).

Writer's Role

The writer's role is one of designing and building the message that will be interpreted in the text by readers and teachers.

Table 7.1

Comprehension Levels, Skills, Behaviors, and Tasks (An aid to writing objectives and questions)

Levels	Skills/Behaviors	Tasks (Verbs)
1. *Literal:* Read lines as stated and recall or restate in own words	1. determine explicitly stated details 2. find explicit main ideas 3. follow directions 4. determine sequence	list, recall, restate, name, identify, locate, label, recognize, tell, explain, translate, measure, convert
2. *Interpretive/Applied:* thoughtfully read between lines, exercise judgment in selecting and relating relevant information to produce a conclusion or apply to new situation	5. determine implicit main ideas and details 6. identify cause/effect or effect/cause 7. make inferences 8. predict outcomes 9. describe character, tone, mood, intent 10. explain relationships 11. draw conclusions	classify, outline, organize, summarize, problem solve, infer, compare, contrast, illustrate, select, demonstrate, perform, differentiate, analyze, explain, apply, conclude
3. *Evaluative/Critical:* pass personal judgment on truth, accuracy, worth of text and justify based on own stated criteria	12. compare/contrast 13. generalize 14. make value judgments 15. justify	judge, justify, generalize, compare/contrast, rate, appraise, value
4. *Creative/Personal:* go beyond message to form personal extensions, develop new ways, show emotional response	16. form own extensions 17. explore similar problems 18. synthesize 19. find similarities in unrelated materials 20. examine possible consequences 21. suggest new solutions 22. use visual imagery 23. empathize with characters or situation 24. appreciate	create, design, synthesize, respond with feeling, stand up for, volunteer, empathize, image, appreciate

John McNeil has described conditions for comprehension.[9] As readers interact with the text, often assisted by teacher strategies, comprehension occurs under the following conditions:

Conditions for Comprehension

1. *What we know will determine what we learn.* For example, "The notes were sour because the seams split" has little meaning unless we know it's referring to a bagpipe.

2. *How we perceive the structure or overall plan (schema) of a topic and a text will also determine meaning.* For example, a schema for the notion of bagpipes would have slots for associated objects such as pipes, pipers, Scotsmen, marching, musical instruments.

3. *The more we can elaborate and draw inferences and relate ideas to each other (through recognition of organizational patterns and summary strategies) the more we will be able to recall from the text.* For example, it is difficult to elaborate adequately on a topic without taking information from several sources.
4. *The perspective we bring to the text influences the meanings we will get out of it.* For example, two groups reading a description of a house will have different perspectives of what is important to recall if one group is designated as potential home buyers and the other group as burglars. The home buyers will look at the house in terms of living problems, the burglars in terms of security features. Current practices often seem to ignore these commonsense notions.

Taxonomies for Thinking and Comprehending

In the past, in an effort to better understand dimensions of comprehending, numerous taxonomies were developed, many building on the familiar *Bloom's Taxonomy of the Cognitive Domain* developed in the 1950s, whose sequenced levels of difficulty included *Knowledge, Comprehension, Application, Analysis, Synthesis,* and *Evaluation.*[10] Norris Sanders changed the term *Comprehension* to *Translation* and *Interpretation* and Thomas Barrett revised the order somewhat and added *Appreciation* at the top.[11,12] Others reduced the number of categories to more general, inclusive terms such as *Literal* (reading the lines as stated) and *Higher Level* (reading between and beyond the lines). To comprehend at these higher levels there are said to be three essential conditions:

1. Background knowledge and a schema for the topic
2. A questioning attitude and a willingness to suspend judgment
3. Ability to analyze materials logically and take action when appropriate

The present authors' adaptation of these arbitrary levels as seen in table 7.1 are *Literal, Interpretive/Applied, Evaluative/Critical,* and *Creative/Personal.* This table shows the skills, behaviors, and tasks that might be connected to each level and could form an aid for teachers in writing objectives and questions.

We consider this to be an arbitrary listing of levels and comprehension skills and behaviors, as it can be argued that many will not fit into one tight box. Also, there may be times when questions at the higher levels are easier to answer than literal ones. As stated above, the purpose of this table is to serve as a reference for you when developing lesson plans, objectives, and questions. Some questions you might wish to ask yourself: How much variety do I seek? Can my students really do a good job of synthesizing this material without first having mastered and analyzed pertinent facts? Why do some students dislike reading a particular text or subject? How can I best help them to a more positive attitude?

Workshop Activity 7.6
Levels, Skills, Behaviors, Tasks

In table 7.1, twenty-four skills and behaviors were arbitrarily listed. This is not intended to be a definitive list, nor are the items necessarily hierarchical in nature. The purpose here is to allow you to think about what your students need in order to work successfully at increasingly higher levels.

First, go down the list and circle those items you feel are essential for your students to master. Next, you may wish to rank them in order of most to least significant. Finally, using the tasks (verbs) column, select one topic, or chapter, or short story and write a content question for each category. This final step may be done in pairs, allowing for quiet discussion.

As an alternative to cognitive levels in taxonomical form, P. David Pearson and Dale Johnson divided comprehension into the word or concept level and the propositional or longer discourse level.[13] For a full treatment of each, we refer you to their book, *Teaching Reading Comprehension.* Looking at the adapted tables (tables 7.2 and 7.3), you will note that the word level table (7.2) has much in common with the previous chapter on vocabulary. Table 7.3, dealing with the propositional level, makes an interesting comparison between the tasks for working with larger segments of writing and the terms used at the word level.

Word Level and Propositional Level

As mentioned earlier, the interactive view of reading looks at the process as one in which readers vary their focus depending on purpose, needs, and abilities. Teaching practices inconsistent with this interactive view of reading include:

Teaching Practices Inconsistent with the Interactive View of Reading

1. Use of readability formulas as the only determiner of text difficulty level for a particular group of readers, with little regard for familiarity, interest, purpose, needs, and abilities.
2. Assessing or "teaching" comprehension by presenting a brief passage followed by multiple choice questions with only one correct response indicated.

Table 7.2

Word Level (Vocabulary)

Category	Relation	Example	Task: The student recognizes that
A. Simple Associations	1. synonym (longer discourse would be a paraphrase)	walk-stroll	two words have similar meanings
	2. antonym	hot-cold	two words have opposite meanings
	3. association	green-grass	two words often appearing together are linked by some relationship
	4. classes	anthropods crustaceans arachnids	there are class labels for various examples belonging to that class
B. Complex Associations	5. analogies	Father is to son as mother is to _____	pairs of words can be related in a similar way
	6. connotative denotative	walk-amble-trudge	words can denote the same thing but have different connotations
C. Ambiguous Words	7. multiple meanings	root-tree root-origin	a given word can have different meanings
	8. homographs	pro jéct pró ject	words with same spelling can have different pronunciation and meaning
	9. homophones	pear, pair	words sounding the same can have different spelling and meaning

Adapted from P. David Pearson and Dale Johnson, *Teaching Reading Comprehension* (New York: Holt, Rinehart, & Winston, 1984). Used with permission.

3. Use of lesson plans featuring teacher questions and lecture, ignoring student-initiated questions and discussion.
4. Failure to discover what in students' background is relevant to the content of the text.
5. Failure to help readers learn how to connect their prior experience and background knowledge to the text, so they will use what they already know as a bridge to the new information.

Table 7.3

Propositional Level (Longer segments)

Task	Word Level Analogue	Example	Description: After reading a paragraph, students:
1. Paraphrase	synonym	The man put the hammer on the table. The hammer was placed on the table by the workman.	recognize the equivalence in meaning between two or more sentences.
2. Association	association		select the one inappropriate sentence in the paragraph.
3. Main Idea—Details	classification		select the main idea or supporting details.
4. Comparison	analogies	One paragraph is about Handel, a second about Bach. Question: How is Handel's music like that of Bach's?	compare relationships between one paragraph, story, or experience with another.
5. Figurative Language	connotation denotation	She is a veritable wizard. She is very bright.	recognize that a figurative and a literal statement mean essentially the same thing. recognize that the tone and feeling communicated by the two sentences are different.
6. Ambiguous Statements	multiple meanings	Military police are asked to stop drinking on base. (Either they are asked not to drink themselves or to stop others from drinking.)	recognize that one sentence can have more than one meaning. select the appropriate meaning for a given context.
7. Causal Relations		When the Japanese attacked Pearl Harbor the president called for a declaration of war. —Why did the president declare war? or —What happened when the Japanese attacked Pearl Harbor?	can identify causes or explanations (answer "why" questions). can identify effects (answer "what happened because of" or "what will happen next" questions).
8. Sequence		Before starting the car, make sure seat belt is fastened. Next check to see that the gear is in the "park" position. —What should be done after fastening your seat belt?	place events in the sequence explained in the paragraph. answer "when" or "what happened after" or "before" questions.
9. Anaphora (substitution of word(s) for a preceding word or group of words)		His poetry enthralls me. "It" was a delightful escape. Joe is an excellent student. "So is" Janice.	recognize what the anaphoric term stands for.

From P. David Pearson and Dale Johnson, *Teaching Reading Comprehension* (New York: Holt, Rinehart & Winston, 1984). Used with permission.

Comprehending Written Discourse: An Interactive Process 199

Failures to Adequately Comprehend

One way to get a sense of some of the processes of comprehending is to look at a few reasons why we may fail to comprehend.

1. *Unfamiliar or ambiguous words.* Individual words have many, often ambiguous, meanings depending on their context. Words become defined only as they are related to one another in the sentence, paragraph, or lengthier discourse. For example, "good play" will be interpreted differently in the ballpark, playground, or theatre. But intersections between meanings are not always enough (play the horses versus the horses play).[14] Syntax, or the way words are placed in sentences, is the primary means by which we specify the intended meanings among words. Words in isolation do not give us precise meanings. What is the precise meaning of the word "root"? How can you tell? What is a light-house keeper? Where do you put the emphasis? However, traditional emphasis on decoding skills in reading instruction, where focus is on each separate word, comes from the view that written language is no more than speech written down. If readers break the code (translate letters into corresponding sounds) then the reading problem is supposedly solved. This way of thinking relates the rest of the task to merely applying previously acquired language skills to the deciphered text. The validity of this rests on two suspect assumptions: one, that beginning readers only lack decoding skills so if they can recognize words *per se* they can get meaning from the text; and second, that the processes readers use to interpret a spoken string of words are adequate for interpreting a written string of words.

2. *Overreliance on listening cues.* Reading requires a syntactic awareness not generally required for listening. When we listen we are given many valuable cues to meaning through expression and emphasis of the speaker. That is one reason why some students prefer getting their information from listening rather than reading, because the speaker has helped in the interpretation.

3. *Unable to see relationships between and among sentences or how the whole text fits together.* Word-by-word readers too often get mired in individual words or phrases without seeing the larger picture. Those readers who have difficulty differentiating between main ideas and details or between facts and generalizations will have difficulty mastering a subject area, whether it is through reading or any other mode such as listening. This thinking skill is basic to general comprehension.

Table 7.4

Examples of Types of Cohesive Ties

Type	Example
Reference (includes many types of pronouns)	John went to the store. *He* bought an apple.
Substitution (the replacement of one word or within another)	Joan already knows. Everyone *does*. ("does" substitutes for "knows")
Ellipsis (the omission of a repeated word or phrase)	Would you like an apple? I have twelve. (implied repetition of apple)
Conjunction (includes additive, adversative, causal, and temporal links)	John went to the store *before* the rain began.
Lexical—Reiteration	An apple is a fruit. *All fruits* contain seeds.
Lexical—Collocation (co-occurrences of words which co-occur in the language)	The apple cost fifty cents. *I had a dollar.*

From Alden J. Moe and Judith Irwin, "Cohesion, Coherence and Comprehension," in *Understanding Teaching Cohesion Comprehension*, ed. J. Irwin (Newark, Del.: International Reading Association, 1986), pp. 3–6.

Cohesion and Cohesive Ties

M. A. K. Halliday and Rugalya Hasan state that the cohesion that binds individual sentences together is achieved where interpretation of one idea in the text depends on ability to interpret another.[15] It can also be seen as a type of redundancy that links one sentence or phrase with another. As Alden Moe and Judith Irwin state, if educators understand cohesion, they can predict comprehension problems; write clearly understood materials; and teach students to heed cohesive ties, which are the links that establish cohesion.[16] Table 7.4 illustrates examples of these ties.

Problem Comprehenders and Comprehension Difficulties

When there is an absence or sparseness in the text of cohesive ties, problems can occur for poor readers, for good readers processing text, and for bilingual readers who need such signposts in their second language.[17]

David Shepherd compiled a list of comprehension difficulties common to all content areas.[18]

1. *Word calling.* Word callers do not realize that moving their eyes rapidly across the print, reading aloud fluently, even recognizing all the words, is not reading. In linguistic terminology they are concerned more with the surface structure, the actual words.

Using mainly the graphophonic (written-sound) cues, they claim indignantly that they have read the chapter twice but still do not understand the material. If they could be taken back through the reading step-by-step, they would be amazed to realize that much of the time their minds were elsewhere, at the football game or last week's social event. They need to realize that comprehending requires getting at the meaning and the thoughts behind the aggregate of individual words—the deep structure—as mentioned earlier.

2. *Purposeless readers* are not aware that it is essential to have some reason or purpose clearly in mind before reading content material for comprehension and retention. Without this purpose as a focus, information "goes in one ear and out the other." Telling them to read the next chapter for a quiz on Monday is not giving them a purpose; rather, they need to know what to look for in the reading (e.g., find three reasons why or how the problem was solved or concentrate on the imagery of the descriptive passages). Content teachers need to recognize that many students have had years of school in which purposes were not set, and therefore they can assist their students by helping them define their purposes. A few lessons may also be planned that require students to articulate the significance of a reading or the author's point of view.

3. *Isolated facts.* These readers read material with understanding but do not perceive that the facts or details are interrelated or how they are tied to main ideas. For this reason they retain very little useful information. Directing them to try to ascertain the connections between ideas can be helpful.

4. *Miss the point.* Readers also understand what they read but do not see the significance of the material or why these facts are important. They are not able to draw inferences or conclusions adequately or see the author's point of view.

5. *Not organized.* When these readers do not spot the author's organization plan, they may be in the same spot as "isolated-facts readers." Many facts and ideas seem unrelated, and thus only rote memorization is accomplished, without any lasting, meaningful learning.

6. *Word-needy.* When the reading assignment contains too many unknown words (more than one out of any twenty running words), word-needy readers are likely to become frustrated and will cease reading. Special connotations of words can prove to be confusing, too, such as *rooting out, root of the problem,* or *square root.*

7. *Experience-needy.* Adequate comprehension requires that experience-needy readers have background experiences they can relate to new ideas. If they don't, these new ideas may have little significance to them. It is often necessary to directly point out the relationships between past experiences and what is being read.

8. *Syntax-confused.* Because reading involves an interaction between thought and language, syntax-confused readers need an understanding of how language is structured, not only the meanings of words but also how these meanings interact in each incident. Oral interpretation may help here. Actually, it is often the text itself that is the culprit in terms of confused syntax.

9. *Nonvisualizing.* Nonvisualizing readers do not react to words with sensory images. They are thus unable to sense the tone or mood of the selection. Being able to construct mental pictures not only aids comprehension but triggers interest, too.

1. *Word calling.* Ask students to look for specific information to help refocus their attention on the meaning rather than words alone. Getting the gist of the paragraph may be more important than knowing all the words in that paragraph.

Recommendations for General Difficulties

2. *Lack of purpose.* As a part of your regular teaching procedure, always state specific purposes of reading and lead students to set up their own questions, such as in the SQ3R strategy (see the chapter on study skills for a more complete explanation of SQ3R).

3. *Isolated facts.* To find main ideas, ask students to try to anticipate what the author will say and have them list before reading what type of information they expect. For those who have trouble sifting through the information, some directed practice in recognizing different paragraph patterns (e.g., summary, cause/effect, etc.) will usually help.

4. *Missing the point.* Often in textbooks the author's purpose is stated in the preface or foreword section or sometimes in an introductory section of a chapter. In many articles some background about the author is given first from which an inference about the author's point of view may be drawn. This should be pointed out to students.

5. *Organization of material.* When students have trouble with the author's organization of ideas, a number of techniques should prove helpful.
   a. Study the table of contents as an outline, a scope, and a sequence of material to be covered.

b. Have them go through a chapter reading only the subheadings first.

c. Apply basic knowledge of composition to a chapter, having the student note its basic structure—introduction, body, and summary.

d. Work out practice sessions in categorizing and classifying key concepts.

6. *Vocabulary lack.* This is such a broad topic you will need to refer to the chapter on vocabulary development for full treatment. As a reminder:

a. Develop background knowledge of vocabulary prior to reading using audiovisual aids.

b. Call attention to the graphic aids within the text that make abstract concepts more concrete.

c. Explain necessary background information prior to reading.

d. State reading purposes for students.

e. Point out the handy glossary in the text.

7. *Lack of experiential background.* As with the development of vocabulary, your responsibility here is to make sure the background base is adequate for comprehension of the new material. Use any appropriate aids—audiovisual, field trips, experiments, discussions—and be sure to help the students make the transfer by directly stating it.

8. *Syntax complexity.* When students have trouble with complex sentences, three techniques can help them:

a. Start with a kernel (noun-verb) sentence and continue to add to it (adverbs, adjectives, clauses, etc.) discussing how each addition expands, extends, or changes the prior meaning.

b. Another strategy is to ask the students to restate the sentence(s) in their own words. (There are two types of sentences: one denoting action, and the other attributive, which identifies, characterizes, or describes.)

c. Note structure words (connectives) such as *but, and, because, if, however.* Point out how these words carry or change the thought of the sentence.

9. *Lack of visual imagery.* To help students use visual imagery:

a. Discuss word meanings, asking them to quickly describe the feeling or image that the word gives them (for example: *exquisite*).

b. Alert students to the emotional or connotative impact of words (for example: *pig*).

c. Ask "How would you feel if . . . ?" "Describe your feelings when . . . " "Sketch the way you see . . . "

d. Dramatize situations from literature, social studies, and science.

e. Have students role-play famous characters, key content figures. In a psychology class one student might be Freud, another Jung, and so on. Given a specific written situation, they would each have to address the problem as the person would whose role they are playing.

f. Have students listen to descriptions with eyes closed and then have them discuss or draw what they have "seen."

Text as Blueprint for Meaning

Reading Like a Writer

The commonality of reading and writing has recently become a popular subject for exploration. John Guthrie talks about how increased proficiency in one may influence awareness of the other.[19] When reading like a writer we anticipate what the writer will say. Readers who write often can gain a better perspective of sense of audience, self, and subject. Knowing who will be reading your work (who is your audience) will influence the style, the simplicity or complexity, and the amount of explanation needed. It is seemingly almost impossible to write on a subject without recognizing your own position or lack of position. Putting thoughts to print can help writers see the total picture, the organization of information, and what is still unknown or unclear. The big questions for readers are: What is the writer trying to help me learn, see, or feel? What is my relationship to the writer? What does the writer know of me? What action does the writer want me to take? What attitude is the writer expressing? How does the writer feel? How accurate is this writing? Are the conclusions drawn important to this writer? If such questions are asked, the reader is participating in the reading like a writer.

Good readers may compose their own texts as they read. Looking at both actions—reading and writing—we can see similarities in the tasks of planning, composing, and revising. Writers plan by gathering information, establishing a writing purpose, and visualizing the potential audience; whereas good readers plan their reading through such prereading activities as recalling what they already know about the topic, establishing a reading purpose, and checking vocabulary. Writers compose print, whereas readers compose tentative meanings as they read. Writers revise what they have written, whereas readers revise meanings in their heads according to the new information read. Readers may also evaluate as they read (see figure 7.2).

Figure 7.2
Reading like a writer.

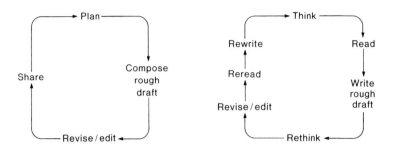

Types of
Paragraphs

The following workshop activity concerns types of paragraphs found in expository writing. It should be read for understanding even if this workshop is not assigned. The twelve types of paragraphs explained in the workshop include: introductory, definition, transitional, illustrative summary, main ideas supported by details or examples, chronological order, comparison/ contrast, cause and effect, problem/solution, descriptive, and narrative. When readers can readily identify different types of paragraphs, they can more easily comprehend expository text.

Workshop Activity 7.7
Types of Paragraphs

The most common types of paragraphs are listed and described below. As you read each one, think about how it might relate to your content area. After completing this section, take one of the textbooks you use or might use with your students and find at least two examples of each relevant type of paragraph. Then, working in pairs or triads with classmates in similar fields, evaluate each other's choices, combining or eliminating when necessary. The object of this activity is for you to have, in writing, several content-related examples that you can use with your students. Be prepared to discuss the reasons for your choices with the whole class.

As an alternative, take a stack of old newspapers with twelve envelopes, each labeled for one type of expository paragraph. Allow students to find appropriate samples of each, working in pairs. After cutting them out of the newspaper and placing in appropriate envelopes, groups may then decide which is the best example of each type. The discussion of why one is better than another is the most important aspect here.

1. *Introductory.* This type of paragraph is generally found at the beginning of selections, chapters, and units. It is useful because in introducing the topic it will give the reader a mental set or a focus for comprehending. A preview of ideas is often given, and the author's purpose or organizational plan is described. Sometimes questions are given to guide the reading. If not, the reader should ask, ''What will this cover? What will the organization plan be?'' This type of paragraph prepares the reader for what is to come.

2. *Definition.* Developed to define technical terms or explain concepts, this paragraph is important to the reader as a foundation for later comprehension. The technical terms or concepts are usually printed in italics or underlined the first time they are used.

3. *Transitional.* The function of a transitional paragraph is to shift the reader's attention from one aspect of a topic, point of view, or time to another. This type often has one sentence that calls attention to the upcoming change.

4. *Illustrative.* Here the author tries to make an abstract process or principle more concrete by giving examples or illustrations. Sometimes readers will confuse the examples with the principle because the language of the illustration is easier to understand and thus more interesting. It is important to point out the difference between the thought and the illustration of that thought.

5. *Summary.* Main ideas are reinforced, restored, and summarized. This paragraph generally comes at the end of the chapter or a section of a long chapter. Because of the concentrated compilation of main ideas contained in a summary paragraph, the reader should read it very slowly and thoughtfully, with full concentration for retention of ideas. A common study strategy has been to have students read the summary first, before reading the chapter. Some recent writing now places the summary paragraphs at the onset of the chapter as a form of advance organizer.

These five paragraphs just described pull together ideas that the author wishes to convey. They show writing patterns that are intended to organize the content into an integrated whole.

Other expository types of paragraphs help to unify closely related ideas.

6. *Main ideas supported by details or examples.* The most common type of general paragraph structure is the one in which one sentence states the topic and the rest of the sentences in the paragraph support that main idea. Topic sentences are usually found at the beginning or the end of the paragraph, although at times they can be found imbedded in the middle. When no main idea is explicitly stated, the reader must take all the examples and put them together to form a main idea.

7. *Chronological order.* This pattern of sequential order of events can help the reader place an event in perspective in relation to what occurred before or after, thus organizing information for later recall.

8. *Comparison/contrast.* These paragraphs are helpful in clarifying points that the writer wishes to get across. Readers might make a rough table or diagram as they read, listing likenesses in one column, differences in another.

9. *Cause and effect.* In this type of organization pattern, the reader needs to see certain relationships between or among facts. Often the writer does not label which is the effect and which the cause, so the reader must be alert to these relationships.

10. *Problem/solution.* These paragraphs present a problem first and then offer solutions for the problem. The reader needs to identify the problem and realize that the suggested solutions are those of the author. Emphasis here is on looking for evidence that the problem exists and that there is support for the solutions suggested.

11. *Descriptive.* The purpose of this type of paragraph is to assist the reader in forming a mental picture of what the writer is trying to convey. Descriptions are used to set the mood or tone for what is to come. Many of these paragraphs do not contain a topic sentence but merely designate what is being described.

12. *Narrative.* Story-type paragraphs relate an anecdote or sequence of events. They are often used in texts to capture attention and arouse interest in the topic. These, like descriptive paragraphs, often do not contain a topic sentence.

Written Discourse: An Overview

To better understand written discourse, it may be helpful to consider the general types, purposes, and cues for each. William Brewer developed a simplified psychological classification for types of discourse, shown in table 7.5. The three major categories or structures refer to the underlying structure of the writing: description, narrative, and exposition. Four general purposes are also outlined: to inform, entertain, persuade, or present a literary, aesthetic experience. Examples are given for different categories. Note that exposition has no entertainment or literary/aesthetic purpose given. Such discourse types as science fiction, although placed under entertainment here, could easily be placed in the informing category, too. Cues that readers may note in helping to determine the type of structure and force or purpose are also shown. The intent of this table is to give you an overview prior to looking further at types of discourse.

Differences Between Narrative and Expository Writing

Young children usually learn to read through contact with narrative material found in basal readers. Generally they first encounter serious expository material around third or fourth grade.[20] Often little or no attempt is made to teach them to be aware of the differences between narrative and expository text, which may seriously impede their ability to use reading in order to learn. Table 7.6 delineates some major differences between narrative and expository writing. Research often suggests the importance of

Table 7.5

A Psychological Classification of Written Discourse Types

	Purpose: Inform, give information	*Purpose:* Entertain, amuse, frighten, excite	*Purpose:* Persuade, convince, concentrate action or idea	*Purpose:* Present literary/ aesthetic experience, work of art
Type of Discourse (Structure)	*Formal Vocabulary* "stand of coniferous saplings on a 50-meter moraine"	*Colloquial Vocabulary* "little old mole hill dressed up fit to kill with pine trees"	*Persuasive Vocabulary* "our forests must be preserved"	*Aesthetic Vocabulary* "sublime sylvan knoll"
Description (space) picture *Locative cues:* near, above, to right of	* technical * botany * geography	* ordinary description	* house advertisement	* poetic description poem
Narration (time-events) motive picture *Time cues:* before, then, while	* newspaper story * history * instructions * recipe * biography	* mystery novel * western novel * science fiction * fairy tale * short story * "light drama" * riddles	* message novel * parable * fable * advertisement * drama	* literary novel * short story * serious drama * science fiction
Exposition (logic) abstract form of representation, e.g., map, table, or chart *Logic cues:* thus, because, since	* scientific article * philosophy * abstract		* sermon * propaganda * editorial * essay	

Adapted from William F. Brewer, "Literary Theory, Rhetoric, and Stylistics: Implications for Psychology," in *Theoretical Issues in Reading Comprehension*, ed. Rand J. Spiro; Bertram C. Bruce; and William F. Brewer (Hillsdale, N.J.: Lawrence Erlbaum Associates, 1980), pp. 221–243.

two instructional strategies, both of which are acts of reading and composing. These are revising and peer editing. We cannot effectively revise our own writing if we cannot critically read our own texts. Nor can we do peer editing if we cannot evaluate the text prose of others.

Because selections in most basal reading programs have been up to 95 percent narrative,[21] there is a need for more exposure to expository writings in developmental reading programs. Expository writings are far more critical to academic achievement in areas other than English and for civic preparation than narrative writing.

Stotsky proposes a revision of our reading and writing curriculum by turning to a dual literacy. The first program would be a complete literature on K–12 for English and Language Arts, where literature is taught solely as literature. The second program would be developmental reading and

Table 7.6

Narrative versus Expository Writing: What Are the Differences?

Narrative Trade Books Story Grammar (Literary)	*Expository* Textbooks Schemata
• Based on life experiences	• Abstract concepts
• Person-oriented (dialogue, familiar language)	• Subject-oriented (little dialogue)
• Purposes: to entertain, give literary or aesthetic experience	• Purposes: to explain or present information, inform, persuade
• Time—past tense or historical present ("There once was")	• Time—not focal, various tenses used
• Vocabulary—anglo-saxon origin, related	• Vocabulary—latinate, more complex structurally and semantically
• Vocabulary—less essential	• Vocabulary—essential to comprehension
• Chronological links ("first," "one day," "then")	• Logical links—(sentence topic and parallel structure keep discourse moving)
• Sentence complexity—sometimes less	• Sentence complexity—sometimes greater
• Density of concepts—sometimes less	• Density of concepts—sometimes greater
• Thought patterns—less varied	• Thought patterns—more varied
• Questions—"Who is the main character?" "What happened next?"	• Questions—"What is the subject?" "Focus?" "Topic sentence?"

Adapted from Carolyn Kent, "A Linguist Compares Narrative and Expository Prose," *Journal of Reading* 28 (December 1984): 232–236; and Sandra Stotsky, "A Proposal for Improving High School Students' Ability to Read and Write Expository Prose," *Journal of Reading* 28 (October 1984): 4–7.

writing K–12 with a focus on expository writing that draws from all content areas. Here, reading and writing would be integrated across the curriculum. This would not be just skills oriented; the major focus would be on historical or scientific information and nonliterary concepts, and could also include creative, imaginative, and informational writing assignments.

Text Structure and Background Knowledge

Those texts that are more highly organized or more closely connected to the reader's knowledge and expectations are better remembered.[22]

In a study with ninth graders, Bonnie Meyer, David Brandt, and George Bluth found that good and average readers were more sensitive to text structure than poor readers.[23] It would seem to follow that if poor readers were given more instruction in thought patterns or structure, their comprehension and recall would improve.

Text grammar has a different focus and organization than story grammar.[24] Three major components of most expository text chapters are:

1. A short beginning, introducing main ideas to be discussed and possibly how the chapter is organized.
2. A lengthy development of several interrelated major ideas.
3. A conclusion or summary of main points, sometimes including the authors' viewpoint.

Usually the basic unit for presenting meaning in texts is the paragraph. Identifying types of paragraphs can thus signal the beginning or end of certain ideas and can serve to break up the print into manageable units for comprehending.

All content areas have many paragraphs that function as definers, the purpose being to define a word, group of words, or concept. A small number of paragraphs introduce ideas, form transitions from one group to another, and summarize or conclude a discussion.

Narrative and descriptive paragraphs are found occasionally in expository text writing, but most often in literature. Persuasive paragraphs are usually found in editorials, essays, and primary source material in history texts.

As Margaret Early has noted, "The ability to perceive patterns of organization is as essential in reading as is reasoning. Patterns occur in word lists, sentences, paragraphs and longer units of discourse."[25] Examples include:

> patterns in pictures
> topics/subtopics
> arranging topics in patterns
> observing topics in tables of contents
> arranging sentences in patterns
> identifying patterns in paragraphs, selections, chapters

Four major generalizations made by Dorothy Grant Hennings for teaching writing as part of content learning are:[26]

The Role of Writing in Content Learning

1. Mastery in composition writing in content areas requires assistance in gathering information, prewriting, drafting, and rewriting.
2. Teachers should provide such tools as data retrieval charts, categorized lists made from brainstorming data, and word charts.
3. Frameworks for teaching writing in content areas include teacher-guided group writing and rewriting, and small-team writing.
4. Writing in the content areas cannot be divorced from the other communication skills of reading, listening, and speaking. While practicing writing, students can be simultaneously learning essential content.

Most of the thinking skills used in reading are the same thinking skills used in writing. Writing is first of all a thinking process, a way of dealing with subject matter to express new relationships. It is also a craft, a way of putting appropriate words and thoughts together to create a lasting impression in an organized fashion.

Writing and Thinking Skills

Table 7.7

Checklist of Writing Skills

This checklist of writing skills can serve as a handy reference guide for both teachers and students.

A good writer in content classes is able to:

I. organize ideas into related wholes in paragraphs
  _____ A. compose while focusing on one main topic
  _____ B. compose so that points develop logically
  _____ C. sequence a series of paragraphs so that ideas develop progressively
II. use words that communicate or give cues to organization
  _____ A. sequence relationships (first, next; finally)
  _____ B. contrast relationships (on the other hand, in this case)
  _____ C. use cause and effect relationships (as a result of, thus, therefore)
  _____ D. compare relationships (in the same way, similarly)
III. compose in meaningful sentence units
  _____ A. write complete sentences
  _____ B. avoid strings of ''ands'' to connect sentences
  _____ C. combine thoughts by subordinating ideas
IV. handle basic punctuation/capitalization patterns for clear communication of meaning
  _____ A. end sentence punctuation
  _____ B. addresses
  _____ C. dates
  _____ D. appositives
  _____ E. parenthetical expressions
  _____ F. direct address
  _____ G. direct conversation, quotations
  _____ H. imbedded sentences
V. select words that communicate with force and clarity
  _____ A. use appropriate synonyms
  _____ B. avoid wordiness
  _____ C. find the best word to convey real meaning

Adapted from Dorothy Grant Hennings, *Teaching Communication and Reading Skills in the Content Areas* (Newton, Mass.: Allyn and Bacon, 1983).

If students are to learn how to express themselves adequately, they need opportunities to write in every area of the curriculum.[27] Writing serves as a diagnostic instrument that can provide teachers with information on how well a topic is understood. Writing demonstrates that students can see relationships between main ideas and details, draw conclusions based on given information, and apply this understanding by explaining or interpreting a related situation.

Teachers in science and social studies often talk about teaching students to think in the modes of their particular disciplines. By integrating their communicative skills of writing and reading, students clarify their understanding of concepts. This involves observing, describing, retelling, summarizing, relating, hypothesizing, generalizing, designing, personalizing, and inventing. These modes of thinking then are those also needed for writing about science, social studies, and other related content fields. Table 7.7 delineates a checklist of writing skills.

Content is communicated through different modes of writing/thinking. These may include reflective, relational, projective, personal, and inventive modes.[28] How many of the following relate to your content area?

Modes of Writing/ Thinking

1. *Reflective* thinking/writing describes what the writer observed, heard, or read and requires a particular style of thinking. Examples include being able to
   - report on events
   - tell how to do something
   - retell something heard or read
   - summarize
2. *Relational* thinking/writing requires perceiving thought relationships, such as
   - compare/contrast
   - likenesses/differences
   - classify
   - analyze
   - explain events
3. *Projective* writing/thinking requires the writer to propose ideas that go beyond observable data, such as being able to
   - predict
   - guess
   - generalize
   - design plans for action
   - devise original classification schemes
4. *Personal* mode of writing/thinking requires the writer to
   - state attitudes
   - express feelings
   - reveal preferences
   - indicate beliefs or judgments (e.g., poems, editorials, essays)
5. *Inventive* writing/thinking requires true originality, being able to
   - create novel descriptions
   - use new analogies
   - build new patterns of organization
   - invent new solutions/problems

No piece of writing necessarily requires only one mode of thought. Sometimes modes are shifted within a single paragraph. Examples include starting a paragraph with a series of specific observations and then concluding with a generalization. A scientific article, for example, may be projective or inventive at the start and reflective at the end.

Workshop Activity 7.8
Modes of Writing/Thinking

Ask students to each bring in a school text in their content area. Have them arrange texts into categories of English, science, social studies, math, other. Divide class into groups and assign each group to find, if possible, the best example of each mode of writing/thinking. Ask that these be labeled and written on the board for class discussion. Categorize modes with specific content areas. Is there a pattern?

Teaching writing as a thinking process makes the passage much easier to read. Each discipline has special concerns and styles, and students will benefit from being taught directly not only to read in that discipline but also to recognize and be able to produce the kinds of writing which that discipline demands. Becoming a better writer can positively affect comprehension.

Summary

Comprehending written discourse is a complex, interactive process involving a number of mental actions readers engage in to get meaning from print. Successful comprehension depends on the readers' existing, organized background knowledge or schemata, and on their purpose, motivation, and the type of writing in question.

Key elements in the comprehending process are active readers who are metacognitively aware; teachers who act as tour guides; writers who are architects of meaning; and texts that are blueprints to meaning. Failures to comprehend depend partly on unfamiliar or ambiguous words; overreliance on listening cues; and unclear relationships between sentences or sections. Knowledge of cohesive ties may help with unclear relationships. When reading as writers, do we anticipate what the writer will say? By writing we are better able to see others' organization. In both writing and reading we plan, compose, and revise.

Structures in written discourse include description, narrative, and exposition, with several purposes for each type. Knowledge of types of paragraphs, the differences between narrative and expository writing, and the differences between text and story grammars assist readers and writers alike.

Writing and reading have similar thinking skills. Most writing has more than one mode of thought. Five modes are seen in writing/thinking across content areas, with a variety included in most texts. No longer are we separating the teaching of reading from the teaching of writing. Both belong in all content classrooms, not just in English classrooms.

Passage A: Washing clothes
Passage B: Flying a kite

References

1. Frank Smith, *Reading without Nonsense* (New York: Columbia University Teachers College Press, 1978), pp. 85–86.
2. Kenneth Goodman, *The Psycholinguistic Nature of the Reading Process* (Detroit: Wayne State University Press, 1968), pp. 23–24.
3. J. D. Bransford and M. K. Johnson, "Contextual Prerequisites for Understanding: Some Investigations of Comprehension and Recall," *Journal of Verbal Learning and Verbal Behavior* 11 (1972): 717–726.
4. Ibid.
5. Marian J. Tonjes, "Metacognitive Strategies for Active Reading," *The New Mexico Journal of Reading* VI (Fall 1985): 5–8.
6. Dolores Durkin, "What Classroom Observations Reveal About Reading Comprehension Instruction," *Reading Research Quarterly* 14 (1978–1979): 481–538.
7. P. David Pearson, "A Context for Instructional Research on Reading Comprehension," in *Promoting Reading Comprehension,* ed. James Flood (IRA, 1984): 1–15.
8. Richard Anderson; R. E. Reynolds; D. L. Shallert; and E. T. Goetz, "Frameworks for Comprehending Discourse," *American Educational Research Journal* 14 (1977): 367–382.
9. John D. McNeil, *Reading Comprehension: New Directions for Classroom Practice* (Glenview, Ill.: Scott, Foresman and Co., 1984).
10. Benjamin Bloom, ed., *Taxonomy of Educational Objectives: Handbook 1, Cognitive Domain* (New York: Longman, Green, 1956).
11. Norris Sanders, *Classroom Questions: What Kinds?* (New York: Harper and Row, 1966).
12. Thomas C. Barrett, "Taxonomy of Cognitive and Affective Dimensions of Reading Comprehension," discussed by Theodore Clymer in "What Is Reading?: Some Current Concepts," in *Innovation and Change in Reading Instruction,* ed. Helen M. Robinson, 67th Yearbook, National Society for Study in Education, part II (Chicago: University of Chicago Press, 1968), pp. 1–30.
13. P. David Pearson and Dale Johnson, *Teaching Reading Comprehension* (New York: Holt, Rinehart & Winston, 1984).
14. Marilyn Jager Adams, "Failures to Comprehend and Levels of Processing in Reading" in *Theoretical Issues in Reading Comprehension,* ed. Rand J. Spiro; Bertram C. Bruce; and William F. Brewer (Hillsdale, N.J.: Lawrence Erlbaum Associates, Inc., 1980), pp. 11–32.
15. M. A. K. Halliday, and Rugalya Hasan, *Cohesion in English* (London: Longman Group, Ltd., 1976).
16. Alden J. Moe and Judith Irwin, "Cohesion, Coherence and Comprehension," in *Understanding and Teaching Cohesion Comprehension,* ed. J. Irwin (Newark, Del.: International Reading Association, 1986), pp. 3–6.
17. H. Alan Robinson, *Teaching Reading, Writing and Study Strategies: The Content Areas* (Newton, Mass.: Allyn and Bacon, Inc., 1983).

18. David L. Shepherd, *Comprehensive High School Reading Methods,* 3d ed. (Columbus, Ohio: Charles E. Merrill Publishing Co., 1982).
19. John T. Guthrie, "Rhetorical Awareness," *Journal of Reading* 28 (October 1984): 92–93.
20. Donna E. Alvermann, and Paula R. Boothby, "Text Differences: Children's Perceptions at the Transition Stage in Reading," *The Reading Teacher* 36 (December 1982): 298–302.
21. Sandra Stotsky, "A Proposal for Improving High School Students' Ability to Read and Write Expository Prose," *Journal of Reading* 28 (October 1984): 4–7.
22. Ernest T. Goetz, and Bonnie M. Armbruster, "Psychological Correlates of Text Structure," in *Theoretical Issues in Reading Comprehension,* ed. Rand J. Spiro; Bertram C. Bruce; and William F. Brewer (Hillsdale, N.J.: Lawrence Erlbaum Associates, 1980).
23. Bonnie J. F. Meyer; David M. Brandt; and George J. Bluth, "Use of Top Level Structure in Text. Key for Reading Comprehension of Ninth-Grade Students," *Reading Research Quarterly* 16 (1980): 72–103.
24. Robinson, *Teaching Reading.*
25. Margaret Early, and Diane Sawyer, *Reading to Learn in Grades 5 to 12* (Orlando, FL: Harcourt Brace Jovanovich, Inc., 1984).
26. Dorothy Grant Hennings, *Teaching Communication and Reading Skills in the Content Areas* (Newton, Mass.: Allyn and Bacon, 1983).
27. Ibid.
28. Ibid.

Recommended Readings

Allen, JoBeth. "Inferential Comprehension: The Effects of Text Source, Decoding Ability, and Mode." *Reading Research Quarterly* 20 (Fall 1985): 603–615.

Baker, L., and Brown, A. L. "Comprehension Monitoring and Critical Reading." In *Understanding Reading Comprehension: Cognition, Language and the Structure of Prose,* J. Flood, ed. Newark, Del.: IRA, 1983.

Chapman, John. "Comprehending and the Teachers of Reading." In *Promoting Reading Comprehension,* James Flood, ed. Newark, Del.: IRA, 1984: 261–272.

Crafton, Linda K. "Learning From Reading: What Happens When Students Generate Their Own Background Information?" *Journal of Reading* 26 (April 1983): pp. 586–592.

Gahn, Shelley Mattson. "A Practical Guide for Teaching Writing in the Content Areas." *Journal of Reading* 32 (March 1989): 525–531.

Garner, Ruth. *Metacognition and Reading Comprehension.* Norwood, N.J.: Ablex Publishing Corp., 1987.

Heller, Mary F. "How Do you Know What You Know? Metacognitive Modeling in the Content Area." *Journal of Reading* 29, no. 5 (February 1986): 415–422.

Hill, Margaret. "Writing Summaries Promotes Thinking and Learning Across the Curriculum–But Why Are They So Difficult to Write?" *Journal of Reading* 34 (April 1991): 536–539.

Horowitz, Rosalind. "Text Patterns: Part I." *Journal of Reading* 28, no. 5 (February 1985): 448–454. "Text Patterns: Part II." *Journal of Reading* 28, no. 6 (March 1985): 534–541.

Irwin, Judith W. *Teaching Reading Comprehension Processes.* Englewood Cliffs, N.J.: Prentice Hall, 1986.

Irwin, Judith W., ed. *Understanding and Teaching Cohesion Comprehension.* Newark, Del.: International Reading Association, 1986.

Kent, Carolyn E. "A Linguist Compares Narrative and Expository Prose." *Journal of Reading* 28 (December 1984): 232–236. (Figure 3 shows concisely the four differences in person, orientation, time, and linkage.)

Kolker, Brenda, and Terwilliger, Paul N. "Visual Imagery of Text and Children's Processing." *Reading Psychology* 7, 4 (1986): 267–277.

Moffet, James. "Integrity in the Teaching of Writing." *Phi Delta Kappan* 61 (December 1979): 276–279.

Nist, Sherrie L.; Kirby, Kate; and Ritter, Annice. "Teaching Comprehension Processes Using Magazines, Paperback Novels and Content Area Texts." *Journal of Reading* 27 (December 1983): 253–261.

Pearson, P. David, and Johnson, Dale. *Teaching Reading Comprehension.* New York: Macmillan, 1984.

Pearson, P. David. "Changing the Face of Reading Comprehension Instruction." *The Reading Teacher.* Newark, Del.: IRA, 38 (April 1985): 724–738.

Peters, Charles W. "Developing a Conceptual Framework for Applying Text Related Research to Classroom Instruction." In *Reading Expository Material,* Wayne Otto and Sandra White, eds. New York: Academic Press, 1982, pp. 147–151.

Pitts, Murray M. "Comprehension Monitoring: Definition and Practice." *Journal of Reading* 26 (March 1983): 516–523.

Raphael, Taffy E., and Englert, Carol Sue. "Writing and Reading: Partners in Constructing Meaning." *The Reading Teacher* 43 (February 1990): 388–400.

Ruddell, Robert B., and Boyle, Owen F. "A Study of Cognitive Mapping as a Means to Improve Summarization and Comprehension of Expository Text." *Reading Research and Instruction* 29 (Fall 1989): 12–22.

Rumelhart, C. E. "Towards an Interactive Model of Reading." In *Attention and Performance VI,* S. Dornic, ed. Hillsdale, N.J.: Erlbaum, 1977.

Singer, Harry, and Donlan, Dan. "Active Comprehension: Problem-Solving Schema with Question Generation for Comprehension of Complex Short Stories." *Reading Research Quarterly* 17 (1982): 166–187.

Stein, N. L., and Glen, C. G. "An Analysis of Story Comprehension in Elementary School Children." In *Multidisciplinary Approaches to Discourse Comprehension,* R. Freedle, ed. Hillsdale, N.J.: Ablex, 1977.

Taylor, Karl. "Can College Students Summarize?" *Journal of Reading* 26, no. 6 (March 1983): 524–528.

Tchudi, Stephen N., and Huerta, Margie C. *Teaching Writing in the Content Areas.* Washington, D.C.: National Educational Association, 1983.

Tonjes, Marian J. *Secondary Reading, Writing and Learning.* Needham Heights: Allyn and Bacon, 1991, Chapters 5 and 6.

Tregaskes, Mark R., and Delva Daines. "Effects of Metacognitive Strategies on Reading Comprehension." *Reading Research and Instruction* 29 (Fall 1989): 52–56.

Tway, Eileen. *Writing Is Reading: 26 Ways to Connect.* National Council of Teachers of English, 1985.

Figure 8.1
Improving study skills:
a cognitive map.

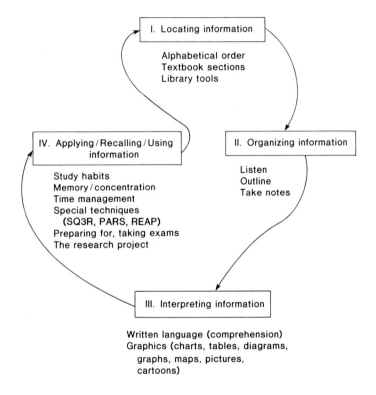

I. Locating information

Alphabetical order
Textbook sections
Library tools

II. Organizing information

Listen
Outline
Take notes

IV. Applying / Recalling / Using
information

Study habits
Memory / concentration
Time management
Special techniques
  (SQ3R, PARS, REAP)
Preparing for, taking exams
The research project

III. Interpreting information

Written language (comprehension)
Graphics (charts, tables, diagrams,
  graphs, maps, pictures,
  cartoons)

Improving Study Skills

8

Anticipatory Questions

(Literal)
1. What is meant by "study skills" as used in this chapter? Show relationships among topics.

(Applied)
2. Select one specific study skill and describe how you would instruct your students in its use, using your content material.

(Applied)
3. How would you incorporate in your content area knowledge about the library?

(Creative)
4. Create in writing a motivating handout (notes facilitator) for a lecture on one particular study skill you wish to teach to your students. An illustration or other graphic map may help.

(Creative)
5. Design a new model for study skills using different categories and interrelationships.

Technical Terminology and Concepts

concentration

Cornell note-taking system

graphic types

listening barriers

mapping

mnemonic devices

notes facilitator

outlining systems

PARS

REAP

retroactive/proactive interference theory

SQ3R/SQ4R

study habits

testing

time management

TQLR

Introduction   A major goal of teaching is for students to become independent learners and be able to apply knowledge when needed. In our constantly changing world the processes for obtaining, integrating, and reviewing information are much more important than the mere memorization of specific data that may soon be obsolete. Guiding students in the use of the essential techniques for mastering school subjects should facilitate their becoming independent learners.

When a problem has been defined or an assignment accepted, students must then

1. *Locate* needed information.
2. *Organize* information in ways that will enhance efficient recall.
3. *Interpret* written information through language or graphics. (Written material has two types of structures—internal and external. The internal is what is actually said, the language and its meaning. The external is the format, the physical features, and graphic aids.)
4. *Use* and/or *apply* the information.

How unfortunate it is that many students finish high school without having learned to read comprehensively, to organize information, or to interpret it effectively. It has been suggested that the difference between "A" and "C" students may not be intelligence or motivation as generally believed, but rather how well study skills have been mastered.

Study strategies, however, are still rarely taught directly throughout the grades as a part of the regular curriculum; or, if introduced in one class, the strategies are not consistently followed up in the next one. One possible reason for this might be found in a fascinating but disturbing study by Eunice Askov, Karlyn Kamm, and Roger Klumb of elementary teachers' own knowledge of the study skills that sixth graders should know.[1] It was found that the teachers themselves lack basic knowledge in areas such as use of the card catalog and map skills.

Another reason for inconsistency in the teaching of study skills might be that because these skills cut across all subject areas, the responsibility for teaching them is not always clearly determined. When we surveyed reading classes in teacher education about the study skills our university students were taught, we found that less than 2 percent remember any direct instruction except in the use of the library, locating information, and map reading.

As you study the cognitive map in figure 8.1, try to recall the content area with which you have had the most trouble in school. What direct teaching could teachers have given you that would have made your work easier or more productive?

After examining the cognitive map, workshop activity 8.1, study skills checklist, should be read. Be sure to give yourself time to react to this workshop before reading the rest of the chapter. The map and the checklist can serve as two kinds of advance organizers to aid in retention of information.

Workshop Activity 8.1
A Study Skills Checklist

Before using this with your students, try it yourself. Wherever you are uncertain of your own abilities, you will want to read that part of the chapter
more carefully. The criterion for "superior" would
be that you would feel comfortable teaching it to
someone else.

1 = superior
2 = adequate
3 = below average
4 = very poor
5 = don't know

The good student knows how to:	Your present ability 1/2/3/4/5	Your projected students' ability 1/2/3/4/5
I. Efficiently *locate* needed information using: A. Alphabetical order		
B. Book parts Table of contents		
Index		
Appendixes		
C. Library tools Dictionary		
Encyclopedia		
Almanac		
Card catalog		
Reader's guide		
II. *Organize* the information through: A. Listening		
B. Outlining		
C. Note taking		

The good student knows how to:	Your present ability 1/2/3/4/5	Your projected students' ability 1/2/3/4/5

III. *Interpret* the information through:
  A. Written language
    (comprehension)		

B. Graphics Charts		
Graphs		
Tables		
Maps		
Diagrams		
Cartoons		
Pictures		

IV. *Apply/Recall/Use* the information
  through:
  A. Use of good study habits
    Memory
    Mnemonic devices		

B. Exams Preparing for		
Writing		
C. Special techniques		
SQ3R		
PARS		
REAP		
Others		

One basic locational skill is using the sequence of the alphabet to find a reference or word in the dictionary. Whereas most students do know how to locate information using the first letter of a word, many do not alphabetize beyond this, nor have they stopped to think of the relative positions of letters, such as *M* being close to the middle in a dictionary.

At the beginning of every course, it may help to review the various parts of the text with students. First, you may wish to ascertain how well your students can use textbook aids. A quick inventory asking a few questions such as the following should suffice:

1. On what page would you find information about _____ ?
2. Where in the index would you look to find the following: (list topics not specifically stated in index) _____ ?
3. How many subtopics are there for _____ ?
4. Is the information in this text up to date? How might you tell?

Sections of a text include the elements listed below. If you find that they are lacking in any of the aids, you might share the following with them. This list and questions should prove helpful as a guideline for presentation.

1. *Title page.* This contains the title or subject, the author's name, and publisher.
   ("What is this all about? Who is the author?")
2. *Copyright.* This is always located on the back of the title page except in very old books. This shows when the first and last editions of the book were printed.
   ("Is this up-to-date information?")
3. *Table of contents.* Here is the organizational outline of the complete text, often with main categories and subcategories. It is a type of map of the domain that should be read prior to reading the first chapter.
   ("How many chapters are there? What do the titles tell me?")
4. *Preface.* The preface should not be overlooked because this is where the authors state why they wrote the book, how the material was gathered, what the emphasis or bias will be, and who contributed material to the book. In addition to an explanation of organizational features, there will sometimes be suggestions for using the text.
   ("What is the approach of the authors of this text?")
5. *Index.* A valuable tool for rapid location of specific topics, the index contains alphabetical listings of subjects and authors with page numbers.
   ("Where will X topic be discussed?")

6. *Glossary.* Definitions are given for the specific technical vocabulary of this particular text. The glossary is often more accurate and less confusing to students than the dictionary, which gives a variety of meanings.
   ("What does 'set' mean in the context of this subject?")
7. *Appendixes.* Included here are such things as tables, maps, illustrations, lists, and supplementary materials.
   ("Where will I find . . . ?")
8. *Bibliography.* Here is a complete record of books, periodicals, papers, and other resources researched by the authors in compiling the text. This is often found at the end of each chapter.
9. *Suggested additional reading.* This is valuable to the student who wants to delve more deeply into a topic, clarify thinking, or get a better grasp of the concepts by reading other materials.
10. *Questions and suggested activities.* The student who reads the authors' questions before reading the chapter has a head start on what the key ideas will be. A normal text chapter will generally have eight to ten major ideas. Reading the questions first alerts the reader to key points to be met while reading the chapter.

The School Library

Another mark of an independent learner is the ability to make effective use of the library. Students need proper instruction in research procedures from early grades through high school. (See also chapter 11, "Enriching Content Classrooms Through Collateral Reading" and the appendix on research papers by Enid Haag.)

Some activities structured by the teacher that students may engage in include:

1. *Learning how to use the library reference books.* This might be accomplished by assigning a report that includes the use of each.
2. *Finding information or answers to a specific question in class.* An example would be to send a student to the library to find the median age of Washington state's population.
3. *Studying assignments, locating information for a report or paper.* A sheet of fifty questions about the Civil War, for example, can be handed out. Students must locate the answers using a variety of sources.
4. *Viewing audiovisual materials.* In some schools these are part of the library, in others they are housed in a learning resource center. Students can use a catalog to locate a filmstrip to be used with their reports on Egypt.
5. *Reading books for information, enjoyment, and relaxation.*

Table 8.1
Dewey Decimal System

Classification	Subject
000	General
100	Philosophy
200	Religion
300	Social Sciences
400	Philology
500	Science
600	Useful Arts
700	Fine Arts
800	Literature
900	History

6. *Reading and browsing through newspapers and magazines.* Students may need to find current information on a topic in geography, for example. High school students can use *Facts on File* as an index to news.
7. *Meeting with an assigned group to develop a class activity.*
8. *Drawing a map of the library* that includes where various things can be found.

Organization of Libraries

A review of the key aspects of the library is provided below. Libraries generally use one of two major systems for cataloging books: the Dewey Decimal System (devised by Melvil Dewey in 1873) or the Library of Congress System. The latter is most often used by large libraries containing many scholarly works.

In the Dewey Decimal System, books are divided into ten subject areas with each area having a set of numbers. These ten large divisions of the field of knowledge are then subdivided into smaller divisions (see table 8.1).

For example, a science book would be numbered between 500 and 599. It would have another set of numbers directly below, preceded by the first letter of the author's last name. Thus 570.8/L342 would be a book on science written by a person whose name begins with L.

The National Library in Washington, D.C., has its own system of classification called the Library of Congress System. In this system, major subject headings are shown by capital letters of the alphabet rather than by numbers. For example, A = General Works, B = Philosophy, C and D = History, E and F = America, and so forth. Subdivisions are then made by different combinations of letters.

The Card Catalog

The card catalog is indispensable to library use. It lists all the books, reference works, and sometimes periodicals the library possesses. Books are listed by author's name and cross-referenced by subject, and sometimes by

Figure 8.2

Reader's Guide entry sample.

	Main Heading	Subheading	Author's Name
Title of Article Name of Periodical			
		Volume Number Page Number	Date of Issue

title, with a separate card for each. If, for example, you wanted to look up information about an American winemaker, Walter Pauk has suggested four successive steps:

1. Look up the name in the card catalog.
2. Look under "American winemakers" for books about people in that field. The winemaker may be included.
3. Look under "wine."
4. Look under "grape-growing," because most winemakers grow their own grapes.[2]

A catalog card includes the following information:

1. Call number of the book
2. Author's name, dates of birth and death
3. Title
4. Publisher, place, and date of publication
5. Number of pages
6. Inclusion of maps or illustrations
7. Contents of the book in general
8. Other card entries for this book

The Reader's Guide

The Reader's Guide to Periodical Literature gives titles of articles appearing in about 125 American and Canadian periodicals such as *Popular Mechanics, Time, Reader's Digest, National Geographic,* and others. Articles are listed alphabetically by author and subject and in some cases by title. A sample of a typical entry is shown in figure 8.2.

Vertical File Index

The filing cabinets in which pamphlets, pictures, and newspaper clippings are stored alphabetically by subject are called the vertical file index. All material in a vertical file index is classified in the card catalog, or you can go directly to the files and look up the subject alphabetically.

Sometimes sufficient information can be readily provided in a reference book, a collection of information arranged by topic. *Encyclopedias* are often a first resource and, although they offer an excellent starting point for investigating a topic, there are other more specialized references such as dictionaries, specialized encyclopedias, yearbooks, almanacs, atlases, and indexes. When students are uncertain about where to start their search, a good dictionary will give them a quick clue. Specialized encyclopedias on specific topics will give special interpretations or more detailed information.

Yearbooks are published annually to supplement and bring up to date the information in the encyclopedia. The most commonly used yearbook is the *almanac,* which contains the latest statistical and miscellaneous information on almost everything—business, education, government, population, sports, and the like. Besides containing maps, *atlases* give information concerning agriculture, industry, natural resources, population distribution, land use, topography, language, and religion. (See the "Test the Atlas" crossword puzzle in figure 8.3.)

Indexes list available materials and their whereabouts. *The Reader's Guide*, discussed previously, is an especially useful index for tracing trends and popular public opinion. *The New York Times Index* is a subject index of newspaper articles from that newspaper. *Who's Who* gives pertinent information about prominent people in the news. There are special indexes for almost every topic, and it is best to consult the librarian as to whether a topic has such an index.

Using the school library efficiently and effectively, then, is one mark of a good student. Each autumn, when the first research assignment is made, it would be beneficial to review these library tools and their proper use with the students. (See chapter 11 on collateral reading for a more detailed treatment of this topic.)

Organizing Information

Listening

What we hear is usually more difficult to remember than what we have read. This is true in part because when listening we usually hear material only once, whereas when reading we can pause and reflect, slow down, or reread. As a reader, then, we control the situation. A standard dictionary definition of listening is "applying oneself to hearing, paying attention, or heeding."

Why teach listening skills? An enormous amount of time is spent each day by all of us in just listening. Numerous studies have shown that we spend more time listening than we do reading, writing, or speaking. Thomas Devine noted in his study of critical listening that the professional persuaders, whether they be politicians, pleaders of causes, teachers or professors, or even barkers at country fairs, all have learned—as did Hitler—that it is in listening that people are most vulnerable.[3]

Yet listening is not generally accepted as part of the regular school curriculum. It is one of the most neglected language arts at all school levels.

Figure 8.3

Test the Atlas.

Jan Foresman Watson, unpublished activity (Burlington, Wash.: Western Washington University, 1977).

All answers to this crossword may be found in the *Goode's World Atlas*. Remember to use the appendix and table of contents to find information.

Note: Your life is not endangered by answering 8-across honestly.

ACROSS

1. Country in which Sulo is located.

2. On a metropolitan area map, the area colored brown means that the area is _____ .

3. Does the atlas contain maps of the ocean floor?

4. The area along the 0 degree parallel is known as the _____ .

5. Which country has the densest population per square mile?

6. Country in which Pandu is located?

7. Both Norway and Sweden speak a language that belongs to what group?

8. This exercise is fun and exciting. Are you glad you are doing it?

DOWN

9. What type of agriculture or farm use does western Washington State have?

10. Is the life expectancy for Australia higher or lower than for Mexico?

11. Abbr. for the United States.

12. Abbr. for Hawaii.

13. The abbreviation ARG stands for what country?

14. On an environmental map, the color red represents what type of area?

15. On a physical-political map, χ represents a _____ .

16. What is the largest country according to land mass? Abbr.

According to Devine, listening and reading are alike in that each is a complex of related skill components.[4] Both reflect the same higher mental processes and can be broken down to almost the same subskills, such as listening to find supporting details, to distinguish fact from opinion, or to note a speaker's bias. In other words, reading and listening have a common thinking base.

Students should benefit from a discussion of bad listening habits and ways to correct them. The following points have proved helpful for discussion:

Bad Listeners

1. *The attention faker.* Too often the listener simply blocks out a message. Although receiving the message, the mind is so wrapped up with its own thoughts that it does not interpret the symbols received or act on them. By simply being present and awake, many of us feel we can pass ourselves off as "listeners."
2. *The "detail" person.* Many listeners think they know what is being said only if they can remember and "spit back" the facts. This results in intense attention to detail that, being difficult to maintain, often results in losing the overall view. This can be a primary problem with students who are unable to locate main ideas in messages.
3. *The tuned-out listener.* Listening requires energy. When students are not willing to exert this energy, the message is simply "turned off." The more difficult the communication, the more likely it will be blocked out.
4. *The bored listener.* Just as difficult material may be turned off, so may an uninteresting subject. Any time a message seems to lack a purpose, or importance, the mind can wander.
5. *The distracted listener.* Very often a listener may be distracted from a message by the speaker's appearance, gestures, accent, and posture, and the listener's attention is drawn away from the topic to the person delivering it. Many forms of interference can inhibit successful listening: noise, motion, visual distractions—all of these can divert attention and make listening impossible.

The following list may be used either as a lecture or as a handout for students.

Correcting
Listening Barriers

1. *Be aware of bad habits in listening.* We are all probably guilty, to some extent, of not listening as well as we could. To improve, we should be aware of our problem areas. (The teacher should discuss the bad habits previously outlined.)
2. *Be ready to listen.* Whenever possible, prepare yourself for listening. Know beforehand that much of your success in listening is due to your own effort toward understanding.

3. *Know what you are listening for.* Purpose is essential if anything is to be gained. Just as we see what we are looking for, we tend to hear what we are listening for. A student listening for the end-of-class bell is certain to hear the bell, but little else.

4. *Listen critically.* Take an alert attitude at all times. Question what the speaker is saying. Analyze and challenge what you are hearing.

5. *Develop skill in note taking.* Do not try to remember all the details, but do identify the main ideas supported by the details. Try to outline the message.

6. *Find your own gimmicks.* Find out what helps *you* to be a better listener. Play a "guessing game" with the speaker, trying to anticipate the purpose, message, actions. Maintain eye contact. Watch for visual clues to meaning. Relate what is being said to what you already know.

7. *Make yourself comfortable while listening.* Relax. If possible remove anything that could be distracting.

8. *Use the better listening formula*—TQLR, which stands for Tune in, Question, Listen, and Review.[5] First, you must be ready and alert to what is being said. Or ask yourself what this will be about and what position the speaker will take, and then listen attentively for answers to your questions. Keep adding new questions as the talk proceeds. This is listening for specific purposes and helps to keep your mind from wandering. Mentally reviewing key points as you leave the lecture helps to remember them.

Skill in listening can be learned, thereby increasing comprehension and retention of information and ideas. In any situation that requires communication, whether on a formal or informal basis, listening plays a crucial part.

Workshop Activity 8.2
The Good Listener

Some people feel pressured to speak up in a class or group. Actually, it is possible to be an active participant without giving a spiel. The following exercise will demonstrate the skills it takes to be a supportive listener. As you participate in this activity, keep in mind the following four points (you may wish to have them written on the chalkboard).

Good listeners will:

1. *Ask* clarifying questions ("Did you mean . . . ?")
2. *Express* support and understanding ("I know how you feel," "I see what you mean")

3. *Reflect* what the speaker says or feels ("I hear you saying . . . " "It appears you feel strongly about . . . ")
4. *Look* directly at the speaker and nod or indicate nonverbally that they are really listening intently

In triads, number off one, two, three.

–number one is the *talker* for three minutes;
–number two is the listener/responder, trying to practice all four rules;
–number three is the referee, making certain that the other two follow directions, and jotting down the examples when the listener uses each of the four rules.

The talker's topic should be decided ahead of time. Some suggestions for topics include a value they hold dear or a teaching problem such as discipline or recalcitrant students. After three minutes of talking, with the listener periodically responding, the referee shares results with the other two. Then roles are rotated until each has played each role. General learnings should then be shared by each group with the total class.

Outlining is a way of logically organizing or categorizing information that is similar to summarizing. It is a dual process of dividing and classifying that forces a person to ferret out or develop main ideas and their supporting details. Basically, there are two types of notations used in outlining: a standard system of indentation, using roman numerals, capitals, and arabic numbers, and a newer form that uses a numbering system. In both types, items closer to the left margin will be superordinate (above in importance) to items further from the margin, the subordinate ones. Learning to outline begins in primary grades when students find the topic sentence for a short paragraph, then identify three items subordinate to the topic sentence. In some ways this is analogous to putting things in categories: fruit is the category, and apple, pear, and peach are the examples. Christian Gerhard suggests teaching students to: (1) look over the whole category, (2) read the label and the topic sentence carefully, (3) decide on the logical order of the items, (4) choose a topic for the paragraph.[6]

Outlining

Sounds at Night
Dogs barking
Footsteps
Police cars
Rustling
Cats meowing
Creaks on the stairs
Owls hooting
Fire trucks

Topic Sentence
At night when you lie in bed, you can
hear all kinds of noises.

Standard Outline

I. Main topic
  A. Subtopic
    1. Supporting detail
    2. Supporting detail
  B. Subtopic
  C. Subtopic
    1. Supporting detail
      a. Explanatory detail
        i. Further support
        ii. Further support
      b. Explanatory detail
II. Main topic, etc. . . .

Number System of Outlining

1. 0 Main topic
1. 1 Subtopic
1. 1. 1 Supporting detail
1. 1. 1. 1 Explanatory detail
1. 1. 1. 1. 1 Further support
2. 0 Main topic

The advantage of the standard system is that in appearance it is neater and less cluttered, whereas the number system has the advantage of making it easier to note outline headings on note cards. For the body of the outline, there are two major styles: the sentence outline, which records complete sentences, and the topic outline, which uses only words and phrases. Examples are shown in figure 8.4, which is an example of a worksheet that can be used with students.[7]

Teaching
Outlining Skills

Never assume that students have learned this necessary skill, even though they have been exposed to outlining at every grade level. The ability to form an outline is a prerequisite skill to good note taking. A suggested sequence of steps for teaching outlining is presented below.

  1. First, provide students with a complete outline for one part of their text chapter. Have them compare the outline to the text, noting the relationships among the elements and the major ideas versus their supporting details. Encourage their questions.

Figure 8.4

Outlining activity for students.

Organizing Facts with Outlines

Have you ever had to collect facts for a social science report? After the facts were gathered, did you have trouble organizing your information so that it could be presented in report form? If you've ever felt confused about how to handle a large amount of material, the skill of outlining can help you. Two types of outlines will be presented in this lesson. Both can help you to recall facts in an orderly manner.

The Sentence Outline

It is important to keep in mind that not every single word of a selection needs to be restated in your outline. An outline is a record of only the main ideas, subtopics, and most important details.

The sentence outline is exactly what its name implies—an outline made up of complete sentences. Read the selection that follows, and then try your hand at completing a sentence outline based on it. Parts of the outline are already filled in to help you get the idea.

> Unfortunately, the residents of the city seem to care no more about keeping the river clean than their rural neighbors upstream. Garbage and human waste from city homes come gushing out of huge sewer pipes. And are those small islands of snow whirling along with the current? No. They are not snow islands. They are billows of suds from man-made household detergents. Water will not dissolve these suds.
>
> Apparently, some people in the city think the river is a good place to dispose of things they no longer want. Cans, oil drums, tires, mattresses, bottles, furniture, and even old automobiles make a floating junkyard of the river. River ships and barges going to and from the city add more pollution to the waters.
>
> A short distance downstream from the city, a long, wide strip of sand lines one bank of the river. Refuse from the river litters the sand. This must be a beach, or the remains of one. The sun has come out again. It is warm. But no people sit and sun themselves on the sand. No one is swimming in the water, either. A high fence keeps people away from their river for their own good.

A Sentence Outline
(To be completed)

I. The residents of the city seem to care no more about keeping the river clean than their rural neighbors upstream.

   A. _____

     _____

   B. Billows of suds from man-made household detergents whirl along with the current.

     1. _____

     2. _____

II. Some people in the city think the river is a good place to dispose of things they no longer want.

III. (Is there a second main idea introduced in paragraph 2?)

   _____

   _____

   _____

   _____

Figure 8.4—*Cont.*

IV. _____
_____
_____

    A. This must be a beach, or the remains of one.
        1. _____
_____

        2. No people sit and sun themselves on the sand.
        3. _____
_____

    B. _____
_____
_____

Keep in mind that the presentation of main ideas, subtopics, and details may vary somewhat from one outline to another. This is usually because the importance of particular information may be judged differently by various people. In other words, outlines of the same selection may vary according to what the main ideas, subtopics, and details are thought to be by each individual. Your outlines of the selection in this lesson might differ some from the outline shown here. Both may be correct.

Topic Outlines

The type of outline you may already be familiar with is the topic outline. This type of outline also has as its main purpose the organization of information. The major difference between the sentence outline and the topic outline is brevity. This means that in a topic outline, the main ideas, subtopics, and supporting details are stated in the briefest or shortest possible way.

Rather than whole sentences, just words and phrases are used. Reread the selection on pollution. Then try to fill in the missing parts of the topic outline that follows.

  I. River unclean
    A. _____
_____

    B. Suds from detergents in current
        1. _____
        2. _____
 II. Unwanted goods thrown into river
III. _____
_____

IV. _____
_____

    A. Remains of beach
        1. Refuse from river on sand
        2. No people on sand
        3. No one swimming
    B. _____
_____

2. Next, give students another outline that has only labels for major sections (main and subtopics) and the number of points to be found. Have them fill in the missing points from their text. For example,

Chapter 23. *Life's Beginnings*

 I. Origins of the Universe
  A. Big bang theory
   1.
   2.
   3.
  B. Development of the solar system
   1.
   2.
   3.
   4.
 II. Et cetera

3. Next, supply students with a list that has only the main topics stated but with letters and numbers to be filled in.
4. Then, only the form of the outline is given with the number of points still indicated.
5. Finally, have them create an outline on their own. Compare these in class.

If some students are unable to do the first two activities, it may be necessary to work with them on these prerequisites: (1) Have students organize a series of objects into specific categories and explain their reasons for that organization; (2) Find three or four main ideas in a section or chapter; and (3) Return to the section or chapter and list or group details around these main ideas.

Note Taking

Good note-taking strategies are important to good study techniques. It is a useful skill whether students plan to further their education or not. Efficient note taking requires many cognitive skills: listening attentively or reading carefully, thinking clearly, discriminating among key thoughts, digesting ideas, and condensing or summarizing them. After reading this section, you may wish to refer back to workshop activity 1.4, page 25.

Why learn to take notes? Students need to know *why* it is important to learn to take good notes. Here are three good reasons.

1. *To organize information.* Organizing the information makes it much easier to comprehend and remember, whether obtained orally or from a reference or text.

Figure 8.5

The Cornell System format for note taking.

_____ 2–½″ _____   _____ 6″ _____

Recall Column:
Key words   Lecture notes

    2. *To hold attention.* Taking notes keeps students actively involved and forces them to listen when their minds might otherwise tend to wander.

    3. *To study material for exams.* Notes are a valuable way for students to capture their teacher's thoughts about what should be emphasized in studying for an exam.

Of the note-taking procedures developed over the years for lectures, one of the most practical is described by Walter Pauk, titled the Cornell System.[8] It is uncomplicated, efficient, logical, and can be adapted to almost every lecture situation (see figures 8.5 and 8.6).

In general there are three stages in note taking: the preparation stage, the recording stage, and the reviewing stage.

Stage One: Preparation

A large, loose-leaf notebook is used to allow room to insert handouts as well as ample space for recording notes. Using only one side of the page, a vertical line is drawn two and one-half inches from the left side of each sheet.

Before each lecture, students should review the previous lecture in order to connect mentally. This can be done easily by overlapping each page so that only the key word columns are uncovered.

Stage Two: Recording

1. Notes are recorded in simple paragraph form, making them as complete and clear as possible.[9]
2. Elaborate outlines and roman numerals should not be used here, as it will not always be an accurate representation. These may be filled in later when notes are reviewed.
3. Major ideas are emphasized rather than every minor detail.
4. Abbreviations are used and supporting details are indicated by numbers or letters under the main idea.
5. Writing should be legible so that time will not be wasted copying or typing notes, a mechanical process that does little to enhance learning or retention.

Figure 8.6

Class lecture notes.

Walter Pauk, *How to Study in College*, 2d ed. Copyright 1974 Houghton Mifflin Company. Used by permission.

October 10, (Mon.) – Soc. 102 – Prof. Oxford

A. Animism

Stick has mind-power.	1. Object has supernatural power.
Power – mana	2. Belief object has mind – a power.
	3. Animism associated with Polynesia.
	4. Power called mana. (not limited to objects)
	a. Objects accumulate mana.
	Ex. Good canoe has more mana than poor one.
Can gain or lose mana	b. Objects can lose mana.
	c. People collect objects with lots of mana.
	d. Good person's objects collect mana.
	e. People, animals, plants have mana, too.
	Ex. Expert canoe builder has mana – imparts mana to canoe.
Good people have lots of mana	f. Chief has lots of mana – too dangerous to get too close to chief – mana around head.
Too much mana = Tabu.	5. Tabu
	a. Objects with powerful mana are tabu.
Use Tabu to regulate economy	b. Chief can manipulate mana – If certain animal becoming scarce, can place tabu on animal for a while.

B. Magic

Cause & Effect (mixture) (rain)	1. Science of primitive man – cause & effect.
	2. Make mixture (cause); Then it rains (effect).
	a. Don't know why it works, but when mixture made, rain comes.
	3. Two kinds magic.
Sympathetic = clay model	a. Sympathetic – make model or form of person from clay, etc., then stick pins into object to hurt symbolized person.
Contagious = fingernail clippings	b. Contagious magic
	(1) Need to possess an article belonging to another person.
	(2) Ex. Fingernail clippings. By doing harm to these objects, feel that harm can be thus transmitted.
Good or evil uses.	c. All magic not necessarily evil – can be used for both good and evil.

Figure 8.6—*Cont.*

Key Terms:
apocalypse
millennium
regenerate
cataclysmic

Def. of
Apocalypse

Origin of idea
of apocalypse

Idea of
apocalypse in
theories of
history:

2 Greek ideas:
1. ___
2. ___

Hebrew view —

2 peculiarities
of Hebrew view:

(Biblio.)

Modern idea —
man taking
over.

Romantic Masterworks – Abrams   9/30/74
Topic: Background for Reading Apocalyptic Literature

[Assignment:]
Read Genesis and Revelations before next class meeting.

I. Def. of apocalypse: a vision of a new world —
the last days in which world is regenerate and (in New
Testament) all time stops and we're back in infinity.

II. Idea of apocalypse a Hebrew invention. Greeks
had nothing like it.

III. Various views of hist. & how apocalyptic idea
figures in them.

   A. First Greek view: the "cycle pattern" —
   "everything repeats itself:" "there's nothing
   new under the sun." Goes on w/o end:

   B. 2nd Greek view: the "primitivists" – the best
   days were in the beginning & things going from
   bad to worse ever since.

   C. Hebrew view:
   1. History has beginning & an end – this peculiar
   to them. In the beginning, a heaven & earth –
   in the end, a new heaven & earth:
   2. Diagram of Hebrew view:

   but restoration delayed until "second coming."
   After the end, time stops and those deserving
   return to eternity – either to heaven or hell.

   3. Two peculiarities
      a. beginning and end – finite.
      b. right angle – fall and restoration sudden,
      not gradual. History changes at once.
   4. Like second Greek view in that best was
   in beginning — but Hebrew fall is sudden
   rather than gradual.

In Pursuit of the Millenium (Sp?)

   D. 17th Century idea (up to modern times)
   1. Gradual progress can be brought about by
   man's own efforts. Man can achieve return to
   felicity by getting rid of evil — man, by
   taking things in his own hands, can change
   environment and change it from bad to
   perfect. [Note: God left out of this scheme.
   Man, not God, effects change.]

Notes should be reviewed as soon after class as possible, filling out abbreviations or adding thoughts to blank spaces. Key thoughts are underlined.

Stage Three: Reviewing

Then, using the recall column on the left (figure 8.5), key words or phrases are filled in as cues for the ideas in the right-hand portion of the page. When notes are covered up, the key words are used to assist memory. After reciting these aloud, the student should uncover the notes and check for accuracy.

The following may be used as a handout or reworded and placed on a chart.

General Hints for Note Taking

1. Do not try to take down everything the speaker said, or your notes will be too cumbersome for efficient review.
2. Always label and date your notes for future convenience.
3. Taping lectures is a waste of future time because you must listen to the entire lecture again when reviewing. (Of course, taping is appropriate in special cases, such as for hard-of-hearing students or so absent students can make up a missed lecture.)
4. Material written on the chalkboard is generally considered important and should be copied.
5. Develop your own convenient set of abbreviations. Certain key terms appear over and over in any subject. Eliminate vowels ("imprvmt" for *improvement*). Use symbols (∴ for *therefore;* + for *and;* w/ for *with*).
6. Do not forget the TQLR formula of tune in, question, listen, review. As you listen with a questioning mind, you will not be likely to daydream and miss key points.

Good note taking requires practice. Eventually everyone adapts techniques to their own style and needs. Just like handwriting, one person's notes will always differ somewhat from another's.

A few things that teachers might do to make the teaching of note taking more productive:

Teaching Note Taking

1. Start practice in note taking with a simplistic and familiar story such as "The Three Bears."
2. Use textbooks or references with good subheadings, or use clearly labeled talks to forestall confusion.
3. Demonstrate good examples on the chalkboard or overhead projector, using the students' own contributions.
4. Encourage students to make use of their notes during class discussions or individual conferences.

Note taking is a difficult and complex skill. Generally, teachers have been found to overestimate their students' abilities in this area. If you doubt the truth of this statement, why not try a little experiment. Briefly lecture to your class and then without warning collect their notes. It is the authors' belief that from that point on you will always include some sessions on how to take good notes (see figure 8.6).

Mapping

As a substitute for outlining or note taking, the **mapping** technique structures information in graphic form. Mapping a chapter can be an exercise in critical thinking, asking for judgment and discrimination about the material. It is also a powerful tool for helping students find main ideas and supporting details. Mapping is similar to designing a flowchart in that there is hierarchical order and words are minimal.

The three basic steps for mapping a chapter are:

1. *Identify the main idea* and write the title on a 5″ × 8″ card or 8½″ × 11″ paper. Place it toward the center of the paper in order to be able to build around it. Draw a circle or square around it. On the other side of the paper jot down a few questions that come to mind about the topic. This step should be easy.
2. *Categorize the supporting details* by hypothesizing first and then skimming the chapter to check accuracy. If the chapter has no subdivisions, the reader must group and label the information. Categories should not exceed six or seven. Draw these secondary categories around the main idea.
3. *Read the chapter carefully for further details.* Add these to the map from memory. This way the reader is held immediately accountable for the reading and receives feedback on which sections need rereading. The completed map is a one-page graphic summary of the chapter. Figure 8.7 illustrates this technique.[10]

Workshop Activity 8.3

Mapping

With a partner, try applying the mapping technique illustrated in figure 8.7 with a topic that really interests both of you, such as dinosaurs, environmental problems, operatic theories, or international sports. After twenty minutes, share and discuss problems and observations.

As a follow up, you may wish to try mapping a chapter in this text.

Figure 8.7

Mapping.

From "Mapping," *Journal of Reading* (January 1971), p. 228. Reprinted with permission of Marilyn Buckley Hanf and the International Reading Association.

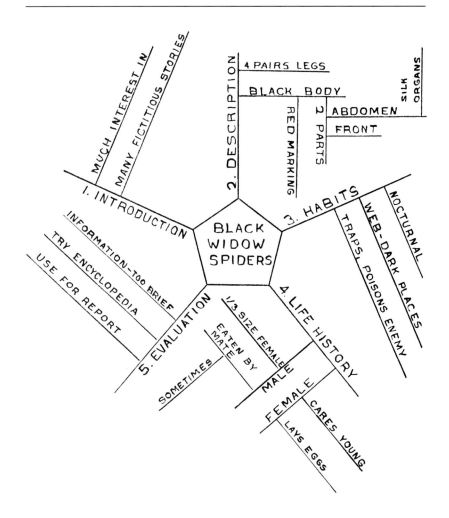

This third general area of study skills, interpreting information, includes two categories—written language and visual aids or graphics. Because interpretation of written language is discussed in the chapter on comprehension, the focus here is on graphics.

Interpreting Information (Graphics)

As the saying goes, a picture is often worth a thousand words. However, how many times do you remember being assigned thirty pages of text and thinking to yourself as you skimmed over the chapter, "Thank goodness for those pictures, graphs, maps, and charts, because I can skip them, so there will be that much less reading!" But look at figure 8.8—which depicts

Figure 8.8
Broad-based constituency.
From *A Political Bestiary*, by Eugene J. McCarthy and James J. Kilpatrick. Copyright McGraw-Hill Book
Co. Used with permission.

The Broad-Based Constituency

A cow never voluntarily sits down. Because it has several stomachs, when it lies down it does so first with its front half and then with its rear half. The Broad-Based Constituency, on the contrary, never voluntarily stands up. Its strength and appeal lie in its broad base. Its movement consists principally in a slow pivot on its nether quarters.

Politicians constantly make the mistake of seeking Broad-Based Constituencies. The thought is that a BBC is reasonably stable and not likely to wander off, as narrow-based or narrow-hipped Constituencies often do. In time, however, Broad-Based Constituencies become a burden on their owners. As they become broader and broader their mobility decreases until in some cases they cannot move, even in search of food. They have to be fed incessantly.

Possessors of Broad-Based Constituencies frequently develop nervous habits. They worry whether the Constituency is happy, whether it needs water, or more food, or just reassurance. Often they will leave in the middle of a party just to run home and give the Constituency a few biscuits and kibbles and a glass of cold milk.

In consequence of its sedentary existence, the Broad-Based Constituency suffers from nerve and muscle deterioration in its lower back and demands to be regularly stroked or massaged. BBCs also become calloused and insensitive in their basic areas, developing an ailment comparable to bargeman's bottom, which is in turn comparable to housemaid's knee or barfly's elbow. It is very painful—so painful that it sometimes drives a Broad-Based Constituency to overcome its inertia and move—leaving the politician who has nurtured it, bereft.

a visual image for the term "The Broad-Based Constituency." As you read the description you will keep associating the words with the gross image. Perhaps you will have a clearer understanding of this political concept than you did previously.

Thus, graphics or visual aids can be of great value to readers in communicating or in making the concepts of abstract written material more concrete. Visual aids range from simple to complex; some have become so symbolic and overgeneralized that they are abstract themselves and must therefore be clarified.

Types of Graphics   Graphic aids may include charts, diagrams, graphs, tables, maps, pictures, and cartoons.

Figure 8.9

Tree chart.

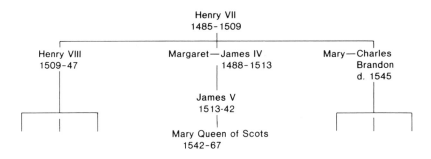

Genealogy of the Tudors

Figure 8.10

Stream chart.

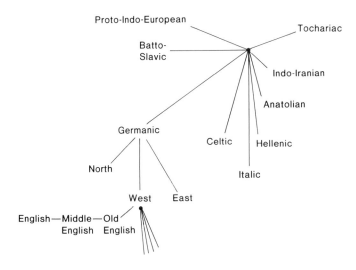

Development of the English Language

Charts and diagrams organize information by focusing on relationships. They are particularly valuable when used with information that is constantly changing. One step beyond a drawing, they coordinate words with graphics in a summary or overview fashion. Types of charts include: flow, tree, stream, time, comparison, sequence, process, organization, and diagram. Several types of charts appear in figures 8.9, 8.10, and 8.11.

Charts and Diagrams

Figure 8.11
A flowchart on how to use flowcharts.

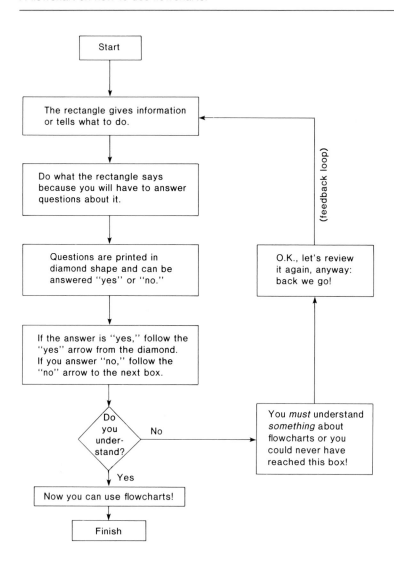

Graphs compare things and show quantitative information in a more dramatic fashion. Because they are a visual representation, size and shape may sometimes give an inaccurate impression if not pointed out. A graph enables us to see at a glance important trends, positions, or history. Types of graphs include bar, circle or pie, line, and pictographs. A *bar* graph as shown in figure 8.12 uses vertical or horizontal bars to compare sizes of items or change in size. *Circle* or *pie* graphs are shown in figure 8.13.

Figure 8.12

Bar graph.

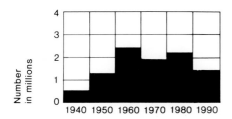

Figure 8.13

Circle on pie graph.

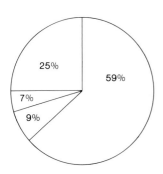

Figure 8.14

Line graph.

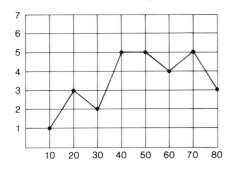

Line graphs (figure 8.14) are the most accurate and are used to show the relations between any two variables. They have vertical and horizontal scales and points are plotted along these.

Pictographs are easier to read but may not be as accurate as other types of graphs. A common type is the repeated symbol pictograph shown in figure 8.15.

Figure 8.15
Pictograph.

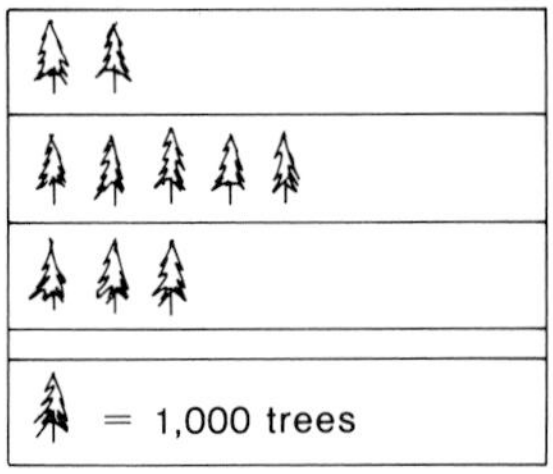

Figure 8.16
Table.

Year	Cost	% change
1970	10.40	.....
1975	10.00	−3.8
1980	9.75	−2.5
1990	9.24	−5.2

Tables

Tables contain information arranged in columns and rows in a systematic fashion (figure 8.16).

Maps

Maps are important tools for aiding understanding in many content areas and are essential in daily life (figure 8.17). They are the oldest written language, having been tracked back to Babylonian times. Examples of the wide variety of maps include road maps, physical maps, political maps, historical maps, and weather maps. Students need to be aware of the type of map, title, legend, direction, distance, scale, and location.

Pictures/Illustrations

Most content texts today contain pictures to interest, motivate, and extend the knowledge of readers. Effective pictures enable students to recognize the subject of the picture, examine details, make inferences, and form generalizations. Figure 8.18 shows one example of how illustrations can extend or clarify information, in this case multiple meanings of the word *trunk*.

Figure 8.17
Map for a map-reading exercise.

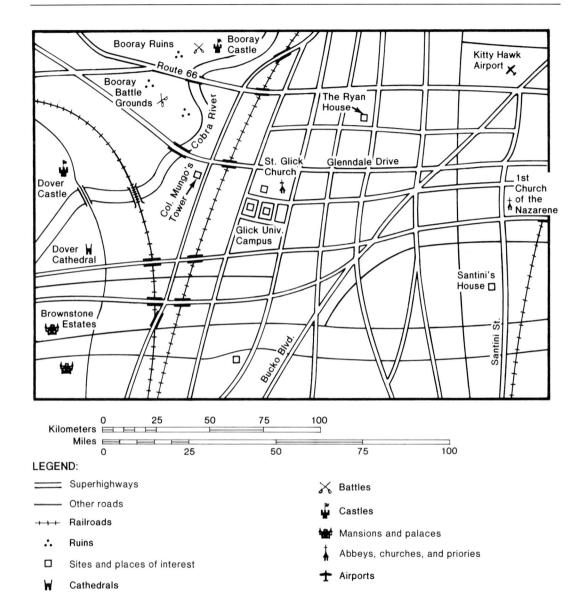

Kilometers

```
0       25      50      75      100
```

Miles

```
0          25         50         75         100
```

LEGEND:

═══ Superhighways

─── Other roads

+++ Railroads

∴ Ruins

□ Sites and places of interest

♖ Cathedrals

⚔ Battles

♜ Castles

🏰 Mansions and palaces

♦ Abbeys, churches, and priories

✈ Airports

Figure 8.18
Multiple meanings of "trunk": illustration that extends and clarifies information.
Tom K. Yazzie. Used with permission.

Pictures
Trunk

Trunk in automobile
storage compartment

Suitcase trunk

Swimming trunk

Elephant trunk

Cedar trunk

Trunk line
railroad switch

Another type of illustration is seen in the Frost/Jeffers children's edition of *Stopping by Woods on a Snowy Evening* (see figure 8.19). This is a beautiful example of enhancing imagery through illustration, and it is ageless. Jeffers has captured the essence of Frost's message. Readers may well feel as if they physically enter the snowy world she depicts.

Cartoons   Cartoons are a special type of picture or pictograph that may contain bias or propaganda. To interpret and judge cartoons, readers must decide: (1) What assumptions are being made by the cartoonist? (2) Are the symbols used clear and appropriate to the message? (3) If it is a political cartoon, are the facts accurately portrayed? (4) Did the cartoonist

Figure 8.19

Illustration that enhances imagery.

The woods are lovely, dark, and deep,

Figure 8.20
Illustration that may contain bias or propaganda.
Gary Glasgow, Staff Member, *The New Mexico Lobo*, Sept. 7, 1977.

overgeneralize? Explain your reasons. Refer to the Jules Feiffer cartoon, chapter 2, page 39 and judge it according to the questions on the previous page (also see figure 8.20).

D. Reinking describes the need for instructional activities that help students make connections among the text, the graphic, and the reader's prior knowledge.[11] His graphic information lesson follows.

Graphic Information Lesson

1. *Select* maps, charts, or graphs that are important to understanding major concepts.
2. *Explain* why these are important to understanding major concepts so that students can transfer this knowledge when reading on their own.
3. *Model* for them your analysis of the graphic, whether the title is accurate, what the basic message is, how the information is organized, and any problems with possible interpretation.
4. Show how the information gleaned from the graphic *supports* a main concept or idea, citing the supporting evidence.
5. *Group* students and have them go through the whole process with another graphic, their goal being to try to reach consensus.

Suggested steps for using the various types of graphics are: (1) extract the information contained and (2) seek the deeper meanings, generalizations, conclusions. For example, students might be asked:

Teaching Tips

1. What type of chart is this? If they identify it as a comparison chart, they will be forewarned to look for what is being *compared*. When they have trouble discerning this, point out how the title often helps.
2. What special devices or symbols are used?
3. What is the significance of _____ ?

In other words, they are shown how to analyze, make inferences, and draw conclusions from these visual aids. As Edward Summers suggests in his outstanding article on this topic, if teachers want to maximize learning from graphics, they should teach students to

1. recognize and interpret the various elements presented;
2. analyze and comprehend relationships between or among these elements;
3. ask questions and search for answers by using the graphics;
4. make inferences and draw conclusions in the light of the particular problem.[12]

It is often necessary to show directly how to move back and forth between print and diagram. ("Arrange the apparatus as shown in figure A" directs them to do it.)

Graphics should never be overlooked in the study of reading because, if used effectively and interpreted correctly, they will significantly improve comprehension, retention, and enjoyment of the material.

Workshop Activity 8.4
Interpreting Charts

The following activity is taken from a discussion of how the polls did in the 1976 presidential election. It is used here as an excellent example of how it is possible to obtain more relevant information from a graphic than from the print describing that graphic—in this case a chart.

In his final sampling for TIME, completed Oct. 19, Pollster Daniel Yankelowich found Jimmy Carter ahead of Gerald Ford, 45% to 42%. That lead was precisely the margin by which the Democrat, according to nearly complete returns, won the popular vote (51% to 48%). George Gallup continued polling until three days before the election and gave Ford an edge of 47% to 46%. Louis Harris wound up a day later and found Carter ahead by 46% to 45%. Given the standard 3 point margin for error, all three polling organizations did well in detecting a close race.

In their final soundings, both Gallup and Harris termed the election too close to call. Each had given Carter a lead of 30 or so points immediately after the Democratic National Convention in July, and each had traced the

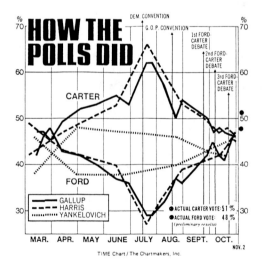

*Reprinted by permission from TIME, The Weekly News Magazine. Copyright Time Inc. 1976.

steady—and inevitable—erosion of that lead. Yankelovich did not poll immediately after the Democratic Convention, when Ford had not yet been chosen, and consequently never found more than a 10-point lead for the Democrat. Nonetheless, he too picked up the falling-off to a dead heat but also registered Carter's rebounding to the 3% lead.

The singularities of the 1976 election—with two candidates who displayed well-developed capacities for blundering—gave pollsters their sternest test. They appear to have earned good grades.

Here is an opportunity to practice and compare findings with classmates. Take ten minutes to: (refer to the Carter-Ford chart)

1. Study the chart and key individually.
2. Write three comments or conclusions.
3. Read the left-hand column to verify and compare.
4. Compare conclusions with the class.

A sample of comments and conclusions for the *Time* chart might be:

1. Carter and Ford started out in March fairly close according to three major polls.
2. The gap widened by the July Democratic Convention, with Carter having a thirty-point lead.
3. The gap quickly narrowed to a photo finish. Overall the polls did very well in their predictions.
4. Overall the polls were very accurate.
5. Other _____

Workshop Activity 8.5
Interpreting Maps

This activity was designed to give students an opportunity to enjoy working with maps in a creative manner before exposing them to the possible drudgery of tracing and drawing maps of countries about which they know little and may care even less. Students are given a chance to exercise their skills in both areas of interpretation: written language and graphics. The directions can be modified to fit different skill levels, student needs, content areas, or a combination of these.[13]

Students are asked first to fold their paper in thirds and put their name on the top. Then they are asked to write a one- or two-paragraph description of a mythical country of their own creation. The description might include approximate or exact size and shape of country, large cities, natural formations, and border countries and their locations in respect to one another. The directions can be specific

Step I
Written
Description

or vague according to your content objective. An English teacher might stress use of unusual adjectives and descriptive imagery, whereas a geography or history teacher might ask for mileage scales and concrete data.

**Step II
Sketch**

The students now pass their completed descriptions to the student on the left. Each student then draws a map of this fictional country according to the details given. Let them choose their own symbols for such things as major highways, cities, and natural formations. They use the second third of the paper for this.

**Step III
Written
Description**

When the maps are completed, students fold down the first third and pass them (without their original descriptions) to the person on the left. The students will now write a description of that country using the map only. They should include all the details that the drawings include. When they have finished this written description, have students compare the original description to the one based on the maps. The class can then discuss their results and see how differently people interpret written and graphic material.

For Example:

"My country is actually a small island off the Bahamas, of approximately twenty-five square miles. It is subtropical and has many indented coves; white, soft, sandy beaches; and crystal clear aqua-purple water. The foliage is dense because of the amount of rainfall. There are two small villages on opposite sides of the island with a total population of 150. My plantation is on a hill in the center of the island with a 360-degree view of the water. One deeply indented cove is directly in front of the main house."

**Applying/
Recalling/Using
Information**

What conditions do you think are most conducive to study? Before commencing to read this section, list a few that come immediately to mind.

Establishing Study
Habits for Better
Concentration

_____ _____ _____
_____ _____ _____
_____ _____ _____

Physical Conditions

Finding a specific spot associated only with study is important to concentration. Students should select a spot in an environment that is completely quiet, free from disruption, comfortable in terms of ventilation and temperature, well lighted without glare, furnished with desk or table and comfortable chair, and supplied with all needed equipment such as sharpened pencils, notebook paper, 3×5 cards, dictionary, clock, and calendar.

Specific study site. Psychologists have found that there can be a conditioning effect between students and the study location.[14] If students allow themselves to daydream a great deal at the desk, then the desk can be a cue for daydreaming. To avoid negative conditioning, students should plan that only work and study be done there. If their minds start to wander, suggest that they get up and go elsewhere for a brief change of pace.

Noise versus quiet. Most studies support the thesis that the quieter the spot, the more efficient it is for study. Many students, however, claim that background music helps them concentrate by blotting out intermittent sounds. Even the soft background music used in industry to alleviate the boredom of repetitive chores is still noise and may interfere with higher cognitive learning tasks. Music of any kind requires expending extra energy to keep one's mind on the studies rather than on the music.

Light. Poor lighting with little contrast causes eye strain, headaches, and fatigue. This in turn can interfere with concentration. Good lighting is glare- and flicker-free. A good shade over the bulb should eliminate glare. Two lights (e.g., ceiling and desk) are recommended to control contrasts or shadows, and a two-tube rather than a one-tube fluorescent lamp is recommended to eliminate flicker.

Comfort and equipment. Real concentration means becoming unaware of the physical surroundings. This is easier to attain when the student is physically comfortable. Also, having needed equipment on hand ahead of time saves wasted minutes and unwanted interruptions later on.

More important to concentration than all the physical conditions mentioned above is mental attitude toward the subject and studying in general. If students are really interested in a subject, they will not have difficulty studying it. But what can they do about required courses? And how can teachers help generate interest?

Frame of Mind

1. Students may ask what benefits they can accrue from mastery in a particular content area. It can be pointed out that good grades in all subjects will help later in the job market.
2. When students ask questions about the courses—and then read to find the answers to their own questions—they often find that the more they learn about a subject, the more interesting it becomes. So, encourage them to ask questions.

Other factors interfering with interest and concentration are poor health, fatigue, and personal problems. Remind students that it is possible to study in spite of these problems if they are willing to persevere. When they are tired, suggest that they take short breaks, such as a brief walk, to change the activity. Study time can be spread out, and a temporary switch can be made to another subject when interest lags. Study can actually be a temporary escape from pressing personal problems.

Efficient Time Use

A dictionary definition of *study* is the *process* of applying the mind to acquire knowledge. The term *process* tells us that study is not one activity but a series of activities. Organization is always necessary wherever steps in a process are involved.[15]

Ask your students if they recognize themselves in either or both of these situations.

1. "I must turn down a fascinating invitation because there was no extra time left to study for an exam. While studying my mind kept wandering, thinking about the fun I might have had."
Or,
2. "I accept the fascinating invitation but do not enjoy it because I feel guilty thinking of how I should really be studying for that exam."

Better organization and planning could have eliminated either unhappy situation.

Time Schedules

The following activity works well with middle school and high school students. Ask your students if they are able to account for the amount of time they spend on different activities. Suggest as an experiment that they try the following activity for one week. When this activity was used with a number of classes at a local high school, the students were amazed to discover how much time was unaccounted for and how little time was actually spent studying (see figure 8.21).

Students should fill in the chart keeping a daily record and total each day in the right-hand column. At the end of the week, they total each activity along the bottom row. When completed, they are led to think about the conclusions to be drawn about efficient use of time.

At this point they are then ready to set up a schedule to fit their own specific needs. Characteristics of a good schedule include:

1. Time allotted for all activities.
2. Enough time for studying each subject (on the average of one-half to one hour daily per subject for high school, two hours for every credit hour for college).
3. Efficient use of small slots of "free" time for study, such as while waiting for a bus.
4. Scheduling study time according to the laws of learning, studying a subject as soon as possible after class with a brief review just before the next class, "overlearning by frequent review," and alternating types of material to be studied, such as math and literature.
5. Time for relaxation and rewards for diligence.[16]

Instruct students to first fill in the blocks in figure 8.22 with fixed activities, then fill in study sessions, recreation, and other flexible activities.

Figure 8.21

Time study blank.

One week schedule	Hours devoted to:												
	Sleeping	Eating	Home chores	Outside jobs	Travel to and from school	Classes	Extra cur. school actv.	Studying	TV/movies	Other recreation	Total	Unaccounted for time	Grand total (Must equal 24 hours)
Monday													
Tuesday													
Wednesday													
Thursday													
Friday													
Saturday													
Sunday													
Total hours spent per week													

Figure 8.22

Trial schedule.

Time	Mon.	Tues.	Wed.	Thurs.	Fri.	Sat.	Sun.
7:00 a.m.							
8:00							
9:00							
10:00							
11:00							
12:00							

etc.

Check it against the list of characteristics of a good time schedule, try it out for one week, and revise where needed. They should remember to break up long study periods into blocks of forty-five minutes to an hour each, with a short break in between of five to ten minutes. This will prevent boredom or tiredness and will allow time to absorb what they have been learning.

The students should spend the first few minutes in a warm-up, where they review the previous assignment and rapidly reread their latest notes. This mastery technique helps bridge the gap between old and new material and will help them see existing relationships.

Some people find it beneficial to estimate before starting how much time will be needed for a specific assignment and then work to complete it within the allotted time—a "beat the clock" game.

Memory: Forgetting and Remembering

Memory is a *process,* a complex system concerned with the "selection, acquisition, retention, organization, retrieval, reconstruction and utilization of all our knowledge and beliefs about the world, including our past experience."[17]

Forgetting is one of the biggest problems that students face in school. By understanding more about this phenomenon, students should be able to lessen its impact. As Pauk states, the fact that we have a memory of a previous experience shows us that the brain does keep a record, or a neural trace.[18] But, like the traces on a recording tape, the brain traces can be erased.

Without periodic review, what we learn fades away over time. Hermann Ebbinghaus, the German psychologist, used nonsense syllables in his research to show how rapidly forgetting takes place.[19] In only four weeks' time we lose 80 percent of the total sum of ideas entering our brain. He also concluded that the greatest amount of forgetting happens immediately after completing the learning task, and then the forgetting process slows down. He constructed the first curve of forgetting, based on years of research and statistics. Figure 8.23 shows this curve. Other more recent studies, using regular words, have come to the same conclusions.

Of the various theories of forgetting, Pauk describes only one, the "interference theory."[20] This theory demonstrates *retroactive interference,* where new learning interferes or covers up the old, and *proactive interference,* where earlier learning interferes with later learning. (This is also referred to as *proactive inhibition.*)

Retroactive interference operates when students learn certain facts at the beginning of the course and do not review them. After a week of learning newer material, they can only remember a few of those initial facts.

An example of proactive interference is learning French and then switching to Spanish and confusing the two.

Figure 8.23

Curve of retention (Ebbinghaus) for nonsense syllables after various time intervals.

From Henry E. Garrett, *Great Experiments in Psychology* (New York: Appleton-Century-Crofts, 1941), p. 273.

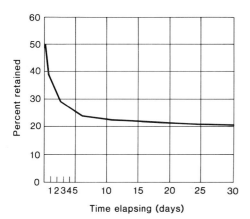

For students who want to remember, here are some suggestions based on learning theory that you may share with them: Retention

1. *Purpose.* Always have a purpose in mind when reading study materials. When not stated in the text or by the teacher, you must set your own purpose to ensure that the material has meaning for you in order to be remembered longer.
2. *Author's organization.* Try to grasp how the concepts are organized and what the main ideas and supporting details are. A helpful procedure is to outline the chapter first.
3. *Notes.* Jot down important points to help fix them in your memory. The act of writing aids memory. It is easier to remember what you have *read* than what you have *heard*.
4. *Summarize.* Upon completion of the chapter, summarize it in your own words. This will indicate that you have the main ideas in mind and understand their relationships.
5. *Discuss or recite.* Talking about the material to yourself or to classmates is another way to enhance your memory of it. This should be done as soon as possible after reading it.
6. *Apply.* Interacting with the material and applying the concepts will also facilitate retention.

We need to remember the psychologist's edict, "No learning takes place without a motive." Then we should be ingenious in generating learning that will be of real interest. One way to make a subject come alive is to find two other students who are enthusiastic and meet with them to discuss assignments. Their attitude may rub off. Another way is to find an alternate text written in an easier style and read the topic from that text before reading your own assignment.

Concentration Aids   To focus our attention effectively, we must have a purpose and not allow inner conflicts to interfere with this attention. Some aids to concentration are: jotting down key thoughts as they occur, underlining key words or ideas, and always reading with a questioning mind. When a text is uninteresting, poorly written, poorly organized, or written at an advanced readability level, we can aid concentration by building a background first. This may be done by reading supplementary material. Workshop activity 8.6 presents a workbook page addressed to college freshmen on practicing concentration.

Workshop Activity 8.6
Practicing Concentration

The following activities will help you develop your ability to concentrate more effectively.

1. Close your eyes and picture a large blackboard in your mind. Visualize numbers being written on the blackboard one at a time: 100, 200, 300, and so on. See how far you can get before stray thoughts push the number pictures from your mind. Then start over again, concentrating harder, and try to get farther the second time, and still farther the third time.
2. Concentration is an important part of careful observation and is essential for good remembering. Look at a picture of a group of people in a magazine or newspaper. Read the caption that gives the names of the people. Study the picture and caption for thirty seconds, concentrating on them as intensely as you can. Without looking at the picture, name and describe each person.
3. Many popular meditation systems promote deep relaxation by teaching you how to concentrate on relaxing. Because everyone's concentration wanders after a time, a preselected number, word, or nonsense syllable can be used to return your concentration to what you are attempting to master. Try the following procedure at a time when you are reasonably alert. (If you are tired, concentrating on relaxing will probably put you to sleep!)
   a. Sit in a comfortable position with your eyes closed. Choose any word, name, number, or nonsense syllables—Shangri-La would do, for example.
   b. Concentrate on relaxing every muscle in your body, starting with your scalp and moving slowly down to your toes.
   c. Once completely relaxed, think of something pleasant; a friend, a country scene. You will find you cannot concentrate on the subject very long before distracting or unpleasant thoughts push it from your mind and your relaxed muscles begin to become tense again. This is where you use your word or number.

d. Drive out the distracting thoughts by saying the word or number until you can return your concentration to relaxing and your pleasant thought. Each time you try, you will find your span of concentration becomes longer.

4. Check the quality of your concentration with and without distractions. Select any two pictures in this book that have similar subjects. Study one of the pictures for one minute in a quiet atmosphere. Write as complete a description of the picture as you can under the same quiet circumstances. Do the same with the second picture, but have loud music playing all the time. Which is the better description? Which took longer?[21]

Testing in some form is generally a part of classroom learning. Students are rarely ecstatic about this state of affairs; nevertheless, there can be significant benefits for students as well as for teachers. Good teachers test to find out which students have learned what and to discover how well they have taught. For the results of tests to be a true reflection of what has occurred, students should have been shown how to study as well as how to prepare for and take a test. It is remarkable how many students have learned this only by a process of trial and error. The greatest advantage to students is that, forced to review and reorganize material they might never have looked at again, they are able to remember the ideas over a long term.

Assuming that your students have been exposed to the study skills previously discussed and that they have learned how to organize their time, listen or read efficiently, take good notes, use a study strategy to enhance concentration and memory, and periodically review their readings and notes, it is now time to help them study for the test.

Remind students that the ideal time to organize and consolidate learnings is several days prior to taking the test. This means that all material should have been read, all notes are in order, and other assignments are completed and turned in—a clearing of the deck, so to speak.

They must synthesize, find the organizing principles, and see relationships in order to successfully handle large bodies of material. If they have not been reviewing the material periodically, they will be forced to "cram," which will work only if they are able to select the vital information. Trying to memorize too much detail in a short time can lead to a failure to remember any of it well. The best they can do is skim over the text and their notes and make a summary sheet of key points with supporting details, then use this for study, reciting the material over and over again.

In preparing for the day of the test, students should get a good night's sleep and get up early enough to avoid rushing. For those who dislike eating breakfast, this is the day to make an exception. They should be sure to include protein, which is nourishing, whereas coffee and a sweet roll are not.

Testing

Preparing for Tests

Some tension is good in that it will keep the students alert, but too much tension is a distraction. If panic arises, tell them to talk positively to themselves and take a few deep breaths and hold them for a short count.

Writing Essay Tests

Many students dislike essay-type tests because they involve much writing, composition, spelling, and punctuation. However, essay tests offer several advantages to students once they have learned some techniques. First, because of time limitations the number of questions will be limited, and those included will cover the most important points. Second, a choice of questions is often given, thus allowing them to write on the areas they know best. Third, it is possible to prepare many answers in advance, because only major ideas are usually included (see table 8.2).

There are three major tasks involved in taking an essay test: recalling material, organizing it, and writing (ROW). Note that writing comes last,

Table 8.2
Key Words for Essay Questions

Clue Words	Meaning

1. Describe
  define
  trace
  discuss
  examine
  analyze
	Give in words a picture of an idea, a concept, or an object. Give clear, concise definitions. Record careful observation. Give the important ideas and show how they are related.

2. Compare and contrast
  differentiate
  distinguish
	Give likenesses and differences. Show differences between items, groups, or categories.

3. Enumerate outline	Use lists, outlines, main and subordinate points, and details.
4. State relate	Write concisely and clearly, connecting ideas or concepts. Use chronology of events or ideas where it applies.
5. Prove justify	Use facts, or logic, or cite authorities to justify your thesis.
6. Evaluate criticize	Make value judgments but use logic to explain. Criticize, pro or con, the merits of a concept or a theory.

7. Review
  summarize
  synthesize
	Summarize main points concisely, restate judgments or conclusions, integrate arguments from different sources.

after time for thinking about the answer and organizing it into an outline. The following steps are suggestions for writing successful essay questions.

1. *Estimate the time.* Look over the entire test and the amount of credit allowed for each question. Spend proportionately more time on the ones that are worth more. (This might seem too obvious, but it is amazing how many students will agonize over initial questions, leaving little or no time for the all-important thirty-point question at the end.)
2. *Outline all answers before writing.* Using only headings and subheadings, quickly write the key points in the sequence to be used. (This step cannot be overstressed, because it is essential to well-organized writing and will demonstrate to the reader a control over the material.)
3. *Writing.* Starting with the easiest question first, begin writing with a thesis statement. For example, "There are many useful suggestions for taking exams," or "Comparing and contrasting *x* with *y,* many similarities and several differences can be found." Then fill in from this outline the supporting details, leaving a blank space for whatever detail cannot be remembered at the moment. Use transitional words such as "thus" to lead the reader from one idea to another. Finish the essay with a summary statement.
4. *Review.* Try to leave a few minutes at the end of the test period to read over the paper, inserting a missing word or phrase and correcting misspelling or punctuation.

Objective tests require short answers about specific facts. This kind of test includes true/false, multiple choice, matching, and completion or fill-in questions. Students often prefer this kind of test, thinking that it is easier to answer and that they do better on it. Actually they have more control over their grade with essay questions. Where essay tests can only cover major ideas, objective tests can probe for the minutest of details.

Objective Tests

1. *True/false.* These questions are absolutely true or false, so look for the clue words to see how they change the meaning:
   a. Extreme expressions, such as *none, all, never, always, every* ("Women are *never* taller than men"), are often false.
   b. More moderate expressions, such as *many, some, few, rarely, often, usually* ("*Some* women are taller than men"), are often true.
   There will generally be more true questions than false, and longer questions are more likely to be true. The reasoning behind this is that test-makers dislike taking up too much space with negative learning.

2. *Multiple choice.* If one thinks of these as being a series of true/false questions, then the choices that are clearly false can be eliminated first (usually three of the possible responses), narrowing the field down to the best answer and the almost correct one. This gives a fifty-fifty chance of being correct rather than a 20 percent chance!

3. *Matching.* In linking up two items of information, first read both columns quickly. Starting at the top of the left column compare it with each item on the right until a match is reached, then fill in the correct letter of the right column by the one in the left. Cross out the matched items as you go along.

4. *Completion or fill-ins.* Here the missing word(s) are supplied in the sentence provided. The whole sentence should be read first to determine what is being asked for, such as a number in the item "A U.S. senator serves a _____ year term."

Advantages to teachers of objective tests are that they are easy to correct using a scoring key and that once constructed they can be reused if copies are numbered and collected. The major disadvantage is the difficulty in constructing valid, reliable test items. The major advantage to students is that the test is scored objectively, with no room for misinterpretation or bias on the part of the scorer. When reviewing with the class for this type of test, let them know the type of question you, the teacher, favor, such as multiple choice or fill-in. It is also helpful to give them one or two examples.

Taking the Objective Test: A Worksheet for Students

1. *Read directions carefully.* This is the most crucial point and one where students most often have problems. Find out, for example, how to mark the true/false, whether more than one multiple choice answer is correct, or if more than one word is allowed in a fill-in.

2. *Skim the entire test* to determine what types of questions are asked and what type of information is sought. Some students have been known to "freeze" when confronted with the first question when they think they do not know the answer to it, thus wasting precious time.

3. *Allot time* to different sections, depending on the number of points. Maintaining a schedule keeps you from spending too much time on one area and running out of time to complete the test.

4. *Answer easy questions first.* Moving rapidly, answer those you feel comfortable with, leaving a small mark by the ones you need to return to. Often the answers will come to you after having gotten into the test.

5. As a rule, *do not change the first answer* to any question unless you are very certain it is incorrect. Statistics indicate that the first hunch is usually better than the second guess.

A number of study strategies have been designed by reading authorities over the past thirty years or so. The forerunner and foundation, *SQ3R,* was developed by Francis P. Robinson in 1941. He was concerned about the lack of reading comprehension and memory of his high school students. The typical reader remembered one-half of what was asked for on a quiz given immediately following the reading assignment. This was found to be true for average and superior students.

Overall Study Strategies

Thus Robinson devised the SQR (Survey, Question, Read), but found it was not totally satisfactory because 80 percent of what the students read was forgotten within two weeks. By adding a test type of review, RR (Recite, Review), forgetting was reduced from 80 percent to 20 percent after two weeks.

Among other strategies inspired by SQ3R are: (1) PQRST, for science; the steps are Preview, Question, Read, Summarize, and Test;[22] (2) SQRQCQ, especially for math; Survey, Question, Read, Question, Compute, Question;[23] and (3) OK5R, Overview, Key ideas, Read, Record, Recite, Review, Reflect.[24]

The SQ3R (SQ4R) method is described here.

SQ3R/SQ4R

1. *S—Survey* (or preview). Read the title, the introductory paragraph, the headings and subheadings; look at pictures and other graphics, reading the explanation beneath each; read the summary and questions. Ask yourself what major points are to be developed. Have an overall picture or map in your mind.
2. *Q—Question.* Turn each subheading into a question. Avoid closed questions that can be answered by a mere yes or no. Instead ask the "who," "what," "where," "why," or "how" types of questions.
3. *R—Read.* Read to find the answer to your first question. This is active reading. Reading for your own purposes (to answer your own question) keeps your mind on the material at hand. Be aware that your question may not cover all the important material so that you may have to add a question or revise your original one.
4. *R—Recite.* Cover up what you have just read under the first subheading and try to answer your question from memory. Check back on those items that you do not remember. Always master one section before moving on to the next one. Repeat steps 2, 3, and 4 with each successive section.
5. *R—Review.* Upon completion of the chapter, spend a few minutes going back over the text and your notes to try to get the overall picture. Knowing that some forgetting will always occur, occasional review keeps this to a minimum.

To this basic strategy some have added a sixth step, *reflect.*

      6. *R—Reflect.* Personalizing what has just been learned by mentally manipulating ideas, reorganizing into larger or smaller categories, playing with these categories, and tying them to existing knowledge makes it possible for knowledge to be retained more effectively.

PARS

Using all five steps in SQ3R may be too complicated or time consuming for some students. Thus, a simpler, alternate strategy, *PARS,* is presented here. The four steps basically are:

1. Set a *Purpose.*
2. *Ask* questions related to the purpose.
3. *Read* to find answers to questions.
4. *Summarize* in your words what has been learned.

REAP

REAP was devised by Marilyn Eanet and Anthony Manzo as a strategy for improving reading/writing/study skills.[25] It was based on the idea that you must process information and organize it in a way that is useful to you as well as to others. The steps in this strategy are:

1. *R—Read* to discover author's message.
2. *E—Encode* the message by putting it into your own words.
3. *A—Annotate* by rewriting the message in notes for yourself or for others.
4. *P—Ponder* or process the message by thinking about it yourself or discussing it with others.

The key step in REAP is annotation, where readers differentiate the writer's ideas, translate them into their own language, and then summarize the results in writing.[26] Of the seven kinds of annotation, three examples are:

1. *Summary,* or condensing in a concise manner. In nonfiction, main ideas are stated so as to make relationships clear but no details are given.
2. *Thesis,* a clear statement, much like a telegram.
3. *Questions,* state significant questions that the reader thinks the author is addressing and direct attention to the answers given.

The sequence of steps for teaching students how to write annotation is as follows:

1. *Recognize and define.* Students read a selection while the teacher writes a summary annotation on the chalkboard. This is then discussed with the students when they have finished reading.

Figure 8.24
REAP: Using a notes facilitator.

Eanet and Manzo (1976) developed a strategy for improving reading/ writing/study skills, based on the idea that we need to process information and organize it so that it is useful to ourselves and others. Use the existing spaces to take notes as we talk about each aspect.

Steps

      R—(read)—

      E—(encode)—

      A—(annotate)—

      P—(ponder)—

Types of Annotations (samples):

    1. Summary—

    2. Thesis—

    3. Questions—

Steps for teaching students to write summary annotations:

    1. Recognize and define—

    2. Discriminate—

    3. Model—

    4. Practice—

---

2. *Discriminate.* Students read a second selection, and this time several summary annotations are presented, one good and the others poor. Students must select the best and defend their choice, explaining why the others are not satisfactory.

3. *Model.* Students read a third selection, and the teacher shows them how to get at the summary annotation by thinking aloud and noting their thought processes when trying to pull out the main ideas and how they are related. They write one together and then rewrite for more exactness or conciseness.

4. *Practice.* With the fourth selection students write their own summary annotation. Then they pair off to compare and come up with the best annotation possible.

In teaching these strategies, you must lead students through the various steps until they can begin to see the value of the strategy. As an aid in taking more precise notes, you may wish to hand out in advance an outline such as the "notes facilitator" in figure 8.24. Students taking notes are then more aware of any key points that they may have missed.

| Notes Facilitator for REAP | In this text the term *notes facilitator* refers to a partial outline of the information to be imparted to them in lecture form. By having the outline in front of them, students can fill in pertinent details where they belong and can return later to study these notes more easily for an exam. |

| Putting Study Strategies to Work | None of these efficient and effective study strategies have "caught on" in public schools and colleges for numerous reasons. Aside from the fact that too few teachers learned about the techniques during their own schooling, many of those who did were merely told about them rather than having experienced them. Those who did experience them were often not informed that using a strategy would be time consuming at first and that they would eventually be able to tailor it to their own needs, eliminating steps not needed. |

It is important, then, that you try out these strategies first in your own work. When you become a believer, your enthusiasm will be contagious to your students.

Summary

The topic of study skills is an immense and diverse one whose range may best be seen in restudying the cognitive map at the beginning of the chapter. The four major categories are (1) locating information, (2) organizing information, (3) interpreting information, and (4) applying/using information. Numerous items are clustered under each heading.

From grade four through college, teachers should determine student needs and teach and review appropriate study skills and strategies needed for their content areas.

References

1. Eunice Askov, Karlyn Kamm, and Roger Klumb, "Study Skill Mastery among Elementary School Teachers," *The Reading Teacher* 30 (February 1977): 485–488.
2. Walter Pauk, *How to Study in College,* 2d ed. (Boston, Mass.: Houghton Mifflin Co., 1974), p. 189.
3. Thomas G. Devine, "The Development and Evaluation of a Series of Recordings for Teaching Certain Critical Listening Abilities" (Ph.D diss., Boston University, 1961).
4. Thomas G. Devine, "Listening: What Do We Know after Fifty Years of Research and Theorizing?" *Journal of Reading* 21 (January 1978): 296–304.
5. Science Research Associates, *III B Laboratory Manual.*
6. Christian Gerhard, *Making Sense: Reading Comprehension Improved through Categorizing* (Newark, Del.: International Reading Association, 1975), p. 76.
7. Ginn and Co. *Read Better—Learn More.* Workbook Series for Reading in Content Areas. Book C, 1972, pp. 160–161.
8. Pauk, *How to Study,* p. 126.
9. Ibid., pp. 130, 131.

10. M. Buckley Hanf, "Mapping: A Technique for Translating Reading into Thinking," *Journal of Reading* 14 (January 1971): 224–230, 270.

11. D. Reinking, "Integrating Graphic Aids into Content Area Instruction: The Graphic Information Lesson," *Journal of Reading* 30 (1986): 146–151.

12. Edward Summers, "Utilizing Audio-Visual Aids in Reading Materials for Effective Learning," in *Developing Study Skills in Secondary Schools* (Newark, Del.: International Reading Association, 1966).

13. Cynthia Abbot, unpublished activity (Bellingham, Western Washington University, 1978).

14. Julia Florence Sherbourne, *Toward Reading Comprehension,* 2d ed. (Lexington, Mass.: D.C. Heath & Co., 1977), p. 5.

15. Carl B. Smith, *Teaching Reading in Secondary School Content Subjects: A Book Thinking Process* (New York: Holt, Rinehart & Winston, 1978), p. 65.

16. Pauk, *How to Study,* p. 50.

17. Ibid.

18. Ibid.

19. Hermann Ebbinghaus, see Henry Garrett, *Great Experiments in Psychology* (New York: Appleton-Century-Crofts, 1941), p. 273.

20. Pauk, *How to Study,* p. 149.

21. Edward Spargo, *The Now Student: Reading and Study Skills,* rev. ed. (Providence, R.I.: Jamestown Publishers, 1977), p. 149.

22. George Spache, *Toward Better Reading* (Champaign, Ill.: Garrard, 1963), p. 94.

23. Leo Fay, "Reading Study Skills: Math and Science," in *Reading and Inquiry,* ed. J. A. Figurel (Newark, Del.: International Reading Association, 1965), p. 93.

24. Pauk, *How to Study,* p. 151.

25. Marilyn Eanet and Anthony Manzo, "REAP, A Strategy for Improving Reading/Writing/Study Skills," *Journal of Reading* 19 (May 1976): 647–652.

26. Lawrence Hafner, *Developmental Reading in Middle and Secondary Schools: Foundations, Strategies and Skills for Teaching* (New York: Macmillan, 1977), p. 179.

Recommended Readings

Alvermann, Donna E. "The Discussion Web: A Graphic Aid for Learning Across the Curriculum." *The Reading Teacher* 45 (October 1991): 92–99.

Blanchard, Jay S. "What to Tell Students about Underlining . . . and Why." *Journal of Reading* 29 (December 1985): 199–203.

Davey, Beth. "Using Textbook Activity Guides to Help Students Learn From Textbooks." *Journal of Reading* 29 (March 1986): 489–494.

Eanet, Marilyn, and Manzo, Anthony. "REAP, A Strategy for Improving Reading/Writing/Study Skills." *Journal of Reading* 19 (May 1976): 647–652.

Fry, Edward B. "Graphical Literacy." *Journal of Reading* 24 (February 1981): 383–390.

Funk, Hal D., and Funk, Gary D. "Guidelines for Developing Listening Skills." *Reading Teacher* 42 (May 1989): 660–663.

Jacobowitz, Tina. "Using Theory to Modify Practice: An Illustration with SQ3R." *Journal of Reading* 32 (November 1988): 126–131.

Manzo, Anthony V. "Expansion Modules for the Re Quest, CAT, GRP and REAP Reading/Study Procedures." *Journal of Reading* 28 (March 1985): 498–502.

McAndrew, Donald A. "Under-lining and Notetaking: Some Suggestions for Research." *Journal of Reading* 27 (November 1983): 103–108.

Nist, Sherrie L., and Simpson, Michele L. "Plae: A Validated Study Strategy." *Journal of Reading* 33 (December 1989): 182–186.

Rogers, Douglas, B. "Assessing Study Skills." *Journal of Reading* 27 (January 1984): 346–354. (The detailed checklist at the end of the article should prove useful.)

Schmidt, Cynthia Maher et al. "But I Read the Chapter Twice." *Journal of Reading* 32 (February 1989): 428–433.

Simpson, Michele L. "The Status of Study Strategy Instruction: Implications for Classroom Teachers." *Journal of Reading* 28 (November 1984): 136–142.

Simpson, Michele L. et al. "An Initial Validation of a Study Strategy System." *Journal of Reading Behavior* 20, 2(1988): 149–180. (Examines effectiveness of PORPE—predict, organize, rehearse, practice, evaluate.)

Stahl, Norman A., James R. King, and William A. Wenk, "Enhancing Students' Notetaking Through Training and Evaluation," *Journal of Reading* 34 (May 1991): 614–622.

Taylor, Karl K. "Teaching Summarization Skills." *Journal of Reading* 27 (February 1984): 389–393.

Classroom Applications

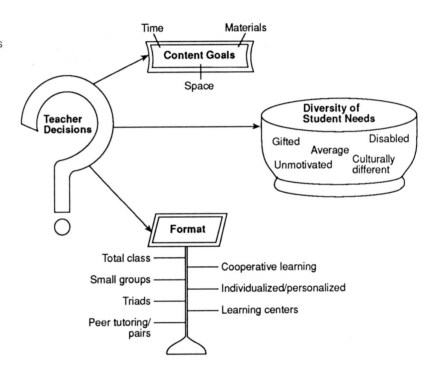

Figure 9.1
Meeting diverse needs through classroom organization: a cognitive map.

Time   Materials

Content Goals

Space

Teacher Decisions

Diversity of Student Needs

Gifted   Disabled
        Average
Unmotivated   Culturally
                        different

Format

Total class ——————— Cooperative learning

Small groups ——————— Individualized/personalized

Triads ——————— Learning centers

Peer tutoring/
pairs

Meeting Diverse Needs Through Classroom Organization

9

Anticipatory Questions

(Literal)

1. List specific suggestions for assisting disabled readers to handle the information load in your classes.

(Literal)

2. How would you describe a content classroom technique for conserving teacher energy?

(Interpretive)

3. Explain what is meant by the statement "The variety of students and the selection of teaching formats should bring together the knowledge, content, and process of learning so that all may learn productively."

(Applied)

4. How would you apply specific cooperative learning activities in your classroom?

(Creative)

5. Design an outline on only one page for a nine-week teaching plan or unit that takes into account the variety of students; organizes time, space, and materials; and uses several teaching formats.

Technical Terminology and Concepts

alternative grouping methods

cooperative learning

culturally diverse/disabled/gifted readers

flexible small group instruction

individualized educational program (IEP)

individualized/personalized learning

learning centers

mainstreaming and Public Law 94–142

pairs, peer tutoring, triads

Introduction

Organization is crucial to effective teaching and learning. At the core of the problem faced by teachers is the vast variety of individual differences found in any given content classroom—differences in knowledge, abilities, and interests. Also, each classroom has a set of content goals. Teachers who are concerned that each of their students meet or move toward these goals must organize their classrooms around existing diverse needs. This is as true for secondary classes as it is for upper elementary ones.

The cognitive map in figure 9.1 shows major organizational concerns for setting up the learning environment to meet these needs. These concerns include time, space, and materials, and they serve as the background for the fourth ingredient, the students—the average as well as the gifted, disabled, and culturally different. Teachers must make decisions about the teaching format that best meets the students' needs and the content goals. Major teaching formats include total class, small groups, triads, peer tutoring/pairs, cooperative learning, individualized/personalized, and learning centers. A mixture of these formats will generally benefit students and lead, it is hoped, to more efficient learning for all.

Organizing Time

How many more slow-learning students might master the content if given more time? How many more gifted students might be less bored and extend their knowledge if given the choice of spending less time (but all that is needed) on the required task and the rest of the time on some type of enrichment? How many students of normal learning aptitude have short attention spans that cause them to tune out halfway through a fifty-minute lecture? Questions such as these are important to teachers who hope to reach most or all of their students.

A traditional time plan for a week of fifty-minute classes in science might look something like the one shown in table 9.1. This plan does not allow for student flexibility in pursuit of learning goals. All students must do the same things, at the same time, for the same amount of time, whether or not it meets their needs. The sequence built into this traditional classroom organization means that when a student misses a class or daydreams through a lecture, it is often impossible to recapture the information. On the other hand, the same science class could be organized around a flexible time plan, where specified activities must be completed by Friday but students have some choice as to how much time is spent on each (see table 9.2).

Organizing Space: The Workroom

A classroom should be designed to emphasize its function as a workroom. This requires a division of space often quite different from the traditional rows of desks and chairs. These should be stations or learning centers, a large group meeting area with demonstration facilities, a reference corner, and some privacy spaces.

Table 9.1
Traditional Time Plan

Time	Monday	Tuesday	Wednesday	Thursday	Friday
9–9:50	lecture discussion	lab	lecture discussion	lab	quiz

Table 9.2
Flexible Time Plan

Time	Monday	Tuesday	Wednesday	Thursday	Friday
9:00–9:05	Vocabulary Activity ⟶				Quiz or small group contest
9:05–9:15	Summarize previous week's learning or return quiz and answer questions		Small groups meet for developing questions, getting classifications, planning, helping each other, correcting other group's work.		
9:15–9:45			mini-lecture labs—in pairs relistening (could be on tapes at listening posts) collateral reading work on study guides		Go over study guides or advance organizers for next week's reading assignment.
9:45–9:50			Cleanup, questions, hand in assignments		

This week's tasks, topics:

_____   _____

Assignments for the Week:
1. Perform labs 24 and 25 and write up
2. Read chapters 9 and 10
3. Complete study guide pages 17–21

To assist in making these divisions it is helpful to have movable dividers, homemade folding screens, bookcases, carrels, a portable chalkboard, small and large tables.

An English class held in the basement of a San Diego area high school made use of huge supporting pillars to divide usable space. In the creative writing area there were numerous homemade carrels, whereas the general discussion area in the center was filled with overstuffed sofas and chairs donated by parents. Long tables around the periphery served as learning centers or for small group discussions.

Organizing Materials

The way in which print materials are placed and categorized for availability and ease of access in the classroom is an important consideration for content teachers.

Collateral materials (see chapter 11) may be collected for free reading time or extra credit reading in areas of interest. These might include such things as historical novels in a history class or an article from a popular magazine on the current speculations on black holes for a physics class.

Another area might contain materials to be used to enhance skill development, such as booklets on map-reading skills for social studies or programmed workbooks on basic computational skills for a math class.

It is helpful to students when some sort of readability designation is made for reading materials, if not by grade levels then at least with the three categories of introductory, average, and advanced. These may be labels or stickers placed on the book spine and may be color coded. The school librarian will be ready to assist and make suggestions for each individual classroom.

Workshop Activity 9.1
Content Materials File

1. In pairs or triads based on the same or similar content areas, select a theme or topic in one course you teach or hope to teach, such as Foods 1 in Home Economics, beginning Spanish, or Art Appreciation.
2. Using annotated lists from professional organizations (see the curriculum librarian), create a card file system for describing content classroom materials that will enrich your unit.

Workshop Activity 9.2
Brainstorm Timesaving Devices

1. Remind students that in any brainstorming activity, the more ideas the better, and no judgments should be made as to the quality or correctness of the suggestions.
2. Ask the focus question: "How many classroom teacher tasks do you think could be successfully delegated to students?"
3. List the ideas on the board as rapidly as possible, repeating the question when necessary. Allow for thinking time.
4. Suggested tasks may then be organized into categories and labeled (list-group-label).

In1900 only about 10 percent of our total population graduated from high school, whereas by 1990 we were encouraging over 90 percent to stay in school through the twelfth grade. Furthermore, we expect these 90 percent to achieve as well as the 10 percent! Educating all the children of all the people is an extremely complex dilemma for educators. How do we try to meet the wide diversity of needs found in schools today? Before attempting to answer that question, let us first look at the range of abilities in any given class.

The public schools have generally followed the practice of using chronological age as the primary criterion for assigning students to grade levels in school. It is sufficiently routine so that when Mrs. Gonzales tells Mrs. Jones that her son is thirteen now, Mrs. Jones can immediately reflect, "Oh, he's in the eighth grade this year." The only logic for this method of assigning students is that it is simple and convenient. With most thirteen-year-olds assigned to the same grade, there will quite obviously be a wide divergence of needs—intellectually and psychologically. Their interests and background experiences may also vary greatly. Divergences among students tend to increase in higher grade levels, particularly in reading ability levels.

Range of Abilities and Needs

Let us look briefly at several diverse groups included in most classrooms: gifted, disabled, uninterested or unmotivated, and culturally different.

William Cruickshank and G. Orville Johnson have suggested that students with high mental ability be recognized as either *talented* or *gifted* or as both *talented and gifted*.[1] James Dunlap suggests:

The Gifted: Challenging the Upper Limits

> The "talented" need experience directed toward their special abilities; the "gifted" require a broad and varied program directed toward their general development. . . . The term "superior" refers to those markedly above the average who should complete college and assume leadership positions; the term "gifted" is applied to the top fraction of the superior group; the "extremely gifted" is that very small fraction who have exceedingly high levels of ability and should be able to make original and significant contributions to the welfare of their own and succeeding generations.[2]

Keeping these students on the growing edge of learning takes serious thought and planning. It is crucial that they not be stifled by hours of "busy work," or going over material they mastered long ago. Instead, they should be allowed to exercise options, to become involved in innovative and creative thinking activities, and to be challenged.

One way we have handled the extremely gifted in the past is to promote them beyond their age group or even allow them to enter college at an early age. David Nevin, reporting on prodigies in science and math, described a boy who entered Brooklyn College's science program after sixth grade and another fourteen-year-old who entered Johns Hopkins to specialize in mathematical reasoning.[3]

It is, of course, preferable to challenge these students in the regular classroom through guided collateral reading and a flexible classroom organization, as described later in this chapter.

Average/
Unmotivated
Students

Average students are often caught in the middle, doing well enough so that scant attention is paid to them. They need special recognition and praise and an opportunity to shine at some task or project. Unmotivated students may have the ability to succeed but due to some unpleasant past experiences have decided it is not worth the effort to try. (See the section on "Motivation" in chapter 2 for guidelines in motivating.)

The Disabled
Reader and
Avenues to Learning

There are students in any class with a great deal of innate ability and considerable talent in certain areas who still do not achieve well in the *print-oriented* situation. Content teachers are *not* required to turn these students into readers, but there are things to be done that may keep from making matters worse.

Any student who is reading at least two years below grade level and who has the capacity to read at or above grade level should be referred to the special reading teacher for help. But that special teacher cannot be a miracle worker, teaching the student all that has been missed over the years. The content teacher, whose job it is to transmit specific knowledge, can assist by doing the following:

1. Avoid the "round-robin" type of oral classroom reading, which will embarrass the poor reader and which is not an effective learning device for *any* student.
2. Provide alternative print materials on the same topic but at lower readability levels, making certain that these alternative materials do not appear childish to other classmates. Many professional organizations provide book and material lists for slower readers.
3. Supplement printed materials with nonprint media, such as listening tapes, movies, television, radio, and records. For example, R. Baird Shuman suggests that students may listen to a cassette on which a competent mathematician explains the binomial theorem, and gain the same or better understanding than if they read the explanation in a textbook.[4]

Mainstreaming,
Public Law 94–142,
and IEP's

Mainstreaming is the process of integrating students with special educational problems into a regular educational setting for all or part of the school day.[5]

Classroom Applications

Congress passed a law, in effect since September 1980, requiring that all handicapped students between the ages of three and twenty-one be given, in school, whatever services they most need. One of the major thrusts of this legal requirement is that school systems can no longer refuse to accept handicapped students in local school programs. The law further provides that students must be evaluated in a manner acceptable to their parents or guardian and that parents will be partners to the decisions made in planning for these students' education.

The evaluation must ensure that biases in intelligence testing are minimized and that physical development, sociocultural background, and personal behaviors are considered in conjunction with test scores. Parents must be provided with results of tests, conferences, and all decisions about placement. After such an "acceptable" evaluation, each student is required to have an *individualized educational program (IEP)*, which must be reevaluated, adjusted, or extended at regularly scheduled time periods each school year. The establishment of IEPs for each student, if cooperatively achieved, should ensure that students work at achieving tasks within their levels of ability and that they make progress toward behavioral goals.

The law, P.L. 94–142, requires that students be placed in school in what is the *least restrictive environment* for them, which has sometimes been misinterpreted by school administrators as requiring mainstreaming for everybody. Some research in the past has indicated that special education students assigned to segregated classes have not always made significantly greater gains than mainstreamed students who stayed in regular classes.[6] Some handicapped students assigned to regular classes may be accommodated either with or without supportive therapy in remediation, counseling, or medicine. However, the least restrictive environment also includes any of the following: (1) attendance in a regular class with supplementary instructional service; (2) part-time special class attendance; and (3) a full-time special class. There are also services for homebound students, instruction in hospital settings, and welfare care and supervision services.

As mainstreaming is extended to more and more classrooms, teachers must be aware of the students who are being accommodated. They must have IEPs, and content teachers certainly should be involved in the formulation of the IEP for their own students. The Association for Children with Learning Disabilities (ACLD) provides guidelines for parents and teachers to help meet student needs.[7] ACLD also cautions about shortcomings occasionally observed in programs for disabled students. Some of these cautions are:

1. As IEPs become established operating procedure, the school administration may not always maintain the high quality of diagnosis and prescription delineated at the beginning of the program.

2. Key personnel who work most directly with the students, that is, classroom teachers, must attend the conferences relative to the IEPs of their own students.
3. The evaluation effort requires constant, continuing study. The breadth of the evaluation is often narrow, and the instruments used may lack validity.
4. Parents may provide their own independent evaluation. Although schools might like to ignore the findings brought in by the parents, parents are protected under the law.
5. Placement in any school situation must follow careful determination of the student's needs along with provision of all the needed services within the school.
6. IEPs must include adequate related services—physical therapy, speech or hearing therapy, drug therapy, or special tutoring.
7. All teachers must be informed of their responsibility in meeting the needs of a given student. They must participate in preparation of an IEP for any student in the courses they teach.

Culturally Diverse Students

Students who have a cultural background different from the main culture of the school may have problems with the text material. They may not have the experiential background needed to deal with the concepts, or it may well be that there is a cultural conflict between what they have experienced and what they are reading.

Language and culture are highly interdependent. Students of linguistically different backgrounds often have more difficulty mastering "standard" English. Because mastery of written language is built on the student's oral language, it is not hard to see why those with a variant dialect (such as "I be here") will have more trouble making the transfer from the oral to the written. Also, negative attitudes are developed toward school and learning if students feel their home language is denigrated.

Teaching Formats

As mentioned in the previous section, once the teacher has organized time schedules and planned the use of classroom space and related learning material—the backdrop for classroom learning—there comes the critical decisions relating to people, or how best to bring together the content information and the students.

Although classroom organizational patterns can be affected by school administrative decisions (e.g., mandated team teaching, integration of supplementary instructional services), our major concern here is *within-class* teaching formats: total class, small groups, triads, pairs/peer tutoring, cooperative learning, personalized/individualized, and learning centers. As we look at each, it is well to remember that no single format is recommended, but rather a flexible combination that can be used as the need

Table 9.3

Teaching Formats

Type	Description	Activities/Materials
Total Class (30 +)	Large time blocks	Lecture, lecture discussion, demonstration, student presentation, debate, panel discussion, diagnosis, evaluation, field trip, outside speaker, viewing audiovisual presentations
	Smaller segments of time	Announcements, directions, explanations, brainstorming, sharing, summarizing
Small Groups (4–10)	General types. Achievement Skill Social interest Both homogeneous and heterogeneous	Research/information search, role playing, simulation, discussion, project construction, workshops
Triads	Permanent, heterogeneous helping groups	Correct, review each other's work before handing in; generally assisting each other in problem solving
Pairs, Peer Tutoring	Pairs—random temporary assignment to solve specific problem	Problem solving
	Peer tutoring—heterogeneous pairing where stronger helps the weaker	
Individualized/ Personalized	Working alone; self-seeking, self-selecting, self-pacing, within content area limits	LAPS (learning activity packets) Developing research papers (see appendix 7)
Learning Centers	Individual or small group works around a table that includes instructions and materials for independent activities	Task cards, learning packets, listening posts, schedule, check sheets
Cooperative Learning	Used with any of the above groupings	Peer teaching, noncompetitive tasks

arises. Teachers need to keep in mind the following questions: Will this activity lend itself best to a total class session with lecture and/or demonstration, to small groups exploring and discussing, to triads or pairs helping each other, or to individual work? How will I mix these up for variety? How might I incorporate cooperative learning into any of these formats? (Refer to table 9.3.)

It is a sad fact that although elementary teachers use, as a matter of course, a variety of teaching formats, the variety decreases as students advance through the grades. And this is so even though we are well aware that the higher the grade level the greater is the diversity of needs. Thus, where variety is needed most, it is often used least.

Let us look now at each organizational pattern for the content classroom. Figure 9.2 attempts to show each pattern.

Figure 9.2
Organizational patterns.

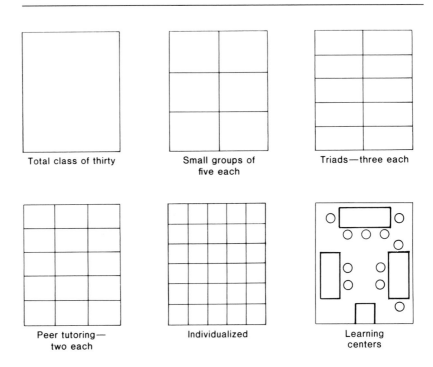

Total class of thirty

Small groups of five each

Triads—three each

Peer tutoring—two each

Individualized

Learning centers

Total Class

Even though there will usually be an extreme range of knowledge, skills, and attitudes in any given content class, there are still many times when it is more efficient and effective to use the total class mode of instruction. This includes large blocks of time for lecture, lecture-discussion, demonstration, student presentation, evaluation, field trips, outside speakers, and viewing audiovisual presentations. It also includes the smaller segments of time devoted to such things as announcements, directions, explanations, brainstorming, sharing, or summarizing. Total class activities, then, are numerous and necessary.

Flexible Small Group Instruction

Breaking up the class into small groups of four to ten students each is an important consideration for any content teacher. Some say five is the ideal number for effective involvement. Two advantages for student learning are: (1) more opportunity for active student participation and (2) more ways to meet student needs.

Recently, one high school teacher was heard to say, "When I stopped talking at the whole class and let groups work together to get their reports ready to present to the class, I found that I had freed myself to circulate, answer questions, and make suggestions. I also found I was not having to spend so much time disciplining!" Breaking up the class into small groups means that the teacher is changing the method to *how* students will learn, rather than *what* they will learn.

There are numerous ways to group students: by achievement, skill needs, social needs, or interests. The student makeup of these groups may be heterogeneous (at different levels) or homogeneous (at the same level).

Students reading at approximately the same levels (as determined in the initial diagnosis when the Content IRI was administered) may be grouped homogeneously so that they may share the same reading materials. At times it might be more advantageous for groups to consist of a variety of achievement levels so that a cross-sharing or pooling of information occurs.

Achievement Grouping

All content subjects have specific skill areas needed for knowledge mastery. For example, these include interpreting diagrams in an auto mechanics class; knowing the translation and interpreting the meaning of Italian words of expression in music; spelling in a composition class; or using a microscope in a science class. Because some students will already have mastered these particular skills, it would be a boring waste of time to practice them in a whole-class setting. Instead, skill groups can be organized to give everyone something they need to work on. For the gifted, some type of enrichment activity or advanced skill practice may be devised. This type of grouping is always a temporary one. As soon as the particular skills are mastered, the group is disbanded.

Skill Needs

Grouping by social needs can be extremely beneficial to students' interpersonal development. One way to develop leadership qualities in the more reticent students might be to place them together in a group where of necessity some must take on the leadership responsibility. Class leaders, on the other hand, might learn cooperation strategies if placed together. Cultural or social cliques can be broken up by dispersing the members among the groups.

Social Needs

An important grouping consideration is the students' own interests as they relate to the subject in question. An English class studying short stories can be successfully subdivided into groups based on areas of interest— mysteries, adventure, romance, or sports. Each group has certain tasks to

Interest Groups

perform in reading and processing learnings, then the groups can come together for a total class session to compare and contrast these learnings. To find out students' subject-related interests, a simple brief interest inventory can be administered beforehand, asking if they would like to read about specific things. Lou Burmeister developed interest inventories in geometry, history, science, and English that could be easily adapted to your class.[8]

Triads

Daniel Fader has described a specific type of permanent grouping that involves no more than three students in each heterogeneous group.[9] The main task for these triads is to care for each other for the duration of the term. This means assisting each other by correcting and reviewing each other's papers before handing them in. It means answering many of the minor questions that continually appear, and it can be especially helpful to those shy students who would rarely ask questions in front of the whole class. This triad support system works well when students understand their cooperative roles—that no one student is to be leaned on to do most of the work and that it is a shared responsibility.

Peer Tutoring or Pairs

Many processing tasks assigned in class can be handled at least as well by allowing students to work in pairs. At times this means one student helping the other, but often it should be a two-way street. The pairs should be changed often so that students have the opportunity of being the helper, the helped, or the equal.

Individualized/ Personalized Learning

Students benefit at times from the opportunity to work alone on a task. Individualized instruction means that students are allowed to seek their own area of interests within the content structure, selecting their own materials, and working at their own rate. A key to this type of instruction is the individual conference with the teacher, when progress is checked and questions dealt with. In content classrooms there is usually a limit to this absolute freedom of choice. For that reason it is often termed *personalized* rather than strictly individualized.

Related to classroom organizational patterns and individualized or personalized classrooms are *learning activity packets* (LAPs) and the *language experience approach* (LEA).

Language Experience Approach

The *language experience approach* (LEA), used successfully for many years by primary teachers to clarify for the student the relationships between speech and print, has more recently been adapted by some content teachers of older students. LEA combines listening, speaking, writing, and reading into a larger structure of language instruction with an instructional sequence something like the following:[10]

1. Generate or evoke the memory of an experience.
2. Stimulate analysis of that experience through questions and probes.
3. Elicit oral statements from students about the experience.
4. Record these statements.
5. Use the written record for group practice or review.
6. Illustrate, tape, dramatize, make a book.
7. File and reuse the written record for individual rereading or reference.

Some applications of this approach follow:

In an English class it can be an appropriate vehicle for creative writing; in social studies for critical thinking analysis; in a science class, following a field trip, for group summary and categorization of key concepts observed; or in any content class as a readiness technique before reading a difficult text assignment. Severely disabled readers can be helped when time and student resources are allotted for dictating and typing main ideas from a lecture to be used later for review.

A non-college-bound eleventh-grade English class, many not reading above a fourth-grade level, listened to a short story entitled "Dream Car." Following a general discussion, students made elaborate plans and sketches of their own dream car. A description was then written to accompany the final drawing and was presented to the class and then posted around the room. These turned-off students became highly motivated with this project and hidden talents emerged.

Students involved in a language experience will listen, think, speak, write, read, illustrate, share, and sometimes tape what they have learned.

Those who would like to break away from the lecture-centered syndrome— without bedlam—might well consider establishing *learning centers* in their classroom. With a little ingenuity and time, content teachers may develop a variety of centers where students pursue learning either individually or in small groups.

Learning Centers

Figure 9.3 summarizes purposes and advantages of learning centers, physical setup, learning components, and steps in developing them. Figures 9.4 and 9.5 show examples. Those of you who are novices should start out with just one center, gradually adding others. For more detailed instructions, refer to the recommended readings at the end of this chapter.

Figure 9.3

Learning centers in content classrooms.

Purposes/Advantages	Physical Setup
Meets diverse needs	Use tables, chairs, desks pushed together, walls, floor, bookcases, bulletin boards, folding screens.
Provides variety	
Individualizes learning, encourages independent study	Arrange for small group or individual work.
Reinforces learnings	
Introduces new concepts	
Allows for investigation, exploration, decision making, active involvement	
Motivates	
Encourages student responsibility	

Learning Components	Steps in Developing
1. Introductory poster explaining learning tasks in general.	1. Select topic or concept: e.g., Math: computational shortcut English: humor in poetry History: the roaring twenties Science: arthropods
2. Center rules—directions for proper use.	
3. Resource materials including pictures for advertising.	2. Decide on main ideas within the topic selected.
4. Learning activity packets, task cards, readings.	3. Develop or gather materials to teach these ideas at the knowledge, interpretive, and applied levels.
5. Schedule for use by assignment, self-selection contract, or rotation.	4. Develop evaluative criteria.
6. Check sheets for record keeping.	5. Decide on rules and regulations for use of center, best done in cooperation with students. This includes traffic patterns and amount of talking allowed when working.

Figure 9.4
Learning center on learning centers.
From C. M. Charles, *Individualizing Instruction* 2d ed. (St. Louis: C. V. Mosby, 1980), p. 134. Used with permission.

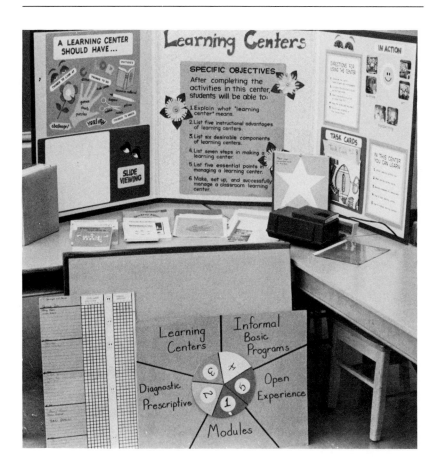

Much has been said recently about the value of cooperative learning for both elementary and secondary students. Students are placed together in pairs, triads, or small groups to work toward common goals. This allows for high social interaction, more individual emotional involvement, and more possibility of risk taking. Cooperative processes mean that students learn how to work productively with others, receiving the support of the study group; they can share what they have learned, hear others' opinions, and teach and be taught by peers. Research consistently shows that students in cooperative learning situations score higher on achievement tests.[11]

Cooperative Learning

Figure 9.5

An example from an excellent sourcebook on secondary learning centers.

From Don M. Beach, *Reading Teenagers: Learning Centers for the Secondary Classroom* (Santa Monica, Calif.: Goodyear Publishing Co., Inc., 1977), pp. 160–61. Used with permission.

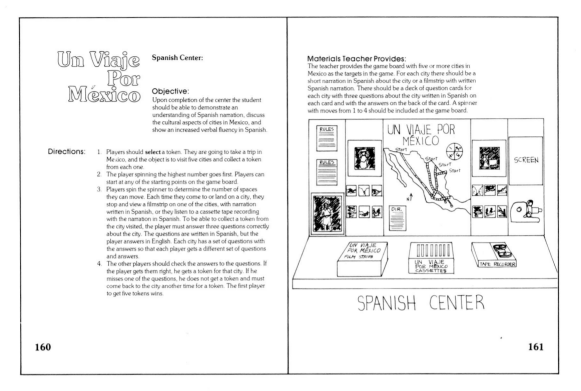

Un Viaje Por México

Spanish Center:

Objective:
Upon completion of the center the student should be able to demonstrate an understanding of Spanish narration, discuss the cultural aspects of cities in Mexico, and show an increased verbal fluency in Spanish.

Directions:
1. Players should **select** a token. They are going to take a trip in Mexico, and the object is to visit five cities and collect a token from each one.
2. The player spinning the highest number goes first. Players can start at any of the starting points on the game board.
3. Players spin the spinner to determine the number of spaces they can move. Each time they come to or land on a city, they stop and view a filmstrip on one of the cities, with narration written in Spanish, or they listen to a cassette tape recording with the narration in Spanish. To be able to collect a token from the city visited, the player must answer three questions correctly about the city. The questions are written in Spanish, but the player answers in English. Each city has a set of questions with the answers so that each player gets a different set of questions and answers.
4. The other players should check the answers to the questions. If the player gets them right, he gets a token for that city. If he misses one of the questions, he does not get a token and must come back to the city another time for a token. The first player to get five tokens wins.

Materials Teacher Provides:
The teacher provides the game board with five or more cities in Mexico as the targets in the game. For each city there should be a short narration in Spanish about the city or a filmstrip with written Spanish narration. There should be a deck of question cards for each city with three questions about the city written in Spanish on each card and with the answers on the back of the card. A spinner with moves from 1 to 4 should be included at the game board.

160

161

Advantages of Cooperative Learning

There are at least eight advantages to using cooperative learning:

1. Higher scores on achievement tests
2. Greater motivation to learn and greater intrinsic motivation
3. More positive attitudes toward instruction and instructors
4. Academic improvement (The best way to learn a subject is to have to teach it to others.)
5. Increased self-esteem
6. Peers seen as more helpful and caring
7. Decrease in competitiveness (Students realize that others' learning can increase their own.)
8. Decrease in dependence on the teacher as they become more aware of their own ability to problem solve[12]

Despite these significant advantages, Johnson and Johnson found that small group learning techniques were used only between 7 and 20 percent of the class time.[13] Slavin said that even with an excellent research base, many forms, and hundreds of thousands of enthusiastic teachers, potential pitfalls remain.[14]

Potential Pitfalls

1. Many teachers with a half knowledge may use ineffective forms of the approach and thus experience failure and frustration.

2. Teachers may place students in groups with materials and problems to solve and then just allow them to discover; or they may have groups produce a single product or solution. Neither of these approaches is supported by research. As a matter of fact, successful models always include good instruction, with cooperative activities supplementing, not replacing, instruction. Groups should include individual accountability. Real group success depends on the sum of all group members' quiz scores or contributions to a team task.

3. Methods may be oversold and undertrained and be promoted as an alternative to tracking and class grouping as a means of mainstreaming academically handicapped students, improving race relations in desegregated schools, solving problems of those at risk, increasing prosocial behavior among students, or increasing student achievement. Cooperative learning *can* accomplish these objectives, as mentioned earlier, but not as a result of one three-hour inservice session.

Lasting success requires in-class follow-up over time from expert or peer coaches. It requires strong administrative support and available materials designed or adapted for cooperative learning. Also, there needs to be a match between the right methods and the right objectives.

Success Requisites

Along with the more commonly used grouping methods—random, achievement, skill needs, social needs, and interests—Wood has gathered several alternatives that deserve consideration.[15]

Grouping Methods

1. *Group retellings.* In pairs, triads, or small groups, each student reads silently a different piece of material from magazines, newspapers, etc., on the same topic. They prepare to retell in their own words to their group what they have read. At any point others may add such items as a similar fact from their own article or an anecdote from their own experience.

2. *Associational Dialogue.* This is a component of what is called *free associational assessment* and can be used instead of

traditional testing. This group method assesses expository material through free recall and associational thinking. Give students a list of key concepts from their reading and instruct them to take notes on a separate sheet of paper when reading or listening to lectures and discussions. They must then form clusters of data by organizing details around main concepts. Using the teacher's original list, with a partner, they try to recite main facts for each concept.

3. *Dyadic learning.* Here students read two pages of their text in pairs; one recalls facts by orally summarizing from memory, and the other listens and facilitates (corrects, clarifies, or elaborates). They switch roles every two pages.

4. *Buddy system.* This system pairs together students of varied ability levels and lets them know they are now responsible for each other's learning. It is also a good idea at the beginning of the term to randomly assign buddies (partners) who are responsible to each other for notes, handouts, and tasks when one buddy is absent.

5. *Problem solving.* In this method thought-provoking questions that have more than one possible response are developed and one is distributed per group, written on large, poster-sized sheets and taped to the walls. The class is divided into groups of five to six, and each group is seated around its home base question. One group member is designated as recorder; another as reporter. As students discuss and respond to the written question, the recorder writes responses on the poster paper. Then, limiting each move to five minutes, groups move around the bases, responding to each question by writing their agreed-upon response on the poster sheet. When they all return to home base, they synthesize all responses to their question and the reporter reports to the whole class at the end.

Cooperative Learning/ Teaching Scripts

Dansereau developed two scripts differentiating cooperative learning and cooperative teaching.[16] The first enhances transfer to individual reading and study, whereas teaching brings about masters of content. He gives examples of the differences. In the cooperative learning script, partners A and B read passage I and when finished, close their books. Partner A orally summarizes, and B corrects any errors or omissions. Both then develop analogies or images to help them remember the information, then move on to passage II and reverse roles. In cooperative teaching, partner A reads passage I, B reads passage II. They take turns teaching their passage to each other while the other asks clarifying questions such as "Did you mean . . . ?" After forming images and analogies, they then reverse roles, each reading the passage they did not read originally in order to further modify, extend, clarify.

An alternative approach to dealing with diverse needs in a content classroom has been suggested by Carl and Sharon Smith.[17] Who learns most? The one who is most active. Who is most active in a teacher-centered classroom? The teacher who has searched, selected, gathered, rewritten, and presented materials. Here is a way to turn this around, where students do most of the reading, writing, comparing, as well as the usual teacher tasks of correcting and grading.

Conserving Teacher Energy— A Content Classroom Technique

Working in groups, students will rewrite and edit portions of textbook chapters. The organizing steps follow:

1. Review with the whole class how to use chapter headings and subtitles as aids to outlining a chapter.
2. Have students individually preview and outline the chapter to be read. Using triads or pairs, the students exchange outlines and assess or correct each other's work during the last ten minutes.
3. As homework, or for the class activity for the following day, small groups of around five students are assigned portions of the chapter to rewrite and condense into one or two pages. Remind students that the goal is to pull out main ideas, using complete sentences. After correcting each other's work in the group, each group selects two of the best papers. Students have thus read that portion of the text and its condensation many times.
4. The third day is spent rotating the paraphrased student condensations among groups, each group selecting the two best ones of each set. The result is a tremendous amount of reading and reinforcing of main ideas by each student, and the teacher has been free to work individually where needed.
5. Now that everyone is well grounded with the factual level, the teacher can ask higher-level questions. As a bonus for the teacher, the best student condensations can be retained and used in the future as low-readability rewrites of the chapter for disabled readers. The rewrites may be typed as a special project by the typing class.

Workshop Activity 9.3
Role Playing Using Triads

1. Divide the class into triads and have each group number off 1, 2, 3. All number ones are assigned the role of a culturally different student. Number twos are disabled readers, and number threes are gifted students.
2. Using these assigned roles, groups are given one of the assigned tasks on page 292. While working on the task for the allotted time (e.g., twenty minutes) each must respond or make suggestions according to its assigned role.

3. When time is up, each group should take five minutes to discuss briefly the problems and feelings encountered. Following this, a general class discussion may be held.

Suggested Tasks

a. Write one paragraph explaining the topic which will be drawn from a grab bag of topics (e.g., *bibliotherapy, the mature reader, readability*). Describe it so that it will be clearly understood by other classmates.

b. Each group is given a card on which the same problem is typed. (As an alternative each group could be given a different problem.) For example:

 (i) You are three students in a combined history/English class studying poverty in Mexico. The culturally different student is from a middle class family from Tijuana, Mexico; the gifted from a wealthy Bostonian family; and the disabled reader from a migrant worker's family. The teacher has assigned your group to write a report and present it to the class next week. Your task is to decide which jobs are best suited to each of you and be ready to defend your decisions.

 (ii) As three teachers on the faculty of a middle or high school, one of you is from Europe and English is your second language; one of you is a former "whiz kid" in electronics; and one of you had to overcome a reading handicap years ago as a high school student. In your roles, and helping each other, develop three higher-level comprehension questions to ask students about a topic in yesterday's newspaper.

Workshop Activity 9.4
Mini-Learning Centers

1. Pass around a sign-up sheet, with general topic headings such as technical vocabulary development, critical-creative comprehension, adaptable rates, locational study skills, organizational study skills, motivational strategies. Ask that no more than five people sign up for any one group. With large classes, there might be two groups labeled "adaptable rates," for example. Groups may be all one content specialty or mixed.
2. The task for each group is to develop a mini-learning center on its general topic, but using its content specialty: for example, the technical vocabulary of biology for the science teacher, figures of speech for English teachers.
3. Allow thirty minutes of class time initially for small group planning. Have outside reading resources available to be checked out or have them on reserve in the library. Large posters or pictures showing examples of a learning center would be helpful.
4. At the next class session allow ten to fifteen minutes for groups to reconvene and refine their plans including individual task responsibilities.

5. During a later class session each group might set up the center and briefly describe it to the rest of the class in three minutes. The last time segment might be reserved to allow each group to try out one other center. As an alternative, show the need to be concerned with efficient *traffic patterns* from one center to another by demonstrating this with the class. Assign groups to centers, and allow them several minutes to examine the material. Ring a bell, or make some signal that they have one minute to "clean up," and then move to the next center on their left, for example.
6. Follow up with a general evaluative discussion of merits and disadvantages of using learning centers in content classrooms.

Summary

As a quick overview of major concepts discussed in this chapter, refer to the cognitive map at the beginning of the chapter. This shows the three organizing elements for which teachers must make decisions as to how to meet diverse needs through classroom organization. These three elements are (1) content goals, including time, space, and materials; (2) the diversity of student needs, from gifted to disabled, average, unmotivated, and culturally different; and (3) format, which includes the many varied ways to organize students for productive, active learning. Whether total class, small group, or smaller, cooperative learning can be adapted to each format. Finally, the language experience approach can be adapted to content classrooms and may involve students in listening, thinking, speaking, writing, reading, illustrating, and/or taping. The key idea of classroom organization is variety.

References

1. William M. Cruickshank and G. Orville Johnson, eds., *Education of Exceptional Children and Youth,* 3d ed. (Englewood Cliffs, N.J.: Prentice-Hall, Inc., 1975).
2. James M. Dunlap, "The Education of Children with High Mental Ability," in *Education of Exceptional Children and Youth,* ed. William M. Cruickshank and G. Orville Johnson, 3d ed. (Englewood Cliffs, N.J.: Prentice-Hall, Inc., 1975), pp. 152–154.
3. David Nevin, "Young Prodigies Take Off Under Special Program," *Smithsonian* 8 (October 1977): 77.
4. R. Baird Shuman, *Strategies in Teaching Reading: Secondary* (Washington, D.C.: National Education Association, 1978), p. 16.
5. John F. Savage and Jean F. Mooney, *Teaching Reading to Children with Special Needs,* Chapter 2, "Learning Problems" (Boston: Allyn & Bacon, 1979), pp. 41–70.
6. Lloyd M. Dunn, "Special Education for the Mildly Retarded: Is Much of it Justifiable?" *Exceptional Children* (October 1968): 5–22.
7. The address of the national association is: Association for Children with Learning Disabilities, 5225 Grace Street, Pittsburgh, Pennsylvania 15236.

8. Lou Burmeister, *Reading Strategies for Middle and Secondary School Teachers,* 2d ed. (Boston: Addison-Wesley, 1978), pp. 75–79.

9. Daniel Fader, *The New Hooked on Books* (New York: Berkley Medallion Books, 1976).

10. Walter Hill, *Secondary School Reading: Progress, Program and Procedure* (Boston: Allyn & Bacon, 1979), p. 234.

11. Karen D. Wood, "Fostering Cooperative Learning in Middle and Secondary Classrooms," *Journal of Reading* 31 (October 1987): 10–18.

12. Ibid.

13. Roger T. Johnson and David W. Johnson, "Student-Student Interaction: Ignored But Powerful," *Journal of Teacher Education* 36 (July–August 1985): 22–26.

14. Robert E. Slavin, "Here Today or Gone Tomorrow?" *Educational Leadership* 47 (December 1989, January 1990).

15. Wood, *Cooperative Learning.*

16. Donald F. Dansereau, "Transfer from Cooperative to Individual Studying," *Journal of Reading* 30 (April 1987): 614–619.

17. Carl B. Smith, Sharon L. Smith, and Larry Mikulecky, *Teaching Reading in Secondary School Content Subjects: A Book Thinking Process* (New York: Holt, Rinehart & Winston, 1978), p. 395.

Recommended Readings

Alvermann, Donna E., and Hayes, David A. "Classroom Discussion of Content Area Reading Assignments: An Intervention Study." *Reading Research Quarterly* 24, 3 (1989): 305–335.

Andersson, Billie V., and Barnitz, John G. "Cross Cultural Schemata and Reading Comprehension Instruction." *Journal of Reading* 28 (November 1984): 102–108.

Bates, Gary W. "Developing Reading Strategies for the Gifted: A Research-Based Approach." *Journal of Reading* 27 (April 1984): 590–593.

Beach, Don M. *Reaching Teenagers: Learning Centers for the Secondary Classroom.* Santa Monica, Calif.: Goodyear Publishing Co., 1977.

Conley, Mark W. "Promoting Cross Cultural Understanding Through Content Area Reading Strategies." *Journal of Reading* 28 (April 1985): 600–605.

Earle, Richard A., and Sanders, Peter L. "Individualizing Reading Assignments." *Journal of Reading* 16 (April 1973): 550–555.

Educational Leadership 47 (December 1989–January 1990). The entire issue contains articles on the theme of cooperative learning.

Flynn, Linda L. "Developing Critical Reading Skills Through Cooperative Problem Solving." *Reading Teacher* 42 (May 1989): 664–669.

Hawley, Robert C., and Hawley, Isabel L. "Scissors, Glue and English Too." *The Independent School Bulletin* 33 (October 1973): 41–43. Describes activities that enhance self-concept while stressing use of metaphor, connotation, imagery, grammar.

Howard, E. R. "Developing Sequential Learning Materials." *National Association of Secondary School Principals Bulletin* 54 (May 1970): 159–168. Discusses ways to create spaces in the classroom for seminars, individual studying, working on projects.

Judy, Judith E. et al. "Effects of Two Instructional Approaches and Peer Tutoring on Gifted and Nongifted Sixth Grade Students' Analogy Performance." *Reading Research Quarterly* 23 (Spring 1988): 236–256.

Kagan, S. *Cooperative Learning: Resources for Teachers.* Riverside, Calif.: University of California, 1988. A handy manual full of ideas and resources on team investigation and learning.

Kline, A. A. "Individualizing Chemistry—A Method Used in an Open High School." *Science Teacher* 39 (March 1972): 61–62. Describes a modulated program that mixes teacher-directed days with individualized learning days.

Larson, Celia O., and Dansereau, Donald F. "Cooperative Learning in Dyads." *Journal of Reading* 29 (March 1986): 516–520.

Maring, Gerald H., and Furman, Gail. "Seven 'Whole Class' Strategies to Help Mainstreamed Young People Read and Listen Better in Content Area Classes." *Journal of Reading* 28 (May 1985): 694–700.

Maring, Gerald; Furman, Gail Chase; and Blum-Anderson, Judy. "Five Cooperative Learning Strategies for Mainstreamed Youngsters in Content Area Classrooms." *The Reading Teacher* 39 (December 1985): 310–313.

Moller, Barbara M. "An Instructional Model for Gifted Advanced Readers." *Journal of Reading* 27 (January 1984): 324–327.

Reimart, Harry. "Practical Guide to Individualization." *Modern Language Journal* 55 (March 1971): 156–163. Tells how to arrange and manage individualized instruction in foreign language.

Reis, Ron, and Leone, Peter E. "Teaching Text Lookbacks to Mildly Handicapped Students." *Journal of Reading* 28 (February 1985): 416–420.

Samway, Katherine Davies, et al. "Reading the Skeleton, the Heart, and the Brain of a Book: Students' Perspectives on Literature Study Circles." *The Reading Teacher* 45 (November 1991): 196–205.

Shuman, R. Baird. "English Instruction Can Be Individualized." *Peabody Journal of Education* 69 (July 1972): 307–313. Explains student-to-student contact with the class.

Slavin, R. E. et al. eds. *Learning to Cooperate, Cooperating to Learn.* New York: Plenum Press, 1985. Covers basic concepts, internal dynamics, how to use in math and science and with multiethnic students.

Stanley, Julian C.; George, William C.; and Solano, Cecilia H., eds. *The Gifted and the Creative: A 50-Year Perspective.* Baltimore: The Johns Hopkins University Press, 1977.

Steuber, Stephen J. "Learning Centers in the Secondary School." *Journal of Reading* 22 (November 1978): 134–139.

Tiedt, Pamela L., and Tiedt, Iris M. *Multi-Cultural Teaching: A Handbook of Activities, Information and Resources.* Boston: Allyn & Bacon, Inc., 1979.

Weber, Kenneth J. *Yes, They Can: A Practical Guide for Teaching the Adolescent Slower Learner.* Ontario: Methuen Publications, 1974.

Wheeler, Patricia M. "Matching Abilities in Cross-age Tutoring." *Journal of Reading* 26 (February 1983): 404–407.

White, Oscar, and White, Sonja. *Learning English as a Second Language: For Secondary Schools and Continuing Education.* Dobbs Ferry, N.Y.: Oceana Publications, 1976.

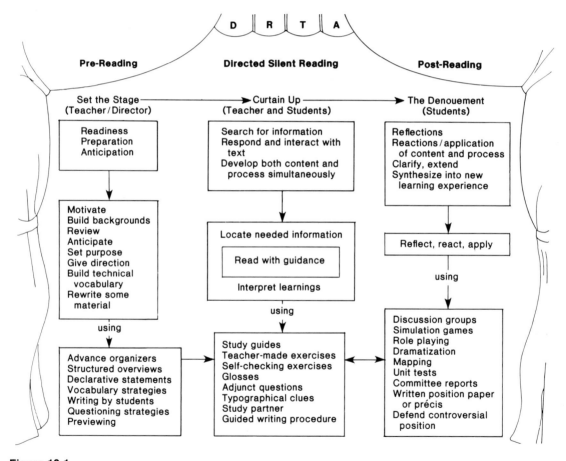

Figure 10.1

Teaching strategies for content classrooms: directed reading-thinking activities for student involvement and successful learning: a cognitive map.

Using Comprehension Teaching Strategies

10

Anticipatory Questions

(Literal)

1. List and briefly describe learning principles underlying proposed teacher strategies.

(Literal)

2. What are five things teachers can do at the prereading stage to get students ready to read? Briefly describe each one in one sentence.

(Applied)

3. Select one strategy and develop a content lesson plan delineating how that strategy is or will be applied in your classroom.

(Evaluative)

4. List and evaluate two specific prereading, two directed reading, and two postreading strategies in terms of your own stated criteria. Be prepared to defend your choices.

(Evaluative)

5. How would you rank order the four types of textbook analysis as described in workshop activity 10.1? Justify your choices.

Technical Terminology and Concepts

advance organizer/ schematic organizer

cinquain summaries

concept analysis/ structure and mode analysis

concept/organizational patterns/three-level study guides

declarative statements

DRTA

gloss

guided writing procedure

inquiry approach

question types: open, focusing, interpretive, capstone

structured overview/ cognitive map

textbook analysis

types of thinking

Introduction

Because they really want students to learn their subject matter, content teachers will try to assist them in preparing for reading the text, guide them through the reading, and allow for their reaction and integration following the reading. The strategies to be discussed in this chapter are based on the principle that to learn and retain new material, students must be able to organize it and connect it in some way to what is already known.

The overall structure of this chapter is based on a synthesized format of a *directed reading-thinking activity (DRTA),* which is an adaptation of a directed or guided reading lesson used by elementary teachers.

Because no single strategy will be able to satisfy all teachers or all students, you will need to select and adapt these ideas to fit your own teaching style as well as what you perceive to be your students' needs.

Workshop Activity 10.1

Textbook Analysis

Introduction

Before reading this chapter on strategies, it will help you organize your thoughts if at first you become aware of the various aspects of the content text used by students in your subject and grade level. This may be done independently, in pairs, or triads. The following text analysis adapted from Smith, Smith, and Mikulecky may be used on one chapter or on an entire text.[1] The four main categories are:

1. Content analysis
2. Structure and mode analysis
3. Cognitive operations
4. Planned applications

*Content Analysis
(major learnings)*

Survey (skim) the chapter or text for the major ideas and information that the writer hopes to get across.

A. *Key concepts* (4 to 8 total): Go through the chapter or text first to list principal concepts of what is to be learned.

1. _____	5. _____
2. _____	6. _____
3. _____	7. _____
4. _____	8. _____

B. *Primary Supporting Material:* Go through the chapter or text to find important data to support and develop the above concepts.

1. _____	5. _____
2. _____	6. _____
3. _____	7. _____
4. _____	8. _____

C. *Vocabulary:* List key terminology needed to develop the concepts stated in "A." You may wish to note those definitions given in context.

_____   _____   _____

_____   _____   _____

_____   _____   _____

D. *Assumptions of Prior Knowledge* (entry behaviors): List the terms, concepts, or specific information that the text assumes your students will already know. (These will be the items you might use in a pretest or preliminary review.)

_____

_____

_____

_____

Noting how the text is written and put together is the next task. Check if the following learning aids have been provided:

Structure and Mode Analysis (Textbook Organization)

A. *Organizational Aids*
   1. How have the chapters been organized (e.g., sequenced)?

   _____

   2. How complete is the table of contents in outlining the material?

   _____

   3. Are subheadings used as clues?

   _____

   4. What typographic aids are used to signal key ideas (e.g., capitals, italics, indentations)?

   _____

   5. Does the index include both topics and names?

   _____

   6. Is the glossary adequate? _____

   7. Other: _____

B. *Written Study Aids*—(Which of the following are included?)

   _____ 1. Introductory paragraphs

   _____ 2. Summaries

   _____ 3. Questions, problems, and follow-up activities

   _____ 4. Marginal notes, footnotes

   _____ 5. Other: _____

C. *Graphics*

    1. What kind are used?

        ____ photographs   ____ tables

        ____ illustrations   ____ maps

        ____ graphs   ____ diagrams

        ____ charts   ____ cartoons

    2. Are they clearly delineated? _____

    3. Are they adequately explained in the text? _____

Cognitive Operations

As you think of the types of comprehension you want to emphasize, which are most adequately provided for in the text? (See the comprehension chapter for more detailed information.)

A. *Levels*

    _____ literal (recognize, recall)   _____ applied

    _____ interpretive   _____ creative

B. *Cognitive operations to be emphasized at each level*

    ____ concrete   ____ inductive   ____ convergent

    ____ abstract   ____ deductive   ____ divergent

                                                   ____ evaluative

Planned Applications of Reading

What do you expect of your students as a result of reading this material?

_____

_____

_____

Which of the following modes will you be using?

    ____ a. lecture   ____ e. individual written assignments

    ____ b. discussion   ____ f. simulation/role play

    ____ c. problem solving   ____ g. pairs/triads

    ____ d. small group projects   ____ h. other _____

How well does the text lend itself to the use of the activities you marked?

_____

Workshop Activity 10.2
Cognitive Organizers

After you have studied how to develop a variety of organizers, we want *you* to practice developing them—with an opportunity, of course, for comparison and feedback from instructor and classmates. We suggest that upon completion of the chapter the class be divided into small groups, each group cooperatively developing a different organizer for this chapter, or another agreed-upon topic. The total class discussion following the completion of this activity should be quite fruitful in terms of which type of organizers are preferred. An example would be:

Group 1	structured overview
Group 2	cognitive map
Group 3	advance organizer (Ausubel)
Group 4	structured overview
Group 5	cognitive map
Group 6	advance organizer (Ausubel)

Selected Learning Principles Underlying Strategies

When your goals include helping students improve study procedures and become independent learners, certain learning principles will underlie the strategies you select to use. Four crucial concerns are *motivation and purpose, experiential background, individual differences,* and *practice.*

Motivation and Purpose

Two prerequisites to meaningful learning are student motivation and purpose. Students must want to learn the material. They must be able to relate it in some way to their own concerns, so from the very beginning they must know the reason or purpose for learning it.

Experiential Background

There is always a need to bring some background information to any new topic. One problem some students have is not realizing how much they already know about any given topic. It is your job to convince them otherwise. If, however, they really are lacking the experiential background, this must be supplied before a reading assignment is given.

| Individual Differences | With a wide range of abilities and interests in any one classroom, some attempt must be made, difficult as it may be, to meet those individual needs. If you use diagnostic techniques, flexible grouping, and a variety of multilevel material, you are probably meeting those needs to the best of your resources. |

| Practice | The skills needed for mastering your subject area need to be practiced consistently during class time. Remember, merely telling students is not teaching; you must allow them time to try out strategies with your guidance. |

Directed Reading-Thinking Activities (DRTAs)

In the remainder of the chapter we will look at ways to guide students through a textbook reading assignment. The *directed reading-thinking activities* (DRTAs) are founded on the idea of reading as reasoning. We guide students through the reading assignment to familiarize them with those reading or study strategies that will help them to be better, independent readers. There is a dual purpose in DRTAs of helping students understand content while acquiring necessary skills.

The DRTA can be divided into three major categories: (1) before, *prereading* (readiness, anticipation, preparation); (2) during, *directed silent reading* (information search); and (3) after, *postreading* (reflections, reactions, applications, and extensions).

Table 10.1 gives a number of strategies for teaching reading/thinking/study skills before, during, and after reading an assigned text.

Setting the Stage: Prereading

We need a frame of reference to relate to when reading. The major purposes of this first stage are to help students realize what they already know about a topic and to trigger their curiosity as to what is to come.

It is difficult to learn much from a reading task if you have not previously given it much thought. A prestructure points the way, allows the reader to associate and categorize, and separate the major from the minor. Without this initial stage students will read blindly through a chapter, remembering little when they are through. Prereading strategies bridge the gap between what is known and what is to be learned.

The kinds of things teachers do at this prereading stage are:

1. Motivate
2. Build a background of experience
3. Revive related concepts
4. Anticipate
5. Set purposes

Table 10.1

Strategies: Teacher/Student/Text

Prereading—Orient to Print	During Reading—Guided Reading	Postreading—Process the Reading
Build, activate, and enrich background information	Focus	Provide feedback
	Rehearse	Elaborate
Preview/survey	Recite	Stimulate thinking by asking reflective questions
Predict/question	Guide reader/text interactions	
Motivate with concrete examples, objects, etc.	Induce imagery	Lead discussion
Preteach key vocabulary	Model self questions/adjunct questions	Summarize
Use analogies	Provide notes facilitators/lesson frameworks	State major concepts and generalizations
State objectives		Use mapping
Provide pretests/prequestions	Gloss	Use cinquains as synthesizers
Use advance organizers	Provide study guides	Use English debates
Brainstorm	Guide writing	Use simulation/role play
Dress as a character		Use visual imagery
Provide attention-getting skit		Draw, illustrate
Write		Dramatize
		Integrate/synthesize with other subjects

6. Give reading/study directions
7. Build up key technical vocabulary
8. Rewrite portions of material when necessary
9. Have students write

The strategies we develop for the prereading stage all serve to set a frame of reference, interest, and feeling of confidence in the reading to be done. The strategies described include the following:

1. Previewing (*inspectional* reading, or thumbing through)
2. Advance organizers (Ausubel)
3. Cognitive maps
4. Structured overviews
5. Use of questions, declarative statements, and inquiry
6. Spotting typographical clues
7. Writing before reading

Curtain Up: Directed Reading	Reading silently to search out information is usually the only part students normally do. And even then they often have little direction from the teacher about the most efficient, effective way to go about the search. An effective teacher can in this instance help students learn to select the most appropriate strategies for their purposes. As they read silently they are interacting with the text, searching for answers to questions posed. It is a matter of developing content and process simultaneously.

Aiding students in this directed or guided reading may be done orally, through teacher questioning, by student self-checking, or by the use of written study guides.

The Denouement: Postreading	The final stage of a directed reading-thinking activity is a most important segment, although it may be more difficult to deal with. Having students spend time reflecting on their reading and reacting to it significantly aids retention. Applying learnings to new situations puts it all into perspective. As shown by Ebbinghaus' Curve of Forgetting, most of what we understand as we read is forgotten within a few hours unless we reflect and react to it.[2] When we do this we are reorganizing our cognitive structure or framework to assimilate the new learning with the old.

Follow-up activities include discussion groups, simulations, role plays, or debates, as well as the processing of what was written in study guides or the reexamination of an advance organizer.

With this brief description of the stages of a directed reading-thinking activity, let us turn now to specific strategies for each stage. (See appendix 6 for an illustrated DRTA lesson.)

Part I: Prereading Strategies	The following strategies may fall under more than one category. One way of guiding students in extracting from the text what you want them to know is to construct a type of cognitive organizer that will help build a frame of reference, a guide for classifying incoming information as reading takes place. Two general types of organizers are *textual* and *schematic*.

Textual Organizers	Textual organizers are a written expository type of material that can be either a *preview* to inspect major ideas and formulate *questions* to answer, or a type of *advance organizer* written at a higher level of generality and abstractness than the topic to be read.[3]

Previewing	When previewing, students skim a chapter searching for the structure, deciding what is important to read more thoroughly and what may be skimmed. We use this type of strategy when we look over the newspaper, deciding what to read and what to ignore.

When students are first asked to survey a chapter to get a frame of reference, they will need teacher guidance. The information students acquire from the skimming survey will alert them to what to look for when they read the chapter.

Previewing (or thumbing through) a chapter to find out its general thesis will help students better understand and remember the information. Making up their own questions will aid concentration and allow them to locate relevant information rather than insignificant details.[4]

The following are guidelines that students may use with three types of material: textbooks, reference materials, and fiction.

Textbooks
1. What is the general topic of the reading assignment? _____ _____ . Thumb through the chapter, reading just the subtitles and visual aids (maps, graphs, charts, pictures).
2. Study the table of contents in order to put the chapter in perspective. How does it seem to relate to what came before? ___ _____ . How does it seem to relate to what will follow? _____
3. Read the summary (if there is one) at the end or beginning of the chapter. This should contain main ideas only. How many are there? _____ List them. _____ _____
4. Read the questions the authors have posed in order to determine what they think is important. How do these differ from the above points? _____ _____

Reference Materials—Nonfiction
1. Look up the topic in the encyclopedia first.
2. Read only the first and last sentence of each paragraph.
3. From this overview, make up your own questions that you want answered. _____ _____

Fiction—Novel or Play
1. Read the synopsis (plot summary) in such sources as *Oxford Companions, Masterplots,* or *Masterpieces of World Literature.*
2. Ask the librarian to help you find a source containing critical commentaries on the book and/or author; for example, *Twentieth Century Views Series* or *Book Review Digest.*
3. Use study-guide notes to direct your prereading.
4. Jot down the questions to answer when you go back to reading it carefully and in depth.

Short Stories, Essays, Poetry
Rapidly read through the entire work with the purpose of determining only
the main idea or general theme. Post your own questions in writing before
the careful rereading.

Advance Organizers

The second type of textual organizer is an advance organizer. The basic
theoretical work on *advance organizers* was done by David Ausubel, who
believed that we have cognitive structures or hierarchies to which any new
material must fit if it is to be meaningful.[5] His concept of an advance organizer is that it is a piece of introductory material written at a higher level
of abstraction or generality than the reading itself. The notion of communicative diseases is more abstract and general than a description of the
common cold, for example.

Ausubel describes two types of advance organizers: *expository* and
comparative. Expository ones are used with completely unfamiliar new material to provide an ideational scaffolding. Comparative organizers are used
with new learning material that is somewhat familiar or relatable to previously learned ideas, with the purpose being to increase discrimination between new and old ideas. This is done by explicitly stating the similarities
and differences. Advance organizers, then, aid students in recalling relevant
principles. They are definitions, concepts, or principles that provide a conceptual framework for explaining and organizing the new material to be
read.

We comprehend better and retain more if we can relate ideas to a cognitive framework or hierarchy, so if this is lacking it should be provided by
the teacher. The old parlor game of a memory tray is a simplistic example
of remembering by associating and categorizing. A covered tray is brought
out, filled with a multitude of small, diverse items. Everyone is given one
minute to look at it, and it is then removed. People then attempt to write
down as many items as they can recall. Those who have labels for categories
are usually more successful in recalling than those who try merely to list
items. The "listers" have no framework onto which to attach the items.

An example of an advance organizer in art, developed by Marsha Weil
and Bruce Joyce, is presented below.[6]

Advance Organizer Model
Marsha Weil and Bruce Joyce

A teacher-guide beginning a tour of an art museum with a group of children
says, "I want to give you an idea that will help you better understand the
pictures and sculpture we are about to see. The idea is simply that art,
although it is a personal experience, reflects the culture and times in which it

Marsha Weil and Bruce Joyce, "Advance Organizer Model," in *Teaching and Learning: Academic
Models of Teaching,* Center for Urban Education, University of Nebraska, Omaha, 1976, pp. 173–205.

was produced in many ways. This may seem obvious to you at first when you look at Oriental and Western art, and to be sure, the differences between the Orient and the West are reflected in their art. However, it is also true that as cultures change, so the art will change, and that is why we can speak of *periods* of art. The changes are often reflected in the artist's techniques, subject matter, color, and style. Major changes are often reflected in the forms of art that are produced." The guide then points out examples of one or two changes in these characteristics. She also asks the students to recall their elementary school days and the differences in their drawings when they were five and six and when they were older. She likens the different periods of growing up to different cultures.

In the tour that follows, as the students look at pictures and sculpture, the teacher points out to them the differences that are due to changing times. "Do you see here," she says, "how this picture of the body of the person is almost completely covered by his robes, and there is no hint of a human being inside his clothes? In medieval times the church taught that the body was unimportant and that the soul was everything." Later on she remarks, "You see in this picture how the muscularity of the man stands out through his clothing and how he stands firmly on the earth. This represents the Renaissance view that man was at the center of the universe and that his body, his mind, and his power were very important indeed."

The teacher of art is using an "Advance Organizer"—in this case, a powerful proposition used by art historians. This idea has many sub-ideas that can be linked to the particular characteristics of the arts. By providing such an organizer, the teacher hoped to provide what David Ausubel calls an "intellectual scaffolding," a structure on which the students could hang the ideas and facts to which they would be exposed during their lesson.

The art teacher used the Advance Organizer on an idea the students were already familiar with. They had recently completed a ten-week anthropology unit that introduced the concept of culture. During the unit, the students had read case studies of both simple and complex societies, and of Western and non-Western cultures. They compared and contrasted the manifestations of culture in the different cases. The teacher capitalized on this background by presenting an idea that would link art to its cultural matrix.

Cautions Research results on the value of some types of advance organizers have been equivocal, and definitions have not always been consistent. Besides the variations in interpretations, there is the problem that constructing a good organizer for each unit or chapter can be a difficult, time-consuming task. Some authors suggest that once teachers are aware of what makes a good advance organizer they will be on the lookout for ones already written. Advance organizers should only be used with material that would prove difficult to comprehend on its own. Otherwise, we are just giving students extra reading.

Basic Rules for Writing and Using Organizers   When an advanced organizer is needed, some basic rules for writing and using them follows.

1. Read the chapter carefully, noting the major ideas.
2. Reorder these ideas into a hierarchy that will show their relationship to each other or from superordinate (most general) to subordinate (most specific).
3. Write a 50- to 300-word passage showing the relationship, or order, that the reader should understand while reading the chapter.
4. Go over the written organizer with the students before they read the chapter, making sure they understand the purpose and interrelationships.

An advance organizer, then, provides a brief summary at a more abstract level of the more detailed text material. It attempts to relate to students' existing knowledge, while presenting key concepts in either narrative or expository paragraphs. Definitions of concepts are written in simple, rather than complex language.

When creating an advance organizer, ask yourself: (1) Does this organizer help students comprehend better? (2) Can they relate the facts, concepts, and generalizations to the learning task, fitting them into the larger framework? If the answer is yes, you have a powerful tool for assisting your students to comprehend their text.

Schematic Organizers

The second kind of advance organizer is a schematic one. *Schematic organizers* take the form of diagrams, flowcharts, tables, or maps. Two types of schematic organizers are *structured overviews* and *cognitive maps*.

Structured Overviews

Richard Barron conceived the idea of a structured overview, using a diagram to reflect the way parts are related to the whole.[7] It involves a process of associating what students already know with what is to be learned and is a visual or verbal representation of key vocabulary, similar to advance organizers in its role of helping the reader to relate pertinent new information to existing knowledge in a hierarchical form. It differs in two respects: it is an iconic representation (or context clue to meaning, symbolized by a diagram, flowchart, or outline); and it is used more as an adjunct teaching device to be worked together by teacher and student, rather than independently, as is often the case with a written advance organizer.

The effectiveness of the structured overview comes from the fact that students participate cooperatively in its construction; it is rarely done completely in advance by the teacher. It is an inductive *process* (not a product) of getting students to relate the old to the new. (The diagrams preceding

Figure 10.2
Structured overview: mathematics.

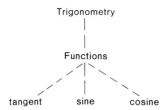

earlier chapters are called *cognitive maps* rather than *structured overviews* because they were done by us in advance with no input from you, the readers.[8] If we could do them cooperatively with you, they would be considered structured overviews.)

Here are the steps for constructing and using structured overviews.

1. List representative vocabulary words that the students will need to understand.
2. Play with the list, rearranging until you have a diagram that shows the interrelationships among the concepts they represent.
3. Simplify or amplify the list as needed.
4. When introducing the assignment, show students initial attempts in diagramming, explaining your arrangement and especially encouraging their reactions, contributions, and suggested changes.
5. Refer to this chart as the reading assignment is carried out.

Figures 10.2 and 10.3 might represent the teacher's initial diagram, with details to be filled in or discussed with the class. Figure 10.4 could represent a finished product after class input.

The second kind of schematic organizer is a cognitive map. Hilda Taba believed that teachers must develop their own cognitive map of the domain before attempting to hold forth in class discussion.[9] We have found this task to be most enlightening when using map construction to organize the chapters of this text; thus we urge you to make it a regular part of your preparation, too. As previously noted, you present the cognitive map as a finished task, whereas structured overviews are discussed and revised with students. Cognitive maps are developed by placing major concepts on a sheet of paper in such a way that relationships among items are shown as well. See the beginning of each chapter for examples.

Cognitive Maps

Figure 10.3

Structured overview: balance of political power.

Harold L. Herber, *Teaching Reading in Content Areas.* Copyright 1978, p. 258. Adapted by permission of Prentice-Hall, Inc., Englewood Cliffs, New Jersey.

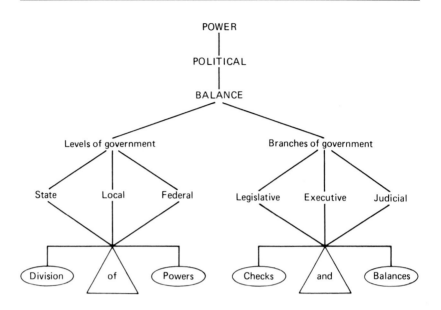

Use of Questions, Declarative Statements, and the Inquiry Process

General questioning strategies are many and diverse. The chapter on comprehension has further explanations concerning levels of questioning as well as additional specific techniques.

Harold Herber makes a cogent case for using declarative statements in lieu of questions at times.[10] The reason for using these declarative statements is that certain skills are necessary before a student can respond appropriately to many types of comprehension questions. Questions, then, reinforce skills already mastered, whereas declarative statements help to build them. Students who do not already have sufficient skills need declarative statements representing information that might be in the text. As they reflect on what the author said or did not say, they are developing both a sense of accuracy in sorting through information to determine what is true and a sense of the relative importance among all the pieces of information presented. With declarative sentences they are reacting to someone else's interpretation, rather than creating it. An example would be, "Put an 'x' by each of the following statements that you can support with evidence from the chapter just read." The students look at each item and select an easier task than if they had been asked what are three important conclusions.

Classroom Applications

Figure 10.4

Structured overview: the twenties and thirties.

Prepared by Nancy Bohlander Willis, graduate student, University of New Mexico. Used with permission.

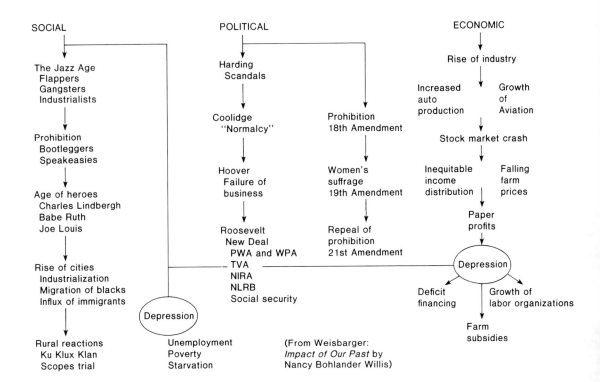

Hilda Taba developed a hierarchical model for narrative or expository material with the purpose of raising students' thinking in social studies.[11] However, the ideas can apply across the curriculum and can help greatly in showing how to sequence questions to get at higher-level thought.

Questioning is divided into three parts: *concept diagnosis, interpretation of data,* and *assimilation of knowledge.* Within each part is contained a sequence of four basic question types.

Sequencing Questions for Higher-Level Thought

1. *Open questions* (cognitive memory). These elicit factual information necessary to reply to all higher-level questions; e.g., "Why must content teachers develop a variety of teaching strategies to accommodate all students?"
2. *Focusing questions.* These designate specific ideas or facts to be compared or contrasted; e.g., ask the students to write one sentence about the type of work they expect to be doing after

they finish school. In what ways will their purposes require the same learnings? In what ways will they need a "different" education?

3. *Interpretive questions* (lifting). These questions help students see relationships among facts, ideas, events; e.g., "Why will those enrolled in college preparatory courses need to use a wide range of study and comprehension skills?"

4. *Capstone question.* This calls for a high level of abstraction or generalization (convergent or divergent evaluative thinking); e.g., "For school success, what *levels* of value (from little to great) do you place on the following: (a) understanding your objective; (b) making a work-study schedule; (c) using critical reading skills; (d) selecting the important, relevant information to remember; (e) measuring success or failure? State your conclusions."

Developing Question Types

Step One—Spend much time involving students, getting from them the important needed facts. Your role is to facilitate participation, not to drag answers out of them! You acknowledge at this point whatever is given, without value judgment or any attempt to clarify. This is similar to brainstorming.

Step Two—Choose convergent, comparison, or contrast questions, focusing only on relevant data that need clarification or elaboration. Before leaving this stage, you paraphrase relevant information elicited from the students. Students must then decide whether they are satisfied with this information.

Step Three—Use convergent thinking again, this time by asking students to clarify relationships. You may need to refocus, paraphrasing the original relationship question, which can be accomplished by giving the information to the students or asking them to recall it.

Step Four—The stage is set now for predicting, evaluating, or generalizing.

Reduction Questioning Strategy

Walter Hill suggests a straightforward reduction questioning strategy where the teacher uses the walk-through process.[12]

1. The teacher and class skim-read together to identify the entry question, which most likely will be concerned with the main theme or scope. Other questions are also written on the chalkboard as they are offered and saved for later clarification.

2. The meanings of the questions are clarified.

3. Students read selectively to answer the questions.

4. Tentative answers are given, examined, clarified, and converted into supporting structure questions.
5. The process is repeated until all are ready to construct their own hierarchy of questions for independently studying the selection.
6. The group summarizes based on the questions raised and investigated.

Inquiry as a process is an excellent comprehension and study tool. The term implies finding out, problem solving, discovering for oneself. It also means that students are actively involved, not passive listeners/observers. Six steps, similar to the scientific method, include: (1) realize what we need to know; (2) specifically identify the problem; (3) collect and organize pertinent data; (4) consider hypotheses and choose the most likely one; (5) draw conclusions, make generalizations; (6) implement the conclusion in thinking about subsequent information. Inquiry Process

In the inquiry process (also known as the discovery method), you inductively develop a generalization about phenomena that share a common element, as opposed to deductive teaching where facts, concepts, and principles are presented, illustrated, and their implications and uses are pointed out.

J. P. Guilford explains three major types of thinking related to the inquiry process.[13] Types of Thinking Related to Inquiry

1. *Convergent thinking.* Gathering together various aspects of a topic from numerous sources to arrive at the best conclusion or generalization in view of evidence given; e.g., "On the basis of the information we have about solar heating, do you think Mr. West's plan will work for New Mexico? Why or why not?"
2. *Divergent thinking.* Elaborating on given information that may go in many different directions; e.g., "Because you now understand the general principles of solar heating, design a working model of a heating system for a building of your choice. What auxiliary services will it need?"
3. *Evaluation.* Knowing whether two units are exactly the same, whether there is a logical consistency in relationships, whether the information is workable; e.g., "Mr. Smith and Mr. Jones each took advantage of federal grants and tax write-offs to renovate their houses in order to use solar heating. Mr. Smith is pleased, but Mr. Jones does not feel that the system works. Both conformed to federal guidelines. List the criteria by which you could begin to evaluate the relative reasons for success or failure of their solar heating units."

Improving Questioning Skills for Testing Comprehension

Questions are important tools in any teacher's repertoire. We show students what we consider important by the types of questions we ask. We can manipulate the learning environment by the type of questions that we choose, by which students we ask, and by the timing and manner of our questioning.

Although the process of questioning will be similar in most subject areas, specific questions may differ according to the organization of thought within that body of knowledge. For example, questions in literature may deal with interpreting figurative language, the feel and tone of the discourse. In math, questions may emphasize information needed for problem solving. Art, drama, or music may center on aesthetic judgments. Science will be concerned with exact details and cause-and-effect relationships. Social studies concentrates on problem solving and value judgments involving no single correct response. (For examples, see workshop activity 10.3, "Content Questions Worksheet.")

Textbooks used in content areas can sometimes be deterrents to good questioning at higher levels when facts are presented in an orderly fashion with detailed explanations given of complex ideas, for the work of interpretation has already been done by the writer. When this is the case, questions can be developed to accompany supplementary material being used, such as trade books or films. These questions can help students relate knowledge they gain from these collateral sources with the basic text information.

A Planned Sequence

Questions may be grouped together in a planned sequence of *focusing, extending,* and *raising.*[14] It is best to start with a focus question ("What do you see?" "What is interesting about . . . ?"). How students respond to the focus question will show whether they are knowledgeable enough about the topic to pursue it further at a more demanding level. If not, additional questions may be asked at the same cognitive level—these additional questions are extending questions ("What else do you know about . . . ?" "Why do you suppose . . . ?"). When you wish to move students to higher levels, you ask a raising question that calls for relating the knowledge to past thoughts and developing new thought ("Why do these . . . ?" "How might we change . . . ?").

Closed Questions

One way to evaluate the effectiveness of your questioning strategies is to focus on the number of words in students' responses: the more words they respond with, the better the question is considered to be. A question requiring a "yes" or "no" answer, for example, is called a closed question. It allows for a 50 percent chance of being correct, whether the student really knows the answer or not.

"Is it true that . . . ?" is an example of a closed question because it requires merely a "yes" or "no" response. On the other hand, "What does this remind you of?" is open-ended and usually gets a longer, descriptive response.

When a question elicits a one-word response, you can follow it up immediately with a "Why?" question. We can all benefit from additional practice in asking and responding to the "Why?" question, of having to justify our responses ("Why is that so?" or "Why do you suppose that to be so?").

Whatever your particular questioning techniques are, they will be less effective if students feel they cannot afford to risk being wrong. Do not play the familiar game of "Guess What's in My Head." For example, we might ask you how many cognitive levels there are. If we believe there are four, and you say seven, you are wrong according to the way we see it (even though you could justify your response if we gave you a chance). Instead, we might better ask you to give an example or two and explain them. If you ask students for their opinion on a topic, verbally reward whoever responds just for offering an opinion. Even if it does not agree with your line of thought, you can always say, "I hadn't thought of that," "Interesting idea," or "I appreciate your efforts," while skillfully pointing out or leading them to see errors in judgment or views unacceptable to the majority. One of the worst practices, in our view, and still used far too often in the schools, is allowing questioning to be a discipline device. Calling on the daydreamers and embarrassing them because they were caught with their minds elsewhere will not enamor the students with your class or subject matter.

When you throw out a difficult question to the whole class, it is vital that you allow time for the students to think about it ('wait time'). The more difficult the question, the longer amount of silence you should tolerate. Usually allow for volunteer responses, but when you feel you must call on a student, try to tailor your question to what you believe can be responded to correctly. Another way to ask a question is to pose it so that no wrong answer is possible, such as "How do you feel about that, John?" "Do you want to add anything to this discussion, Ann?" If she says "no," accept that for the time being. When you do call on students, do not give their names first before asking the question, or else the rest of the class may tune out. "Frank, what is the sequence?" No one else has to worry, it's Frank who is on the spot.

An Accepting Environment

Workshop Activity 10.3
Content Questions Worksheet

Now, having read a bit on comprehension skills, questioning, cognitive levels, and taxonomies, it is time to try to apply your understandings to your own subject. The following questioning worksheet brings together Bloom's taxonomy, Helen K. Smith's comprehension skills, and Thomas and Robinson's examples.[15,16,17,18] After reading it once carefully, decide on one specific topic in your content field. Then, using the sample questions as a reference, devise a question of your own for each skill and level on your selected topic. The first four questions are at the literal level and are generally quite easy to construct; these are the types most often found in texts and most frequently asked by teachers. The remaining eight questions go beyond what was literally stated and require higher-level thinking abilities: interpretive, evaluative, or applied comprehension.

A. Literal Comprehension

Your topic for these twelve questions: _____

1. Grasping directly stated details or facts

Science:	What conditions are probably necessary for a volcano to erupt?
Art:	Draw the heroes just as they are described in
English:	this novel, jotting down details the writer uses to help you visualize them.

Your Question: _____

2. Understanding the main idea

English:	What is a good title for this essay?
Science:	Read the lab procedures for this experiment and describe its purpose.

Your Question: _____

3. Grasping the sequence of ideas, events, or steps

Social Studies:	In this selection concerning the Boston Tea Party, note important events in order, associate each with their dates, and think how each event led up to the next one.
Mathematics:	Read this explanation of the derivation of a formula to see whether you can follow the reasoning that leads to its final form.

Your Question: _____

4. Understanding and following directions

Photography:	Study the directions for mixing the photodeveloper. Write your own list of things to do in order.
Science:	What procedures do you follow in order to focus your microscope on this slide?

Your Question: _____

5. Grasping implied meanings or drawing inferences

B. Interpretive
and Applied
Comprehension

Social Studies: What can you learn about the customs and
                           values of the Athenian people from reading this
                           funeral oration?

English: What truth about our inner lives is suggested by
                           Hawthorne in the "The Minister's Black Veil?"

Your Question: _____

6. Understanding character (emotional reactions, motives, personal traits, and
    setting)

English: Imagine yourself as Brutus when he heard
                           Caesar say, "And you too, Brutus!" How do you
                           think Brutus felt? Explain.

Your Question: _____

7. Sensing relationships of time, place, cause and effect, events, and
    characters

Social Studies: What causes led to our purchasing the Louisiana
                           Territory, and how did this purchase affect our
                           national growth?

Science: If you drop a needle carefully on the surface of
                           the water, will it float? If so, why?

Your Question: _____

8. Anticipating outcomes

English: After the murder of Duncan, who will stand the
                           strain of guilt better—Macbeth or Lady
                           Macbeth? Why?

Math: Cover up the proof of this theorem. Read the
                           statement, examine the diagram, and decide
                           what you have to prove and what is already
                           given. Then guess what the author's first
                           statement will be, write it down, and check it
                           out. Next, ask yourself, "What will the author
                           give as a reason?" Jot down and check.

Your Question: _____

9. Recognizing author's tone, mood, and intent

All Subjects: Is the reporter unbiased or biased? If so, how
                           can you tell?

English: Sometimes a writer says one thing although the
                           exact opposite is meant. Find an example in this
                           passage where the writer uses irony to make the
                           point.

Your Question: _____

10. Understanding and drawing comparisons and contrasts

Science: Compare the telephone transmitter to the human
                           ear, and list all the similarities and differences.

Social Studies: Where would you prefer to live in ancient
                           Greece—ancient Athens or Sparta? Explain.

Your Question: _____

11. Drawing conclusions, making generalizations

Science: What general rule can you make concerning the effect that heat has on molecules?

All Subjects: Examine the conclusion stated in the text, then find the facts given in the passage. Together, do they warrant this conclusion? Why or why not?

Your Question: _____

12. Making evaluations

All Subjects: Which report is more reliable? Before answering, set up your own standards or criteria for judging a reliable statement.

Science: Should we be trying to engineer man's heredity? If so, what kinds of people should we be engineering for? Explain your philosophy about this.

Your Question: _____

Table 10.2 is included as a further aid and reference for writing questions at a variety of levels. The sample listing of verbs to use should be most helpful.

Structured Comprehension for Problem Readers

For students who have difficulty in verbalizing what the sentence has told them after reading the words, Marvin Cohn describes a technique called *structured comprehension.*[19] Students read one sentence and must answer the question, "Do I know what this sentence means?" This forces them early in their learning to begin the habit of talking back to the writing and, with the help of the teacher, learning that each sentence tells something and that as sentences accumulate they build sequences of ideas. Teachers should also ask questions about the sentence. After students are successful with this technique, they should then be required to write brief answers to some of the questions. Cohn states that in the beginning teachers should be satisfied with literal-level questions.

Hypothesis Testing

The hypothesis-testing model for teaching paragraph comprehension was successfully used with dull-normal children. It may be adapted for use with all students when they encounter complex material. The steps are:

1. Read the first sentence and assume it is the main idea.
2. Read the second sentence and
   a. if the meaning of the first sentence encompasses the second one, continue to think of the first sentence as stating the main idea;

Table 10.2

An Aid to Writing Questions and Objectives

Taxonomy Level	Emphasis	Objective	Sample Verbs to Use
1. Knowledge (facts, rote memory)	recognize and recall facts in a form close to the way they were first presented	show how you know by:	list, tell, define, identify, label, locate, recognize
2. Translation and interpretation (put in own words)	grasp the meaning and intent of information, tell in your own words	show that you understand by:	explain, illustrate, describe, summarize, interpret, expand, convert, measure, translate, restate
3. Application (use what you know)	use information—ability to apply learning to new situations and real-life circumstances	show that you can use what is learned by:	demonstrate, apply, use, construct, find solutions, collect information, perform, solve, choose appropriate procedures
4. Analysis (take apart to solve problem)	reasoning—ability to break down information into component parts and to detect relationships of one part to another and to the whole	show that you can pick out the most important points presented or solve the problem by:	analyze, debate, differentiate, organize, determine, distinguish, take apart, figure out, solve
5. Synthesis (put together in a new way)	originality and creativity—ability to assemble separate parts to form a new whole	show that you can combine concepts to create an original idea by:	create, design, develop a plan, produce, synthesize, compile
6. Evaluation (make value judgment based on criteria)	criteria or standards for evaluation and judgment—ability to make judgments based on your stated criteria or standards	show that you can judge and evaluate ideas, information, procedures, and solutions based on your own stated criteria by:	judge, rate, compare, decide, evaluate, conclude, appraise (with reasons given)
7. Appreciation (attitudes, feelings)	psychological and aesthetic impact, emotional sensitivity, attitudes, and reactions	indicate verbally or nonverbally that you are emotionally involved with the content and language imagery by:	respond with interest, excitement, anger; volunteer; stand up for; describe with feeling; identify with; emphasize

   b. if the first sentence is too narrow, combine the two sentences
      to state the main idea.
3. Continue with each sentence as in step 2, asking the students to
   read the first sentence and tell you what it means in their own
   words. Ask them to do the same with the second sentence. Then
   ask which ideas are more important. Can these be put together
   to form a main idea? Continue this pattern to the end of the
   paragraph. At the end of the paragraph, ask which is the topic
   sentence or if there was one.[20]

Reciprocal Questioning (ReQuest)

This procedure was developed by Anthony Manzo to improve reading comprehension and help students develop questioning techniques. It is a one-to-one teaching technique that helps students think critically and formulate questions. Brief instructions follow.

1. Have copies of the selection to be read available for everyone.
2. Everyone reads the first sentence silently. Students ask the teacher questions about that sentence. They should ask not only questions they think teachers might ask, but also the way teachers might ask them.
3. Teachers answer the questions, requiring students to rephrase any questions that cannot be answered because of incorrect logic or poor syntax.
4. After all the students' questions are answered, the second sentence is read and the teacher asks questions of students (as many as needed to ensure that they comprehend the content).
5. Periodically the teacher asks students to verify responses by asking them the reasons why they responded that way and what proof they have.
6. After reading the second sentence, the teacher requires integration of ideas from both sentences.

It must be reinforced that student questioning should model teacher behaviors— "That's a good question"—or the teacher should give the student the fullest of replies. The procedure is continued until the student can read all the words in the first paragraph, can show literal comprehension of what is read, and can formulate a reasonable purpose for reading the rest of the selection.[21]

Slicing

When you ask a question of a class and the response is utter silence, what does it mean? Did they understand the question? Are they afraid to answer? What can you do? You might ignore it, or you could answer it yourself and go right on to the next question. Better yet, do what Pearson and Johnson suggest and *slice*.

Basically, there are two ways to "slice" a question. You can restate it, asking for a smaller part of the total issue, or you can change the task from one of recall to one of recognizing from alternatives. This last option can be one of multiple choice or simply a yes/no response. Pearson and Johnson's example explains it clearly. Here are four questions that a teacher might ask. Try to put yourself into the position of a student being asked this all-encompassing question: "What were the causes of the Civil War?" (You might hesitate trying to respond because you are not certain you remember *all* the causes.) Thus, this question is met with silence. The teacher then slices it in one of the following three ways:

1. "Who can think of *one* cause of the Civil War?" (much less frightening), or

2. "Was it states' rights? Railroad routes? Slavery? Which?" And as a last resort:
3. "Was slavery one of the causes? Why? Who had slaves—the North or the South? Who thought that slavery was wrong?"

As students are successful with one aspect, they are more likely to try to expand on their responses. Changing the focus may also help. "How did they get rails from Pittsburgh to California in 1865?" This question calls for one correct response, which may keep students from attempting to answer. "How do you think they *might* have moved rails from Pittsburgh to California in 1865?" By changing the focus and asking them to speculate, there can be no incorrect answer.[22]

The *maze* strategy developed by J. Guthrie is based on the cloze procedure, which was described in Chapter 4. Maze is intended to be an easier task than a cloze because it involves just recognition rather than recall. It consists of a series of sentences extracted from a passage that the student has not yet read. The text is altered by substituting three alternative words for every fifth or tenth word, using the cloze deletion techniques. The three choices substituted are:

Maze Strategy

1. Correct word
2. Incorrect word from the same word class (noun, verb, etc.)
3. Incorrect word from a different word class

The order of choices is altered at random. Example:

	1. *sidewalk* (correct)
The girl hurried down the	2. *sideboard* (incorrect but also a noun)
	3. carefully (incorrect and a different word class)

The student should read the passage silently and select the alternative believed to be correct. The percentage of correct choices is commensurate with the comprehension of the material in the passage. Scoring is based on at least twenty items:

Above 85% = independent reading level
60–75% = instructional reading level
below 50% = frustration reading level

Caution: The reliability and validity is based partly on 0.82 correlation with the Gates-MacGinitie comprehension subtest, a reputable test, but a similar procedure was used to determine the comprehension score on it as was used in the maze technique. Thus, it should actually have an even higher correlation than 0.82. Also, the validation was done on six- to eight-year-olds, not on upper-grade students.[23]

When we ask students to write before reading, it may increase their motivation by stimulating their curiosity; it may also activate their prior knowledge and improve learning from text by giving a permanent record of thoughts. Several examples of writing tasks include:

1. *Displaying key words* from a unit, asking students to write a short essay using all these words. Then, after reading about the topic, readers check their essays for accuracy and modify where needed.
2. *Brainstorming* what should be included in an explanatory brochure on the topic. Then they read to determine what else their brochure might contain.
3. Asking them to *write all the positive things* they can think of for the topic. They then read to verify or modify.
4. *Assigning free writing on the topic before reading.*

These four tasks define what the finished *product* will be, but they do not specify the *process* students are to follow. As we know, merely telling is not teaching. For example, telling students to produce a brochure on a topic is quite different from teaching them how to produce this brochure. The "how to" steps should also be included.

Part II: Directed Silent Reading Strategies

Three general types of study guides are: (1) the *three-level study guide* (literal to critical), (2) *organizational patterns study guide,* and (3) *concept study guide* (remembering through "chunking" or associating). Mostly, these are developed to be used during and after the reading assignment.[25]

Three-level
Study Guide

Herber bases his notions about reading and reasoning guides on a hierarchical relationship among what he defines as literal, interpretive, and applied levels of comprehension.[26] This means that to be able to handle higher levels we need to have mastered the literal level first. It is the difference between being able to state the facts (literal), and then state what they mean (interpretive), or how they can be used (applied). The belief that greater sophistication is required of the reader at each succeeding level means that some teachers will keep the slower student at the literal level but will ask the advanced group the highest level questions. We do not agree, because studies such as the one done by King, Ellinger, and Wolfe show that the students can handle all levels if they are working with material at their ability level.[27] Thus, we recommend differentiating the material used so that all students can work at any level.

*How to Construct
a Three-level
Study Guide*

Working backwards is the key to constructing a three-level study guide.

1. Carefully analyze the selection to be read, looking for possible generalizations that can be made.
2. Decide on purposes for the lesson.

3. Think of your students' needs in relation to that purpose.

4. Starting with a higher-level question, move from the general to the specific. This is because specific details are important only as they relate to the major ideas.

5. When the purpose is to help students generalize, work with them as to what inferences might be drawn, bridging the gap between the literal and applied.

6. Finally, examine what the writer said, selecting only those details essential to making those inferences.
(Some of the thinking in these steps may occur simultaneously.)

Remember that you do not want to limit your students' thinking.

Teach, don't just tell.
Instruct rather than indoctrinate.
Stimulate *how* to think, not *what* to think.

As your students become more familiar with the procedures, you may loosen the structure, allowing them more freedom with open-ended questions. Finally, let students write some mini-guides themselves.

Knowledge of the way material is organized and the pattern of thought used may help students better comprehend the material. (Writing patterns and signal words are discussed more fully in other chapters.) Four common patterns found in expository material are: compare and contrast; cause/effect; chronological order; and listing. Often these patterns are mixed within a paragraph or longer discourse, but generally one pattern predominates. Those patterns may not apply as often to reading in certain content areas such as math as they will for social studies, science, or English.[28]

Organizational Patterns Study Guide

There are several ways to teach students to note organizational patterns.

1. Show short examples of each from the textbook. Often these patterns are evident in the writer's use of "signal words" (see the chapter on vocabulary). For example, "but" means contrast; listing is identified by the words "first, second, third," etc.

2. Take students through the process of inspecting what they are about to read in an assignment.

3. Have students look for examples of patterns in other sources such as newspapers or magazines to cut out and include in a folder.

To construct an organizational patterns guide:

How to Construct an Organizational Patterns Study Guide

1. Analyze carefully the purpose of the lesson and the nature of the reading selection. Ask yourself, "What is the underlying logic? the key vocabulary?" Use a pattern guide only where the organization is clearly shown.

2. Search for key statements reflecting the pattern where you can safely draw inferences about it.

Concept Study Guides

These stimulate understanding because they are based on the premise that for learning to occur, new ideas must be associated with known ones. Learning then is a two-step process: (1) Trigger—we become aware of an idea; (2) Frame—we categorize it by relating it to our past knowledge and experience.

This psychological process is termed *chunking,* coming from information theory. It attempts to describe what the brain does to compensate for the limitations in processing and storing pieces of information. We regroup the data into a sequence of chunks. *It is awareness that triggers learning; it is association that synthesizes it.*[29]

How to Construct a Concept Study Guide

To construct concept study guides:

1. Analyze the reading material for a limited number of major concepts, listing them.
2. Reread to find statements that underline the concepts.
3. Arrange the guide so that the statements are the first part and categorization the second part.

Adjunct Questions Strategy

During the guided reading, if you do not wish to use study guides, another strategy is to stay with the students as they read, asking adjunct questions as they proceed.

Besides wanting students to retain major concepts, we also want them to integrate the information presented. We may do this by directing their attention to specific relationships while reading and by asking different levels of adjunct questions that guide them in reviewing and integrating facts. These questions are used to guide readers *while* they read, not before or after. These questions are usually not given to students prior to reading but are offered intermittently at crucial points during the chapter.

Whereas prereading questions alerts readers by giving them a framework, adjunct questions are used to process information. Questions used after the reading may serve to facilitate reflection, reaction, and application. The common way to give students these questions is in the form of a reading guide. As an example of adjunct questioning have them read specific pages to answer explicit questions given to them in writing.

Typographic Clues

Textbook writers today attempt to help students in the interpretation and mastery of the material by including such typographic devices as previews, summaries, outlines, lists, illustrations, subheadings, and boldface type. More abundant use of graphic aids is evident, too, in the modern text.

However, this does not mean that students automatically benefit from these clues and aids. This may be due to the fact that the readability level makes the material too hard for the student to grasp. Another reason may be the rigid approach to which some students are exposed while reading during their early elementary years.

At any rate, teachers need to take a strong position in directing students in the benefits of these aids, at the same time stressing that reading in their content area needs to be purposeful and adaptable to circumstances.

To teach the use of typographic clues:

Using Typographic Clues

1. Identify the aid (for example, the summary).
2. Assess students' competence in using it.
3. Develop interest and conceptual background.
4. Demonstrate the functions.
5. Provide guided practice in its use.
6. Provide delayed practice as a follow-up.

Walter Hill suggests dividing the class in half, giving one group a content selection with textual aids, the other without.[30] Time the reading and give a quiz emphasizing main ideas that are identified by the textual aids. Let the students compare results and reach their own conclusions.

Glossing, a very old technique of using notes written in the margins of the text to guide the reader, has recently reemerged as a viable reading strategy.[31,32] Using notations in the margins and underlining key ideas and vocabulary in the text or on an inserted sheet are a means of directing readers while they read rather than before or after the act. In a way, it is like having the teacher personally walk through the material with each student. A gloss may define or give synonyms for technical terms; it may clarify concepts; it may point out needed comprehension or study strategies; or it may ask provocative questions of the reader.

Glossing or Gloss

To construct a gloss, teachers should read over the chapter and

1. Identify terminology, concepts, and skills with which students will need assistance.
2. Write glosses on ditto masters, identifying page and line numbers, or write them in the text itself if permitted.
3. Have students insert each ditto copy in their text opposite the page to be read or under the page so that the margin shows.
4. As one alternative, dictate glosses to students, who will write them in their texts or notebooks.
5. Another alternative is to have students in groups gloss a difficult chapter for future readers.

An example of a glossed text is shown in figure 10.5.

Figure 10.5
Glossing.
From Wayne, Otto, White, Sandra, and Camperell, Kaybeth. "Text Comprehension Research to Classroom Application. A Progress Report." Theoretical Paper No. 87, Wisconsin Research and Development, Center for Individualized Schooling, University of Wisconsin, Madison, October 1980, p. 119.

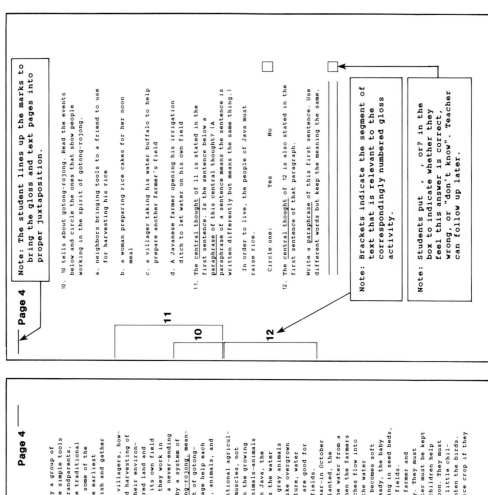

Page 4

been used for a long, long time by a group of people. The villagers use the same simple tools and methods that their parents, grandparents, and great-grandparents used. These traditional Javanese farmers are also part of some of the natural food chains. Just like the earliest people on Java, they also catch fish and gather fruits to eat.

The survival of the Javanese villagers, however, depends upon the growing and harvesting of rice. The Javanese have changed their environment to grow rice. They have cleared land and irrigated fields. Each family has its own field of about two acres. On most days, they work in the rice paddies. Growing rice is a never-ending job. The planting is made easier by a system of work which the Javanese call gotong-rojong, meaning community help. In this spirit of gotong-rojong all the people of the village help each other by sharing irrigation water, animals, and tools.

The power used in their traditional agriculture comes from human and animal muscles, not machines. The animal power used in the growing of rice comes from domesticated animals—animals that have been tamed by people. On Java, the most common domesticated animal is the water buffalo. Water buffaloes are big, gray animals with long horns. They look much like overgrown cows. In spite of their gentle nature, water buffaloes are very powerful. They are good for the hard job of plowing wet rice fields.

Rice is planted twice each year—in October and May. Before the rice can be planted, the irrigation ditches, which bring the water from a nearby stream, must be checked. Then the farmers let water from the irrigation ditches flow into their paddies. Next they harness the water buffaloes and plow until the soil becomes soft and muddy. When the paddies are ready, the baby rice plants, which have been growing in seed beds, can be transplanted to these rice fields. While the plants are growing, the farmer and his wife keep working in the paddy. They must keep it free of weeds, and the water must be kept about six inches deep. The older children help care for the plants in the afternoon. They must go to school in the morning. Even little children help by making noise to frighten the birds. Hungry birds can eat up a whole rice crop if they

Page 4

Note: The student lines up the marks to bring the gloss and text pages into proper juxtaposition.

10. 10 tells about gotong-rojong. Read the events below and circle the ones that show people working in the spirit of gotong-rojong.

   a. neighbors bringing tools to a friend to use for harvesting his rice

   b. a woman preparing rice cakes for her noon meal

   c. a villager taking his water buffalo to help prepare another farmer's field

   d. A Javanese farmer opening his irrigation ditch to let water on his own field

11. The central thought of 11 is stated in the first sentence. Is the sentence below a paraphrase of this central thought? (A paraphrase of a sentence means the sentence is written differently but means the same thing.)

   In order to live, the people of Java must raise rice.

   Circle one: Yes   No

12. The central thought of 12 is also stated in the first sentence of that paragraph.

   Write a paraphrase of this first sentence. Use different words but keep the meaning the same.

11

10

12

Note: Brackets indicate the segment of text that is relevant to the correspondingly numbered gloss activity.

Note: Students put , , or? in the box to indicate whether they feel this answer is correct, wrong, or "don't know". Teacher can follow up later.

326

In this final portion of directed reading-thinking activities, it is often a good idea to use small groups for processing information without attaching grades to responses. These postreading activities are crucial to long-term retention and should not be neglected or squeezed into the end of a class period.

This is the time when students examine relationships, seeing connections between what they know and what they read. The guide material or organizers used in the previous part of the lesson can well be the stimulus for small group reactions and reflections. Students should be asked to explain and defend their responses, as well as to understand the reactions of others that differ from their own (e.g., "This is how it seems to me. How does it seem to you?") They need to make value judgments as to the future worth of the information as well as how well the material came across. Thus, postreading activities call on students to reflect, react, apply, and judge.

Part III: Postreading Activities

Grouping allows more students to be actively involved in reflecting, reacting, and evaluating the reading. Two ground rules for students participating in group reactions are:

Using Small Groups

1. Have a reason behind your disagreement, do not argue just for the sake of arguing.
2. Try to understand and hear out others who do not agree with you. On the other hand, stand up for your own beliefs, too. The synthesizing that comes about from this type of postdiscussion can be a potent and productive learning for all.

Mathew Miles has classified discussion groups into three broad categories:

Types of Discussion Groups

1. *Training groups.* Students with the same strengths and needs are instructed in an activity or concept by the teacher.
2. *Work groups.* Students of comparable abilities are given a task to work at without direct teacher instruction, because they have the needed skills to accomplish it.
3. *Work-training groups.* Combining both training and work groups, students will need a great deal of structure and guidance.[33]

Teachers who get training and work groups mixed up are being assumptive teachers, because some students will be asked to do some group work without the skills or support of the teacher, whereas others would benefit from making their own decisions because they have the needed skills to carry out the task.

Group Membership Roles

Teachers must be cognizant of roles that individual group members may play. When discussing a topic, there is a general sequence of task roles that are guided by the leader—either teacher or student.

Leader Roles

1. Initiate discussion.
2. Give and ask for information.
3. Give and ask for reaction.
4. Restate and give examples.
5. Confront and reality test.
6. Clarify, synthesize, summarize.

Individual Task Roles (Concern for group problem— "Let's get to work")

1. *Recorder*—Takes notes on the discussion.
2. *Reporter*—Reports to class at end.
3. *Gatekeeper/expediter*—Keeps the group aware of purposes and operations as well as of its criteria for effectiveness.
4. *Timekeeper*—Alerts the group when it is time to move on.
5. *Evaluator/diagnostician*—Keeps the group on the track to meet its stated goals.
6. *Standard-setter*—Pushes when the product is not sufficient.
7. *Illustrator*—Develops/draws a poster or handout.

Maintenance Roles (agreeable, supportive, and concerned for others in the group)

8. *Sponsor/encourager*—Praises contributions.
9. *Tension reliever*—Often uses humor.
10. *Active listener*—Uses good listening skills.

Negative Roles (concerned with self only)

11. *The "star"*—Tries to dominate the discussion.
12. *The blocker*—Stubborn, overcritical, blocks discussion.
13. *The withdrawer*—Shows lack of interest, refuses to participate.
14. *The nitpicker*—Overemphasizes details, keeps the group on one topic when the rest are ready to move on.

None of these rules are mutually exclusive; group members may exhibit a combination throughout the discussion and work time.

Teacher's Role in Grouping Strategies

Leadership styles can vary considerably and may include the following types:

1. *Autocratic.* Dictates the task, makes the assignments, evaluates the results, "Do it my way."
2. *Laissez-faire (assumptive).* Supplies no function, does nothing to help group members supply them. "What shall we do today, gang?"

3. *Cooperative problem solver (democratic).* Works together with students to solve problems. Allows for shared decision making.
4. *Paternalistic.* Benevolent autocrat. Still "hogs" the leadership but in a kindly manner.
5. *Bargainer.* Uses rewards and punishments, agreeing to meet group members' needs if they will work on the group task.

When grouping the class, the effective teacher:

1. *Initiates.* Keeps groups moving or gets them going, suggests steps to take, points out goals, clarifies.
2. *Regulates.* Influences groups' direction by pointing out time limits, summarizing, or restating.
3. *Informs.* Brings information or opinion to the group.
4. *Supports.* Creates a good emotional climate to hold groups together (relieves tension, voices groups' feelings, encourages).
5. *Evaluates.* Helps the groups evaluate decisions, goals, or procedures (for example, tests for consensus and notes the group processes being enacted).

Table 10.3 shows a variety of ways in which students might be grouped, depending on the purpose of the assignment.

Table 10.3
Flexible Grouping
(How many of these have *you* tried or experienced?)

Type of Group	Purpose or Description
Skill Deficiency	Gives specific instruction to those who have a noted deficiency in some skill area.
Reading Level	Uses books at a variety of readability levels according to each student's needs.
Interest	Extends interest in a topic by having a chance to investigate additional information with others of the same interest.
Social	Motivates students by allowing them to work with peers of their choice, or developing leadership or helping qualities.
Psychological	Allows students of divergent backgrounds, abilities, and interests to experience working together.
Research	Gives practice and application in reading/study skills with an in-depth investigation of a topic.
Triads, Pairs	Allows more active involvement and mutually beneficial help, usually over a longer period of time.
Peer Tutoring	An adept student gives intensive help to one who lacks competence or skill in an area.

Ability Groups
in Science

An example of tasks for three ability groups in a science classroom follows.

Group 1 (Advanced, experienced, with ability to do abstract thinking):
1. Analyze the usefulness of _____ as described in the text.
2. Analyze the values of _____ in other fields.

Group 2 (Some scientific experience, understands major concepts)
Explain the definition and main idea of _____ and its possible value to our lives.

Group 3 (Concrete thinkers with little background experience)
Find examples of _____ in the text and list examples from real life.

Which would you find more interesting to do? What if it was in an area in which you knew little? Which would be the easiest?

Workshop Activity 10.4
Role Playing Ability Grouping

Number off by threes into arbitrary groups. Group 1 will be the advanced, group 2 will have some competency, and group 3 will have little background or ability.

Take a topic from this chapter, such as "advance organizers." Each group addresses questions posed under the above heading "Ability Groups in Science." For example, group 1 will analyze the usefulness of advance organizers. Appoint a moderator, a recorder, a reporter, and a timekeeper in each group. When all groups feel they are ready, reconvene for a general class discussion about the ease or difficulty of the tasks and how much time should be allotted for each. How did group 3 feel about being classified as the lowest group? Compare their feelings to those in the middle and advanced groups.

Synthesizing
or Summarizing
Using Cinquains

Thomas Estes and Joseph Vaughn describe an interesting strategy for synthesizing or summarizing using the idea of *cinquains*.[34] Cinquains are five-line poems with specific limitations:

Line 1—One-word title
Line 2—Two-word description of topic
Line 3—Three words expressing action
Line 4—Four words showing feeling for a topic
Line 5—One-word synonym, restating the essence of the topic

Used not only in English classes but in all content areas, this strategy has proved to be a powerful tool for getting the gist of the information read.

(Title:) _____ Volcanoes
(Description:) _____ Red hot
(Action:) _____ Erupting from within
(Feeling for topic:) _____ Nature's furnace of fire
(Synonym, restating essence:) _____ Inferno

Ecology
Cycling, recycling
Intense land-use planning
Energy, diversity, nutrient, development
Bio-geo-chemical.

DRTA
Organized plan
Helping learning stick
Motivating, purposeful, familiarizing, associating
Teaching

After sharing some examples, have students work in pairs or triads to develop a cinquain on a unit, chapter, or topic.

A *simulation* represents a real experience artificially, putting together a contrived series of activities to approximate a situation or process as closely as possible. It is a "you are there" type of phenomenon, where students, for example, are told that they are now living under an absolute dictator and that they must perform certain tasks. *Role playing,* then, becomes a part of the simulation.

Simulations/Role Play

An excellent example of simulation is in the training of airline pilots, where an artificial environment is set up to approximate actual flying conditions. Pilots must attempt to handle simultaneously a fire in the cabin, an electric storm with buffeting downdrafts, and a highjacking.

Designed to help readers synthesize and retain information, this two-day guided writing procedure includes these steps.

Guided Writing Procedure (GWP)[35]

First day:
1. *Brainstorm* what is known about an upcoming topic, recording responses on the board or overhead.
2. *Identify categories* by grouping items and labeling them.
3. Using labels and the items under them, *form a cognitive map* (graphic organizer).

4. With the cognitive map as a guide, *write* about the topic.
5. *Supply additional reading material* on the topic to use for expanding or modifying papers.

Second day:
1. *Display* a few papers from former students on an overhead projector, showing good and poor writing examples.
2. *Revise* papers according to the content and two or three writing criteria, such as: main ideas and minor ones are distinguishable in expository writing; story plot has a clear beginning, middle, and end in narratives; sentences are well-formed, complete thoughts; words are spelled correctly.
3. Students *evaluate* partner's paper before the actual rewrite.

Free Writing

A final note—the opposite of the guided writing procedure is free writing, as found generally in English classrooms. When students say they do not know what to write, try playing music to stimulate images; or provide the class with a list of 300 topics or story-essay starters to choose from; or have students keep a reaction or content journal containing insights and elaborations of topics or eras being studied.

English Debate

An English debate can be a motivating strategy when there are definitely two sides to a question. The class is divided into two sections facing each other according to the position taken on the topic. Each side has a leader who fields questions. If someone's argument convinces anyone that they should change sides, they literally get up and move to the other side. A count is taken at the beginning and end to note changes made. A total class discussion of the pros and cons can be the final synthesizing activity. This debate technique can last several days, allowing time for students to read more on the topic for persuasive argument.

The KWL Strategy for Mastering Expository Text

Assessing our prior knowledge of a topic to be read in an expository text is important for mastery of the material. Donna Ogle developed the KWL three-step strategy to show students the importance of background knowledge.[36]

Step K—What I Know (Prereading: Five Categories)
1. Brainstorm what the class already knows about the topic to be read, recording responses on the board. Be specific as to the concept selected. If there is little response, slice back to a more

general question and then ask if these new facts can apply to the original concept. Ogle suggests that volunteers be asked where they learned their fact or how it could be proved.

2. Have students look at their list on the board of what they already know and group items into a general category. If this proves difficult, model an example or two by picking out a category apparent from the list such as eating habits, caring for young, natural enemies for a study of animals or one kind of animal. Then ask students to find other categories and again, if they have trouble, give them other articles to read on the same subject in order to identify and anticipate other categories. Knowledge of general categories available helps students store new data for future study.

Step W—What Do I Want to Learn? (Prereading: Purpose and Guidance)
Discuss questions and problems that have arisen and then, before reading, have students write on their worksheet specific questions they want answered. After focusing on their purpose (their question), they can begin reading.

Step L—What I Learned (Postreading)
Ask students to write what they learned from reading and to decide whether the article answered their questions. If not, suggest further reading on the topic to show them that their own need to know has priority over just what the author decided to include.

Here are some reminders. What might you add?

Improving
Comprehension:
A Checklist

___ 1. Capture the students' interest—give an exciting or provocative preview of the topic or story to be read.

___ 2. Build a background of mutual experience through films, brainstorming, speakers, or field trips.

___ 3. Help set a purpose for reading and remind students to formulate their own questions.

___ 4. Use broad, open-ended questions that do not require merely a yes/no answer or one correct response. Keep the environment as free of anxiety as possible. Reward students verbally for volunteering answers, even when it is not exactly what you wanted, by such statements as "good try" or "you're getting there."

___ 5. Use techniques such as role playing or simulation to get your students more actively involved in the reading process.

_____ 6. Include strategies such as glossing, the maze technique, or the ReQuest procedure in your monthly plans.

_____ 7. Remember to be a model for asking higher-order, provocative, open-ended questions.

_____ 8. Include more writing activities to help in thinking and retention.

_____ 9. _____

_____ 10. _____

Summary

Comprehension teaching strategies can be used before reading, during reading, and after reading. When we use the format of a directed reading-thinking activity (DRTA), we direct students to read for a specific purpose, we prepare and motivate them for the reading assignment, we may use some type of guide for them to refer to while silent reading, and we follow up and enrich through reflections, reactions, applications, and extensions. Some of the prereading strategies include advance or schematic organizers and questioning. Examples of strategies during reading include study guides and adjunct questions. Postreading strategies include such activities as synthesizing using cinquains, having discussion groups, or using role plays or simulations. (See the cognitive map at the beginning of the chapter for further details.)

References

1. Carl B. Smith, Sharon L. Smith, and Larry Mikulecky, _Teaching Reading in Secondary School Content Subjects_ (New York: Holt, Rinehart & Winston, 1978), pp. 318–319.

2. From Henry E. Garrett, _Great Experiments in Psychology_ (New York: Appleton-Century-Crofts, 1941), p. 273.

3. David P. Ausubel, "Use of Advance Organizers in the Learning and Retention of Meaningful Verbal Material," _Journal of Educational Psychology_ 51 (1960): 267–272. Quoted in _Educational Psychology: A Cognitive View_ (New York: Holt, Rinehart & Winston, 1968).

4. Thomas H. Estes and Joseph L. Vaughn Jr., _Reading and Learning in the Content Classroom_ (Boston, Mass.: Allyn & Bacon, 1978), pp. 151–152.

5. Ausubel, "Advance Organizers."

6. Marsha Weil and Bruce Joyce, "Advance Organizer Model," in _Teaching and Learning: Academic Models of Teaching_ (Teacher Corps—Corps Member Training Institute, 1976), pp. 173–205.

7. Richard F. Barron and V. K. Stone, "The Effect of Student-Constructed Graphic Post-Organizers upon Learning Vocabulary Relationships," in _Twenty-Third Yearbook of the National Reading Conference,_ ed. P. L. Nacke (Clemson, S.C.: National Reading Conference, Inc., 1974), 172–175.

8. Hilda Taba, _Teaching Strategies and Cognitive Functioning in Elementary School Children,_ Cooperative Research Project #2404 (San Francisco: San Francisco State College, 1966).

9. Taba, *Teaching Strategies.*

10. Harold Herber, *Teaching Reading in Content Fields* (Englewood Cliffs, N.J.: Prentice-Hall, 1978), p. 56.

11. Taba, *Teaching Strategies.*

12. Walter Hill, *Secondary School Reading: Process, Program, Procedure* (Boston, Mass.: Allyn & Bacon, 1979), p. 139.

13. J. P. Guilford, "Frontiers in Thinking That Teachers Should Know About," *The Reading Teacher* 13 (February 1969): 176–182.

14. Benjamin S. Bloom, ed., *Taxonomy of Educational Objectives: Handbook I, Cognitive Domain* (New York: Longman, Green, 1956).

15. Ibid.

16. Helen K. Smith, *Sequential Development of Reading Abilities* (Chicago: University of Chicago Press, 1960).

17. Ellen Lamar Thomas and H. Alan Robinson, *Improving Reading in Every Class,* 2d ed. (Boston, Mass.: Allyn & Bacon, 1977), pp. 134–142.

18. David L. Shepherd, *Comprehensive High School Reading Methods,* 2d ed., (Columbus, Ohio: Charles E. Merrill Publishing Co., 1978).

19. Marvin L. Cohn, "The Structured Comprehension," *The Reading Teacher* 22 (February 1969): 440–444, cited in Eldon E. Ekwall, *Diagnosis and Remediation of the Disabled Reader* (Boston: Allyn & Bacon, 1976), p. 145.

20. Lawrence Hafner, *Developmental Reading in Middle and Secondary Schools* (New York: Macmillan Co., 1977).

21. Anthony V. Manzo, "The ReQuest Procedure," *Journal of Reading* 13 (November 1969): 123–126.

22. P. David Pearson and Dale Johnson, *Teaching Reading Comprehension* (New York: Holt, Rinehart & Winston, 1978).

23. J. Guthrie et al., "The Maze Technique to Assess, Monitor Reading Comprehension," *The Reading Teacher* 28 (November 1974): 161–168.

24. David Moore, John Readence, and Robert Rickelman, "Writing Before Reading," *Prereading Activities for Content Area Reading and Learning,* 2d ed. (Newark, Del: International Reading Association, 1989), pp. 62–74.

25. Estes and Vaughn, *Reading and Learning,* p. 153.

26. Herber, *Teaching Reading,* pp. 55–57.

27. Martha L. King, Bernice Ellinger, and Willavene Wolfe, *Critical Reading: A Book of Readings* (Philadelphia: J. B. Lippincott, 1967).

28. Herber, *Teaching Reading,* pp. 77–78.

29. Estes and Vaughn, *Reading and Learning,* p. 168.

30. Hill, *Secondary School Reading,* p. 136.

31. Wayne Otto, Sandra White, and Kaybeth Camperell, "Text Comprehension Research to Classroom Application: A Progress Report," Theoretical Paper No. 87 (Madison, Wis.: Wisconsin Research and Development Center for Individualized Schooling, October 1980).

32. Harry Singer and Dan Donlan, *Reading and Learning from Text* (Boston: Little, Brown & Co., 1980), p. 56.

33. Mathew Miles, *Learning to Work in Groups* (New York: Columbia University Teachers College Press, 1967).

34. Estes and Vaughn, *Reading and Learning,* pp. 182–184.

35. C. C. Smith and T. W. Bean, "The Guided Writing Procedure: Integrating Content Reading and Writing Improvement," *Reading World* 19 (1980): 290–294.

36. Donna M. Ogle, "KWL: A Teaching Model that Develops Active Reading of Expository Text," *Reading Teacher* (February 1986): 564–570.

Recommended Readings

Alvermann, Donna E., and Swafford, Jeanne. "Do Content Area Strategies Have a Research Base?" *Journal of Reading* 32 (February 1989): 388–394.

Applebee, A. N. "Writing and Reasoning." *Review of Educational Research* 54 (1984): 577–596.

Atwell, Margaret A., and Rodes, Lynn K. "Strategy Lessons As Alternatives to Skill Lessons in Reading." *Journal of Reading* 27 (May 1984): 700–705.

Balajithy, Ernest. "Using Student-Constructed Questions to Encourage Active Reading." *Journal of Reading* 27 (February 1984): 408–411.

Beach, Don M. *Reaching Teenagers: Learning Centers for the Secondary Classroom.* Santa Monica, Calif.: Goodyear Publishing Co., 1977.

Birken, Marcia. "Teaching Students How to Study Mathematics: A Classroom Approach." *Mathematics Teacher* 79 (September 1982): 410–413.

Blanton, William E.; Wood, Karen D.; and Moorman, Gary B. "The Role of Purpose in Reading Instruction." *The Reading Teacher* (March 1990): 486–493.

Fulwiler, T. "Journals Across the Disciplines." *English Journal* 69 (1980): 14–19.

Gauthier, Lane Roy. "Helping Middle School Students Develop Language Facility." *Journal of Reading* 33 (January 1990): 274–276.

Gebhard, Ann O. "Teaching Writing in Reading and the Content Areas." *Journal of Reading* 27 (December 1983): 207–211.

Haggard, Martha Rapp. "An Interactive Strategies Approach to Content Reading." *Journal of Reading* 29 (December 1985): 204–210.

Josel, Carol A. "A Silent DRTA for Remedial Eighth Graders." *Journal of Reading* 29 (February 1986): 434–439.

Karahalios, Sue; Tonjes, Marian; and Towner, John. "Using Advance Organizers to Improve Comprehension of a Content Text." *Journal of Reading* 22 (May 1979): 706–708.

Kormanski, Luethel M. "Using the Johari Window to Study Characterization." *Journal of Reading* 32 (November 1988): 146–153.

Raphael. Taffy E. "Teaching Learners About Sources of Information for Answering Comprehension Questions." *Journal of Reading* 27 (January 1984): 303–311.

Richgels, Donald J., and Hansen, Ruth. "Gloss: Helping Students Apply Both Skills and Strategies in Reading Content Texts." *Journal of Reading* 27 (January 1984): 312–317.

Richgels, Donald J., and Mateja, John A. "Gloss II: Integrating Content and Process for Independence." *Journal of Reading* 27 (February 1984): 424–431.

Santa, Carol Minnick; Dailey, Susan C.; and Nelson, Marylin. "Free Response and Opinion-proof: A Reading and Writing Strategy for Middle Grade and Secondary Teachers." *Journal of Reading* (January 1985): 346–352.

Simpson, Michele L. "PORPE: A Writing Strategy for Studying and Learning in the Content Areas." *Journal of Reading* 29 (February 1986): 407–414.

Slater, Wayne H. "Teaching Expository Text Structure with Structural Organizers." *Journal of Reading* 28 (May 1985): 712–718.

Strahan, David B. "Guided Thinking: A Strategy for Encouraging Excellence at the Middle Level." *NASSP Bulletin* (February 1986): 75–80.

Tonjes, Marian J. "Using Advance Organizers to Enhance the Processing of Text." In *The Reader and the Text,* John Chapman, ed. Heinemann Educational Books (1981): 131–141.

Tonjes, Marian J. "Metacognitive Modeling and Glossing: Two Powerful Ways to Teach Self-Responsibility." In *Reading: The ABC's and Beyond.* Christine Anderson, ed. London: Macmillan, 1988, pp. 24–30.

Tonjes, Marian J. "Selected Instructional Strategies for Promoting Content Reading and Study Skills." In *Teaching Reading: The Key Issues.* Alastair Hendry, ed. London: Heinemann Educational Books, 1982, pp. 97–106.

Figure 11.1
Developing collateral reading: a cognitive map.

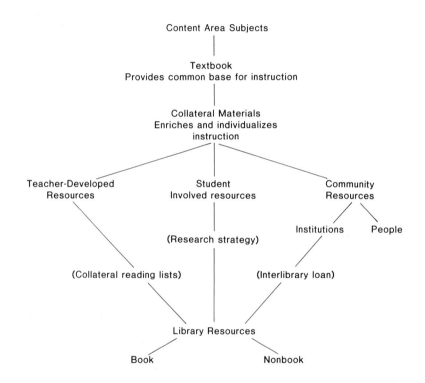

Content Area Subjects

Textbook
Provides common base for instruction

Collateral Materials
Enriches and individualizes instruction

Teacher-Developed Resources

Student Involved resources

Community Resources

Institutions

People

(Research strategy)

(Collateral reading lists)

(Interlibrary loan)

Library Resources

Book

Nonbook

Enriching Content Classrooms Through Collateral Reading

11

by Enid E. Haag

Anticipatory Questions

(Literal)

1. What are the five steps in searching for the related reading material needed?

(Applied)

2. Select a specific topic and develop a two-page annotated bibliography.

(Evaluative)

3. Delineate and discuss three ways you expect to change or adapt your teaching behavior following the reading of this chapter.

Technical Terminology and Concepts

annotated bibliography

book review index

book selection

CD-ROM

collateral reading

handbooks

multiethnic material

periodical index

school media center

search strategy

special encyclopedias

standard catalog

trade book

Introduction

Formal education applies its patterns to the mind; but only through books does the mind itself enrich, deepen, apply, modify, and develop those patterns in individual life fulfillment. Intelligence must be kept active, playing over the education it is receiving, drawing its own conclusions, making its own observations and its own test; otherwise, we have simply a thin surface coating of applied instruction. Books are the instrument of intelligence.[1]

Helen Haines urges all of us to reach out to the rich world of books to provide students with opportunities to experience concepts, ideas, and adventure beyond the traditional scope of classroom instruction. She invites teachers to extend their students' interests and intellects by introducing them to appropriate books and writers in the various subject fields. Science teachers should introduce students to popular science writers such as Allan E. Nourse, Isaac Asimov, James Herriot, or Carl Sagan. Social studies teachers should introduce students to the novels of writers such as Laura Ingalls Wilder, Irene Hunt, Howard Fast, MacKinley Kantor, and James A. Michener, who make historical events live for the reader.

Traditional or formal education has always relied heavily on the textbook, which is a concise and overly factual presentation of the subject matter. Because so much information must be covered in one book, many facts are briefly presented without meaningful explanation. "Dry facts are soon forgotten; attitudes, feelings, and general concepts can remain forever."[2] Regardless of which textbook is used to teach a particular subject area, it needs to be supplemented by a large and varied collection of pertinent collateral material.

Textbooks

Assets

The function of any textbook is to provide a skeleton of subject information that all students are exposed to and expected to master. The information given in the textbook should be the "basics" of the subject matter. In other words, the textbook provides for the students a common background of knowledge, a common base from which they may then build and expand according to interest, need, experience, or future development. It presents data and facts concerning a particular subject and then either explains or shows the relationships between the data and facts. From the explanations or the relationships, students learn basic concepts, thought patterns, and/or philosophies that are supposed to provide them with the "basic education" from which they will draw during the rest of their lives. And with mastery of these concepts and knowledge, the students should satisfy the performance objectives of the course or unit.

Limitations

Instruction utilizes all forms of media, including nonbook materials, textbooks, and trade books. The textbook has been the primary method of imparting information since the first school opened in the American colonies.

Of course, early in this century, all the necessary information on a particular subject could be contained in a minimum of space. The body of knowledge up to the mid-twentieth century was relatively small compared with the second half of the twentieth century. The student today has to master more information than did the student even ten years ago. And the students ten years from now will have to master more than the students of today. Because the textbook is expected to do so much in so little space, there are, naturally, some inherent problems.

1. The textbook, on the average, is likely to be too concise or bland, a bare skeleton of facts.
2. Reading levels are inconsistent and may even vary within a single text.
3. Concepts are curtly defined and relationships between concepts seldom explored.
4. Comprehension levels vary, often making learning difficult for even the "average" student.
5. In some subject fields, textbooks may be outdated, incomplete, or in error, even prior to publication.
6. Replacement of textbooks by newer editions may not be possible because new editions are not yet on the market.
7. The textbook may not be the choice of the teacher but of a former teacher; or the teacher may not have been included in the selection process.
8. Replacement of textbooks by later editions is often dictated by economics, rather than educational need.
9. Textbooks are often chosen because of political pressures or partisan group dialogue.
10. The textbook is often inappropriate for the student population presently attending the school or taking the course.

The cognitive map in figure 11.1 details the interdependence of textbook use and collateral reading needs. Workshop activity 11.1 will help you anticipate more specifically the directions this chapter takes in discussing the use of collateral reading materials to enrich content area subjects.

Workshop Activity 11.1
Locating Appropriate Reading Materials

You have been reminded of the wide range of reading abilities that any teacher may expect in any class of unselected students. Now it is suggested that you need to locate appropriate reading materials to meet the individual differences and needs of these students.

You may work independently or join with two or three other teachers to complete the following:

1. Select a topic that is a part of or a unit within your course of study.
2. If you have no topic of interest, you or your group may want to use one of these:
   a. minorities
   b. environmental issues
   c. death or separation
   d. pioneer life
   e. politics
3. Brainstorm, developing a list of books, fiction and nonfiction, that you already know of that are directly related to your topic.
4. Using your school library card catalog, check under the appropriate subject. Locate titles you have not considered.
5. When you rejoin the class, be prepared to tell them
   a. how materials chosen might add to the students' understanding of the topic that the textbook does not;
   b. what you or your committee was able to list by thinking of books and stories they had read;
   c. what additional materials you located via the card catalog;
   d. what additional materials the group would like in order to round out a possible unit on the subject.

Using Collateral Material

There has always been a need to individualize the curriculum in our schools. Students are not uniformly endowed. They learn through different methods, at different rates, and with different capacities. Success in learning requires a combination of textbook and collateral reading. Kenneth Goodman was advocating this when he said that "textbooks could become elements in resource kits to provide more specific focus on single concepts or depth treatment of groups of related concepts."[3] Whereas the teacher can use the textbook as a common point of reference for the entire class, the use of collateral material rounds out and fills in the details left out by the textbook.

The term *collateral reading* means reading material related to the main topic or theme being studied—that is, reading that supports and enriches or broadens the experience of the reader. Collateral materials may be books, magazines, or teacher-created materials used to enrich instruction. There are three broad categories of books: textbooks, trade books, and reference books. The last two can be considered collateral reading materials. Reference books provide quick or ready answers to questions (e.g., How long is the Mississippi River? Who was the fifth U.S. president? What kind of government does Mexico have?). Reference books are not meant to be read from cover to cover. They are to be consulted for specific questions. Trade books are written for pleasure reading and fall into two types, fiction and nonfiction. The fiction includes novels and short stories. The nonfiction trade books include such subject areas as philosophy, psychology, religion, sociology, science, technology, literature, biography, autobiography, and history. When we talk about trade books being used as collateral reading material, we are referring to both fiction and nonfiction.

Since the advent of television, teachers have been competing with the media for students' learning time and energy. Television entertainers rely on acting techniques to hold their audiences. Teachers are professional educators and should take advantage of all their subject knowledge to guide students in the exercise of their talents. During the first few years of teaching, most educators have little trouble being enthusiastic. So it is not only important for the student, but also for the teacher, that the vitality be maintained as an integral part of the learning atmosphere every day of every term of the school year. For teachers, one way of maintaining this vitality over the years is to be co-learners with their students. Using collateral reading materials in conjunction with a textbook allows teachers to be active co-learners, because locating suitable collateral materials is intellectually stimulating. It allows teachers to be exposed to new ideas and thoughts of writers, to struggle with difficult new concepts, and to apply concepts learned during the academic years.

Teachers must constantly be aware of materials that might be used alone or adapted to fit into a particular unit being taught. For example, an airline magazine might provide an article explaining a trip to Shakespeare's theatre in England; such an article could be used in an English literature class. Or a publication from an insurance company might give some excellent parking tips useful in a driver education class. Perhaps while thumbing through one of the small press poetry magazines, a poem is located, the theme of which is the same as a well-known poem, and could be compared by students in a poetry unit.

Developing Collateral Reading Lists

Collateral reading, when appropriately planned by either the teacher or both the students and the teacher, may make many specific positive contributions to the course of study. Such reading may (1) extend vividness, clarity, and a sense of reality to the topic; (2) add many details that enrich and clarify cognitive information; (3) add completeness and extend the students' interests in further reading; (4) not only provide knowledge, per se, but also give practice in its application; (5) give the student opportunities to read and evaluate competent writing about topics being studied; and (6) necessitate ability to discriminate among fiction and nonfiction materials, authoritative and superficial writing, and to establish guidelines for evaluating a published work. For example, college bound high school students will enjoy reading *Shōgun* by James Clavell, a novel that was on the best-seller lists for many weeks and was then made into a television series. The book portrays feudal seventeenth-century Japan through the eyes of an English sea pilot. The book helps foster an appreciation for non-Western cultures. *Shōgun* can also be compared with James Michener's *Hawaii* or his *Chesapeake,* for all three have themes concerning cultural and social change. *Chesapeake,* on the best-seller lists for many weeks, chronicles four centuries of life on Maryland's eastern shore. Both lend themselves to introducing students to tracing their own cultural roots. Elementary or middle school students will enjoy the series of books by Laura Ingalls Wilder: *Little House in the Big Woods, Little House on the Prairie, Farmer Boy, On the Banks of Plum Creek, By the Shores of Silver Lake, The Long Winter, Little Town on the Prairie, First Four Years, On the Way Home, These Happy Golden Years.* The *Little House* books, once a television series, have been extremely popular with young readers ever since the first book was published in 1932. Through these books students vicariously experience the settlement of the Midwest rather than reading dry facts and figures.

In developing lists of available resources, teachers should first consult the card catalog and the periodical indexes. What reference tools in science does the library have? What trade books are available on insects, birds, automobile repairs, or the civil rights movement? What magazines contain articles on the above subjects that the students can consult without having to go to another library? What clippings are available in the vertical file on the subject being studied? (See figure 11.2.)

If the school library does not have sufficient materials available on a topic, the teacher may check the local public library to see what is available. Many times a phone call to the public library is all that is necessary to discover if a trip to the library is worthwhile or necessary. If the library has a wealth of materials, teachers naturally would want to review the materials prior to including them on the list (see figure 11.3).

In some states, school libraries may borrow materials from other libraries in the state or from the state library. Ask your school librarian if this is possible. Together with your school librarian, a list of requests may be drawn up and sent off to various state, university, or public libraries. In some cases, the list of materials requested can include magazine articles, audiovisual material, and artifacts. Large-print books, taped books, video, and Braille materials may also be borrowed.

Figure 11.2

Collateral materials include teacher-made materials, library resources, community resources, and student-made materials. The library resources include both book and nonbook media. (This diagram was prepared by Ruth Powers and Enid Haag.)

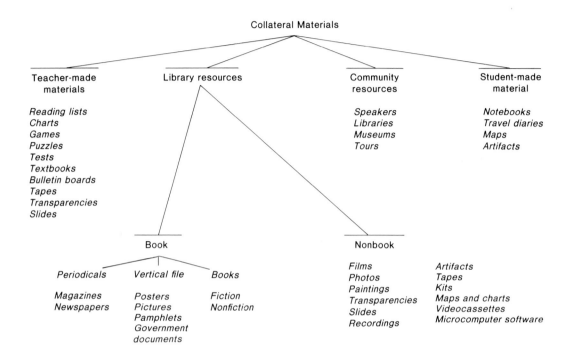

Many selection aids exist that assist teachers and librarians alike in the location of collateral reading materials for students.

Becoming familiar with these aids will not only assist the teacher in locating appropriate collateral materials, but also make much easier the teacher's job of giving suggestions for purchases to the school librarian. The school library collection supports the curriculum taught at that school. The school librarian, along with the teachers, must select materials each year that are appropriate for the curriculum. Librarians cannot do the job alone, and they need the active participation of all teachers. Librarians are not subject specialists in all areas. They need the expert input of the subject specialists—the teachers. To give suggestions and to know what is being published in a given subject area, teachers need to know what new trade books are currently being published. The best way to do this is to read book reviews of newly released titles.

Reference Sources: Aids to Developing Reading Lists

Figure 11.3

Developing reading lists requires knowing what is available in the school and community libraries, what should be in a basic school library collection, and what new materials are being published which you would like to see added to the second library collection.

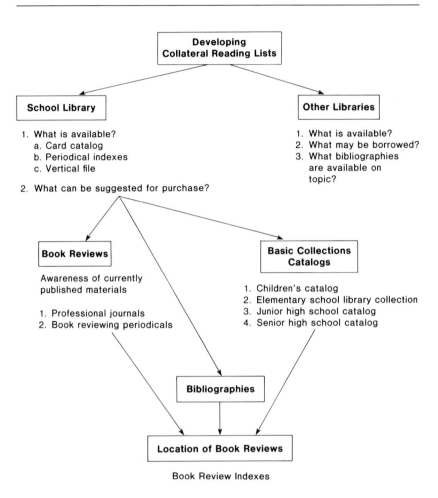

Book Review Indexes

Book Reviews

Periodicals

There are several excellent periodicals that review trade books, both fiction and nonfiction. *Booklist,* which is published by the American Library Association, is one of the best for both elementary and high school level. Published twice monthly from September through June and monthly in July and August, it reviews current materials that are worthy of purchase by small and medium-sized public libraries, school libraries, and community college libraries. In each issue, there is a section entitled "Books for Youth," with six subsections entitled: Adult Books for Young Adults, Books for Older

Readers, Books for Middle Readers, Starred Reviews: Books for Youth, Books for the Young, Series Roundup. A separate section reviews nonprint materials. The young adult and youth sections are cross-referenced with each other. And the young adult section is cross-referenced with the adult book reviews. Annually in a January issue a "Booklist Editors' Choice" is published that includes young adult, youth, and nonprint materials. "Best books for young adults" and "Notable children's books" listings are published annually in the March 15 issue. There is also a section that reviews new reference books. Special features of *Booklist* include books for the handicapped, bilingual books, easy reading, biographies, adult literacy books, high-low reading, professional material, and nonprint media including: film and video, filmstrips, and microcomputer software. In November 1990 *Booklist* Publications launched a new publication, *Book Links: Connecting Books, Libraries, and Classrooms.* The intent of the publication is to help teachers and librarians identify good books—older titles as well as new titles—that will support the curriculum and encourage reading. The first five issues appeared as inserts in the fifteenth of the month issues of *Booklist.* In September 1991 it began as a separate bimonthly publication. Sections giving teaching strategies using grade-appropriate trade books appear in each issue.

The Bulletin of the Center for Children's Books is published monthly except during August. Although the books reviewed are mostly for preschool through junior high school, many are of interest to high school students. Code symbols before recommended grade levels provide instant evaluation of each title. One code identifies titles useful to the curriculum. On the inside of the back cover, each issue publishes a short bibliography of recently published books and journal articles relevant to children's literature. This includes special subject bibliographies of interest to teachers.

The Horn Book Magazine, published six times a year in January, March, May, July, September, and November, reviews books for children of elementary school age and is valuable for all wishing to keep abreast of high-quality children's books. Each issue reviews from seventy to 120 books, mostly fiction but with a few nonfiction, too. *The Horn Book Magazine* features columns about young adult issues, children's book publishing, Canadian children's literature, Spanish books, and picture books. There is also a column about sharing books with children in the classroom. Midyear in 1989 the editors came out with *The Horn Book Guide* that covers six months of short critical reviews of children's and young adult hardcover trade books. Arrangement is by grade level or genre for fiction and the Dewey classification for nonfiction.

The *Kliatt Young Adult Paperback Book Guide* is useful in locating collateral materials for middle school and high school students. Published eight times a year, the January, April, and September issues are especially well organized for easy use because the paperbacks reviewed are placed under subject categories corresponding to the general subject areas taught in the public schools. Each of these three issues also contains an "Issues and Comments" column which may cover curriculum areas of interest; e.g., novels of the Vietnam War; reading for the male reluctant reader; the morally serious novel; or memorable female protagonists of the 1980s in science fiction and fantasy. Reference and professional paperbacks are also reviewed in *Kliatt's*.

The Council of Interracial Books for Children irregularly publishes the *Interracial Books for Children Bulletin*. The *Bulletin* not only reviews books of interest to minority children, but also publishes feature articles pertinent to the education of children. For example, volume 16, no. 8 (1985) included lesson plans for celebrating Martin Luther King's birthday.

The *School Library Journal* is the counterpart to the well-known *Library Journal*. It is published monthly except June and July, and includes reviews of new books for preschool through high school. Several times a year the *School Library Journal* also publishes a list of "best books of the year" for both elementary and secondary students.

Science Books and Films, published by the American Association for the Advancement of Science, is an excellent source of reviews of science and mathematics books for elementary, junior high, and secondary school. Published five times yearly, it reviews trade, textbook, and reference books in addition to films, video, and filmstrips. The November/December issue features a list of "best children's science books" for the year.

One periodical which publishes feature articles concerning literature for children and young adults is the *Wilson Library Bulletin*. It is published monthly except in July and August. The *Wilson Library Bulletin* publishes noteworthy features such as: "Current Reference Books," "picture books for children," and "the young Adult Perplex." Starting in September 1989 a feature called "The Booktalker" was introduced. It is devoted entirely to booktalks and booktalking.

Although not all of these periodicals can be found in any one school or public library, an occasional check of even one—say, *Booklist*—will assist teachers in keeping current with children's literature. Reviews of books found in educational periodicals are also very helpful and should not be overlooked. The *English Journal, Language Arts, Young Children, Reading Teacher, Science and Children, The Mathematics Teacher, Journal of Physical Education and Recreation*, and *Journal of Reading* represent only a few titles that provide regular book reviews for teachers.

Indexes

Many times we wonder about the quality of a book. What do other people think of the book? In other words, we want to read reviews other than the one encountered. Several annotated indexes are published to assist the reader in locating a review. However, not all indexes cover all the periodicals, as can be seen from figure 11.4. The *Book Review Index, Children's Literature Review,* and *Children's Book Reviews Index* do a better job of indexing the periodicals mentioned previously in the chapter than does the

Figure 11.4

Reviews of books located through indexes. The list of periodicals mentioned in the chapter, along with a list of the common indexes to book reviews, is keyed so that the reader can see where each periodical is indexed.

Periodicals Publishing Book Reviews

1. *Booklist*
2. *Bulletin of the Center for Children's Books*
3. *Horn Book*
4. *Interracial Books for Children Bulletin*
5. *Kliatt Young Adult Paperback Book Guide*
6. *School Library Journal*
7. *Science Books and Films*
8. *Wilson Library Bulletin*

Indexes to Book Reviews

Book Review Digest (annual)
   Does not index 2, 4, 5, 7, or 8 of the above
Book Review Index (annual)
   Does not index 2 or 4 of the above
Children's Literature Review (annual)
   Does not index 5 of the above
Children's Book Reviews Index (annual)
   Does not index 4 or 5 of the above

Book Review Digest. Book Review Digest provides brief descriptive notes of each book reviewed, along with quotations from selected reviews and references to the periodicals in which the review appeared. *Book Review Index* is published bimonthly with annual cumulative volumes. Arrangement is alphabetical by author's last name. Most of the periodicals indexed cover the fields of fiction and nonfiction, humanities, social sciences, library science, bibliography, and juvenile and young adult books.

Two indexes cover children's literature exclusively. The first is *Children's Literature Review*. The index presents significant excerpts from reviews, criticism, and commentaries published in journals and newspapers on books for children and young adults. Preceding each author's listing of writings is a paragraph identifying the author's nationality, principle writing genre, and major awards received. Cross-references are made to *Contemporary Authors* and *Something about the Author*. Each entry consists of three parts: general commentary; excerpts pertaining to individual titles; and locator or index citations of materials that might be of further interest to the reader. The second index in the field is *Children's Book Review Index*. Published annually, it cites reviews of children's books appearing in more than 230 periodicals (i.e., those noted in figure 11.4) plus *English Journal,*

Time, Saturday Review, New York Times Book Review, Newsweek, and the *Christian Science Monitor,* to name only a few. If working in a library with a small periodicals collection, users of the two indexes may find the *Book Review Index* more fruitful.

Workshop Activity 11.2
Locating Reading Materials Through Book Reviews

To fully understand how reading book reviews can assist in developing reading lists or suggesting good books to students, examine several of the periodicals publishing book reviews.

1. Locate as many of the book-reviewing periodicals mentioned in the chapter or listed in figure 11.4 on the previous page as you can.
2. Read the book reviews published in the appropriate section for the grade level being taught.
3. Choose twelve to fifteen titles that could be used to enrich units you are presently teaching or are planning to teach.
4. Answer the following questions regarding each of the books chosen:
   a. In which unit of study would the book be useful?
   b. What would the book add to the content of the unit that the textbook does not?
   c. Would the book replace an older book used presently in the unit?
   d. What type of student do you think might enjoy reading the book? Why did you think of that type of individual?

Bibliographies

Bibliographies and indexes share the responsibility for listing books, articles, and other material according to some pattern: author, subject, title, and form. Bibliographies vary in scope, purpose, and makeup. In older bibliographies, the books cited may be out of print but that does not mean that children will not enjoy and appreciate reading them. A good example is *Children's Books Too Good to Miss,* last published in 1979. This slim bibliography is now considered a classic. From a bibliography, teachers can quickly become aware of collateral reading materials available for a particular unit, on a particular reading level, or on varying levels of ability.

Standard Catalogs of School Library Collections

The H. W. Wilson Company publishes three important catalogs for schools: the *Children's Catalog,* the *Junior High School Library Catalog,* and the *Senior High School Library Catalog.* Each is a bibliography of suggested resource materials for the particular grade level it serves. A new edition of

Table 11.1

Bowker's Indexes to *Books in Print*

Books in Print
Subject Guide to Books in Print
Children's Books in Print
Subject Guide to Children's Books in Print
Paperbound Books in Print
El-Hi Textbooks in Print

---

each catalog is published every five years with annual supplements published in the intervening years. The edition, plus the four supplements, may be considered a basic collection for the school library. The *Catalogs* have two parts to them. The user first looks in part II of the volume, in which there are author, title, subject, and analytical indexes, to find titles and portions of books dealing with any subject taught on the particular grade level. After locating the pertinent entry or entries, the user consults part I of the bibliography, which is arranged by the Dewey classification system, and which contains complete bibliographic information about the title and a brief description of each book's contents.

The Brodart Foundation publishes *The Elementary School Library Collection,* which is similar in format to the *Children's Catalog,* but with the added advantage of listing titles of other media such as films, filmstrips, videocassettes, recordings, multimedia kits, realia, and games. The appendixes even include a section listing media for use with preschool children and another section suggesting titles of books for independent reading for grades one and two.

Whenever a new course or unit is being offered or planned, it is advisable for the teacher to go through the appropriate catalog to see how many of the suggested titles the school library or public library has. A request can then be made for pertinent and recently published titles to be added to the library collection. Older titles may be out of print and unavailable except through chance encounters in secondhand bookstores or as gifts from private libraries.

R. R. Bowker Company publishes a group of books that index books that are still in print and available for purchase. They include *Books in Print, Subject Guide to Books in Print, Children's Books in Print, Subject Guide to Children's Books in Print, Paperbound Books in Print,* and *El-Hi Textbooks in Print* (see table 11.1). These reference books serve only to provide information for ordering books. They are incomplete in that they do not list all books published, because many publishers do not provide Bowker with a list of the titles they have published that year. Titles of books for collateral reading lists should not be picked from one of these indexes without reading several reviews of the titles from one of the sources listed previously in the chapter.

Indexes to Books in Print

Categories of Bibliographies

Numerous bibliographies have been published and are available to academic or large public libraries. These fall naturally into two categories, general or special. They serve as excellent reference tools because they have been critically compiled by experts in the field.

General

General bibliographies cover all subjects. Because of this they are usually revised frequently to include recently published titles. Teachers will also find it easier to locate general bibliographies in their local libraries. Good examples of bibliographies falling into the "general" category are three by John T. Gillespie. The books are annotated briefly with easy subject access. Appropriate age level is given for all book titles. With the three titles, grade levels from preschool through high school are covered: *Best Books for Children: Preschool through Grade 6; Best Books for Junior High Readers; Best Books for Senior High Readers.*

Other general bibliographies of interest include: *Adventuring with Books: A Booklist for Pre-K-Grade 6; Eyeopeners! How to Choose and Use Children's Books About Real People, Places, and Things; Using Picture Storybooks to Teach Literary Devices: Recommended Books for Children and Young Adults.*

When looking for particular resources, appropriate general as well as special bibliographies should be consulted. To locate recent publications, book reviewing journals will be helpful.

Workshop Activity 11.3
Using General Bibliographies

You have been introduced to a number of general bibliographies that will assist you in locating appropriate titles for units of study or individual student needs.

1. Scan the titles listed in the bibliography under "General." Check local professional, academic, or school libraries to determine which titles are available.
2. Using the bibliographies available to you, find the titles of three books you would like to read aloud to your students during the coming year that you did not know about before reading this chapter. Be ready to discuss reasons why you chose that particular title.

3. Again scan the general bibliography at the end of the chapter and answer the following questions:
   a. Which tool would most probably assist in locating all the book titles about the struggles of the Moffat family?
   b. You have been given $500 by the principal to purchase collateral reading materials for your school library-media center. Which tools will assist you in selecting the best resources for your content area?

Awareness of published bibliographies on subjects for which teachers have a special need can be a great timesaver. For example, primary teachers who are aware of the books *Beyond Picture Books* by Barbara Barstow or *Books for Children to Read Alone* by George Wilson and Joyce Moss may locate titles of good books to introduce to primary children who are beginning to read on their own. Middle and secondary school teachers using *Junior Plots 3* by Gillespie can find book titles about Vietnam, drugs, pregnancy, or teen problems.

Special Bibliographies

Locating reading material for reluctant readers can be challenging, especially because the reader is older and interested in topics far beyond his or her reading level. The bibliographies cited under "Reluctant Readers" at the end of this chapter will make the task of locating good reading easier. *Choices: A Core Collection for Young Reluctant Readers* annotates the books cited. *Choices* along with the sixth edition of *High Interest–Easy Reading,* published by the National Council of Teachers of English, are the most recently published books for remedial readers.

Reluctant Readers

There are a variety of bibliographies that social studies teachers will find useful in locating collateral materials. Jeanette Hotchkiss has compiled a list of historical fiction and nonfiction in *European Historical Fiction and Biography for Children and Young People,* second edition. Margaret Faissler compiled the useful book *Key to the Past, Some History Books for Pre-College Readers.* Seymour Metzner's *World History in Juvenile Books: A Geographical and Chronological Guide* is excellent for ninth and tenth graders. *A Guide to Historical Reading: Non-Fiction for the Use of Schools, Libraries, and the General Reader,* 9th revised edition, compiled by Leonard B. Irwin, is a continuation of Logasa's *Historical Fiction,* first through sixth editions. *Historical Nonfiction,* a companion to the earlier *Historical Fiction,* can be located in the seventh and eighth edition. This bibliography is selective but covers all periods of history. Each entry gives an author, title, publisher, and a descriptive and evaluative annotation.

Social Studies or History

In 1983 Fred R. Czarra's book *A Guide to Historical Reading, Non-fiction for Schools, Libraries, and the General Reader,* 11th revised edition, was published. This is an annotated bibliography arranged into categories reflecting the major geographic regions of the world. Under each category and subcategory are two groups of books, one for the young adult reader and the other for adults.

U.S. History teachers will find Van Meter's recently published *American History for Children and Young Adults* a key resource for curriculum planning. It is organized by historical periods including the Vietnam Era. *Peoples of the American West* by Cordier is another recent bibliography that will be useful along with the eleven books in the series *Reading for Young People.* Whole language teachers should find Laughlin's *Literature-based Social Studies* helpful.

Science

Finding age appropriate interesting science books for children is challenging. The gifted child with an avid interest in a topic may not read on a level sufficient to allow him to tackle the book he or she wishes to read. Or, the child's narrow subject interest may tax both teacher and school librarian in locating material. Unfortunately it may be that only one or two children's books have been published on a particular topic. And, those may be out-of-print and unavailable if a local library doesn't own a copy. Some children just aren't interested in science but might be guided from an interest in fiction into nonfiction science books. Several recently published books list grade and subject appropriate materials. Carol Kennedy, Stella Spangler and Mary Ann Vanderwerf compiled two excellent volumes: *Science and Technology in Fact and Fiction: a Guide for Young Adults, and Science and Technology in Fact and Fiction: a Guide to Children's Books.* Another recent guide to science literature is the Butzow book, *Science Through Children's Literature: an Integrated Approach.*

Special Students

Since mainstreaming of the handicapped became law, bibliographies assisting that population of our student body are beginning to appear. The most recently published bibliography for handicapped is *More Notes From a Different Drummer, a Guide to Juvenile Fiction Portraying the Disabled,* which expands on the earlier title, *Notes from a Different Drummer: A Guide to Juvenile Fiction Portraying the Handicapped.* The earlier edition identified, described, and critiqued works written between 1940 and 1975. The latest edition examines juvenile titles written between 1976 and 1981 that contain characters with impairments. Books for readers from infants to adolescents including picture books and junior novels are included in the recent edition. Chapter 1 is an essay on the mainstreamed society with a discussion of areas where the disabled person is participating. Chapter 2 is an essay on the disabled in literature. The annotated guide begins with Chapter 3. Lengthy annotations to each title are provided along with reading levels.

There are a number of bibliographies about minorities. *A Guide to Non-Sexist Children's Books* is a briefly annotated list of books for preschool through high school ages. *Books on American Indians and Eskimos: A Selection Guide for Children and Young Adults* lists books published prior to January 1977. However, books dealing with Indians or Eskimos from Canada, Mexico, and Central or South America have been excluded from this bibliography. *Multi-Ethnic Media, Selected Bibliographies in Print* is a bibliography of bibliographies appearing in journal form or book form, which includes both trade books and curriculum materials. *A Selected and Annotated Bibliography of Bicultural Classroom Materials for Mexican American Studies* includes both book and nonbook materials that have as their theme or purpose the enhancement of the self-image of the Chicano student. Part I is a report of research on bicultural classroom materials. Part II is the annotated bibliography of bicultural materials.

Building Ethnic Collections: An Annotated Guide for School Media Centers and Public Libraries is an excellent guide to ethnic book and non-book materials. Part I covers general materials on ethnicity and includes a section on methodology and curriculum materials. The second section is alphabetically arranged under ethnic groups, with cross-references. *Literature by and about the American Indian, an Annotated Bibliography,* by Anna Lee Stensland is the best source of information for any elementary or secondary teacher preparing a unit on Indian literature. Aids for teachers, brief bibliographical sketches of Indian authors, a discourse on the themes found in Indian literature, and graded sections of annotated books are all included in the volume.

Cultural Awareness

An enormous amount of attention is being paid to substance abuse in our country and our schools. Need for appropriate curriculum and collateral reading materials is pressing and constant. Theodora Andrews' recent publication *Substance Abuse Materials for School Libraries, an Annotated Bibliography* is a welcome addition to the professional reference collection. The volume alerts the user to reference tools, periodicals, general informational materials, and special source material by subject area. Two other

Health Education

special bibliographies of interest to the health educator are: *Health, Illness and Disability; a Guide to Books for Children and Young Adults* by Pat Azarnoff and *Sex Education Books for Young Adults 1892–1979* by Patricia J. Campbell.

Sources of Bibliographies

Libraries

Bibliographies from individual libraries, such as the New York Public Library, the Seattle Public Library, and the Denver Public Library, should be collected. Usually the reference departments of any medium-sized or large public library have available for their patrons library-prepared subject bibliographies to assist patrons. By collecting a number of these in a particular subject field, the user can become aware of much of the literature in a given subject field. In libraries where there are children's or young adult collections, there will also be bibliographies available. Teachers of state history should especially take note of bibliographies available from state historical libraries or state libraries. Large metropolitan public libraries very often have city or state historical collections and, because of their demand, have produced historical bibliographies that are valuable. Many secondary librarians make a practice of picking up bibliographies from libraries they visit on vacations or trips. From these, they are able to fill in gaps in their own school library collections because the bibliography draws their attention to a book or books they were unaware of previously. Teachers will find this practice helpful, too.

Curriculum Materials

Curriculum materials can also be a rich source of bibliographies. Committees, in preparing curriculum guides, very often include suggested readings for students. The Association of Supervision and Curriculum Development (ASCD) has a display of curriculum materials at their annual conferences. These are also placed on microfiche and sold to colleges, universities, and school systems by Kraus Microform of Millwood, New York. A general subject index to the collection is helpful in locating a particular curriculum for a specific subject area.

Data Bases and Indexes

The Education Resources Information Center (ERIC) collection of microfiche also contains many curriculum guides and bibliographies of interest and help to the classroom teacher. A search of the ERIC CD-ROM data base to locate entries can be made at a college or school district having this technology. Even a quick search of the "Publication Type Index" of RIE under "bibliographies" will yield useful documents. The advantage of the ERIC CD-ROM search is that it can locate not only ERIC documents but also useful journal articles from the professional literature. When doing an ERIC CD-ROM search, teachers may combine a subject descriptor with a document type number to quickly locate either curriculum or bibliographies. When teachers find it difficult to locate reading lists on current topics, such as AIDS, the ERIC data base is an excellent reference source to search.

This section on bibliographies is not intended to be inclusive, but, rather, to give readers an idea of the kinds of bibliographies available. Other titles have been included in the bibliography at the end of the chapter. By collecting and consulting these and other bibliographies, classroom teachers can develop reading lists of their own, useful as sources of collateral reading materials for units of work with students or groups being taught.

A century ago, students could master all known knowledge about a subject in a short period of time. Now we cannot even hope to learn that much in a lifetime, and we cannot predict what may be needed twenty-five years from now. Knowledge does not remain static. It grows, mushrooms, changes, and even explodes. What is learned one day could be obsolete the next. Recognizing this, educators should spend a lot of time teaching students where to locate information. This exemplifies the importance of the school library or media center. It serves as a reservoir of current, as well as retrospective, reference materials where information may be located. Through the use of encyclopedias, indexes, handbooks, yearbooks, dictionaries, and biographical aids, students discover the wealth of information within their grasp. Properly guided and instructed in a logical search strategy, the entire world of learning opens for students. And this world opens up to students not only while they are in school, but for a lifetime, via the use of the public library.

Teaching Students to Locate Information

The best *search strategy* for acquiring information is one that starts students with a reference tool that presents mostly substantive information (see figure 11.5). In other words, it would be best if students first gained an **overview** of the subject before being exposed to various criticisms of programs, ideas, or methods.

Search Strategy

For example, the *Grolier Electronic Encyclopedia* or the *World Book* in CD-ROM format, contain lengthy articles devoted to subject information in which students acquire a grasp of a topic assigned as well as a familiarity with new vocabulary of the subject field and famous personages in the field. Students should also consult specialized encyclopedias (figure 11.5), where available. Examples of common ones found in secondary schools are: the *Science and Technical Reference Set* or the *McGraw-Hill Encyclopedia of*

Encyclopedias

Figure 11.5
Locating information. Students should start their search for information at point 1, a substantive source, and move along the continuum to the right, so that when they consult a location source of information, they do so only when they know something about their topic.

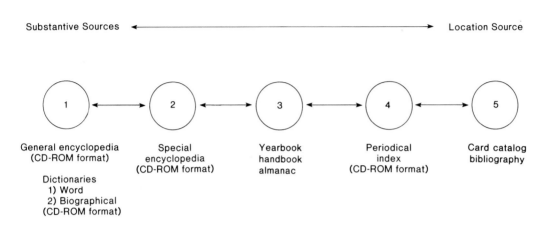

Science and Technology in CD-ROM format. In these specialized encyclopedias, more detailed information is provided for the reader. The specialized encyclopedias are an outgrowth of the information explosion. When the general encyclopedia could not hope to keep up with presenting a synthesized article of the subject matter, the specialized encyclopedia came into being.

When reading encyclopedia articles, students should be instructed to note new vocabulary words. They may have to consult a dictionary to arrive at a clear understanding of the meaning of the terminology presented by the author. Several of the CD-ROM encyclopedic products include a dictionary with the data base. Or students may consult a biographical dictionary to find out more about the life of a particular individual.

Yearbooks and Almanacs

Yearbooks that are published to update the encyclopedias may be consulted. *Collier's Encyclopedia Yearbook,* for example, contains a well-written survey of the past year's happenings. The *McGraw-Hill Yearbook of Science and Technology* updates the parent set in the field of science. Almanacs should be included with the yearbooks. Examples of good almanacs to consult are: *The World Almanac and Book of Facts, Information Please Almanac,* and *Reader's Digest Almanac* (see figure 11.5).

Magazine and journal articles (periodicals) form a very important reservoir of information. Most secondary school libraries contain a substantial collection of a range of periodicals, from more recreational ones, such as *Hot Rod* and *Seventeen,* to the *Atlantic Monthly, Scientific American, Psychology Today,* and *Current History.* The *periodical index* is the locating reference tool of magazines and journal articles whether in print or CD-ROM format. The most commonly found printed periodical index in secondary schools is the *Reader's Guide to Periodical Literature,* indexed by author, title, and subject. The *Abridged Reader's Guide to Periodical Literature,* which began in 1935, may be found in many smaller secondary schools. This abridged edition indexes fewer than fifty titles; the unabridged edition indexes about 160 periodicals. There are annual cumulations for both editions, along with monthly supplements. Students using either edition of the index should be instructed to locate their subject in one of the cumulative editions before going to one of the supplementary monthly updating issues. Neither of the indexes is useful to the student unless the library or media center makes a conscious effort to subscribe to periodicals indexed in them. A number of CD-ROM products are available that offer general periodical indexing. Some even include a subscription to full-text microfiche back files for the magazines indexed. An example is the TOM CD-ROM system. The *General Science Index* is available on CD-ROM. It indexes about 109 science periodicals useful in schools.

Teachers, when making requests for periodical purchases, should make certain that the periodical they request is indexed in one of the indexes taken by their library. If the periodical is not indexed, it may not be used. Selma K. Richardson has compiled and annotated books that list and annotate suggested periodicals for children and schools: *Magazines for Children* and *Magazines for Young Adults: Selections for School and Public Libraries.*

After checking one or more of the periodical indexes, students are ready to use the *card catalog.* Because the card catalog is neither critical nor selective, it should be consulted from the position of an expert at a time when students know what they are looking for—i.e., an actual book title or author. Remind students that *the card catalog is only a location device.* It shows whether the library or a cooperating library has the desired book. And if the library has access to the book, the card catalog notes the location of the book.

The logic of working from a purely substantive source to a location device is self-evident. This strategy allows the teacher to individualize the teaching to fit the needs of the students, and the benefits derived from the teaching of such a strategy are not only surprising, but gratifying.

If a student is assigned a report on crystals, the student should get a general idea of what crystals are by consulting *World Book* (general encyclopedia), and should then get a more scientific explanation by looking at the article on crystals in the *McGraw-Hill Encyclopedia of Science and Technology* (specialized encyclopedia). To find out what has happened with crystals in the past year or two, the student then would consult the *McGraw-Hill Yearbook of Science and Technology* (yearbook) and then go on to the *Reader's Guide (periodical index)* to locate articles on crystals. To identify experiments to do and to learn more about crystals, the student may consult Pilger's book, *Science Experiments Index for Young People* (index). Through a magazine article indexed in a periodical, the student might see a reference to several books about crystals that are considered very good in the field. He or she could then check the card catalog to locate these books on that topic (the final step).

In History

By the time students reach secondary school, U.S. history has been taught two different times in two different years of school, perhaps once in the fourth grade and once in the eighth. It is then taught again in secondary school, perhaps during the junior year of high school. Secondary school history teachers are faced with the task of trying to make that history live for their students. Teachers may plan individualized and group activities structured on the interests of the students. For example, introduce the students to many chronologies that are available. John Clement's *Chronology of the United States,* published in 1975, is well-suited for use with secondary students with reading levels fifth to eighth grade, and it is especially useful with students who have little interest in history. Gordon Carruth's *The Encyclopedia of American Facts and Dates* and Irving Kull's *A Chronological Encyclopedia of American History* are very interesting to the average student or to the above-average student.

Chronologies may impress secondary students because, in many cases, for the first time they can synthesize events in history that they have learned about previously. They can learn what the best-sellers of the era studied were, or what natural disasters happened then, or what sporting events occurred, or what the fashions were. In other words, this is one way to individualize the assignments. By taking a ten-year period in history and allowing students to select such topics as sports events, disasters, leaders, important women, or scientific discoveries, students should research the period so they can make a report orally or in writing.

Gifted students will be able to report on what was happening in the rest of the world during the period being studied in the United States. They could consult chronologies on the topic of world history: I. E. Butler's

Everyman's Dictionary of Dates, Canning's *100 Great Events That Changed the World: From Babylon to the Space Age,* or Longer's *An Encyclopedia of World History: Ancient, Medieval, and Modern, Chronologically Arranged.* Another interesting assignment with chronologies is a crossword puzzle or list of one hundred questions that can be answered via the chronologies.

While a teacher may be attempting to clarify a concept presented in a chapter in the history book for some members of the class, other students could be sent to *The Annals of America,* by Mortimer J. Adler, to trace the history of civil disobedience. Or the nonreaders or reluctant readers can enjoy a pictorial walk through what is being taught by showing them the *Album of American History,* by James Truslow Adams, or the *Pageant of Americans: A Pictorial History of the United States,* by Ralph Henry Gabriel.

The teacher guiding students through the ever changing pains of growing up and maturing will find Dryer's multivolumed set entitled, *Bookfinder: a Guide to Children's Literature About Needs and Problems of Youth Aged 2–15* useful.

In Counseling

Death has become an everyday occurance in our lives. Joanne Bernstein and Masha Rudman's book, *Books to Help Children Cope with Separation and Loss* is now in its 3rd edition. Not only does the book contain annotations of suggested books to be used with children dealing with death, the book also lists resources for adults working with those children.

Music students can trace musical periods via the chronologies and the special encyclopedias in their area, such as *The New Grove Dictionary of American Music,* edited by H. Wiley Hitchcock and Stanley Sadie (encyclopedia).

In Music

The physical education area has a wealth of reference tools: encyclopedias, rule books, yearbooks, record books, and special periodical indexes such as the *Physical Education Index* or *Sport Discus* on CD-ROM.

In Physical Education

In fact, there is not a subject that does not have the standard reference tools appropriate for middle school and secondary use. To become familiar with your particular reference tools, consult one of the many guides to the

Guides to All Subject Areas

literature, such as the *Guide to Reference Books for School Media Centers,* 3d edition, by Christine Wyner where the reference tools are classified by subject and by reference type (e.g., encyclopedia, dictionary, yearbook). Find your particular subject area, read through the annotations, and then locate the reference tools. If you cannot locate them at your school library, go to a nearby larger library.

If you would like to use them in your course of study, request their purchase from your librarian or media specialist. Librarians are always happy to receive suggestions for purchase. Remember, they cannot be subject specialists in all areas and must rely on your judgment as to what to purchase in your subject area. The school library wants to support your curriculum, but to do this, you must make your wants known. As you are going through these reference tools, formulate questions and ideas for incorporation into your units of study. Especially note where facts are presented that perhaps are not present in the textbook you are using. Then you may direct students to these locations. Also, note the different reading and interest levels of the reference tools. You will want to know which tool to direct students to use at any given time.

Summary

No teacher can rely on a textbook to impart all the necessary knowledge in any subject field for a given readership. Teachers need to develop skills in locating and developing collateral reading lists for their subject fields so that the content of the textbook is enriched and the individual interests of students are encouraged and nurtured. Katherine Paterson conveys in her recent book *The Spying Heart* almost the same thoughts as Helen Haines did in 1950 when she writes

> Chimpanzees can make tools and weapons. Computers can decode and compute, but only the human mind can imagine. Our task, as persons devoted to the education of children, is to nourish the imagination. Facts are easily forgotten. Knowledge is replaced by newer information. But the ability—to make connections, to open up closed systems, to discover likenesses that have not been seen before—the ability to imagine will never become obsolete.[4]

This chapter has given some ideas and suggestions of resources to enable teachers to teach a search strategy for locating information. Such efforts on the part of teachers will certainly increase the knowledge base of their students, enhance the reading skills of students, and hopefully encourage lifelong learning.

References

1. Helen E. Haines, *Living with Books, the Art of Book Selection,* 2d ed. (New York: Columbia University Press, 1950), p. 3.
2. Ann Troy, "Literature for Content Area Reading," *The Reading Teacher* 30 (February 1977): 474.

3. Kenneth S. Goodman, "Behind the Eye: What Happens in Reading?" in *Theoretical Models and Process of Reading,* 2d ed., ed. Harry Singer and Robert Ruddell (Newark, Del.: International Reading Association, 1976), p. 486.

4. Katherine Paterson, *The Spying Heart: More Thoughts on Reading and Writing Books for Children* (New York: E. P. Dutton, 1989), p. 161.

Adams, Jane T. "Connecting with a Children's Author." *The Reading Teacher* 37(8) (April 1984): 722–723.

Ahern, John F., and Moir, Hughes. "Celebrating Traditional Holidays in Public Schools: Books for Basic Values." *The Social Studies* 77(6) (November–December 1986): 234–239.

Alvermann, Donna E. "Using Textbook Reading Assignments to Promote Classroom Discussion." *Clearing House* 58(2) (October 1984): 70–73.

Alvermann, Donna E.; Dillon, Deborah R.; O'Brien, David G.; and Smith, Lynn C. "The Role of the Textbook in Discussion." *Journal of Reading* 29(1) (October 1985): 50–57.

Anderson, Nancy. "Using Children's Literature to Teach Black American History." *The Social Studies* 78(2) (March–April 1987): 88–89.

Atwell, Margaret A. "Predictable Books for Adolescent Readers." *Journal of Reading* 29(1) (October 1985): 18–22.

Bachner, Saul. "Sports Literature and the Teaching of Reading: Grab Them and Move Them." *Clearing House* 57(7) (March 1984): 313–314.

Banfield, Beryle. "Books on African American Themes: A Recommended Book List." *Interracial Books for Children Bulletin* 16(7) (1985): 4–8.

Banfield, Beryle. "Children's Books on Martin Luther King, Jr. Offer a One-Dimensional View." *Interracial Books for Children Bulletin* 16(8) (1985): 3–6.

Banfield, Beryle. "Guidelines for Choosing Books on African American Themes." *Interracial Books for Children Bulletin* 16(7) (1985): 9–11.

Banfield, Beryle. "Teaching about Martin Luther King, Jr.: To What End?" *Interracial Books for Children Bulletin* 16(8) (1985): 9–13.

Barrow, Lloyd H.; Kristo, Janice V.; and Andrew, Barbara. "Building Bridges Between Science and Reading." *The Reading Teacher* 38(2) (November 1984): 188–192.

Bechtel, Judith, and Franzblau, Bettie. *Reading in the Science Classroom.* Washington, D.C.: NEA, 1980.

Bernstein, Harriet. "The New Politics of Textbook Adoption." *Phi Delta Kappan* 66(7) (March 1985): 463–466.

Beyer, Barry K. "Critical Thinking: What Is It?" *Social Education* 49(4) (April 1985): 270–276.

Blakeman, John A. "Better Book Reports: Volume Control in the Classroom." *The Science Teacher* 57(6) (September 1990): 54–57.

Braun, Joseph A. Jr., and Cook, Malcolm L. "Making Heritage Experiences Come Alive for Elementary School Social Studies Students." *The Social Studies* 76(5) (September–October 1985): 216–219.

Bristow, Page S., and Farstrup, Alan E. *Reading in Health/Physical Education/Recreation Classes.* Washington, D.C.: NEA, 1981.

Recommended Readings

Brown, Sheldon. "The Depression and World War II as Seen Through Country Music." *Social Education* 49(7) (October 1985): 588–595.

Bullock, Terry L., and Hesse, Karl D. *Reading in the Social Studies Classroom.* Washington, D.C.: NEA, 1981.

Byrnes, Deborah A. "Children and Prejudice." *Social Education* 52(4) (April–May 1988): 267–271.

Calfee, Robert, and Drum, Priscilla. "Research on Teaching Reading." In *Handbook of Research on Teaching,* ed. 3d ed. Merlin C. Whittrock, New York: Macmillan Publishing Company, 1986, pp. 804–849.

Cary, John R. "Supplementary Materials for the American History Survey Course." *History Teacher* 15(3) (May 1982): 385–412.

Chall, Jeanne S., and Conard, Sue S. "Resources and Their Use for Reading Instruction." In *Becoming Readers in a Complex Society: Eighty-third Yearbook of the National Society for the Study of Education.* Part 1. Alan C. Purves and Olive Niles, eds. Chicago: University of Chicago Press, 1984, pp. 209–232.

Charnes, Ruth. "U.S. History Textbooks: Help or Hindrance to Social Justice?" *Interracial Books for Children Bulletin* 15(5) (1984): 3–8.

Chilcoat, George W. "The Images of Vietnam: a Popular Music Approach," *Social Education* 49(7) (October 1985): 601–603.

Clark, Richard E., and Salomon, Gavriel. "Media in Teaching." In *Handbook of Research on Teaching,* 3d ed. Merlin C. Whittrock, ed. New York: Macmillan Publishing Company, 1986: pp. 464–478.

Crook, Patricia R. "On Track with Trade Books." *Science and Children* 27(6) (March 1990): 22–23.

Cudd, Evelyn T. "Research and Report Writing in the Elementary Grades." *The Reading Teacher* 43(3) (December 1989): 268–269.

Cunningham, Patricia M. "A Teacher's Guide to Materials Shopping." *The Reading Teacher* 35(2) (November 1981): 180–184.

Danielson, Kathy Everts. "Helping History Come Alive with Literature." *The Social Studies* 80(2) (March–April 1989): 65–68.

Du Bois, B. De Lin, and McIntosh, Margaret E. "Reading Aloud to Students in Secondary History Classes." *The Social Studies* 77(5) (September–October 1986): 210–213.

Dupart, Annie. "Encouraging the Transition to Pleasure Reading Among Children 10–12 Years." *The Reading Teacher* 38(6) (February 1985): 500–503.

Dupuis, Mary M. "The Problem Reader; Fiction to Challenge Reluctant Readers." *Curriculum Review* 22(1) (February 1983): 59–60.

Eisner, Elliot W. "Art, Music, and Literature Within Social Studies." In *Handbook of Research on Social Studies Teaching and Learning.* James P. Shaver, ed. New York: Macmillan, 1991: 551–558.

Finkelstein, Judy; Stearns, Steve; and Hatcher, Barbara. "Museums Are Not Just For Observing Anymore!" *Social Education* 49(2) (February 1985): 150–154.

Gaug, Mary Ann. "Reading Acceleration and Enrichment in the Elementary Grades." *The Reading Teacher* 37(4) (January 1984): 372–376.

Gay, Carol. "Zane Grey and the High School Student." *English Journal* 70(8) (December 1981): 23–29.

Hanson, Jaci. "Art, Reading, and Kids." *Arts and Activities* 97(2) (March 1985): 28, 37.

Harder, Annie K. "Attitudes Toward Reading Science Textbooks." *The American Biology Teacher* 51(4) (April 1989): 208–212.

Harens, Bonnie et al. "A Symposium on Pre-1900 Classics Worth Using in School." *English Journal* 72(3) (March 1983): 51–57.

Heathington, Betty S., and Alexander, J. Estill. "Do Classroom Teachers Emphasize Attitudes Toward Reading?" *The Reading Teacher* 37(6) (February 1984): 484–488.

Heinly, R. E., and Hilton, K. "Using Historical Fiction to Enrich Social Studies Courses." *Social Studies* 73(1) (January–February 1982): 21–24.

Herber, Harold L., and Nelson-Herber, Joan. "Planning the Reading Program." In *Becoming Readers in a Complex Society: Eighty-third Yearbook of the National Society for the Study of Education.* Part 1. Alan C. Purves and Olive Niles, eds. Chicago: University of Chicago Press, 1984:174–208.

Hill, W. R. "Reading Methods, Secondary." In *The International Encyclopedia of Education: Research and Studies.* Torsten Husen and T. Neville Postlethwaite, eds.-in-chief. Vol. 7. New York: Pergamon Press, 1985:4213–4216.

Hochman, William R. "The Fallible Winds of War." *The Social Studies* 76(3) (May–June 1985): 134–138.

Jacobson, Frances F. "Library Instruction and the Science Classroom: The Ideal Laboratory." *Journal of Youth Services in Libraries* 2(3) (Spring 1989): 234–240.

James, Michael, and Zarrillo, James. "Teaching History with Children's Literature." *The Social Studies* 80(4) (July–August 1989): 153–158.

Jebsen, Harry Jr. "Integrating Sports History into American History Courses." *Social Studies* 75(2) (March–April 1984): 62–67.

Krapp, JoAnn Vergona. "Teaching Research Skills: A Critical-Thinking Approach." *School Library Journal* 34(5) (January 1988): 32–35.

Kretman, Kathy Postel, and Parker, Barbara. "New U.S. History Texts: Good News and Bad." *Social Education* 50(1) (January 1986): 61–63.

Laughlin, Mildred K. *Developing Learning Skills Through Children's Literature: An Idea Book for K–5 Classrooms and Libraries.* Phoenix, Arizona: Oryx, 1986.

Lehman, Barbara A., and Hayes, David. "Advancing Critical Reading Through Historical Fiction and Biography." *The Social Studies* 76(4) (July–August 1985): 165–169.

Levstik, Linda S. "Historical Narrative and the Young Reader." *Theory Into Practice* 28(2) (Spring 1989): 114–119.

Long, Margo Alexandre. "The Interracial Family in Children's Literature." *Interracial Books for Children Bulletin* 15(6) (1984): 13–15.

Long, Roberta. "Soviet Children's Books: Expanding Children's Views of the Soviet Union." *Journal of Reading* 27(5) (February 1984): 418–422.

MacDonald, Margaret Read. *Booksharing: 101 Programs to Use with Preschoolers.* Hamden, Conn: Library Professional Publications, 1988.

Mangieri, J. M., and Corboy, M. R. "Recreational Reading: Do We Practice What Is Preached?" *The Reading Teacher* 34(8) (May 1981): 923–925.

Martin, Charles E.; Cramond, Bonnie; and Safter, Tammy. "Developing Creativity Through the Reading Program." *The Reading Teacher* 35(5) (February 1982): 568–572.

McClure, Amy A. "Integrating Children's Fiction and Informational Literature in a Primary Reading Curriculum." *The Reading Teacher* 35(7) (April 1982): 784–789.

McCutcheon, Randall. "Library Scavenger Hunts: A Way Out of the Bewilderness." *Wilson Library Bulletin* 64(5) (January 1990): 38–40.

McGowan, Tom and Guzzetti, Barbara. "Promoting Social Studies Understanding through Literature-based Instruction." *The Social Studies* 82(1) (January–February 1991): 16–21.

Memory, David M., and McGowan, Thomas M. "Using Multilevel Textbooks in Social Studies Classes." *The Social Studies* 76(4) (July–August 1985): 174–179.

Mikulecky, Larry, and Haugh, Rita. *Reading in the Business Education Classroom.* Washington, D.C.: NEA, 1980.

Morrow, Lesley Mandel. "Promoting Voluntary Reading." *In Handbook of Research on Teaching the English Language Arts.* New York: Macmillan, 1991: 681–690.

Moss, Joy F. "Reading and Discussing Fairy Tales—Old and New." *The Reading Teacher* 35(6) (March 1982): 656–660.

Musser, Louise S., and Freeman, Evelyn B. "Teach Young Students About Native Americans: Use Myths, Legends, and Folktales." *The Social Studies* 80(1) (January–February 1989): 5–9.

Nauman, Ann K., and Shaw, Edward L. "Science in the Library." *Science Activities* 26(3) (September–October 1989): 26–28.

Nist, Sherrie; Kirby, Kate; and Ritter, Annice. "Teaching Comprehension Processes Using Magazines, Paperback Novels, and Content Area Texts." *Journal of Reading* 27(3) (December 1983): 252–261.

Polette, Nancy. *Whole Language in Action!: Teaching With Children's Literature.* O'Fallon, MO: Book Lures, 1990.

Radencich, Marguerite C. "Books That Promote Positive Attitudes Toward Second Language Learning." *The Reading Teacher* 38(6) (February 1985): 528–530.

Read, Donna, and Smith, Henrietta M. "Teaching Visual Literacy Through Wordless Picture Books." *The Reading Teacher* 35(8) (May 1982): 928–933.

Reading in the Content Areas: Research for Teachers. Edited by Mary M. Dupuis. Newark, Del.: International Reading Association, 1984.

Reynolds, Frances E., and Pickett, Ilayna. "Think! Write!: The Reading Response Journal in the Biology Classroom." *The American Biology Teacher* 51(7) (October 1989): 435–437.

Riecken, Ted J., and Miller, Michelle R. "Introduce Children to Problem Solving and Decision Making by Using Children's Literature." *The Social Studies* 81(2) (March–April 1990): 59–64.

Saccardi, Marianne. "Books to Go: A Portable Reading Project." *School Library Journal* 35(13) (September 1989): 168–172.

Scales, Pat. "Children's Novels to Teach." *Booklist* 85(11) (February 1, 1989): 944–945.

Searls, Donald T.; Mead, Nancy A.; and Ward, Barbara. "The Relationship of Students' Reading Skills to TV Watching, Leisure Time Reading, and Homework." *Journal of Reading* 29(2) (November 1985): 158–162.

Seidman, Laurence I. "Folksongs: Magic in Your Classroom." *Social Education* 49(7) (October 1985): 580–587.

Sharp, Peggy Agostino. "Teaching with Picture Books Throughout the Curriculum." *The Reading Teacher* 38(2) (November 1984): 132–137.

Smith, Cyrus F. Jr., and Kepner, Henry S. *Reading in the Mathematics Classroom.* Washington, D.C.: NEA, 1981.

Smith, Richard J. "A Study Guide for Extending Students' Reading of Social Studies Material." *The Social Studies* 78(2) (March–April 1987): 85–87.

Storey, Dee C. "A Legacy of Values: War in Literature for Adolescents." *The Social Studies* 76(2) (March–April 1985): 85–89.

Storey, Dee C. "Reading Role Models: Fictional Readers in Children's Books." *Reading Horizons* 26(2) (Winter 1986): 140–148.

Swartz, B. J., and Zimmerman, Karen J. "Hidden Treasure: Government Documents for Children and Teens." *School Library Journal* 35(12) (August 1989): 40–43.

Vocke, David E., and Hahn, Amos. "What Does Reading Research Say to Social Studies Teachers?" *Social Education* 53(5) (September 1989): 323–324, 326.

Watson, Jerry. "Lies: The Beginning of Honesty." *School Library Journal* 34(3) (November 1987): 33–36.

Whitmer, Jean E. "Pickles Will Kill You: Use Humorous Literature to Teach Critical Reading." *The Reading Teacher* 39(6) (February 1986): 530–534.

Wiesendanger, Katherine D., and Bader, Lois. "SSR: Its Effect on Students' Reading Habits After They Complete the Program." *Reading Horizons* 29(3) (Spring 1989): 162–166.

Wilcox, Fred A. "Pedagogical Implications of Teaching 'Literature of the Vietnam War'." *Social Education* 52(1) (January 1988): 39–40.

Woodward, Arthur. "Improving the Quality of Textbooks: A Brief Reference List." *Social Education* 50(1) (January 1986): 70.

Woodward, Arthur; Elliott, David L.; and Nagel, Kathleen Carter. "Beyond Textbooks in Elementary Social Studies." *Social Education* 50(1) (January 1986): 50–53.

Book Review Digest. Monthly with semiannual and annual cumulations. 1905–.

Book Review Index. Bimonthly with cumulations three times a year and an annual cumulation. 1965–.

Children's Book Review Index. Volume 1–. Gary C. Tarbert, editor. Detroit: Gale Research Company, 1975–.

Children's Literature Review: Excerpts from Reviews, Criticism, and Commentary on Books for Children and Young People. Volume 1–. Gerard J. Senick, editor. New York: Gale Research Company, 1976–.

Part One—Cited and Suggested Bibliographies

Book Review Indexes

Book Links: Connecting Books, Libraries, and Classrooms. Chicago: American Library Association, 1991.

Booklist. Chicago: American Library Association, 1904–.

Bulletin of the Center for Children's Books. Zena Sutherland, editor. Chicago: University of Chicago Press, 1947–.

Horn Book Guide to Children's and Young Adult Books. Boston: The Horn Book, Inc., 1990–.

Book Reviews

Horn Book Magazine. Ethel L. Heins, editor. Boston: The Horn Books, Inc., 1924–.

Kliatt Young Adult Paperback Book Guide. Newton, Ma.: Kliatt Paperback Book Guide, 1967–.

School Library Journal. New York: R. R. Bowker Company, 1954/55–.

Science Books and Films. Michele M. Newman, editor. Washington, D.C.: American Association for the Advancement of Science, 1965/66–.

Wilson Library Bulletin. William R. Eshelman, editor. New York: H. W. Wilson Company, 1921–.

Standard Catalogs

National Association of Independent Schools, Ad Hoc Library Committee. *Books for Secondary School Libraries.* 6th ed. New York: R. R. Bowker, 1981.

Children's Catalog. 16th ed. New York: H. W. Wilson, 1991.

The Elementary School Library Collection: A Guide to Books and Other Media. 17th ed., phases 1-2-3. Edited by Lois Winkel. Williamsport, Pa.: Brodart Co., 1990.

Junior High School Library Catalog. 6th ed. New York: H. W. Wilson Company, 1990.

Senior High School Library Catalog. 13th ed. New York: H. W. Wilson Company, 1987. Supplements: 1988, 1989, 1990.

General Bibliographies

Anderson, Vicki. *Fiction Sequels for Readers 10 to 16: An Annotated Bibliography of Books in Succession.* Jefferson, N.C.: McFarland, 1990.

Apseloff, Marilyn Fain. *They Wrote for Children Too: An Annotated Bibliography of Children's Literature by Famous Writers for Adults.* New York: Greenwood, 1989.

Arbuthnot, May Hill; Clark, Margaret Mary; Hadlow, Ruth M.; and Long, Harriet G. *Children's Books Too Good To Miss.* revised and enlarged, 7th ed. New York: University Press Books, 1979.

Association for Childhood Education International Books for Children Committee. *Bibliography, Books for Children.* Wheaton, Md.: Association for Childhood Education International, 1989.

Association for Childhood International. *Excellent Paperbacks for Children.* Washington, D.C.: The Association for Childhood International, 1979.

Association for Library Service to Children and Young Adults Services Division, American Library Association. *Selecting Materials for Children and Young Adults: A Bibliography of Bibliographies and Review Sources.* Chicago: American Library Association, 1980.

Association for Library Service to Children, American Library Association, Notable Films, Filmstrips and Recordings, 1973–1986 Retrospective Task Force. *Notable Children's Films and Videos, Filmstrips and Recordings, 1973–1986.* Chicago: American Library Association, 1987.

Blostein, Fay. *Connections: Paperback Reading for Young People.* Toronto, Canada: Ontario Library Association, 1988.

Carlsen, G. Robert. *Books and the Teen-age Reader; A Guide for Teachers, Librarians and Parents,* 2d rev. ed. New York: Harper & Row, 1980.

Carroll, Frances Laverne, and Meachan, Mary. *Exciting, Funny, Scary, Short, Different, and Sad Books Kids Like About Animals, Science, Sports, Families, Songs, and Other Things.* Chicago: American Library Association, 1984.

Carter, B., and Abrahamson, Richard F. *Books For You: A Booklist for Senior High Students.* 10th ed. Urbana, Ill.: The National Council of Teachers of English, 1988.

Carter, B., and Abrahamson, Richard F. *Nonfiction for Young Adults: From Delight to Wisdom.* Phoenix: Oryx Press, 1990.

Clark, Catherine H., and Widutis, Florence, editors. *Books for New Age Children and Youth.* College Park, Md.: Beautiful Day Books, 1977.

Elleman, Barbara, editor. *Popular Reading for Children II: A Collection of the Booklist Columns.* Chicago: American Library Association, 1986.

Gillespie, John T. *Best Books for Junior High Readers.* New Providence, NJ: R. R. Bowker, 1991.

Gillespie, John T. *Best Books for Senior High Readers.* New Providence, NJ: R. R. Bowker, 1991.

Gillespie, John T. *The Elementary School Paperback Collection.* Chicago: American Library Association, 1985.

Gillespie, John T. *The Junior High School Paperback Collection.* Chicago: American Library Association, 1985.

Gillespie, John T. *The Senior High School Paperback Collection.* Chicago: American Library Association, 1986.

Gillespie, John T., and Naden, Corinne J. *Best Books for Children: Preschool Through Grade 6.* 4th ed. New York: R. R. Bowker, 1990.

Hall, S. *Using Picture Storybooks to Teach Literary Devices: Recommended Books for Children and Young Adults.* Phoenix: Oryx Press, 1990.

Haviland, Virginia, compiler. *Children's Books, 1979: A List of Books for Preschool Through Junior High School Age.* Washington, D.C.: Library of Congress, 1980.

Helbig, Alethea K., and Regan, Agnes. *Dictionary of British Children's Fiction: Books of Recognized Merit.* New York: Greenwood, 1989.

Hunt, Mary Alice, editor. *A Multimedia Approach to Children's Literature: A Selective List of Films (and Videocassettes), Filmstrips, and Recordings Based on Children's Books.* 3d ed. Chicago: American Library Association, 1983.

Jett-Simpson, Mary, editor, and the Committee on the Elementary School Booklist of the National Council of Teachers of English. *Adventuring with Books: A Booklist for Pre-K–Grade 6.* 9th ed. Urbana, Ill.: National Council of Teachers of English, 1989.

Kobrin, B. *Eyeopeners! How to Choose and Use Children's Books About Real People, Places, and Things.* New York: Penguin Books, 1988.

Laughlin, Mildred K., and Claudia L. Swisher. *Literature-Based Reading: Children's Books and Activities to Enrich the K-5 Curriculum.* Phoenix, AZ: Oryx Press, 1990.

Leonard, Charlotte. *Tied Together: Topics and Thoughts for Introducing Children's Books.* Metuchen, N.J.: Scarecrow Press, 1980.

Lindskoog, John, and Lindskoog, Kay. *How to Grow a Young Reader: A Parent's Guide to Kids and Books.* Elgin, Ill.: David C. Cook, 1978.

MacLeod, Anne S., editor. *Children's Literature: Selected Essays and Bibliographies.* (Student Contribution Series Number 9.) College Park, Md.: College of Library and Information Services, University of Maryland, 1977.

National Council of Teachers of English. *Books for You: A Booklist for Senior High Students,* Richard F. Abrahamson and Betty Carter, Co-chairs, and the Committee on the Senior High School Booklist of the NCTE, 10th ed. Urbana, Ill.: National Council of Teachers of English, 1988.

National Council of Teachers of English, Committee on the Junior High School Booklist and James E. Davis and Hazel K. Davis, editors. *Your Reading: A Booklist for Junior High Students,* 7th ed. Urbana, Ill.: National Council of Teachers of English, 1988.

Olderr, Steven. *Olderr's Young Adult Fiction Index.* Chicago, IL: St. James Press, 1989.

Owen, Betty M. *Smorgasbord of Books: Titles Junior High Readers Relish.* New York: Citation Press, 1974.

Paulin, Mary Ann. *Creative Uses of Children's Literature.* Hamden, Conn.: Library Professional Publication, 1982.

Paulin, Mary Ann. *More Creative Uses of Children's Literature. Vol. 2.* Hamden, CT: Library Professional Publications, in press.

Pettus, Eloise S. *Master Index to Summaries of Children's Books,* 2 volumes. Metuchen, N.J.: Scarecrow Press, 1985.

Polotte, Nancy, and Hamlin, Marjorie. *Celebrating with Books.* Metuchen, N.J.: Scarecrow Press, 1977.

Roman, Susan. *Sequences: An Annotated Guide to Children's Fiction in Series.* Chicago: American Library Association, 1985.

Rosenberg, Judith K. *Young People's Literature in Series: Fiction, Non-Fiction, and Publishers' Series, 1973–1975.* Littleton, Col.: Libraries Unlimited, 1977.

Roser, Nancy, and Frith, Margaret, editors. *Children's Choices: Teaching with Books Children Like.* Newark, Del.: International Reading Association, 1983.

Rudman, Masha Kabakow. *Children's Literature: An Issues Approach.* 2d ed. New York: Longman, 1984.

Sadker, Myra Pollack, and Sadker, David Miller. *Now Upon a Time: A Contemporary View of Children's Literature.* New York: Harper, 1977.

Scott, Jon C. *Children's Literature From A to Z, A Guide for Parents and Teachers.* New York: McGraw Hill, 1984.

Shapiro, Lillian L. *Fiction for Youth: A Guide to Recommended Books.* 2d ed. New York: Neal-Schuman Publishers, Inc., 1986.

Shelton, Helen, editor. *Bibliography of Books for Children,* 1988–89 edition. Washington, D.C.: Association for Childhood Education International, 1988.

Spirit, Diana L. *Introducing More Books, A Guide for the Middle Grades.* New York: R. R. Bowker, 1978.

Sutherland, Zena. *The Best in Children's Books: The University of Chicago Guide to Children's Literature 1973–1978.* Chicago: University of Chicago Press, 1980.

Sutherland, Zena, editor. *The Best in Children's Books: The University of Chicago Guide to Children's Literature, 1979–1984.* Chicago: University of Chicago Press, 1986.

Tiedt, Irish M. *Exploring Books with Children.* Boston: Houghton Mifflin, 1979.

Walker, Elinor. *Book Bait: Detailed Notes on Adult Books Popular with Young Adults.* 4th ed. Chicago: American Library Association, 1988.

Woodbury, Marda. *Selecting Materials for Instruction: Subject Areas and Implementation,* volume 3. Littleton, Col.: Libraries Unlimited, 1980.

Horner, Catherine Townsend. *The Aging Adult in Children's Books and Nonprint Media, An Annotated Bibliography.* Metuchen, N.J.: Scarecrow Press, 1982.

Gallivan, Marion F. *Fun For Kids, An Index to Children's Craft Books.* Metuchen, N.J.: Scarecrow Press, 1981.

Arts and Crafts

Breen, Karen, editor. *Index to Collective Biographies for Young Readers.* 4th ed. New York: R. R. Bowker, 1988.
Siegel, Mary-Ellen. *Her Way, A Guide to Biographies of Women for Young People.* 2d ed. Chicago: American Library Association, 1984.
Silverman, Judith. *Index to Young Readers' Collective Biographies: Elementary and Junior High School Level.* 2d ed. New York: R. R. Bowker, 1975.
Stanius, Ellen J. *Index to Short Biographies: For Elementary and Junior High Grades.* Metuchen, N.J.: Scarecrow Press, 1971.

Biographies

Aubrey, Irene E. *Notable Canadian Children's Books, 1980–1984,* cumulative edition. Ottawa, Canada: National Library of Canada, 1989.
McDonough, Irma, editor. *Canadian Books for Young People.* Toronto, Canada: University of Toronto Press, 1980.
Pederson, Beverly. *Something to Chew On: Canadian Fiction for Young Adults.* Saskatoon, Canada: Saskatoon Public Library, 1979.
Scott, Jon C., and Jones, Raymond E. *Canadian Books for Children: A Guide to Authors and Illustrators.* Toronto, Canada: Harcourt Brace Jovanovich Canada, 1988.
Verrall, Catherine. *Resource Reading List 1990: Annotated Bibliography of Resources by and about Native People.* Toronto: Alliance Canadienne en Solidarite avec les antochtones, 1990.

Canadian

American Association of University Women, Boulder Colorado Branch. *Books with Options: An Annotated Bibliography of Non-Stereotyping Books for Children and Young People.* Boulder: American Association of University Women, 1976.
Buttlar, Lois, and Wymar, Lubomyr R. *Building Ethnic Collections: An Annotated Guide for School Media Centers and Public Libraries.* Littleton, Col.: Libraries Unlimited, 1977.
Chambers, Joanna Fountain. *Hey, Miss! You Got a Book for Me? A Model Multicultural Resource Collection, Annotated Bibliography.* Revised and Expanded, 2nd edition. Austin, Tex.: Austin Bilingual Language Editions, 1981.
Department of Indian Affairs and Northern Development, Education Division. *About Indians: A Listing of Books.* 4th ed. Toronto, Canada: Department of Indian Affairs and Northern Development, 1977.

Cultural Awareness

Duran, Daniel Flores. *Latino Materials: A Multimedia Guide for Children and Young Adults.* New York: Neal-Schuman Publishers, 1979. (Selection Guide Series)

Elleman, Barbara, editor. *Children's Books of International Interest.* 3d ed. Chicago: American Library Association, 1984.

Fitzgerald, Bonnie. *Bibliography of Literature and Cross-Cultural Values.* Urbana, Ill.: Conference for Secondary School English Department Chairmen, National Council of Teachers of English, 1973.

Gilliland, Hap. *Indian Children's Books.* Billings: Montana Council for Indian Education, 1980.

Haller, Elizabeth S., compiler. *New Perspectives: A Bibliography of Racial, Ethnic, and Feminist Resources.* Harrisburg: Pennsylvania Department of Education, 1977.

Hotchkiss, Jeanette. *African-Asian Reading Guide for Children and Young Adults.* Metuchen, N.J.: Scarecrow Press, 1976.

Karolides, Nicholas J. *Black Fiction and Biographies: Current Books for Children and Adolescents,* WCTE Service Bulletin No 28. River Falls: Wisconsin Council of Teachers of English, 1972.

Lass-Woodfin, Mary Jo, editor. *Books on American Indians and Eskimos: A Selection Guide for Children and Young Adults.* Chicago: American Library Association, 1978.

Mills, Joyce White, editor. *The Black World in Literature for Children: A Bibliography of Print and Non-Print Materials.* Atlanta: School of Library Service, Atlanta University, 1975.

National Council of Teachers of English. *Annotated Bibliography.* Urbana, Ill.: National Council of Teachers of English, 1979.

Portland Public Schools. *A Community of People: A Multi-Ethnic Bibliography.* Portland: Educational Media Department, Portland Public Schools, 1974.

Reilly, Robert P. *A Selected and Annotated Bibliography of Bicultural Classroom Materials for Mexican American Studies.* San Francisco: R & E Research Associates, 1977.

Rollock, Barbara. *The Black Experience in Children's Books.* New York: New York Public Library, 1974.

Scherf, Walter, editor. *The Best of the Best: Picture, Children's and Youth Books for 110 Countries or Languages; Catalogs of the International Youth Library 3; Die Besten Der Besten: Kataloge der Internationalen Jugend Bibliothek 3,* enlarged edition. New York/Munchen, Germany: R. R. Bowker/Verlag Dokumentation, 1976.

Schmidt, Velma E., and McNeill, Earldene. *Cultural Awareness: A Resource Bibliography.* Washington, D.C.: National Association for the Education of Young Children, 1978.

Schon, Isabel. *A Hispanic Heritage: A Guide to Juvenile Books about Hispanic People and Cultures.* Metuchen, N.J.: Scarecrow Press, 1980.

Seattle Public Schools. *Books Transcend Barriers: A Bibliography of Books About Africans, Afro-Americans, Japanese, Chinese, American Indians, Eskimos and Mexican Americans for Elementary and Middle School Grades.* Revised. Seattle, Wash.: Seattle Public Schools, 1972.

Spache, George D. *Good Reading for the Disadvantaged Reader: Multi-Ethnic Resources.* Champaign, Ill.: Garrard Publishing Company, 1975.

Tway, Eileen, editor. *Reading Ladders for Human Relations.* 6th ed. Urbana, Ill.: National Council of Teachers of English, 1981.

Washington (State) Department of Education. *A Bibliography of Asian and Asian American Books for Elementary School Youngsters.* Olympia, Wash.: State Superintendent of Public Instruction, 1975.

Wolfe, Ann G. *About 100 Books . . . a Gateway to Better Intergroup Understanding.* 8th ed. New York: American Jewish Committee, 1977.

Wynar, Lubomyr R., and Buttler, Lois. *Ethnic Film and Filmstrip Guide for Libraries and Media Centers: A Selective Filmography.* Littleton, Col.: Libraries Unlimited, 1980.

Bernstein, Joanne E., and Rudman, Masha K. *Books to Help Children Cope with Separation and Loss: An Annotated Bibliography.* 3d ed. New York: R. R. Bowker, 1989. — **Death, Dying, Separation, and Loss**

Fassler, Joan. *Helping Children Cope.* New York: Free Press, 1978.

Gillis, Ruth J. *Children's Books for Times of Stress: An Annotated Bibliography.* Bloomington: Indiana University Press, 1978.

Kerr, Lucille E., and Kaplan, Mimi. *A Bibliography of Resources on the Subject of Death for Children Junior High and Younger.* 1979.

Thomas, James L., editor. *Death and Dying in the Classroom; Readings for Reference.* Phoenix: Oryx Press, 1984.

Wass, Hannelore, and Corr, Charles A., editors. *Helping Children Cope with Death: Guidelines and Resources.* New York: Hemisphere Publishing, 1982.

Wilkin, Binnie Tate. *Survival Themes in Fiction for Children and Young People.* Metuchen, N.J.: Scarecrow Press, 1978.

Cuddigan, Maureen, and Hanson, Mary Beth. *Growing Pains: Helping Children Deal with Everyday Problems through Reading.* Chicago: American Library Association, 1988. — **Everyday Problems**

Dreyer, Sharon Spredemann. *The Bookfinder: A Guide to Children's Literature About the Needs and Problems of Youth Aged 2–15.* Vol. 1—Circle Pines, Minn.: American Guidance Service, Inc., 1977—.

Eastman, Mary Huse. *Index to Fairy Tales, Myths and Legends.* 2 vols. Supplement by Mary Huse Eastman. Boston: F. W. Faxon, 1926. — **Fairy Tales and Folklore**

Ireland, Norma. *Index to Fairy Tales 1949–1972, Including Folklore, Legends and Myths in Collections.* Westwood, Mass.: E. W. Faxon, 1973.

Ramsey, Eloise. *Folklore for Children and Young People: A Critical and Descriptive Bibliography for Use in the Elementary and Intermediate School.* Compiled and annotated by Eloise Ramsey in collaboration with Dorothy Mills Howard, chairman Sub-Committee on Bibliography, Committee on Folklore for Children and Young People of the American Folklore Society. Philadelphia: American Folklore Society, 1952.

Shannon, George. *Folk Literature and Children: An Annotated Bibliography of Secondary Materials.* Westport, Conn.: Greenwood Press, 1981.

Ziegler, Elsie B. *Folklore: An Annotated Bibliography and Index to Single Editions.* Boston: F. W. Faxon, 1973.

Families	Hausslein, Evelyn B. *Children and Divorce: An Annotated Bibliography and Guide.* New York: Garland Publishers, 1983.
	Horner, Catherine Townsend. *The Single-parent Family in Children's Books: An Annotated Bibliography.* 2d ed. Metuchen, N.J.: Scarecrow Press, 1988.
First Readers	Barstow, Barbara, and Riggle, Judith. *Beyond Picture Books: A Guide to First Readers.* New York: R. R. Bowker, 1989.
	Polette, Nancy. *E is for Everybody: A Manual for Bringing Fine Picture Books into the Hands and Hearts of Children.* 2d ed. Metuchen, N.J.: Scarecrow Press, 1982.
	Reasoner, Charles F. *Bringing Children and Books Together: A Teacher's Guide to Early Childhood Literature.* A Yearling Book. New York: Dell, 1979.
	Reasoner, Charles F. *Releasing Children to Literature: The First Teacher's Guide to Yearling Books.* A Dell Yearling Book. Rev. ed. New York: Dell, 1976.
	Reasoner, Charles F. *When Children Read: The Third Teacher's Guide to Yearling Books.* A Dell Yearling Book. New York: Dell, 1975.
	Williams, Helen Elizabeth, with Gloden, Katharine Mary. editors. *Independent Reading, K–3.* Williamsport, Pa.: Bro-Dart Publishing Company, 1980.
	Wilson, George, and Moss, Joyce. *Books for Children to Read Alone: A Guide for Parents and Librarians.* New York: R. R. Bowker, 1988.
Foreign Countries	Schmidt, Nancy J. *Children's Books on Africa and Their Authors: An Annotated Bibliography.* Volume 3. New York: Africana Publishing Co., 1975.
	Schmidt, Nancy J. *Supplement to Children's Books on Africa and Their Authors: An Annotated Bibliography.* Volume 5. New York: Africana Publishing Co., 1979.
	Zekiros, Astair, and Kofi, Mensah. *Children's Books on Africa.* Madison, Wis.: African Studies Program, Wisconsin University, 1978.
Foreign Language	Dale, Doris Cruger. *Bilingual Books in Spanish and English for Children.* Littleton, CO: Libraries Unlimited, Inc., 1985.
	Schon, Isabel. *Basic Collection of Children's Books in Spanish.* Metuchen, N.J.: Scarecrow Press, 1986.
	Schon, Isabel. *Books in Spanish for Children and Young Adults: An Annotated Guide.* Metuchen, N.J.: Scarecrow Press, 1978.
	Schon, Isabel. *Books in Spanish for Children and Young Adults: An Annotated Guide, Series II.* Metuchen, N.J.: Scarecrow Press, 1983.
Gifted	Baskin, Barbara H., and Harris, Karen H. *Books for the Gifted Child.* New York: R. R. Bowker, 1980.
	Halsted, Judith Wynn. *Guiding Gifted Readers: From Preschool to High School: A Guide for Parents, Teachers, Librarians and Counselors.* Columbus: Ohio Psychology Publishing Company, 1988.
	Hauser, Paula, and Nelson, Gail A. *Books for the Gifted Child.* 2 Vol. New York: R. R. Bowker, 1980, 1988.
	Pollete, Nancy. *Books and Real Life, A Guide for Gifted Students and Teachers.* Jefferson, N.C.: McFarland & Company, Inc., 1984.

Baskin, Barbara H., and Harris, Karen H. *More Notes From a Different Drummer: A Guide to Juvenile Fiction Portraying the Disabled.* New York: R. R. Bowker, 1984.

Baskin, Barbara H., and Harris, Karen H. *Notes From A Different Drummer: A Guide to Juvenile Fiction Portraying the Handicapped.* New York: R. R. Bowker, 1977.

Coping: Books About Young People Surviving Special Problems: A Bibliography Based on the Acquisition of EDMARC. Washington, D.C.: U.S. Department of Health, Education and Welfare, 1977.

Friedberg, Joan Brest; Mullins, June B.; and Weir Sukiennik, Adelaide. *Accept Me As I Am: Best Books of Juvenile Nonfiction on Impairments and Disabilities.* New York: R. R. Bowker, 1985.

Horn, Thomas D., and Ebert, Dorothey J. *Books for the Partially Sighted Child.* Champaign, Ill.: National Council of Teachers of English, 1965.

National Library Service for the Blind and Physically Handicapped. *For Younger Readers, Braille and Talking Books.* Washington, D.C.: Library of Congress, 1981.

Pardeck, Jean A., and Pardeck, John T. *Young People with Problems: A Guide to Bibliotherapy.* Westport, Conn.: Greenwood Press, 1984.

Special Students

Altshuler, Anne. *Books That Help Children Deal with a Hospital Experience.* Rev. ed. Washington, D.C.: U. S. Department of Health, Education and Welfare, 1978.

Andrews, Theodora. *Substance Abuse Materials for School Libraries: An Annotated Bibliography.* Littleton, Col.: Libraries Unlimited, 1985.

Azarnoff, Pat. *Health, Illness and Disability: A Guide to Books for Children and Young Adults.* New York: R. R. Bowker, 1983.

Campbell, Patricia J. *Sex Education Books for Young Adults, 1892–1979.* New York: R. R. Bowker, 1979.

Charles, Sharon Ashenbrenner, and Feldman, Sari. *Drugs: A Multimedia Sourcebook for Children and Young Adults.* New York: Neal-Schuman; Santa Barbara, Calif.: ABC-Clio, 1980. (Selection Guide Series)

Health Education

Indiana State Department of Public Instruction. *An Annotated Bibliography of Children's Literature Related to the Elementary School Mathematics Curriculum.* Indiana State Department of Public Instruction, 1979.

Matthias, Margaret, and Thiessen, Diane. *Children's Mathematics Books: A Critical Bibliography.* Chicago: American Library Association, 1979.

Roberts, P. L. *Counting Books Are More Than Numbers: An Annotated Action Bibliography.* Hamden, Conn.: Library Professional Publication, 1990.

Schaaf, William L. *The High School Mathematics Library.* Reston, Va.: National Council of Teachers of Mathematics, 1987.

Mathematics

Adell, Judith, and Klein, Hilary Dale. *A Guide to Non-Sexist Children's Books.* Chicago: Academy Press Limited, 1976.

Bakerman, Jane S., and DeMarr, Mary Jean. *Adolescent Female Portraits in the American Novel 1961–1981.* New York: Garland Publishing, Inc., 1983.

Nonsexist

Davis, Enid. *The Liberty Cap: A Catalogue of Nonsexist Materials for Children.* Chicago: Academy Press, 1977.

Loercher, Donna. *Girls and Boys Together: A Bibliography/Catalog of Non-sexist Children's Literature.* Whitestone, New York: Feminist Book Mart, 1974.

Newman, Joan E. *Girls Are People Too!: A Bibliography of Nontraditional Female Roles in Children's Books.* Metuchen, N.J.: Scarecrow Press, 1982.

Northwest Regional Educational Laboratory Center for Sex Equity. *Bibliography of Nonsexist Supplementary Books (K–12).* Phoenix: The Oryx Press, 1984.

Wilms, Denise, and Cooper, Ilene, editors. *A Guide to Non-sexist Children's Books, Vol. II: 1976–1985.* Chicago: Academy Chicago Press, 1987.

Occupational

Baldauf, Gretchen S. *Career Index: A Selecive Bibliography for Elementary Schools.* New York: Greenwood, 1990.

Bienstock, June Klein, and Bienstock, Anolik, Ruth, compilers. *Careers in Fact and Fiction: A Selective, Annotated List of Books for Career Backgrounds.* Chicago: American Library Association, 1985.

Egelston, Roberta Riethmiller. *Career Planning Materials: A Guide to Sources and Their Use.* Chicago: American Library Association, 1981.

Gersoni-Edelman, Diane. *Work-Wise: Learning About the World of Work From Books—A Critical Guide to Book Selection and Usage.* New York: Neal-Schuman Publishers, 1980.

Picture Books

Cianciolo, Patricia. *Picture Books for Children.* 3d ed. Chicago: American Library Association, 1990.

Lima, Carolyn W. *A to Zoo: Subject Access to Children's Picture Books.* 3d ed. New York: R. R. Bowker, 1989.

Polette, Nancy. *Picture Books for Gifted Programs.* Metuchen, N.J.: Scarecrow Press, 1981.

Roberts, P. L. *Alphabet Books as a Key to Language Patterns: An Annotated Action Bibliography.* Hamden, Conn.: Library Professional Publication, 1987.

Yonkers Public Library Children's Services. *A Guide to Subjects and Concepts in Picture Book Format.* Dobbs Ferry, New York: Oceana Publications, 1974.

Plays

Chicorel, Marietta. *Chicorel Theatre Index to Plays for Young People in Periodicals, Anthologies and Collections.* New York: Chicorel Library Publishing Corp., 1974. (Chicorel Index Series, Vol. 9)

Karp, Rashelle S., and Schlessinger, J. H. *Plays for Children and Young Adults: An Evaluative Index and Guide.* NY: Garland, 1991.

Kreider, Barbara A. *Index to Children's Plays in Collections.* 2d ed. Metuchen, N.J.: Scarecrow Press, 1977.

Sierra, Judy. *Fantastic Theatre: Puppets and Plays for Young Performers and Young Audiences.* NY: H. W. Wilson, 1991.

Abrahams, Roger D., and Rankin, Lois, editors. *Counting-Out Rhymes, A Dictionary.* Austin: University of Texas Press, 1980.

Blackburn, G. Meredith. *Index to Poetry for Children and Young People: 1982–1987.* New York: H. W. Wilson Company, 1989.

Brewton, John E., and Brewton, Sara W., compilers. *Index to Children's Poetry, 2nd Supplement: A Title, Subject, Author and First Line Index to Poetry in Collections for Children & Youth.* New York: H. W. Wilson, 1965.

Brewton, John E., and Brewton, Sara W., compilers. *Index to Children's Poetry: A Title, Subject, Author and First Line Index to Poetry in Collections for Children & Youth.* New York: H. W. Wilson, 1942.

Brewton, John E., and Brewton, Sara W., compilers. *Index to Poetry for Children and Young People, 1964–1969: A Title, Subject, Author and First Line Index to Poetry in Collections for Children & Youth.* New York: H. W. Wilson, 1972.

Brewton, John E., and Brewton, Sara W., compilers. *Index to Poetry for Children and Young People, 1970–1975: A Title, Subject, Author and First Line Index to Poetry in Collections for Children & Youth.* New York: H. W. Wilson, 1978.

Brewton, John E., and Brewton, Sara W., compilers. *Index to Children's Poetry, 1st Supplement: A Title, Subject, Author and First Line Index to Poetry in Collections for Children & Youth.* New York: H. W. Wilson, 1954.

Brewton, John E.; Blackburn II, G. Meredith; and Blackburn, Lorraine A., compilers. *Index to Poetry for Children and Young People, 1976–1981: A Title, Subject, Author and First Line Index to Poetry in Collections for Children and Young People.* New York: H. W. Wilson, 1984.

Delamar, Gloria T. *Children's Counting-Out Rhymes, Fingerplays, Jump-rope and Bounce-ball Chants and Other Rhymes: A Comprehensive English-Language Reference.* Jefferson, N.C.: McFarland, 1983.

Haviland, Virginia, and Smith, William Jay. *Children and Poetry: A Selective, Annotated Bibliography.* Revised, 2d ed. Washington, D.C.: Library of Congress, Superintendent of Documents, Government Printing Office, 1979.

Olexer, Marycile E. *Poetry Anthologies for Children and Young People.* Chicago: American Library Association, 1985.

Shaw, John Mackay. *Childhood in Poetry: A Catalogue, With Biographical and Critical Annotations, of the Books of English and American Poetry Comprising the Shaw Childhood in Poetry Collection in the Library of the Florida State University With Lists of Poems That Relate to Childhood, Notes and Index.* 5 volumes. Detroit: Gale Research Company, 1962–1967.

Shaw, John Mackay. *Childhood in Poetry: A Catalogue, With Biographical and Critical Annotations, of the Books of English and American Poetry Comprising the Shaw Childhood in Poetry Collection in the Library of the Florida State University With Lists of Poems That Relate to Childhood, Notes, and Index.* 1st supplement, 3 volumes. Detroit: Gale Research Company, 1972.

Shaw, John Mackay. *Childhood in Poetry: A Catalogue, With Biographical and Critical Annotations, of the Books of English and American Poetry Comprising the Shaw Childhood in Poetry Collection in the Library of the Florida State University With Lists of Poems That Relate to Childhood, Notes and Index.* 2d supplement, 2 volumes. Detroit: Gale Research Company, 1976.

Smith, Dorothy B., and Andrews, Eva L. *Subject Index to Poetry for Children and Young People, 1957–1975.* Chicago: American Library Association, 1977.

| Reference | Haviland, Virginia, compiler. *Children's Literature: A Guide to Reference Sources, 2nd Supplement.* Washington, D.C.: Superintendent of Documents, U. S. Government Printing Office, 1977. |

Haviland, Virginia, compiler. *Children's Literature: A Guide to Reference Sources, 2nd Supplement.* Washington, D.C.: Superintendent of Documents, U. S. Government Printing Office, 1977.

Sader, Marion, editor. *Reference Books for Young Readers: Authoritative Evaluations of Encyclopedias, Atlases, and Dictionaries.* New York: R. R. Bowker, 1988.

Wynar, Bohdan S. *Recommended Reference Books for Small and Medium-sized Libraries and Media Centers.* Littleton, Col.: Libraries Unlimited, 1984.

Wynar, Christine G. *Guide to Reference Books for School Media Centers.* 3d ed. Littleton, Col.: Libraries Unlimited, 1986.

Religions

Davis, Enid. *A Comprehensive Guide to Children's Literature with a Jewish Theme.* New York: Schocken Books, 1981.

Pearl, Patricia. *Children's Religious Books: An Annotated Bibliography.* New York: Garland Publishing, 1988.

Reluctant Readers

Cummins, Julie and Blair, ed. *Choices: A Core Collection for Young Reluctant Readers.* Vol. 2. Evanston, IL: Burke, 1990.

Flemming, Carolyn S., and Schatt, Donna, ed. *Choices: A Core Collection for Young Reluctant Readers.* Vol. 1. Evanston, IL: Burke, 1983.

LiBretto, Ellen V., compiler and editor. *High/Low Handbook: Books, Materials and Services for the Teenage Problem Reader.* New York: R. R. Bowker, 1981. (Serving Special Population Series)

Nakamura, Joyce, editor. *High-Interest Books for Teens.* 2d ed. Detroit: Gale Research Company, 1988.

National Council of Teachers of English, Dorothy Matthews, Chair, and the Committee to Revise High Interest-Easy Readings. *High Interest Easy Reading for Junior and Senior High School Students.* 5th ed. Urbana, Ill.: National Council of Teachers of English, 1988.

Palmer, Julia Reed. *Read for Your Life: Two Successful Efforts to Help People Read and An Annotated List of Books That Make Them Want To.* Metuchen, N.J.: Scarecrow Press, 1974.

Pilla, Marianne Laino. *Resources for Middle-Grade Reluctant Readers: A Guide for Librarians.* Littleton, Col.: Libraries Unlimited, 1987.

Ryder, Randall J., et al. *Easy Reading: Book Series and Periodicals for Less Able Readers.* 2d ed. Newark, Del.: International Reading Association, 1989.

Spache, George D. *Good Reading for Poor Readers.* 9th ed., revised. Champaign, Ill.: Garrard Publishing, 1974.

Wise, Bernice Kemler. *Teaching Materials for the Learning Disabled: A Selected List for Grades 6–12.* Chicago: American Library Association, 1980.

Withrow, Dorothy W., et al. *Gateways to Readable Books: An Annotated Graded List of Books in Many Fields for Adolescents Who Find Reading Difficult.* 5th ed. New York: H. W. Wilson, 1975.

Butzow, Carol M. and John W. *Science Through Children's Literature: An Integrated Approach.* Littleton, Col.: Libraries Unlimited, 1989.

Higgins, Judith H. *Energy, A Multimedia Guide for Children and Young Adults.* Santa Barbara, Calif.: American Bibliographical Center/Clio Press; New York: Neal-Schumann Publishers, 1979. (Selection Guide Series)

Kennedy, DayAnn M.; Spangler, Stella S.; and Vanderwerf, Mary Ann. *Science and Technology in Fact and Fiction: A Guide to Young Adult Books.* New York: R. R. Bowker, 1990.

Richter, Bernice, and Wenzel, Duane. *The Museum of Science and Industry Basic List of Children's Science Books, 1986.* Chicago: American Library Association, 1986.

Richter, Bernice, and Wenzel, Duane. *The Museum of Science and Industry Basic List of Children's Science Books, 1987.* Chicago: American Library Association, 1987.

Richter, Bernice, and Wenzel, Duane. *The Museum of Science and Industry Basic List of Children's Science Books, 1988.* Chicago: American Library Association, 1988.

Richter, Bernice, and Wenzel, Duane. *The Museum of Science and Industry Basic List of Children's Science Books, 1973–1984.* Chicago: American Library Association, 1985.

Wilms, Denise Murcko. *Science Books for Children: Selections from Booklist, 1976–1983.* Chicago: American Library Association, 1985.

Wolff, Kathryn; Fritsche, Joellen M.; Gross, Elina N.; and Todd, Gary, compilers and editors. *The Best Science Books for Children: A Selected and Annotated List of Science Books for Children Ages Five Through Twelve.* Washington, D.C.: American Association for the Advancement of Science, 1983.

Barron, Neil, editor. *Anatomy of Wonder: A Critical Guide to Science Fiction.* 2d ed. New York: R. R. Bowker, 1981.

Barron, Neil, editor. *Fantasy Literature: A Reader's Guide.* NY: Garland Publishing, Inc., 1990.

Kies, Cosette. *Supernatural Fiction for Teens: 500 Good Paperbacks to Read for Wonderment, Fear and Fun.* Littleton, Col.: Libraries Unlimited, 1987.

Lynn, Ruth Nadelman. *Fantasy for Children: An Annotated Checklist.* New York: R. R. Bowker, 1979.

Pflieger, Pat, editor, and Hill, Helen M., advisory editor. *A Reference Guide to Modern Fantasy for Children.* Westport, Conn.: Greenwood Press, 1984.

Rovin, Jeff. *The Science Fiction Collector's Catalog.* San Diego, Calif.: A. S. Barnes. Distributed in the U.S. by Oak Tree Publications, 1982.

Wehmeyer, Lillian Biermann. *Images in a Crystal Ball: World Futures in Novels for Young People.* Littleton, Col.: Libraries Unlimited, 1981.

Archer, Marion Fuller, regional editor. *Reading for Young People: The Upper Midwest.* Chicago: American Library Association, 1981.

Austin, Mary C., and Jenkins, Esther C. *Promoting World Understanding Through Literature, K–8.* Littleton, Col.: Libraries Unlimited, 1983.

Cordier, Mary H. *Peoples of the American West: Historical Perspectives through Children's Literature.* Metuchen, N.J.: Scarecrow Press, 1989.

Czarra, Fred R. *A Guide to Historical Reading: Nonfiction: For Schools, Libraries, and the General Reader.* Revised, 11th ed. Washington, D.C.: Heldref Publications, 1983.

Dorsett, Cora Matheny, regional editor. *Reading for Young People: The Mississippi Delta.* Chicago: American Library Association, 1983.

Giese, James R. *U.S. History: A Resource Book for Secondary Schools.* 2 Vol. Santa Barbara, Cal.: ABC–CL10, 1989.

Greiner, Rosemarie. *Peace Education: A Bibliography Focusing on Young Children.* 2d ed. Santa Cruz, Calif.: Greiner, 1984.

Harmon, Elva A., and Milligan, Anna L., regional editors. *Reading for Young People: The Southwest.* Chicago: American Library Association, 1982.

Heald, Dorothy, regional editor. *Reading for Young People: The Southeast.* Chicago: American Library Association, 1980.

Hinman, Dorothy, and Zimmermann, Ruth, regional editors. *Reading for Young People: The Midwest.* Chicago: American Library Association, 1979.

Hotchkiss, Jeanette. *European Historical Fiction and Biography for Children and Young People.* 2d ed. Metuchen, N.J.: Scarecrow Press, 1972.

Howard, Elizabeth F. *America As Story: Historical Fiction for Secondary School.* Chicago: American Library Association, 1988.

Laughlin, Mildred. *Literature-based Social Studies: Children's Books and Activities to Enrich the K–5 Curriculum.* Phoenix, Az.: Oryx Press, 1991.

Laughlin, Mildred, regional editor. *Reading for Young People: The Rocky Mountains.* Chicago: American Library Association, 1980.

Laughlin, Mildred, regional editor. *Reading for Young People: The Great Plains.* Chicago: American Library Association, 1979.

McCauley, Elfrieda, regional editor. *Reading for Young People: New England.* Chicago: American Library Association, 1985.

Meacham Mary, regional editor. *Reading for Young People: The Northwest.* Chicago: American Library Association, 1980.

Mertins, Barbara, regional editor. *Reading for Young People: Kentucky, Tennessee, and West Virginia.* Chicago: American Library Association, 1985.

Metzner, Seymour. *World History in Juvenile Books: A Geographical and Chronological Guide.* New York: H. W. Wilson, 1973.

Pennypacker, Arabelle, regional editor. *Reading for Young People: The Middle Atlantic.* Chicago: American Library Association, 1980.

Roskies, Diane K. *Teaching the Holocaust to Children: A Review and Bibliography.* New York: Ktav Publishing House, 1975.

Sutherland, Zena. *History in Children's Books: An Annotated Bibliography for Schools and Libraries.* Brooklawn, N.J.: McKinley Publishing, 1967. (McKinley Bibliographies Vol. 5)

Taylor, Donna, editor. *The Great Lakes Region in Children's Books: A Selected, Annotated Bibliography.* Brighton, Mich.: Green Oak Press, 1980.

VanMeter, V. *American History for Children and Young Adults: An Annotated Bibliographic Index.* Englewood, Col.: Libraries Unlimited, 1990.

World Civilization Booklist Committee of NCSS. *World Civilization Booklist: Supplementary Reading for Secondary Schools.* Bulletin 41. Washington, D.C.: National Council for the Social Studies, 1969.

Blickle, Calvin, and Corcoran, Frances. *Sports, A Multimedia Guide for Children and Young Adults.* New York: Neal-Schuman Publishers; Santa Barbara, Calif.: ABC-Clio, 1980.

Bollas, James A. *Sports Literature: A Recommended List of Books for High School Libraries.* Thesis, Kent State University, 1965. Available from James A. Bollas, 8581 Columbus Rd. N.E., Louisville, Ohio.

Harrah, Barbara K. *Sports Books for Children: An Annotated Bibliography.* Metuchen, N.J.: Scarecrow Press, 1978.

Nunn, Marshall E. *Sports.* Littleton, Col.: Libraries Unlimited, 1976.

Sports

Association for Library Service to Children, Ad hoc committee. *Storytelling: Readings/Bibliographies/Resources.* Chicago: American Library Association, 1978.

Bodart-Talbot, Joni. *Booktalk 3: More Booktalks for All Ages and Audiences.* New York: H. W. Wilson Company, 1988.

Carnegie Library of Pittsburgh, revised and edited by Laura E. Cathon, Marion McC Haushalter and Virginia A. Russell. *Stories to Tell to Children, A Selected List.* 8th ed. Pittsburgh: University of Pittsburgh Press, 1974.

Gillespie, John T., with Naden, Corinne J. *Juniorplots 3: A Book Talk Guide for Use with Readers Ages 12–16.* New York: R. R. Bowker Company, 1987.

Gillespie, John T., and Naden, Corinne J. *Seniorplots: A Book Talk Guide for Use with Readers Ages 15–18.* NY: R. R. Bowker, 1989.

MacDonald, Margaret Read. *Booksharing: 101 Programs to Use with Preschoolers.* Hamden, Conn.: Library Professional Publications, 1988.

MacDonald, Margaret Read. *The Storyteller's Sourcebook: A Subject, Title, and Motif Index to Folklore Collections for Children.* Detroit: Gale Research Company, 1982.

MacDonald, M. R. *Twenty Tellable Tales: Audience Participation Folktales for the Beginning Storyteller.* New York: H. W. Wilson Company, 1986.

Sierra, Judy. *The Flannel Board Storytelling Book.* New York: H. W. Wilson, 1987.

Spirt, Diana L. *Introducing Bookplots 3: A Book Talk Guide for Use with Readers Ages 8–12.* New York: R. R. Bowker Company, 1988.

Thomas, R. L. *Primaryplots: A Book Talk Guide for Use with Readers Ages 4–8.* New York: R. R. Bowker, 1989.

Storytelling

Figure 12.1
Identifying writing
patterns and content-
specific skills: a
cognitive map.

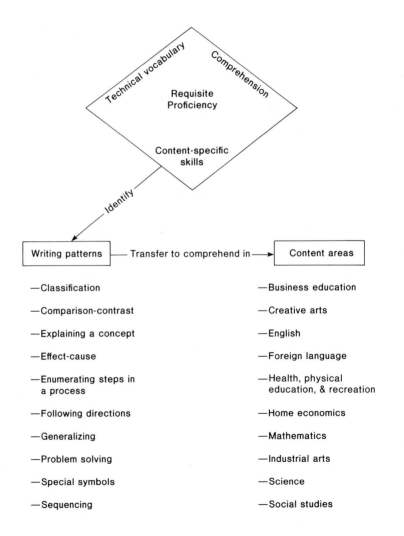

Requisite
Proficiency

Technical vocabulary

Comprehension

Content-specific
skills

Identify

| Writing patterns | — Transfer to comprehend in → | Content areas |

—Classification

—Comparison-contrast

—Explaining a concept

—Effect-cause

—Enumerating steps in
   a process

—Following directions

—Generalizing

—Problem solving

—Special symbols

—Sequencing

—Business education

—Creative arts

—English

—Foreign language

—Health, physical
   education, & recreation

—Home economics

—Mathematics

—Industrial arts

—Science

—Social studies

Identifying Writing Patterns and Content-Specific Skills

12

Anticipatory Questions

(Literal)

1. Using the major writing patterns found in content texts, identify each pattern in one content area.

(Literal)

2. Describe some ways your students can unlock new words in your content area.

(Interpretive)

3. How would you compare and contrast the macro structures of science, social studies, and math texts?

(Applied)

4. Which two writing patterns do you believe to be most prevalent in your subject? Give an example of each and suggest how you would help students identify them.

(Creative)

5. Design a one-page outline of a content-specific lesson plan that incorporates some of the skill tasks delineated in table 12.3.

Technical Terminology and Concepts

abbreviations/symbols/ signs/ratio relationships

classification/ categorizing pattern

comparison/contrast pattern

developing concepts pattern

discourse analysis

cause/effect or effect/ cause

enumerating steps in a process

following specific directions pattern

generalizing pattern

information/concept/ process-centered text

problem-solving pattern

sequencing: interpreting

graphics

verbalism

writing patterns

Introduction

A variety of writing patterns exists in content texts. If students become aware of this and are able to identify pertinent patterns, they may better comprehend their assigned readings and will then be able to study needed concepts independently and with greater proficiency.

Students' ability to effectively perform this analysis may well rest on requisite proficiency in vocabulary and comprehension. Two examples would be (1) identifying signal words (found in the chapter on vocabulary) and (2) discerning paragraph organization (located in the comprehension chapter).

The cognitive map in figure 12.1 provides an overview of the process and the content of writing patterns and content-specific skills.

One requisite proficiency for identifying writing patterns is the ability to discern appropriate meanings of technical vocabulary in the context in which they appear.

Unlocking Meaning

Teachers should recognize that some students have had an excellent preparation for extracting meaning in their textbooks. New words, diacritical markings, syllabication, and selecting the correct definition in the dictionary are all abilities they have mastered, and thus they can work independently. However, there are others who need specific instruction in all of these abilities in order to study effectively. Aspects of word attack skills are shown in table 12.1. If students lack meanings and the word is presented in isolation (without a context), students may be able to break the work into syllables, identify prefixes or suffixes, and discover known parts to arrive at the needed meaning. Generally, with words such as those suggested in table 12.1, students will do well to make habitual use of the dictionary.

Greek and Latin Combining Forms

Graph is used as one example in table 12.1. Students from third or fourth grade, learn that *geo* and *graphy* means literally "to write about the earth." Other common examples might be as follows:

Combining Forms:	*Literal Meanings:*
bio + logy	life + the science of
thermo + meter	heat + to measure
tele + scope	far away + to view

Syllabication

All students need to learn the diacritical markings for pronouncing words in the dictionary. The *schwa* (ə) appears so frequently it should be reviewed and understood. Many words have been marked for the reader in table 12.1 with diacritical markings.

Table 12.1

Unlocking Meanings in New Words across Content Areas—Choose Your Own Subject

Aspects of Word Attack Skills	Subjects of the School Curriculum				
	1—Business Education	2—Creative Arts	3—English	4—Foreign Language	5—Health, Physical Education, and Recreation

Examples of Technical Vocabulary Terms:	depreciation
	accrued revenue
	corporation
	creditor
	flowchart
	merchandising
	posting
		subliminal
		   processes
		proprioceptive
		   level
		multisensory
		   experience
		impulsivity
			bibliography
			colloquial
			capitalization
			complement
			extemporaneous
			nonfiction
			precis
				conjugación
				diálogo
				esdrújulo
				Konjugation
				Zwiegespräch
				Betonung
				conjugaison
					carcinogens
					cholesterol
					conjunctivitis
					diaphragm
					emphysema
					respirator
					riboflavin

1. Context Clues	*Posting:* "Transferring the entries in a journal to the accounts in a ledger is called *posting.* Posting sorts the data in the journal bringing all the data of one kind together."[1]	*Creativity:* (synonym) "Creativity is thus synonymous with power, force, change, relation, organization, purpose and meaning; it is life-giving, rhythmic, constructive, clarifying, flexible, and progressive."[2]	*Macron:* (italics) "To indicate a long vowel, a dictionary generally uses a diacritical mark called a *macron*—a long, straight mark over the vowel."[3]	As in English, attention is directed to *new meanings* by explanation, synonym, italics, boldface type, phrases in apposition, quotation marks, or footnotes.	*Malocclusion:* (contrast) "Facial deformities can result from malocclusion. When the teeth fit together properly on closing the jaws, this is proper occlusion. If the teeth do not fit . . . the person has malocclusion."[4]
2. Multiple Meanings of Common Words (Example: *Prime*)	*Prime* cost *Prime* interest rate *Prime* contract "*Priming* the pump"	*Primary* colors *Prima* donna	He's in his *prime.* "This is the forest *prim*eval." *Prime:* original, first in time	*primo* *prim*acía *prim*ogénito *prim*itivamente *prim*ordial	"In the *prime* of life." *Prime:* in fencing, the first eight defensive positions.
3. Greek and Latin Combining Forms: (Example: *Graph*)	mimeo*graph* steno*graphy* litho*graph*	photo*graphy* choreo*graphy*	bio*graphy* bibliog*rapher* *graph*eme *graph*ic	foto*grafia* mimeo*grafia*	histo*graph* choreo*graph* cardio*graph* encephalo*graph*
4. Syllabication, Pronunciation Symbols, and Stress	appurtenances (ə-pərt-ən-ən(t)s-iz) waybill (wā-bil)	balalaika (bal-ə-li-kə) pianoforte (pē-an-ə-fo-ərt) tarentella (tär-ən-tel-ə)	onomatopeia (än-ə-mat-ə-pē-ə) oxymoron (äk-si-mō-rän)	naivete (nä-ē-və-tā) magnum opus (mag-nə-mō-pəs) caballeros (käb-ə-yā-ros)	immunization (im-yə-nə-zā-shən) fibrillation (fib-rə-lā-shən) emphysema (em-fə-sē-mə)

Identifying Writing Patterns and Content-Specific Skills

Table 12.1—Cont.

Aspects of Word Attack Skills	Subjects of the School Curriculum				
	6—Home Economics	7—Industrial Arts	8—Mathematics	9—Science	10—Social Studies
Examples of Technical Vocabulary Terms	braising riboflavin mercerizing polyesters blanching nutrients epidemiologist	micrometer internal combustion oscilloscope armature crankshaft centrifugal clutch polyethylene	disjunction equiangular exponential hyperbola polynomial quadratic equation trapezoidal	isotopes thermodynamics electromagnetic curvature luminescence microbiology chromatography	bourgeoisie coup d'etat manifesto primogeniture surrogate theocracy
1. Context Clues	*Design:* (description) "The fundamental principles of *design*—balance, proportion, rhythm and emphasis— serve as guides for both creating and evaluating design."[5]	*Vacuum:* (example) "A *vacuum* is the absence of air or any other matter. Astronauts on their way to the moon soon pass through our atmosphere and into the vast region of empty space. This is a vacuum."[6]	*Interior angles:* (explain) "If two parallel lines are cut by a transversal, then the *interior angles* on the same side of the transversal are supplementary."[7]	*Chronology:* (explain) "Basic to the story is *chronology*—a time scale divided into periods and ages in which events can be assigned their proper dates, permitting an analysis of causes and effects."[8]	*Plantation:* (description) "The plantation . . . is a large landed estate, located in an area of open resources . . . in which social relations between diverse racial and social groups are based on . . . "[9]
2. Multiple Meanings of Common Words (Example: *Prime*)	*Prime* rib	*Primer* coat *prime* the carburator	*prime* factor *prime* number: no factors; 53 is a *prime* number.	*Prime* meridian *Prime* coat in finishing surfaces.	*Prime* minister *Prime* meridian He's a *prime* candidate. "The New Deal *primed* the pump."
3. Greek and Latin Combining Forms (Example: *Graph*)	*graph*ics *graph*ic art phono*graph*	*graph*ite *graph*ing histo*graph* litho*graph*y	*graph*s bar *graph*s picto*graph*s	spectro*graph* seismo*graph* helio*graph*y crypto*graph* *graph*itization	geo*graph*y bio*graph*y autobio*graph*y
4. Syllabication, Pronunciation Symbols, and Stress	interior decorating (in-tir-ē-ər-dek-ə-rā-ting) riboflavin (ri-bō-flā-v-ən) economize (i-kon-ə-miz)	motorization (mōt-ə-ra-zā-shən) carburetor (kär-bə-rāt-ər) ignition (ig-nish-ən)	superscript (sū-pər-skript) Pythagorean (pə-thag-ə-rē-ən)	carboniferous (kär-bə-nif-ər-əs) paleobotany (pā-lē-ō-bät-ə-nē) hippopotamus (hip-ə-pät-ə-məs)	sovereignty (sov-ran-te) protectorate (prə-tek-tə-rət)

Many times the context of the sentence explains the meaning of the term in question if students continue reading to the end of the sentence: "The cacique, the chief of the tribe, ordered an inquisition of the intruders who came into the village." The meaning may be given by providing a synonym, a description, an explanation, or an example as shown across table 12.1.

Using Context Clues

The example *prime* is a word that may be used in many subject areas as evidenced in the examples across table 12.1. Also, multiple meanings must be easily understandable when one word is used in very different contexts:

Multiple Meanings

Chicago has a new mayor. (Chicago is a political entity.)
A blizzard engulfed *Chicago*. (Chicago is a geographical entity.)
There were serious riots in *Chicago* last night. (Chicago is a social entity.)

You will find it worthwhile to study table 12.1 carefully and discuss it with a partner.

Verbalism

Beyond considering technical vocabulary, conscientious students who work hard to please may memorize or paraphrase the text without comprehending the underlying concepts that were intended to be conveyed by the chapter or unit. This is *verbalism*. To the extent that it is divorced from genuine thinking and understanding, it is a sheer waste of time and effort for all involved.

Verbalism, then, is reading (or word calling) without understanding the meaning behind the words.

The excellent example of verbalism below was given by Ernest Horn.[10] As you will note, all the words are easy to understand, the estimated readability level is approximately fourth grade, and yet the ideas expressed are abstract and describe a difficult process.

The square of the sum of two numbers is equal to the square of the first added to twice the product of first and second added to the square of the second.

Although there are no difficult words in this sentence, it represents in words the quadratic equation explaining how square root works, or

$$A^2 + 2AB + B^2.$$

Five Forms of Discourse

A recent branch of linguistic and psychological investigations has been labeled *discourse analysis,* which goes beyond consideration of vocabulary terms and sentence structures to look at characteristics of paragraphs and longer passages as well as relationships between sentences.[11]

Jane Catterson describes five forms of discourse: *narration, explanation, classification, description,* and *argument.*[12] She suggests that readers be instructed to scan the material first to identify the form of discourse being used. This helps to develop a "mindset" for the detailed reading to follow. For example, if the discourse is argumentative, readers would set as their purpose to uncover the basic argument and the author's intended meaning.

Workshop Activity 12.1
Forms of Discourse

Individually or in pairs, first skim this text and locate another brief example of each of the five types of discourse, noting the page location of each. Meet with another pair and decide on the one best example of each type. Discuss this with the whole class for consensus.

As a follow-up, using content texts, find further examples in the different subject areas. Present to the class for critique and discussion.

Writing Patterns

(1) Classification

Ten basic writing patterns and examples will be described here. The *classification* pattern is frequently used in science where a common heading has a number of subheadings or subdivisions. *Living things, elements,* or *gases* are common headings that can have subheadings. The subclasses have certain elements in common but vary in certain ways from one another. Students who recognize classification concepts will then concentrate on grasping the relationship between the key idea and the subparts.

Otto et al. provide an example of this pattern in delineating forms of bacteria.[13]

Forms of Bacteria

While bacteria vary greatly in size, their cells are of three basic shapes. Some bacterial cells tend to exist singly when grown in liquid cultures or broths, while others often remain attached after cell division and form colonies of cells. We can classify the basic cell shapes and groupings as follows:

coccus (plural, *cocci*): cells sphere-shaped or globular
diplococcus: cells often joined in pairs or short filaments
staphylococcus: clusters of cells
streptococcus: filaments, or strings, of cells
tetrad: groups of four cells arranged as a square

sarcina: cubes or packets of cells
bacillus (plural, bacilli): cells cylindrical, or rod-shaped
diplobacillus: cells in pairs
streptobacillus: cells joined end to end forming a filament or thread
spirillum (plural, spirilla): cells in the form of bent rods or corkscrews

A common pattern encountered in social studies or many of the practical arts is that of *contrast* of the way in which two things are alike and also different. If this pattern is called to the students' attention, their awareness of it should facilitate their clearer understanding and their ability to recall. Bernard Weisberger provides such a contrast in his discussion of Wilson and Harding as successive presidents:

(2) Compare/ Contrast

> It would be difficult to find two more different men than Woodrow Wilson and Warren G. Harding, who succeeded Wilson as President in 1921. Wilson was an ex-professor, accustomed to lecturing others, especially on their duties. Harding was a likable, easy-going, small-town newspaper owner, at ease bouncing a child or greeting a visiting baseball team.
>
> Although Harding himself was not politically corrupt, he appointed some of his friends to high posts. They betrayed him by taking bribes in return for doing illegal government favors. The President and the country were just beginning to learn of these scandals when Harding suddenly died in August of 1923.[14]

Physical education teachers who encourage students to read about the lives of successful people in sports should take note of books such as *Women Who Win,* in which the author contrasts the old traditional attitudes toward women who became "too athletic" and the attitudes today, which come closer to giving them the same opportunities that men have enjoyed.

> It's not surprising that girls were rarely encouraged to develop their athletic talents. "Don't bother," was the advice given to most of them. "There's no future in sports for you. Even if you become a champion you won't be able to capitalize on your accomplishments. Who ever heard of a woman making a living in sports?"
>
> Girls were also taught that no normal man would want to date or marry a woman who could outshine him physically. While it was considered natural for boys to be competitive, any girl who was at all serious about sports ran the risk of being considered "unnatural." And if that wasn't enough to turn her off, there were still more warnings. Just think of those ugly muscles female athletes develop.
>
> But in recent years, attitudes finally began to change. With the emergence of the Women's Liberation movement of the 1970s, females everywhere started to question some of the assumptions that had shaped their lives. In sports, as well as every other field, they challenged financial inequities, demanding equal pay for equal work. At the same time, they began to re-examine some basic sexual stereotypes. Why should physical

weakness be thought of as a feminine virtue? What was so unnatural about a woman playing to win? Many females even began to question the traditional standards of "feminine" beauty and wondered how a healthy, well-developed body could be considered anything but beautiful.[15]

(3) Explanation of a Concept

The following home economics textbook excerpt provides an example of reading for details to understand a process. Most of us are aware of the reasons for sorting clothes when washing. What we are apt to forget is that youngsters need the instructions and need to be reminded of reasons why certain details are important.

Sorting

Clothes should be sorted according to color, fiber content, fabric finish, garment construction, and amount of soil. These things are important when deciding on water temperature, length of washing cycle, wash and spin speeds, and laundry aids.

Separate white clothes from colored clothes and dark-colored clothes from light-colored ones. Then sort these piles of clothes so that those which are to be washed in hot water are separate from those to be washed in warm water and cold water. Or sort them according to the different cycles on the washing machine, such as delicate or permanent press. Heavily soiled clothes should not be put in to wash with lightly soiled clothes. The heavily soiled clothes may not get clean and may make the lightly soiled ones dingy.[16]

(4) Cause/Effect

In the paragraphs below on listening to music, the writer admonishes us to take time to hear the music. Notice that there is considerable *cause/effect* expressed in these three paragraphs. People cannot have their attention elsewhere and still think about how the sounds of music form patterns, how the patterns are related, and how details may be absorbed by hearing the music repeated over and over again.

How to Listen to Music

A generation ago it was not easy to hear a symphony. You had to go to the concert hall and buy a ticket. When you finally got to the concert, you were likely to *listen* when the orchestra began to play. Today all you have to do is flick a knob, and music comes pouring into the room. On Sunday morning millions of people flick that knob, and for the next ten hours they are surrounded by music. They talk to each other, they eat, they read the funnies and do crossword puzzles, and all the time the sounds are flowing past their ears.

But the great composers did not write their music to serve as a background for other activities. There is only one way to listen to their works, and that is—to listen! When you listen to an important musical work, make sure that you are not doing anything else, such as talking or reading.

The sounds are forming patterns, and you cannot understand them unless you hear how the patterns are related. This you will do only if you give your full attention to what is going on.

In addition, try to hear a piece of music again and again. You will be surprised at how much more the music will mean to you once you become familiar with it.[17]

Major changes in history, past and present, are brought about by some *cause* or *combination of causes*. Thus, we might say that history is made up of causes and their resulting effects. In students' reading, however, they are most often presented with the effects of changes and are expected to think through to the causes that have brought these changes about. We need to guide students when reading about the effects of a social change, so that they become adept in relating the cause or combination of causes to these events. In this example below, Bernard Weisberger discusses the effects on society of the rapid growth of the automobile industry:

Effect/Cause

> Along with its huge economic impact, the automobile had revolutionary effects on society. A car gave any man, regardless of section, class, or background, a 40-mile-an-hour magic carpet to go wherever he wished. It gave young people who were "keeping company" a chance to escape the supervision of older eyes. It thus changed manners and morals by loosening family control of behavior.
>
> The automobile also put suburban living within the reach of the middle class. In the nineteenth century only the well-off businessman could buy a "country retreat." But inexpensive automobiles allowed the ordinary worker to seek fresh air and greenery for himself and his children. He no longer had to live near his job. The automobile sparked a suburban real estate boom which has yet to slow down.[18]

Another pattern that students should recognize is that of explaining the steps of a process, or enumeration. Otto et al. show this in the following explanation of the process of reproduction in the paramecium:

(5) Enumeration of Steps in a Process

> After several months of cell divisions, especially in the same environment, paramecia lose vitality and die, unless they undergo conjugation. This process requires the mixing of two mating types, or sexes, which may be designated as $+$ and $-$ or as I and II. Exchange of nuclear materials during conjugation, resulting in revitalizing of the cells, can be summarized as follows:
> 1) Two cells unite at the oral grooves.
> 2) The micronucleus in each cell divides. The macronucleus degenerates.
> 3) The two micronuclei in each cell divide, forming four micronuclei, three of which degenerate.
> 4) The remaining micronucleus divides unequally, forming a large and a small micronucleus. The cells exchange smaller micronuclei.

5) The large (stationary) and small (migrating) micronuclei fuse in each cell.

6) The cells separate. In each, the fused micronucleus undergoes three consecutive divisions, forming eight nuclei.

7) Of the eight nuclei, four fuse and form a macronucleus, three degenerate, and one remains.

8) Two consecutive cell divisions occur, resulting in the formation of four small paramecia from each of the two original conjugants.[19]

(6) Following Directions

McDermott, Norris, and Nicholas have detailed the steps to follow for making bean soup. It is first necessary to know that all the necessary ingredients have been assembled and then to follow the steps in combining them.[20]

NAVY BEAN SOUP
(Serves 6 or 8)

1 cup dried navy beans	*Sort* and wash beans; cover with six cups
6 c. water	water and soak for several hours; add bone to
small ham bone	beans and simmer for 1 hour.
2 c. canned tomatoes	*Add* tomatoes, salt, and pepper; simmer for ½
1 t. salt	hour or until the beans are tender.
½ t. pepper	*Serve* hot.

Following Specific Directions

A driver education manual explains that drivers can easily change a flat tire if they know the specific tasks to perform.

Changing a Flat. Once your vehicle is off the road you can either call for assistance to change the wheel or you can do it yourself. It is not a difficult procedure. Follow directions and the job can be done in a few minutes.

The equipment you need should be in the trunk—an inflated spare tire, a lug wrench and a jack. You should also have flares for night-time emergencies.

To change a flat:

1. Make sure your car is well off the roadway and on as level a spot as possible.

2. Set your parking brake. Warn approaching motorists by activating the emergency flashers. Use flares if at night.

3. Put an automatic transmission car in "Park." A manual transmission should be put in "Reverse."

4. Wedge a stone, piece of wood, etc., in front and behind the wheel diagonally opposite the one you are changing. This will keep the car from rolling.

5. Take the jack and inflated spare out of the trunk.

6. Follow the instructions in your owner's manual on where to place your jack and how to operate it. In some cars they may also be found on the inside of your trunk lid.

7. Lift the car until its weight is off the flat, but do not raise the tire off the ground.

8. Pry off the hubcap. Place it on the ground. Loosen each lug nut.
9. Use the jack to lift the car so that the flat tire is off the ground.
10. Remove the lug nuts by hand. Place them in the hubcap.
11. Take off the flat. Lift the spare and see that the holding bolts slip into the proper holes.
12. Replace the lug nuts. Tighten two opposite ones with your wrench. This will put the wheel in its proper position.
13. Lower the car. Tighten all lug nuts with your wrench.
14. Replace the hubcap. Put the flat and jack into the trunk.[21]

Most texts have sections that contain detailed, explanatory information. These paragraphs are usually not highly technical nor are they generally densely laden with concepts. The illustration below, taken from a manual for driver training, will be easily understood if readers direct their attention to the author's argument that drivers must be able to "look" around so that they are aware of their position "from all directions at once."

(7) Generalizations

Observing All around the Car

Developing the habit of looking far enough ahead does not mean you should focus your eyes at a specific distance ahead of the car. It does not mean you should ignore everything else around you. The thing to do is look well ahead. But also keep your eyes moving to look in all directions.

A good driver looks to the left and right of the car. This is where some of the signs are located that give information as to what is ahead. It is also important to watch the movement of cars and pedestrians from either side. These things may not be in your path now. But in the next second they very well could be.

And finally, a good driver looks to the rear. Cars behind you can become important if you decide to slow down or change direction. Failure to look to the rear may increase the chance of a rear-end collision.

If you are to see things in time to react to them properly, you must "scan" the scene around you. Scan means to glance quickly. By scanning around you and by looking far enough ahead, you observe the entire driving scene.[22]

Generalizations need to be supported with data or clarifying information. If textbooks are "overstocked" with these generalizations, students are in danger of accepting superficiality in their quest for information. In the article below, Weisberger makes some generalizations about the New Deal as it was introduced in 1933. Students will be provided with supporting or clarifying information later in the text. When you feel the text is inadequate in this regard, this is an excellent opportunity for organizing panel discussions or class debates with extensive reading assignments in collateral materials. The associative thinking diagram presented earlier in chapter 10 (structured overview) is an example of how one teacher got a group of students to suggest concepts and raise questions, which further reading then helped them develop.

Supporting Generalizations

"Action now" was what the nation got. Roosevelt was given sweeping emergency powers. He almost immediately declared a "bank holiday" to give government examiners a chance to eliminate unsound banks and to restore faith in the value of the dollar. Then he brought a stream of special advisors to Washington. Most were young university professors. Hence they were nicknamed the "Brain Trust," and provided good targets for cartoonists. . . . In the New Deal's first hundred days, lights burned late as the Brain Trust boldly planned war on the depression. At first Congress enacted everything the reformers proposed.

The immediate goal of 1933 planning was to get people back to work. Early programs bore down on this task and spent freely to achieve it. One measure set up a Public Works Administration (PWA) and gave it $3.3 billion for immediate work on projects such as constructing roads, bridges, tunnels, post offices, and government office buildings. A Federal Emergency Relief Administration (FERA) got $5 billion to help feed and house the jobless. In his first morning of work, its director, Harry L. Hopkins, authorized the spending of several million dollars. A Civilian Conservation Corps (CCC) swiftly put thousands of young men between the ages of 18 and 25 to work in national and state forests planting trees, fighting fires, and building dams.[23]

(8) Problem-Solving Diagrams

Verbal explanations of processes are often accompanied by diagrams to be read before or simultaneously with the reading of the text. The diagrams themselves often require skill in interpreting in order to match them with the written text. In figure 12.2, taken from a sewing text, students need to alternately read the text explaining the pattern envelope front and the diagram of the front of the envelope, making them fit together.[24]

Pattern Envelope Front

Often a pattern makes two or more different styles. A drawing or photograph on the front of the pattern envelope shows the style or styles the pattern pieces can make. For example, a shirt can be shown with long sleeves and with short sleeves. This means that pattern pieces are included for both styles. If a dress is shown with a V-neck and a round neck, there are pattern pieces for both styles. Sometimes one style of a garment is shown in different fabrics. A blouse may appear in a plain fabric in one style and in a different fabric in another style. Instructions are included for making both styles. The different styles are usually called *views* and may be labeled View 1, View 2 and so on.

The pattern identification number appears on the front of the pattern envelope. This tells you that the envelope contains the design you have selected from the pattern book. Patterns for women and girls show the sizes and figure types. Examples are Junior size 9, Misses size 10, or Young Junior/Teen size 13/14. Patterns for men and boys indicate the body build and size, such as Teen Boys size 16 or Men size 40. When you choose your pattern, check to make sure that it is the style you want and that the size and figure type or body build are correct. Sometimes patterns cannot be exchanged or returned. For this reason be certain that you have made the right choice that will satisfy you.

Figure 12.2
A diagram of the pattern envelope front to be read concurrently with the
reading of the text.
From *Clothes, Clues, and Careers* by Margil Vanderhoff, Copyright 1977, by Ginn and Company
(Xerox Corporation), p. 221. Used with permission.

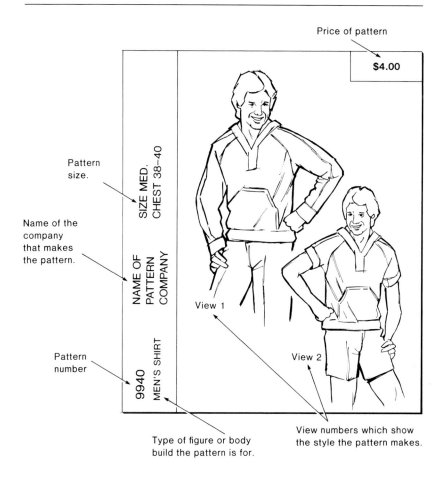

Price of pattern

$4.00

Pattern size.

SIZE MED. CHEST 38–40

Name of the company that makes the pattern.

NAME OF PATTERN COMPANY

View 1

Pattern number

9940   MEN'S SHIRT

View 2

Type of figure or body build the pattern is for.

View numbers which show the style the pattern makes.

Other information may also be shown on the front of the pattern
envelope. A few words may tell you that the pattern should be used only
with knitted fabrics. Or a statement may tell you that the garment is
considered to be one that is easy to make. Sometimes the pattern envelope
indicates that the pattern is especially good for beginners to use.[25]

Part of the technical vocabulary of a class in chemistry will be concerned
with interpreting symbols. Notice on the following page the explanation of
the meaning of the word *calorie,* then the way in which hydrogen molecules
can be released from water molecules (H_2O).

(9) Interpretation of Special Symbols

1. A gain of one calorie of heat raises the temperature of *one* gram of water one Celsius degree. Hence, to find the heat gained by *m* grams of water, undergoing a temperature change Δt, simply multiply $m \times \Delta t$. (The Greek letter delta, Δ, is often used to mean "a change in" something.)
. . .

In each of the preceding reactions, the metal has liberated some of the hydrogen atoms that make up the water molecules. These atoms then form hydrogen molecules, H_2. For every water molecule that reacts, one hydrogen atom is liberated while the other remains attached to the oxygen atom. The resulting compounds, LiOH, NaOH, KOH, $Mg(OH)_2$, are called *hydroxides*. The first three dissolve completely in the excess water.[26]

Understanding Abbreviations, Symbols, and Ratio Relationships

Mathematics and science both require an understanding of specialized terminology including abbreviations, equations, formulas, geometric signs, and others. Otto et al. demonstrate the need to understand symbol and ratio relationships in their biology text:

Two methods are used in the commercial pasteurization of milk. In the low-temperature or *holding* method the milk is heated to 145° F for thirty minutes. In the high temperature or *flash* method the milk is heated to 161° F for fifteen seconds. About 90 to 99 percent of the bacteria present are killed. Rapid cooling retards the growth of surviving organisms. However, pasteurized milk must be kept refrigerated to reduce bacteria growth. It should be covered to avoid the introduction of additional bacteria from the air.[27]

(See also appendix 10.)

Sequencing

An industrial arts text explains steps in the process of sharpening a plane (figure 12.3). This pattern requires not only the careful reading of steps in the process but also the ability to read alternately the step to be completed and the diagram.[28]

Information, Concept, and Process-Centered Texts

According to Jane Catterson, most text writing patterns we have just discussed are in fact subpatterns, used to structure portions of chapters rather than whole chapters.[29] These patterns cannot be fully understood without recognizing the macrostructure—the main topics and subtopics. Whereas texts in social studies, science, and mathematics share a common macrostructure, with each chapter having a single main topic with two or more subtopics, they differ in purpose.

Social Studies

Social studies texts are information centered. Unless chronology is very important, information is divided into logical subcategories using cause/effect, list/enumeration, comparison/contrast, and others. Graphics here emphasize ideas but are not always necessary for understanding the prose.

Classroom Applications

Figure 12.3

Interpreting graphics.

From Chris H. Groneman and John L. Feirer. *General Industrial Education,* 5th ed. (McGraw-Hill Book Co., 1974), pp. 218–20. Used with permission.

a. Testing the sharpness of the plane iron cutting edge on paper.

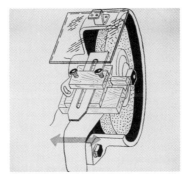

b. Plane iron held in position for sharpening on the grinder.

c. Sharpening a plane iron by grinding the edge.

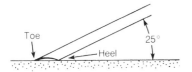

d. The angle for grinding a plane iron.

e. Testing the cutting edge of a plane iron for squareness.

f. Whetting the cutting edge of a plane iron on an oilstone.

g. Whetting the back side of a plane iron on an oilstone.

h. Removing the burr edge from a plane iron.

Workshop Activity 12.2
Finding Specific Writing Patterns

Select one content area, and using a text for that subject, find a sample for each of these patterns. If you have trouble finding a pattern, is it because it is not commonly found in your subject?

Content Area*	(Choose One)
Pattern:	(Example in content area)
1. Classify/ Categorize	
2. Compare/ Contrast	
3. Develop Concepts	
4. Cause/ Effect	
5. Enumerate	
6. Follow Directions	
7. Generalize	
8. Problem Solve	
9. Symbols/ Signs	
10. Sequence	

*Choose one of the following: Business Education; Creative Arts; English; Foreign Language; Health, Physical Education, and Recreation; Homemaking; Mathematics; Practical Arts; Industrial Education; Science; Social Studies; Other.

Science texts since the 1960s have tried to move away from information prose to concepts in order to help students develop a scientific way of thinking. Topics are ordered from simple to complex concepts. Experiments and explanation of the scientific process subpattern is included. Photographs are used to foster conceptual thinking. Experiments are set out as open-ended procedures from which students must formulate their own conclusions. Explanations are accompanied by diagrams to aid comprehension, and sketches or photos are included to develop powers of observation. No actual statements are made as to what should have been observed.

Mathematics texts are process centered with the purpose of developing problem-solving abilities. A concept is first explained, and then sample problems are given with step-by-step solutions, followed by many problems where students can test their problem-solving ability. They can do this by asking, "What am I to find? What am I given? What process will I use? What is an estimate of the correct answer?"[30]

Problems and Strategies for English Classrooms

A major stumbling block for students in English classes may well be the vast variety of writing styles and formats that must be dealt with, each necessitating a different strategy or approach. For example, in table 12.2 from the Myles Friedman and Michael Rowls text, some problems for various types of literature are shown and some suggested strategies for dealing with each are given.[31] This table can serve as a helpful resource when developing relevant lesson plans in English classrooms.

Table 12.2
Writing Styles and Formats: Problems and Strategies in Reading Literature

Type	Problems	Strategies
1. Short Story	a. little background information or buildup given b. few elaborations or details	—introduce background information for readiness and motivation —explain the nature of a short story —have students predict from the title what it will be about —suggest skimming before careful reading
2. Novel	a. length and complexity b. need to assimilate vast amount of information	—assign one segment at a time —establish purposes for reading —follow up silent reading with some oral interpretation —insert opportunities to predict what is to come —give background information and summarize

Table 12.2—Cont.

Type	Problems	Strategies
3. Poetry	a. no logical format b. syntactical patterns vary from usual patterns	—read poems orally in class —establish poet's purpose —discuss difficult words and literary devices —explain format, structure of poetry —select poems carefully to appeal to the age group —have students compose their own poems
4. Drama	a. no benefit from seeing and hearing performance b. tense dialogue is often meant to be conveyed through intonation and gesture	—emphasize the importance of staging information —allow students to cast the play —provide class time for practice reading and performing the play —select relevant plays —encourage attendance at local theatres —summarize frequently —present recordings and films
5. Essay and Biography	a. must understand author as well as the written message	—stress that these are vehicles for authors to express themselves —assist in deciphering author's views, biases, or mood —select relevant material

From Myles I. Friedman and Michael D. Rowls, *Teaching Reading and Thinking Skills.* Copyright © 1980 by Longman Inc. Reprinted by permission of Longman Inc., New York.

Content Area Tasks

Table 12.3 shows selected examples of reading/thinking/study skill tasks commonly needed in ten content areas. It is not intended to be an all-inclusive list. It might be well to select a particular content area of interest and compare/contrast with another subject. What might be added here?

Summary

To be able to effectively analyze writing patterns in content texts, students may first need proficiency in technical or special vocabulary and comprehension of extended discourse. Writing patterns and skills vary according to content areas with some being much more prevalent in one than another. Writing patterns to discern include classification, comparison/contrast, explanation of a concept, effect/cause or cause/effect, enumeration, following directions, generalizations, problem-solving diagrams, interpretation of special symbols, and sequencing. The forms of longer discourse include narration, explanation, classification, description, and argument. Skimming material first to identify the form of discourse will form a mind-set for detailed reading. Examples of specific reading/thinking/study skill tasks in ten content areas are listed.

Table 12.3

Examples of Reading/Thinking/Study Skill Tasks in Content Areas

Business Education	Creative Arts	English	Foreign Language
Learn specialized vocabulary.	Learn specialized vocabulary.	Develop a broad, general vocabulary.	Learn special vocabulary.
Read directions for assembling, cleaning, and repairing machines.	Read to follow precise, difficult directions.	Adapt rates of reading to fit purposes and density of material.	Read to learn stress, pitch, and intonation in the new language.
Reproduce typewriter symbols automatically.	Read words in songs by syllables.	Read to establish sequence.	Learn new vocabulary, figures of speech, idioms.
Practice phrase reading as an aid to copy typing.	Understand symbols and notations.	Read literature for imagery, character portrayal, details.	Study the customs and the culture of the foreign country.
Alphabetize and file.	Read literature to appreciate the setting for creative art.	Understand syntax and semantics in both writing and reading.	Find meanings in dictionaries and resource books.
Scan standard forms quickly.	Read biographies of creative artists.	Identify types of writing, purposes.	Practice using the language.
Read graphs, charts.	Read critical reviews of performances.		
Learn records management.			

Health, Physical Education, and Recreation	Home Economics	Industrial Arts	Mathematics
Learn specialized vocabulary.	Learn specialized vocabulary.	Learn specialized vocabulary.	Learn specialized vocabulary.
Read about sports heroes, sports events.	Adapt reading rates for journal and technical articles.	Follow directions in manuals: how to assemble, how to fix.	Grasp the problem as a whole.
Read biographies.	Read charts, graphs, diagrams, patterns, drawings, and cutaways.	Interpret symbols, abbreviations.	Decide what is to be done.
Understand details for measuring courts, game scores, players.	Read recipes accurately.	Problem solve.	Identify givens.
Read and interpret graphs, charts, diagrams.	Know abbreviations used.	Interpret graphics.	Decide how to find the answer.
Understand nutrition and the body.	Follow directions, sequence steps.		Know symbols and abbreviations.
			Follow directions.
			Use SQRQCQ strategy.
			Use percentages, as in batting averages.

Table 12.3—*Cont.*

Science	Social Studies	Other (Specify)
Learn specialized vocabulary.	Learn specialized vocabulary.	
Read for key idea and supporting ideas.	Identify key ideas.	
Use SQ3R strategy.	Use SQ3R strategy.	
Understand relationships, generalizations, drawing conclusions.	Understand relationships, generalizations, drawing conclusions.	
Interpret charts, maps, graphs, and diagrams.	Use sophisticated library research skills.	
Know symbols, formulas, and abbreviations.	See time and space relationships.	
Anticipate outcomes.	Understand cause/effect.	
Recognize propaganda.	Recognize propaganda.	
Read between the lines.	Read between the lines and draw inferences.	
Problem solve.		

References

1. Robert M. Swanson, Lewis D. Boynton, Kenton E. Ross, and Robert D. Hanson, *Century 21 Accounting* (Cincinnati, Ohio: Southwestern Publishing Co., 1977), p. 124.
2. George Conrad, *The Process of Art Education in the Elementary School* (Englewood Cliffs, N.J.: Prentice-Hall, 1964), p. 121.
3. John E. Warriner and Sheila Laws Graham, *English Grammar and Composition, Heritage Edition* (New York: Harcourt Brace Jovanovich, 1977), p. 460.
4. Jessie Helen Haag, *Focusing on Health,* rev. ed. (Austin, Texas: Steck-Vaughn Co., 1978), p. 89.
5. Irene McDermott, Jeanne L. Norris, and Florence Nicholas, *Homemaking for Teenagers, Book II,* 4th ed. (Peoria, Ill.: Charles A. Bennett, 1976), p. 401.
6. William H. Crouse, *Automotive Mechanics,* 7th ed. (New York: McGraw-Hill, 1975), p. 61.
7. Harold R. Jacobs, *Geometry* (San Francisco: W. H. Freeman and Co., 1974), p. 272.
8. Carl O. Dunbar and Karl W. Waage, *Historical Geology,* 3d ed. (New York: John Wiley & Sons, 1969), p. 9.
9. E. T. Thompson, *The Plantation* (Durham, N.C.: Duke University, 1935), cited in Jan O. M. Broek and John W. Webb, *A Geography of Mankind* (New York: McGraw-Hill, 1968), p. 234.
10. Ernest Horn, *Methods of Instruction in the Social Studies* (New York: Charles Scribner's Sons, 1937), p. 167.

11. P. David Pearson and Dale D. Johnson, *Teaching Comprehension* (New York: Holt, Rinehart & Winston, 1978), p. 17.

12. Jane Catterson, "Comprehension: The Argument for a Discourse Analysis Model," in *Reading Comprehension at Four Linguistic Levels,* ed. Clifford Pennock (Newark, Del.: International Reading Association, 1979), pp. 2–7.

13. James Otto, W. David Otto, Albert Towle, and Robert Weaver, *Modern Biology* (New York: Holt, Rinehart & Winston, 1973), p. 246.

14. Bernard A. Weisberger, *The Impact of Our Past, A History of the United States* (New York: Webster Division, McGraw-Hill, 1972), p. 615.

15. Trancene Sabine, *Women Who Win* (New York: Random House, 1975), pp. x–xi.

16. Margil Vanderhoff, *Clothes, Clues, and Careers* (Lexington, Mass.: Ginn and Co., 1977), pp. 180–181.

17. Joseph Machlis, *Music: Adventures in Listening* (New York: Grosset & Dunlap, 1968), pp. 4–5.

18. Weisberger, *Impact of Our Past,* p. 618.

19. Otto et al., *Modern Biology,* pp. 285–286.

20. McDermott et al., *Homemaking,* p. 619.

21. Center for Safety, New York University, *Driver Education and Traffic Safety* (Englewood Cliffs, N.J.: Prentice-Hall, 1976), pp. 40–41.

22. Robert L. Marshall, Robert L. Baldwin, Richard Tossell, Robert A. Ulrich, and June S. Cunningham, *Safe Performance Driving* (Lexington, Mass.: Ginn and Co., 1976), p. 52.

23. Weisberger, *Impact of Our Past,* p. 649.

24. Vanderhoff, *Clothes,* p. 220.

25. Ibid., p. 221.

26. F. Albert Cotton, C. LeRoy Darlington, and Lawrence D. Lynch, *Chemistry, An Investigative Approach,* rev. ed. (Boston: Houghton Mifflin, 1973), pp. 65, 202.

27. Otto et al., *Modern Biology,* p. 256.

28. Chris H. Groneman and John L. Feirer, *General Industrial Education,* 5th ed. (New York: McGraw-Hill, 1974), pp. 218–220.

29. Jane Catterson, "Discourse Forms in Content Texts," *Journal of Reading* 33 (April 1990): 256–258.

30. Ibid.

31. Myles I. Friedman and Michael D. Rowls, *Teaching Reading and Thinking Skills* (New York: Longman, 1980), pp. 475–476.

Recommended Readings

Bean, Thomas W. et al. "Acquisitions of Hierarchically Organized Knowledge and Prediction of Events in World History." *Reading Research and Instruction* 26 (Winter 1987): 99–114.

Bean, Thomas; Singer, Harry; and Cowan, Stan. "Analogical Study Guides: Improving Comprehension in Science." *Journal of Reading* 29 (December 1985): 246–250.

Bohnning, Gerry, and Radencich, Marguerite. "Information Action Books: A Curriculum Resource for Science and Social Studies." *Journal of Reading* 32 (February 1989): 434–439. (Visual formats of action books motivate reading and provide a unique resource for middle school teachers.)

Briars, D. J., and Larkin, J. H. "An Integrated Model of Skill in Solving Elementary Word Problems." *Cognition and Instruction* 1 (1984): 245–296.

Cook, Linda, and Mayer, Richard. "Teaching Readers About the Structure of Scientific Text." *Journal of Educational Psychology* (December 1988): 448–456.

Curry, Joan. "The Role of Reading Instruction in Mathematics." In *Content Area Reading and Learning: Instructional Strategies,* Diane Lapp, James Flood, Nancy Farnam, eds. Englewood Cliffs, N.J.: Prentice-Hall, 1989.

Duke, Charles R. "Integrating Reading, Writing, and Thinking Skills in the Music Classroom." *Journal of Reading* 31 (November 1987): 152–157.

Earle, Richard. *Teaching Reading and Mathematics.* Reading Aids Series. Newark, Del.: International Reading Association, 1976.

Frager, Alan M., and Thompson, Loren C. "Reading Instruction and Music Education: Getting in Tune." *Journal of Reading* 27 (December 1983): 202–206.

Gentile, Lance M. *Using Sports and Physical Education to Strengthen Reading Skills.* Newark, Del.: International Reading Association, 1980.

Gentile, Lance M., and McMillan, Merna M. "Reading and Writing in the Content Areas of Physical and Health Education." In *Content Area Reading and Learning: Instructional Strategies,* Diane Lapp, James Flood, Nancy Farnam, eds. Englewood Cliffs, N.J.: Prentice-Hall, 1989.

Harms, Jeanne McLain, and Lucille J. Lettow. "Extending the Message: Collaboration of Livingston, the Poet, and Fisher, the Painter. *Journal of Reading* 34 (March 1991): 462–464.

Hayes, Bernard, and Peters, Charles. "The Role of Reading Instruction in the Social Studies Classroom." In *Content Area Reading and Learning: Instructional Strategies,* Diane Lapp, James Flood, Nancy Farnam, eds. Englewood Cliffs, N.J.: Prentice-Hall, 1989.

Hermann, Beth Ann. "Characteristics of Explicit and Less Explicit Explanations of Mathematical Problem Solving Strategies." *Reading Research and Instruction* 28 (Spring 1989): 1–17.

Hollingsworth, Sandra, and Karen Teel. "Learning to Teach Reading in Secondary Math and Science." *Journal of Reading* 35 (November 1991): 190–194.

Horrowitz, Rosalind. "Text Patterns: Part I." *Journal of Reading* 28 (February 1985): 448–454.

Horrowitz, Rosalind. "Text Patterns: Part II." *Journal of Reading* 28 (March 1985): 534–541.

Hynd, Cynthia R., and Alverman, Donna E. "Overcoming Misconceptions in Science: An On-Line Study of Prior Knowledge Activation. *Reading Research and Instruction* 28 (Summer 1989): 12–26.

Kresse, Elaine Campbell. "Using Reading As a Thinking Process to Solve Math Story Problems." *Journal of Reading* 27 (April 1984): 598–601.

Lampert, M. "Knowing, Doing and Teaching Multiplication." *Cognition and Instruction* 3 (1987): 305–342.

Lees, Fred. "Mathematics and Reading." *Journal of Reading* 19 (May 1976): 621–626.

Levine, Isadore. "Solving Reading Problems in Vocational Subjects." *High Points* 12 (April 1960): 10–27.

Lloyd, Carol V., and Mitchell, Judy Nichols. "Coping With Too Many Concepts in Science Texts." *Journal of Reading* 6 (March 1989): 542–545.

Lunstrum, John, and Taylor, Bob. *Teaching Reading in the Social Studies.* Newark, Del.: International Reading Association, 1978.

Mallow, Jeffry V. "Reading Science." *Journal of Reading* 34 (February 1991): 324–338.

Manzo, Anthony V. "Three Universal Strategies in Content Area Reading and Languaging." *Journal of Reading* 24 (November 1980): 146–149.

Maring, Gerald H., and Ritson, Robert. "Ten Teaching Strategies for Combining Reading Skills and the Content of Physical Education." *Journal of Reading* 24 (October 1980).

Moore, David W., and Moore, Sharon Arthur. "Reading Literature Independently." *Journal of Reading* 30 (April 1987): 596–600.

Roe, Betty D.; Stoodt, Barbara D.; and Burns, Paul C. *Secondary School Reading Instruction: The Content Areas.* 2d ed. (Boston: Houghton Mifflin, 1983).

Santa, Carol; Havens, Lynn; and Harrison, Shirley. "Teaching Secondary Science Through Reading, Writing, Studying and Problem Solving." In *Content Area Reading and Learning: Instructional Strategies,* Diane Lapp, James Flood, Nancy Farnam, eds. Englewood Cliffs, N.J.: Prentice-Hall, 1989.

Spiegel, Dixie Lee, and Wright, Jill D. "Biology Teachers' Preferences in Textbook Characteristics." *Journal of Reading* 27 (April 1984): 624–631.

Thelen, Judy. *Improved Reading in Science.* 2d ed. Newark, Del.: International Reading Association, 1984.

Walters, George Lewis. *The Developmental and Refinement of Reading Skills in Business Education.* Cincinnati: Southwestern Publishing Co., 1975.

Figure 13.1
Getting it all together: reading/thinking/study skills across the curriculum: a cognitive map.

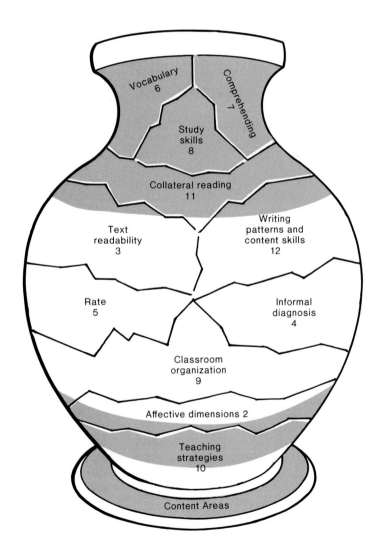

406

Getting It All Together: Reading/Thinking/Study Skills across the Curriculum

13

Anticipatory Questions

(Literal)

1. Describe major approaches for teaching children to learn how to read.

(Literal)

2. State the steps in sequence for setting up a reading program across the curriculum.

(Applied)

3. Discuss some problems occurring in early reading and relate them to your own past experience.

(Applied)

4. From the description of reading in chapter 1, other chapters in the text, and the discussion in this chapter, compose in writing a one-paragraph definition of *content reading*.

Technical Terminology and Concepts

basal/individualized/ language experience/ whole language approaches

comprehensive reading program

developmental/ disabled readers

needs assessment

reading process

To the Instructor: Important!

This final chapter begins with a potent workshop activity that may be used as a means of assisting students to synthesize some major concepts discussed throughout the term. It is strongly recommended that it be assigned by the instructor to be read *during* the last regular university class session, because its impact will be dissipated if assigned as outside reading. If this chapter is assigned to be read prior to the last class, omit this section as required reading and ask students to begin by reading Getting it All Together found on page 411.

We have used this particular workshop activity with great success in numerous inservice workshops. Good teachers and administrators are often shaken by the realization that they may have been assuming student competency in basic areas that did not really exist.

Workshop Activity 13.1
Experience Is the Best Teacher, or The Singletree-Doubletree Anachronism[1]

To the Instructor

1. The instructor announces that during this last class students will be engaging in a group culminating activity, the purpose of which is to bring into sharp focus some major reading/thinking/study problems in content classrooms. Also, students are to note and critique any adverse teacher behaviors or omissions that affect learning.
2. The instructor starts the simulated content class by calling roll.
3. Next, "Today class, we will all read pages _____ to _____ in our text. You will be tested on this section. We will start off by having this student (point to one) in the back row read the first sentence aloud. The person directly to the left will read the second sentence, etc." (Continue this until four or five students have read a sentence orally. The instructor may wish to have instructed two students privately beforehand to read in a stumbling manner.)
4. The instructor stops the oral reading and tells the students that they have four minutes to complete the reading silently before the test is given. There is to be *no* talking or sharing.
5. At the end of exactly four minutes, the instructor stops the reading, asks them to close their books, and hands out the three questions (found at the end of the reading) on a sheet labeled "Test," leaving large spaces after each question for written responses.
6. After two or three minutes, or as soon as most of the class are not writing, the instructor announces, "I see that *most* of you have *not* been concentrating, although 'John' and 'Lucy' have! I have changed my mind— for the next three minutes you may go ahead and refer to your texts for the answers. I will call on several of you to share your answers with the class."
7. After three minutes, the class should be sufficiently frustrated at this point to be audibly relieved when the instructor announces that the simulation is over.

Figure 13.2

Functioning anachronisms.

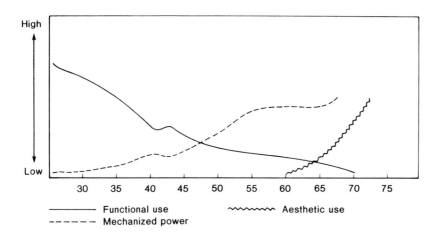

Figure 13.3

Singletree-doubletree use.

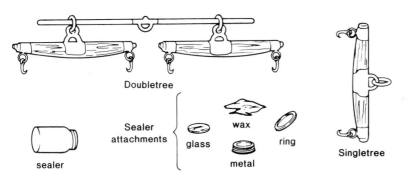

Note the similarity between the singletree and the doubletree.

8. The instructor reads off the correct responses (see end of chapter). A fruitful discussion may then ensue in which not only the faulty teaching techniques are dissected but also the multiple problems met in the reading are identified.

The Singletree-Doubletree Anachronism

The short selection which follows—The Singletree/Doubletree Anachronism—was intentionally written to include many of the problems faced by students when they read subject matter. You can increase your awareness of these problems by reading the selection, studying figures 13.2 and 13.3, and by assessing your ability to answer the questions at the end of the selection.

When is an object an anachronism? Can an object be an anachronism and a functional implement in the same geographical area? In the same time period?

When does an object have aesthetic value? Can an object be both admired and scorned as useless in the same geographical area? In the same time period?

Does the appellation given an object reflect its value? i.e., can a euphemism add value to an object (e.g., "antique" *vis-a-vis* "junk")?

Perhaps the singletree and the doubletree can provide answers. The singletree and the doubletree are like the sealer. The sealer is an anachronism. So are the singletree and the doubletree. They are also functional implements. They are anachronistic and functional in the same areas. They are anachronistic and functional in the same time period. Aesthetically, they are admired by some, they are disdained by others. Discrimination does not seem to be related to geographical location.

The functional decline of the singletree and the doubletree occurred before the advent of VEE.* Machines hastened their decline. Singletrees and doubletrees were not used with machines. The former were abandoned to the ravages of weather and time. Figure 13.3 illustrates the decline of the singletree and the doubletree as mechanized power became available. Aesthetic ascendancy of these objects is also shown.

The functional decline of the singletree and doubletree was not universal in occurrence. The aesthetic ascendancy of these objects was also not universal. In remote areas, both are used today (functionally). Some religious groups have retained them. In these areas, the sealer is also popular. However, although these objects are put to the same uses in different areas, they are called by different names in different areas. Also, where functional use is preeminent, only a modicum of aesthetic appreciation can be found.

Both the singletree and the doubletree can be made from a single tree. Metal rings or hooks are attached to the main object. The singletree is used for light loads. The doubletree is often used for heavier loads. As aesthetic objects, load is a minor factor to be considered. Here either object can be used for a single purpose. Although singletrees and doubletrees can be seen in many places, few traces of singletrees and doubletrees can be found. Weather, of course, is the reason for this.

Answer the following questions:

1. a. Why might some people incorrectly conclude that the 1971 VEE epidemic was the main cause of the decline of the popularity of the singletree and the doubletree?
   b. Why did mechanized power hasten the decline in their popularity?
2. Load is not a factor of major importance in discriminating between the use of a singletree and a doubletree for aesthetic purposes. Yet it is important in relation to their functional value. Why is this so?
3. How is it possible that many singletrees and doubletrees can be found, but few traces of singletrees and doubletrees can be found?

STOP HERE: Wait for further instructions

*Venezuelan equine encephalitis

First elicit from the class and list on the board the reading problems they encountered in this article as well as the teacher behavior that they perceived as having hindered learning. Some possible responses:

Reading Problems	Adverse Behaviors
1. Background or experience	1. Wasting time calling roll
2. Vocabulary (list types and examples)	2. Assigning reading pages without comment
3. Style	3. Using "round-robin" oral reading
4. Graphic aids	4. Making no allowance for variety of reading rates
5. Other	5. Making derogatory remarks about the class
	6. Selecting a few students for praise
	7. Using the threat of a test or being called on as the purpose for reading
	8. Other

1. *Background or Experience:* Those who have been familiar with draft horses used on farms and with antiques should have had less trouble comprehending this selection.
2. *Vocabulary:* (key words, supporting words, multiple meanings, colloquial or unusual terms, abbreviations).
   Key words: "singletree," "doubletree," "anachronism," "functional," "aesthetic"
   Supporting vocabulary: "euphemism," "appellation," "modicum," "preeminent"
   Multiple Meanings: inappropriate definitions of the words "traces," "discrimination," "singletree"
   Colloquial or unusual terms: "sealer" and "vis-a-vis" (in central Canada fruit jars are often referred to as "sealers") *Abbreviations:* "i.e.," "e.g."
3. *Style:* The rhetorical questions used at the onset are easy to forget; the reader would need to return to them while reading. Overall style was difficult.
4. *Graphic Aids:* Not strategically placed in article, incomplete, no referent to indicate relative size of objects, confusion of horizontal fruit jar, vertical singletree.
5. *Interest:* Nothing done to appeal to your interest.

Answers will be found at the end of the chapter.

From Arnold Burron and Amos L. Claybaugh, *Using Reading to Teach Subject Matter* (Columbus, Ohio: Charles E. Merrill Publishing Co., 1974), pp. 10–13.

Throughout this text we have been looking at separate segments of reading/ thinking/study skills as they apply to content teaching, grades four through twelve. These segments include such areas as vocabulary, comprehension,

Getting it All Together

motivation, writing patterns, and collateral reading. In this final chapter we look at reading/thinking/study as a whole entity in a developmental continuum. Included are general definitions of the reading process and developmental versus disabled readers; major early approaches to learning how to read; and steps for incorporating a reading program across the curriculum.

The cognitive map in figure 13.1 is an attempt merely to portray the message that the separate pieces we have examined in this text may fit together in a variety of ways. The size of each piece will depend on your particular subject matter and the needs of your specific students. (This is a general map and is not intended to reflect information found in this final chapter.)

The Reading Process Reviewed

Definition of the Reading Process

In his book, *The Art of Loving,* Erich Fromm describes different kinds of love.[2] He maintains that our theory of love affects our practice of love; our definition of love affects our general attitude toward it, the way we love, whom we love, and why we love. In a similar way we might say that our theory and definition of reading as a process affects our attitude toward it, and the way we read, what we read, how often we read, and why we read. If content teachers think of reading as only a decoding process, it is no wonder that they resist and declare, "I'm not a *reading* teacher!"

Reading is a complex process, one that involves perceiving graphic symbols; interpreting their meanings based on prior knowledge, then predicting, revising, or confirming on that basis; reacting; and applying these meanings to the life situation. It is an active thinking process that demands meaning. *Decoding* is just one aspect, one way to get at meaning, whereas *comprehension* is the vital component. If you can read "the zump was rothing" you are decoding the print into sounds, but you are merely "word calling" without comprehending what the sentence really means. In general we may decode first and then get the meaning from that decoding, a process called comprehending. Many concerns and beginning skills of learning how to read do of course center around decoding aspects: using content clues, phonics, structural analysis, and the dictionary. Later, however, these should have become automatic, and the emphasis is then on the use of reading as a process used to learn some content (reading to learn).

Developmental versus Disabled Readers

We speak of *developmental readers* as those who have made normal progress in reading up to their capacity. These include: (1) the gifted or mature readers who read well above grade level, (2) the average readers who read at or around grade level, and (3) the slower readers who read below grade level, *but* still read up to their potential. On the other hand, *disabled readers* are those reading below their potential and who should profit from a course in remedial reading. Often they have been considered disabled if they are reading two grades below their potential.

Before considering a reading program across the curriculum, let us look briefly at some major approaches to teaching early reading and some of the problems that may emerge for content area students, grades four through twelve.

Why talk about the early school years in a text for teachers of older students? In many places formal instruction in reading for all students has been discontinued by the end of elementary school. Unfortunately, not only are there many who have not completely mastered the requisite skills at this time, but also there are numerous higher-level reading/study skills that all students would profit from if they were taught through the vehicles of specific content. Those of you who are upper elementary teachers will find this section to be a review of your current practices.

Present Practices in Early Primary Grades

1. *Basal readers:* This approach uses a series of reading texts that include readers, detailed teachers' manuals, skill workbooks, and related materials. Vocabulary and skills are carefully sequenced and controlled, and directed reading lessons are taught to several ability groups.
2. *Language experience approach (LEA):* Language experience integrates all aspects of language arts including listening, speaking, writing, and reading. Students dictate or write sentences and stories based on their own experiences and read silently and aloud their own and each other's words. Students often create their own books to be shared.
3. *Individualized reading:* This approach allows children to self-select what they wish to read from a wide variety of trade books, read at their own pace, and then confer regularly with the teacher. It involves detailed record keeping.
4. *Whole language:* This recent movement came about some say as an offshoot of language experience. The philosophy here is that we learn to read by reading, not by taking it all apart and examining the bits or drilling on decoding. Whole language uses good literature as the basic material to be read.

Major Approaches to Teaching Reading

This is an example of writing from a nineteen-year-old high school dropout, using the language experience approach. He wrote about something he felt keenly about and then read what he had written, sharing it with others, too.

> The Diamondback Rattlesnake is very big and can be very scary. They can be found in the rocky areas of New Mexico. I came upon one two years ago in Abo Canyon. Leading the horse across the canyon, I saw his coiled figure in the grass. I dropped the horse's reins and picked up a nearby stick. Knowing how dangerous this snake is, I killed him immediately.

These snakes are very poisonous. They have black and brown spots about the size of quarters on their back. If you come upon one of these snakes, try to turn around and move slowly away. In the summer and early fall months the Diamondback is out of hibernation and can be real trouble. Don't be fooled by this snake not shaking his rattle. In very hot weather they may make no noise but are still coiled to strike. This means to always be on the lookout while walking in the desert.

If you get bit by a Diamondback, *don't panic!* If you get terribly excited this only makes your heart pound faster and the deadly venom races through your body quicker. Stay calm and make a tourniquet. Tie the tourniquet very tightly above the bite. Get medical help as soon as possible then.

Don't stay away from the beautiful deserts of New Mexico. Just make sure you are prepared for emergencies!

Some Problems in Early Primary Reading

1. Readiness for beginning reading is sometimes mishandled. Some children enter school already reading or ready to commence but are stifled by readiness workbooks or related activities. Others might benefit from a lengthy readiness period of being read to, trying to write, illustrating stories, etc., without being forced too soon into formal reading.
2. Three reading ability groups do not encompass all the levels, skills, and interests of children in any given heterogeneous class. They may also be harmful by classifying children as bright, average, or slow.
3. Some teachers place most of their emphasis on just "getting through the book" in the basal series without concern for teaching the related skills.
4. Reading is too often taught as being synonymous only with stories and literature, rather than also with the expository writing of content texts.
5. Many primary teachers have had only one or two general reading courses, with little attention to content area reading.

Workshop Activity 13.2
Learning to Read

For those of you interested in experiencing some of the difficulties and frustrations that a child may go through at the very beginning stages of learning to read, it is suggested that you attempt to read McKee's *Primer for Parents* (see the sample figure 13.4).[3] The dilemma of meeting an entirely new set of symbols is clearly illustrated. This exercise may be done using an overhead projector and asking the class to study each page for a minute and then read it aloud in chorus. Each new word is introduced once with its meaning. Thereafter, students must remember them without aid.

Figure 13.4

Primer for parents.

From Paul McKee, *Primer for Parents* (Boston: Houghton Mifflin Co., 1975), p. 7. Used with permission.

Illustrations by Judy Goodwin

A Content Reading Program across the Curriculum

Regardless of grade level, you should now be well aware that for maximum learning students must be helped with the *process* as well as the *knowledge* of subject matter. Reading/thinking/study skills are not something added to the curriculum and your already crowded schedule, but rather they are pathways leading to successful content mastery, a way to teach and learn.

If your school does not have a comprehensive reading program, you should be aware of some general procedures for establishing one. Possible considerations and procedures follow:

1. Establish a coordinating committee.
2. Reach consensus on a statement of philosophy.
3. Survey content teachers for present reading/study practices and needs.
4. Tabulate the results and prioritize needs.
5. Schedule practical inservice sessions using content-related reading skills and materials.
6. Ascertain that all faculty are clear about existing reading programs, facilities, and staff roles.
7. Provide for anonymous feedback from content teachers as to the worth of inservice sessions for the past year and their recommendations for future sessions.

Establish a Coordinating Committee

Generally, the principal or another chief administrator is an initiator in establishing or changing the reading program. This person is an essential member of the coordinating committee.

Ideally, a school will already have or will be willing to hire a reading consultant, one who is trained to work primarily with teachers, rather than just with disabled and developmental students. This consultant may serve as the coordinator of the committee, laying the groundwork for future work to be accomplished. The consultant will have met the criteria established by the International Reading Association for reading consultants. See *Guidelines for the Specialized Preparation of Reading Professionals,* developed by the professional standards and ethics committee of the International Reading Association, 1985–1986. (International Reading Association, 800 Barksdale Road, P.O. Box 8139, Newark, Delaware 19711.)

If a consultant is not available, the remedial reading teacher or the person designated as the reading "expert" should serve. Whoever serves in this capacity must have had both a developmental reading course and a course in reading in content areas.

Other committee members should include department heads or their representatives, the school librarian, a guidance counselor, with the possible addition of a student, parent, and/or community representative.

The coordinating committee should consider and reach consensus on their beliefs concerning a schoolwide reading program. Consultation should be given to such concerns as accommodating all the students; reading as a continuous developmental process; roles and training of reading personnel; and the importance of content teachers. These beliefs should be written simply and shared with the entire staff.

Develop a Statement of Philosophy for a Sound Reading Program

Two helpful texts that discuss establishing a statement of philosophy in a school include Otto and Smith[4] and Smith, Otto, and Hansen.[5] Otto and Smith postulate six key philosophical concepts on which a sound reading program may be built:

1. The person is the focal point in the reading program (not a curriculum guide, a textbook, or a "program.")
2. The purpose of the reading program is to help each student read as nearly as possible at capacity level.
3. Reading is much more than the simple decoding of printed symbols.
4. A statement of the scope and sequence of reading skill development can serve as a framework for the instructional reading program.
5. Reading is only one of the language arts. Reading, writing, speaking, and listening must be mutually reinforcing.
6. The ultimate product of a successful reading program is a mature reader. (See chapter 1 for a full discussion of the mature reader.)

To help you survey content teachers for present reading and study practices and needs, a needs assessment instrument has been developed by Sheila Allen and Robert Chester that can be used by secondary schools and adapted for the upper elementary grades.[6] This instrument provides important information on present practices in content classrooms, immediate perceived needs of these teachers, and their priorities of need (see appendix 8).

Survey Content Teachers

If you have used the survey instrument or adapted it to your situation, it will be a simple task to tabulate the results and decide on priorities.

Tabulate Results and Prioritize Needs

Next you will need to ascertain that all faculty members are clear about existing reading programs, facilities, and staff roles. This may be done in several ways—in writing or at a general or departmental meeting; by the principal or other concerned administrators, the reading specialist, or the coordinator of the advisory committee. All teachers must be reminded of the referral process and requirements for students to enter a developmental or remedial (disabled) program or class.

Clarify Existing Programs, Facilities, and Roles

Provide Feedback
on Inservice
Sessions

You should also provide for anonymous feedback from content teachers about the worth of inservice sessions for the past year and their recommendations for future sessions. Following a series of inservice sessions, this feedback may be used for decisions for future meetings.

Plan and Schedule
New Inservice
Sessions

Inservice sessions should be ongoing, stretching out over several years. This will occur when topics are dealt with in depth, with opportunity for content teachers to work on and try out the ideas in class. Inservice sessions that try to "cover the waterfront" rarely show practical results in the classroom. Teachers need to practice strategies themselves, adapting as needed, with the opportunity to come back to a later session for feedback and clarification.

**Workshop
Products and
Content Tools**

Now, having just completed this course, which of the following practical products and tools do you possess to incorporate into your content classroom? (This may be used also as a pretest/posttest device by asking students to briefly define or describe each item.)

_____ 1. Annotated bibliography of content topic
_____ 2. Attitude/interest survey forms
_____ 3. Cloze procedure model
_____ 4. Collateral reading strategies
_____ 5. Comprehension strategies
_____ 6. Content IRI (CIRI)
_____ 7. Cooperative learning: working in pairs, triads, committees, or small groups
_____ 8. Directed reading-thinking activity (DRTA) lesson plan
_____ 9. Mini-learning centers
_____ 10. Rate adaptability materials
_____ 11. Readability formulas
_____ 12. Samples of writing patterns that are content specific
_____ 13. Study skill strategies
_____ 14. Text evaluations
_____ 15. Text organization considerations
_____ 16. Timesaving devices
_____ 17. Vocabulary strategies
_____ 18. Writing strategies
_____ 19. Other: _____
_____ 20. Other: _____

Workshop Activity 13.3
Final Self-evaluation

(Note to the instructor: You may wish to consider using this activity at midterm time as well as during the final week. In that way students have the opportunity to practice thinking along these lines.)

The highest level of Bloom's Taxonomy of the Cognitive Domain (see the chapter on comprehending) is *evaluation,* when learners must make value judgments based on their own stated criteria (the plural of criterion). In this activity, you as university students are asked to evaluate in writing your own learning and efforts, and at the same time decide which criteria to use. This is not the time to evaluate the course or text; it is instead a self-searching that requires a decision as to what is worthwhile to you, the student. (An example of a criterion is "interest.")

This self-evaluation should be a thoughtful paper of one or more pages, and you are encouraged to put it together in some creative form, such as a gameboard, cognitive map, report card, puzzle, or seasonal theme. Enjoy this assignment.

Answers to Workshop Activity 13.1

1. A. Singletrees are used with horses. People assumed that the deaths of large numbers of horses created a situation in which few horses were available to be hitched to singletrees.
   B. Machines were used to do much of the work formerly done by horses.
2. A doubletree is used with more than one horse when a heavy load is to be pulled. When decorative objects, such as flowerpots or beer steins, are hung from singletrees or doubletrees, the weight factor of the objects is not of significance in deciding between the use of a singletree or a doubletree.
3. Harnesses—sometimes called "traces"—were usually made of leather and deteriorated when left outdoors for any length of time.

References

1. Arnold Burron and Amos L. Claybaugh, *Using Reading to Teach Subject Matter: Fundamentals for Content Teachers* (Columbus, Ohio: Charles E. Merrill Publishing Co., 1974), pp. 10–13.
2. Erich Fromm, *The Art of Loving* (New York: Harper, 1956).

3. Paul McKee, *Primer for Parents: How Your Child Learns to Read* (Boston: Houghton Mifflin, 1975), p. 7. Translation: "Are you sick? Are you waiting for the doctor?"

4. Wayne Otto and Richard J. Smith, *Administering the School Reading Program* (Boston: Houghton Mifflin, 1970).

5. Richard J. Smith, Wayne Otto, and Lee Hansen, *The School Reading Program* (Addison-Wesley Publishing Co., 1979).

6. Sheilah M. Allen and Robert D. Chester, "A Needs Assessment Instrument for Secondary Reading Inservice," *Journal of Reading* 21, 6 (March 1978): 489–492.

Recommended Readings

Conley, Mark W., and Savage, Peter F. "What's Really New in Models of Content Reading?" *Journal of Reading* 28 (January 1985): 336–341.

Downing, John, and Morris, Bert. "An Australian Program for Improving High School Reading in Content Areas." *Journal of Reading* 28 (December 1984): 237–243.

Farrell, Richard T., and Cirrincione, Joseph M. "State Certification Requirements in Reading for Content Teachers." *Journal of Reading* 28 (November 1984): 152–158.

Henry, Claire. "The Administration Helps Teachers Make a Difference." *Journal of Reading* 20 (March 1977): 508–512.

McDonald, Thomas F. "An All School Secondary Reading Program." *Journal of Reading* 14 (May 1971): 553–558.

Moore, David W.; Readence, John E.; and Rickelman, Robert J. "An Historical Exploration of Content Area Reading Instruction." *Reading Research Quarterly,* Vol. XVIII (Summer 1983): 419–438.

Ratekin, Ned; Simpson, Michelle L.; Alvermann, Donna E.; and Dishner, Ernest K. "Why Teachers Resist Content Reading Instruction." *Journal of Reading* (February 1985): 432–437.

Santa, Carol M. "Changing Teacher Behavior in Content Reading Through Collaborative Research." In *Changing School Reading Programs,* S. Jay Samuels and P. David Pearson, eds. Newark, Del.: International Reading Association, 1988.

Siedow, Mary Dunn; Memory, David M.; and Bristow, Page S. *Inservice Education for Content Area Teachers.* Newark, Del.: International Reading Association, 1985.

Vacca, Jo Anne L. "How to Be an Effective Staff Developer for Content Teachers." *Journal of Reading* 26 (January 1983): 293–296.

Whilhite, Robert K. "Principals' Views of Their Role in the High School Reading Program." *Journal of Reading* 27 (January 1984): 356–358.

Zaleski, Ann Marie. "How to Present a Reading Program to the Administration." *Journal of Reading* 18 (May 1975): 610–614.

Appendixes

Appendix 1

Religion in the Public School Curriculum: Questions and Answers
(See sponsoring organizations listed on page 425.)

Growing numbers of people in the United States think it is important to teach *about* religion in the public schools.[1] But what is the appropriate place of religion in the public school curriculum? How does one approach such issues as textbook content, values education, creation science, and religious holidays?

The following questions and answers are designed to assist school boards as they make decisions about the curriculum and educators as they teach about religion in ways that are constitutionally permissible, educationally sound, and sensitive to the beliefs of students and parents.

There are other questions concerning religion and the schools not addressed here, including school prayer, equal access, and how schools accommodate diverse religious beliefs and practices. For a full discussion of these broader issues, please contact the sponsors listed on the back of this publication.

Q: Is it constitutional to teach about religion in public schools?

A: Yes. In the 1960s school prayer cases (which ruled against state-sponsored school prayer and Bible reading), the U.S. Supreme Court indicated that public school education may include teaching about religion. In *Abington* v. *Schempp,* Associate Justice Tom Clark wrote for the Court:

> [I]t might well be said that one's education is not complete without a study of comparative religion or the history of religion and its relationship to the advancement of civilization. It certainly may be said that the Bible is worthy of study for its literary and historic qualities. Nothing we have said here indicates that such study of the Bible or of religion, when presented objectively as part of a secular program of education, may not be effected consistently with the First Amendment.

Q: What is meant by "teaching about religion" in the public school?

A: The following statements distinguish between teaching about religion in public schools and religious indoctrination:

☐ The school's approach to religion is *academic,* not *devotional.*

☐ The school may strive for student *awareness* of religions, but should not press for student *acceptance* of any one religion.

☐ The school may sponsor *study* about religion, but may not sponsor the *practice* of religion.

☐ The school may *expose* students to a diversity of religious views, but may not *impose* any particular view.

☐ The school may *educate* about all religions, but may not *promote* or *denigrate* any religion.

☐ The school may *inform* the student about various beliefs, but should not seek to *conform* him or her to any particular belief.[2]

Q: Why should study about religion be included in the public school curriculum?

A: Because religion plays a significant role in history and society, study about religion is essential to understanding both the nation and the world. Omission of facts about religion can give students the false impression that the religious life of humankind is insignificant or unimportant. Failure to understand even the basic symbols, practices, and concepts of the various religions makes much of history, literature, art, and contemporary life unintelligible.

Study about religion is also important if students are to value religious liberty, the first freedom guaranteed in the Bill of Rights. Moreover, knowledge of the roles of religion in the past and present promotes cross-cultural understanding essential to democracy and world peace.

Q: Where does study about religion belong in the curriculum?

A: Wherever it naturally arises. On the secondary level, the social studies, literature, and the arts offer many opportunities for the inclusion of information about religions—their ideas and themes. On the elementary level, natural opportunities arise in discussions of the family and community life and in instruction about festivals and different cultures. Many educators believe that integrating study about religion into existing courses is an educationally sound way to acquaint students with the role of religion in history and society.

Religion also may be taught about in special courses or units. Some secondary schools, for example, offer such courses as world religions, the Bible as literature, and the religious literature of the West and of the East.

Q: Do current textbooks teach about religion?

A: Rarely. Recent textbook studies conclude that most widely used textbooks largely ignore the role of religion in history and society. For example, readers of high school U.S. history texts learn little or nothing about the great colonial revivals, the struggles of minority faiths, the religious motivations of immigrants, the contributions of religious groups to many social movements, major episodes of religious intolerance, and many other significant events of history. Education without appropriate attention to major religious influences and themes is incomplete education.

Q: How does teaching about religion relate to the teaching of values?

A: Teaching about religion is not the same as teaching values. The former is objective, academic study; the latter involves the teaching of particular ethical viewpoints or standards of behavior.

There are basic moral values that are recognized by the population at large (e.g., honesty, integrity, justice, compassion). These values can be taught in classes through discussion, by example, and by carrying out school policies. However, teachers may not invoke religious authority.

Public schools may teach about the various religious and non-religious perspectives concerning the many complex moral issues confronting society, but such perspectives must be presented without adopting, sponsoring, or denigrating one view against another.

Q: Is it constitutional to teach the biblical account of creation in the public schools?

A: Some states have passed laws requiring that creationist theory based on the biblical account be taught in the science classroom. The courts have found these laws to be unconstitutional on the ground that they promote a particular religious view. The Supreme Court has acknowledged, however, that a variety of scientific theories about origins can be appropriately taught in the science classroom. In *Edwards* v. *Aguillard,* the Court stated:

> [T]eaching a variety of scientific theories about the origins of humankind to schoolchildren might be validly done with the clear secular intent of enhancing the effectiveness of science instruction.

Though science instruction may not endorse or promote religious doctrine, the account of creation found in various scriptures may be discussed in a religious studies class or in any course that considers religious explanations for the origin of life.

Q: How should religious holidays be treated in the classroom?

A: Carefully. Religious holidays offer excellent opportunities to teach about religions in the elementary and secondary classroom. Recognition of and information about such holidays should focus on the origin, history, and generally agreed-upon meaning of the observances. If the approach is objective, neither advancing nor inhibiting religion, it can foster among students understanding and mutual respect within and beyond the local community.

NOTES

[1] "Teaching about religion" includes consideration of the beliefs and practices of religions; the role of religion in history and contemporary society; and religious themes in music, art, and literature.

[2] This answer is based on guidelines originally published by the Public Education Religion Studies Center at Wright State University.

Religion in the Public School Curriculum: Questions and Answers is sponsored jointly by:

American Academy of Religion
Department of Religion
501 Hall of Languages
Syracuse University
Syracuse, N.Y. 13244–1170

American Association of School Administrators
1801 N. Moore St.
Arlington, Va. 22209

American Federation of Teachers
555 New Jersey Ave., N.W.
Washington, D.C. 20001

Americans United Research Foundation*
900 Silver Spring Ave.
Silver Spring, Md. 20910

Association for Supervision and Curriculum Development*
125 N. West St.
Alexandria, Va. 22314–2798

Baptist Joint Committee on Public Affairs
200 Maryland Ave., N.E.
Washington, D.C. 20002

Christian Legal Society
P.O. Box 1492
Merrifield, Va. 22116

National Association of Evangelicals
1430 K St., N.W.
Washington, D.C. 20005

National Conference of Christians and Jews
71 5th Ave.
New York, N.Y. 10003

*These organizations have materials available for teaching about religion in the public school curriculum.

National Council of Churches of Christ in the U.S.A.
475 Riverside Drive
New York, N.Y. 10115

National Council on Religion and Public Education*
Southwest Missouri State University
901 S. National Ave.
Springfield, Mo. 65804

National Council for the Social Studies*
3501 Newark St., N.W.
Washington, D.C. 20016

National Education Association
1201 16th St., N.W.
Washington, D.C. 20036

National School Boards Association
1680 Duke St.
Alexandria, Va. 22314

*These organizations have materials available for teaching about religion in the public school curriculum.

Appendix 2
Literacy in the United States: What Is the Status? What's Being Done?*
*John Micklos

There has been a lot of discussion in recent years about adult illiteracy in the United States. Depending upon whose figures you use, you might come to the conclusion that illiteracy is extremely uncommon, or you might believe that it is a problem of epidemic proportions.

U.S. Census data show an illiteracy rate of about one-half of one percent. That figure, however, represents only those people with less than six years of schooling who say that they can't read or write. The Census Bureau is quick to state that it doesn't view this as an accurate measurement of adult literacy.

At the other end of the spectrum are the estimates of people such as Jonathan Kozol who claim that 60 million adults in the U.S. are functionally illiterate. In his book, *Illiterate America,* Kozol says that illiteracy reduces the nation's Gross National Product by more than $100 billion per year. He also cites estimates claiming that it could cost at least $5 billion per year to make a real dent in the problem.

One commonly used estimate sets the number of adult illiterates in the United States at between 23 and 27 million. This estimate is based upon the Adult Performance Level study published in 1975. That study also estimated that another 34 million adults functioned "with difficulty." Based on those figures, some critics claim that there are more than 60 million functionally illiterate adults in the United States. The Coalition for Literacy has used the figure of 27 million illiterate adults in its current nationwide public awareness campaign, which is being coordinated by the Advertising Council.

What is the real extent of the problem? It's hard to say. Literacy is, as some experts point out, a rubber yardstick. Literacy levels can vary tremendously depending upon the criteria used to measure it. One problem is the difficulty in determining a definition of literacy.

Perhaps the literacy assessment of young adults currently being conducted by the National Assessment of Educational Progress (NAEP) will shed some further light on the issue. In this study, NAEP defines literacy as "using printed and written information to function in society, to achieve one's goals and to develop one's knowledge and potential."

NAEP is gathering demographic information on a sample of young adults aged 21–25 and measuring simple "core" skills, such as reading street signs and medicine labels. NAEP is also measuring some more sophisticated literacy skills of people in this age range, and findings were scheduled for release in the spring of 1986.

*These organizations have materials available for teaching about religion in the public school curriculum.

Although the exact extent of the problem may be uncertain, one thing is obvious. Everyone would like to reduce the illiteracy rate, whatever it may be. And more than ever before, concerted efforts are being made to do just that. The list of activities mentioned here is not exhaustive, but may be representative of efforts underway throughout the United States.

Federal Government

In September 1983, the federal government announced an Adult Literacy Initiative aimed at reducing adult illiteracy in the United States. The Adult Literacy Initiative is working with the Coalition for Literacy to broaden awareness of the illiteracy problem, and it is also encouraging the development of state and local literacy councils.

Through the Department of Education, the federal government funds the Adult Basic Education program at a level of $100 million per year. Literacy is also a component of the rewritten Vocational/Technical Education Act. "All of these efforts are useful and important," says IRA President John C. Manning. "But they are not enough. Among other things, the federal government should be funding research on reading for the adult reader."

Congress is also showing interest in the issue of adult illiteracy. On August 1, 1985, Manning testified before a Joint House/Senate Education subcommittee on the topic of adult illiteracy. He noted that adult illiteracy is a problem of national scope and that successful programs for teaching adults to read feature one thing in common—a teacher who cares. He stressed that teacher education programs should be more classroom-management oriented and that "methods" courses should be deemphasized.

Manning stressed several points raised in the report, *Becoming a Nation of Readers,* including the need to create a positive literacy environment. He also suggested the creation of a "Literacy Corps" as one method for combating adult illiteracy.

Also testifying at the subcommittee hearing was William Woodside, chairman and chief executive officer of American Can Company. Woodside said that he was "appalled and dismayed" by the extent of illiteracy in the United States, and he pointed out that corporations are spending "hundreds of millions of dollars annually" for in-house basic skills and literacy programs.

"Our so-called literacy gap exists at a time when changes in the labor market are increasing the premium on communication skills and when literacy standards are higher today than they were 10 years ago," added Woodside. He called upon businesses and the federal government to join together in efforts to upgrade and revitalize the public schools, calling such efforts "a strategic national investment for the 1990s."

Efforts of the Business Sector

Businesses are becoming more aware of the importance of good literacy skills in the workplace, and efforts to organize programs in this area are increasing. Harold W. McGraw, Jr., chairman of McGraw-Hill, Inc., organized the Business Council for Effective Literacy (BCEL) in 1984 to focus corporate attention on the area of adult literacy.

The BCEL produces a quarterly newsletter for business leaders, and it is now producing monographs on special issues such as volunteer tutoring and how functional illiteracy hurts business. BCEL has also provided funding to support the Coalition for Literacy's public awareness campaign.

"We've been pretty successful in creating an awareness in the business community of the problem and what can be done to help," says Dan Lacy, vice president of BCEL. "I think we need to realize that no one group alone can make a dent in the problem."

Many individual corporations are also becoming involved in supporting projects relating to literacy. These include such corporate giants as AT&T, Gulf and Western, American Can Company, Time, Inc., Exxon Corporation, Bristol-Myers, IBM and Warner Communications, as well as many others. Often, these companies provide funding and support for ongoing literacy projects that other groups have organized.

Other corporations sponsor their own literacy-related projects. For example, Pizza Hut, Inc. sponsored the "Book It!" program nationwide from October 1985 through March 1986. More than seven million children were expected to participate in the program, which rewarded children for achieving extracurricular reading goals set by their teacher. Students who met their goals received a free Personal Pan Pizza at participating Pizza Hut restaurants. For further information about the "Book It!" program, contact: Pizza Hut, Inc., Corporate Communications, 9111 East Douglas, PO Box 428, Wichita, Kansas 62701, USA.

In the fall of 1985, the Six Flags Corporation sponsored "Read-To-Succeed." Several of the Six Flags theme parks throughout the United States participated in this program, which encouraged students to read more both in and out of school. Noted cartoonist Chuck Jones, creator of Bugs Bunny and Daffy Duck, provided illustrations and artwork for the program. Students who participated in the program received prizes and admissions to participating Six Flags theme parks. For further information about the "Read-To-Succeed" program, contact: Lovetta Kramer, Director of Corporate Communications, Six Flags Corporation, 8700 West Bryn Mawr Avenue, Chicago, Illinois 60631, USA.

IRA is represented on the advisory panels of both the "Book It!" and "Read-To-Succeed" programs by Director of Research Alan E. Farstrup.

Newspapers

Newspapers are also playing an active role in promoting literacy. "Newspapers have always been involved with and concerned about literacy in our country," says Linda Skover, manager of educational services for the American Newspaper Publishers Association Foundation. "We feel it's extremely important that we have a literate society—citizens who read and who know what is going on."

IRA and the American Newspaper Publishers Association cosponsor an annual "Newspaper in Education Week" to stress the use of newspapers in the classroom. Furthermore, more than 650 newspapers throughout the United States and Canada participate in ongoing Newspaper in Education programs. Many newspapers have launched innovative projects. For example, Jan Fenholt, NIE coordinator for the *Columbus Dispatch* in Ohio, developed a program which uses newspapers to teach literacy skills to prison inmates.

In the spring of 1985, the American Newspaper Publishers Association Foundation sponsored a meeting which brought together representatives of newspapers and newspaper-related organizations, education agencies, and literacy groups to brainstorm ideas for ways newspapers can promote literacy. Ideas included creating tutoring programs using newspaper employees, providing more news coverage relating to literacy and education, and publishing easy-to-read sections in the newspaper.

The Gannett Foundation is providing $500,000 to help combat adult illiteracy. Most of the budget for the program is earmarked to support community volunteer tutoring programs and related projects. To date, more than 20 local literacy grants have been awarded.

One project with national ramifications is a conference sponsored by the Gannett Foundation which brought together specialists in applications of microcomputers to adult reading instruction. This meeting took place in Minnesota in November, 1985. Conference goals included setting up a nationwide network through which literacy groups can share computer tutoring methods.

For further information about the Gannett Foundation programs, contact: Christy C. Bulkeley, Vice President, Gannett Foundation, Lincoln Tower, Rochester, New York 14604, USA.

Literacy Programs

There are some national programs which operate to help adult illiterates. These programs, however, reach only a small percentage of adult illiterates in the United States. Here are some of the prominent national programs.

The Coalition for Literacy, of which IRA is a charter member, was founded by a number of education organizations to raise national awareness of the problem of adult illiteracy. The Coalition is currently conducting a national awareness campaign through the auspices of the Advertising Council. Public service announcements have appeared in both print and broadcast media since the beginning of 1985.

People interested in becoming involved in the battle against illiteracy can utilize the Coalition for Literacy's national literacy hotline. Established on November 1, 1983 as part of the national awareness campaign, the hotline had handled approximately 33,000 calls through July 1985. More than 20,000 of the calls were from potential volunteers, 8,000 were from potential students, and the rest were requests for general information.

For further information on the literacy hotline, write to: Contact Literacy Center, PO Box 81826, Lincoln, Nebraska 68501–1826, USA or call (800) 228–8813.

Laubach Literacy Action, the U.S. program of Laubach Literacy International, is a network of 50,000 volunteers who provide tutoring in basic literacy skills to adult illiterates in 46 states. Laubach volunteer tutors work with approximately 60,000 adults in 600 communities each year. The Laubach program emphasizes one-to-one and small group tutoring. For further information about the Laubach program, contact: Laubach Literacy International, 1320 Jamesville Avenue, Box 131, Syracuse, New York 13210, USA.

Another major program is that of the Literacy Volunteers of America, Inc. (LVA). Founded in 1962 in Syracuse, New York, LVA now has 200 chapters in 31 states. More than 30,000 tutors and students are currently involved in LVA's basic reading and English as a second language programs, which use the one-to-one tutoring method.

LVA and the Gannett Foundation joined together to create a tutor's handbook using the daily newspaper as a means of teaching reading and survival skills. The handbook is entitled "Read All About It! Tutor Adults with the Daily Newspaper." For further information about LVA, contact: Literacy Volunteers of America, 404 Oak Street, Syracuse, New York 13203, USA.

A new nationwide initiative, "Battle Against Illiteracy," was launched this June by the Christian Broadcasting Network, Inc. (CBN). CBN plans to establish "Heads Up" literacy centers in a number of major cities throughout the United States. For further information about the "Heads Up" program, contact: CBN Center, Virginia Beach, Virginia 23463, USA.

Another program, Reading is Fundamental (RIF), attempts to stem adult illiteracy by generating reading interest among children. RIF operates on the principle that youngsters will read if they have interesting books to call their own.

Founded in 1966, RIF now has 3,300 local umbrella organizations. RIF programs currently involve 99,000 volunteers and serve nearly 2.3 million children. Since 1966, RIF has provided more than 65 million books to youngsters. For further information about RIF, contact: Reading Is Fundamental, Department I, 600 Maryland Avenue, SW, Suite 500, Smithsonian Institution, Washington, D.C. 20560.

Conclusion

This article is by no means exhaustive; it merely seeks to indicate the level of interest in the issue of adult literacy in the United States and point out some activities currently underway. IRA supports efforts to improve literacy, but does not endorse any particular method or materials for combating adult illiteracy.

Coalition for Literacy Seeks Support

The Coalition for Literacy, of which IRA is a charter member, supports literacy projects such as the national literacy awareness campaign and a national hotline number. The Coalition is now seeking one-time, two-year members to help sponsor its activities. There are a number of membership categories.

Sponsoring member	US$1,000 or more
Sustaining member	US$ 500
Contributing member	US$ 100
Supporting member	US$ 50
Associate member	US$ 10

All members will receive quarterly written information on the activities of the Coalition for Literacy, and all members will be invited to an annual membership meeting. All Coalition memberships are tax deductible.

The Coalition for Literacy operates under the fiscal management of the American Library Association. Make checks payable to the Coalition for Literacy and send them to: Coalition for Literacy, 50 East Huron Street, Chicago, Illinois 60611, USA.

Appendix 3

Content IRI Report*

*Carolyn L. Lauron. Used with permission.

Taffel, Alexander, Ph.D.
Physics It's Methods and Meanings, Allyn
and Bacon, Inc., 1981, pp. 269–271.

A N S W E R K E Y

Name: _____

Class: _____

Date: _____

Content IRI

Part I: Reading

Preparation/Motivation:

Have you ever wondered what happens to ocean waves as they move toward the shore? They aren't the same large, roaring waves you see and hear in the distant; or are they? Read the following paragraphs and discover what can happen to ocean waves as they make their approach to the shore.

15–11 Law of Reflection

When the reflecting wall is very large compared to the wavelengths of the water waves falling upon it, the waves obey a simple law of reflection. This law can readily be observed by means of a series of parallel straight-line wave fronts.

A series of parallel straight-line wave fronts is generated in a ripple tank and directed so that the waves fall obliquely upon a straight barrier. Note that the waves are reflected after they strike the barrier, moving in the direction shown in Fig. 15.6. The waves falling upon the barrier are called *incident waves.* Those that are reflected from the barrier are called *reflected waves.*

Consider the path of a typical ray such as *AB,* which is perpendicular to the incident wave fronts and is called an *incident ray.* After reflection, *AB* turns in the direction *BC* perpendicular to the reflected wave fronts. *BC* is called a *reflected ray.* Let *NB* be the perpendicular to the reflecting wall at *B. NB* is called a *normal.* The angle between the incident ray *AB* and the normal is called the *angle of incidence.* The angle between the reflected ray *BC* and the normal is called the *angle of reflection.* It is seen that, on reflection, a ray obeys the following law: *the angle of reflection is equal to the angle of incidence.*

This law is general and holds true for all possible angles of incidence and for waves of all wavelengths.

*These organizations have materials available for teaching about religion in the public school curriculum.

15-12 Refraction of Water Waves

The speed of water waves depends upon the depth of the water and decreases as the water becomes less deep. When water waves pass from deep water to shallower water or vice versa, the change in their speed usually causes them to change direction sharply. The sudden changing of the direction of the waves is called *refraction*.

Refraction may be illustrated in a ripple tank by lining part of the bottom of the tank with a triangular piece of glass as shown in Fig. 15.7. The water in the tank is now less deep above the glass triangle than it is everywhere else.

When a series of parallel straight waves is now generated at the deep end of the tank, they advance, break, and change direction as they pass into the less deep water. The typical ray *AB* changes direction sharply on crossing the boundary between the deeper and less deep water and takes the new direction *BC*. The ray is said to be refracted as it crosses the boundary between the two water depths. *AB* is called the incident ray and *BC* is called the refracted ray.

15-13 Superposition and Interference

Different waves can travel over a water surface at the same time. If two sets of circular waves are generated at two different points in the pan of water at the same time, each set appears simply to pass through the other. Actually, the effects of the two sets of waves on any small mass of water over which they pass at the same time combine by a process called *superposition*.

Consider a point on the water over which both sets of waves are passing. If a crest of the first set of waves arrives at the given point at the same time as a crest of the second set of waves, the waves will assist each other to produce an especially high crest. At that point, the amplitude of the new crest is equal to the sum of the amplitudes of the two superimposed crests.

If troughs of both sets of waves arrive at the given point at the same time, they will again assist each other to produce an especially large trough equal in amplitude to the sum of the amplitudes of the two superimposed troughs. In these two instances, the two waves are exactly "in step" at the given point and are said to be *in phase*. The net effect of such waves in phase is to assist each other. Such waves are said to *interfere constructively* with each other. (See Fig. 15.8).

If a crest of either set of waves arrives at the given point at the same time as a trough of the other set of waves, the waves will cancel out all or part of each other's effects. The net amplitude produced by the two waves will be equal to the difference between their individual amplitudes and in the direction of the larger one. If the amplitudes of the waves are equal, their net effect is to cancel each other out. Waves that are "in opposite step" with each other in this manner are said to be *in opposite phase* and are said to *interfere destructively* with each other. (See. Fig. 15.9).

An interference pattern formed by two sets of waves may be made by holding the forefinger and middle finger about 5 centimeters apart and dipping both fingers at a regular rate into a rectangular pan of water at a position close to the middle of one of the long walls of the pan. Two sets of half-circular waves are formed and interfere with each other to make a pattern of crisscrossing waves. Where the waves intersect in phase, they produce extra-large crests or troughs. Where they intersect in opposite phase, they tend to cancel each other.

(Please note that diagrams are not shown.)

Questions: Now that you have completed the reading selection, write your answers to the following questions.

(V)   1. Such waves are said to *interfere constructively* with each other.

   Interfere constructively means: (the net effect of two waves in phase to assist each other.)

(I)   2. Other than ocean depth and wave speed, what factors would affect wave refraction?

   (Tides, currents, movement of the ocean floor, and weather.)

(F)   3. What causes waves to change direction sharply?

   (The change in speed of waves as they pass from deeper to shallower water and vice versa.)

(V)   4. Actually, the effects of two sets of waves on any small mass of water over which they pass at the same time combine by a process of superposition.

   Superposition means: (A process in which two sets of waves on any small mass of water pass at the same time and combine.)

(F)   5. What two components determine an angle of incidence?

   (Ray AB)   (Normal)

(I)   6. Why might it be important to know that the angle of reflection is equal to the angle of incidence?

   (To control the reflection of sound waves for concerts or public address systems and to adjust light waves to hit a certain target to draw attention.)

(V)   7. The ray is said to be *refracted* as it crosses the boundary between the two water depths.

   Refracted means: (sudden change of the direction of waves.)

(F)   8. In superposition, what is the amplitude of a large trough equal to?

   (The sum of the amplitudes of the two superimposed troughs.)

(V)   9. NB is called *normal*.

Normal means: (perpendicular to the reflecting barrier.)

(I)   10. How would you think opposite-in-step waves are created?

(By releasing the second set of waves a few seconds after the first set.)

Part II: Reading/Study Skills

A. *Parts of Text:*
   1. When was this book published? By whom? (Copyright)   (Publisher)

   2. Where would you find the answers to the problems presented at the end of selected sections in chapter? (Answers to the Test Yourself Problems)

   3. Where does the text define the boldfaced terms at the end of each chapter? (Glossary)

   4. Where would you find the table of Physical Constants? (Appendix)

   5. Where would you find the chapters dealing with the Methods of Science and Measurement? (Table of Contents)

B. *Interpreting Graphics:*
   1. What is the topic of this diagram? (Reflection of waves)

   2. What does the boxed area represent? (Ripple tank)

   3. What combination of rays represents the angle of incidence? (AB and NB)

   4. What combination of rays represents the angle of reflection? (CB and NB)

   5. What name is attributed to the succession of horizontal lines generated from the bottom of the diagram? (Incident waves)

C. *Translate Symbols or Formulas:*
   1. What is meant by $v = v + at$? (Velocity equals the sum of the initial velocity and the product of the acceleration and time.)

   2. What do the following represent?

N (Newton)   J (Joule)   K (Kelvin)

r (Radius)   G (Gravitational constant)   V (Volume/Velocity)

f (Force)   Δ (Delta)   π (Pi)

3. If pressure is held constant, which formula would you use?

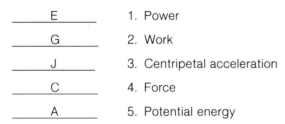

$$\underline{\hspace{3cm}} \quad P_1V_1 = P_2V_2$$

$$\underline{\hspace{3cm}} \quad (P_1V_1)/T_1 = (P_2V_2)/T_2$$

$$\underline{\hspace{3cm}} \quad P_1/T_1 = P_2/T_2$$

$$\underline{\hspace{2.5cm}X\hspace{0.5cm}} \quad V_1/T_1 = V_2/T_2$$

4. Match the following:

$\underline{\hspace{1.5cm}E\hspace{1.5cm}}$ 1. Power

$\underline{\hspace{1.5cm}G\hspace{1.5cm}}$ 2. Work

$\underline{\hspace{1.5cm}J\hspace{1.5cm}}$ 3. Centripetal acceleration

$\underline{\hspace{1.5cm}C\hspace{1.5cm}}$ 4. Force

$\underline{\hspace{1.5cm}A\hspace{1.5cm}}$ 5. Potential energy

a. mgh	b. $(.5)mv^2$	c. ma	d. mg
e. work/time	f. output/input	g. $f \times d$	
h. $d \times a$	i. v/t	j. v^2/r	

Date Administered: Wednesday, 21 March 1990
Academy of Our Lady of Guam
Agana, Guam
4th Period
Physics (Honors class for Seniors)
Mr. Wai Chi Lau, Instructor

I wasn't quite sure what time 4th period started. I was too nervous and excited about going to my alma mater to remember whether Mr. Lau said 11:00 or 11:15. I didn't want to take the chance of getting there late or too early so I decided to leave campus at 10:50.

I arrived at Academy around 11:00. There weren't any ample parking spaces for visitors, so I parked in a teacher's slot and left a note on my dashboard informing him where I could be located if he needed me to move my car.

It was almost uncomfortable returning to my old high school. I remember running up the stairs as a student less than three years ago. Now, I was carefully walking up the same steep staircase as a student teacher.

As I reached the top of the stairs, I stopped a girl and asked her what period it was. She stared at me strangely and said, "It's only third period. In a few minutes, the bell will ring for fourth period." I thanked her and she walked away with the same strange look on her face.

I knew that if the bell rang, I would be pushed and shoved aside by the more than 400 girls making way in the seven foot wide hallway. As if he had heard me, Mr. Lau opened his classroom door and invited me into his 3rd period Computer Programming class. All the girls were busy with their printouts but spared enough time to look at this new face encroaching upon their territory.

Mr. Lau commented that he was glad I was early. He asked me to refresh his memory of what I planned to do today. I grabbed a chair near his desk and proceeded to explain the Content IRI. I gave him a copy and went through the CIRI step by step with him and gave insights as to the purpose of each section. Just when I had finished, the bell rang and the third period class filed out the "exit" door. A few minutes later, the room was filled with the students who make up Mr. Lau's fourth period Physics class.

While Mr. Lau took role, I could not help noticing the inquisitive and analyzing looks the girls gave me. After a short introduction, Mr. Lau directed the girls' attention to me. I told them that what they were about to do today was a Content Informal Reading Inventory which will measure their special needs for this class. They seemed uncomfortable at first but after I passed out the inventory and walked them through each section, they felt a little better. When I announced that the inventory would not be graded but would be used as a tool to develop a means to meet their individual needs, a sigh of relief permeated the room. I reminded them that it was of utmost importance that they do their best so that their true strengths and needs can be determined. I then asked, "What questions do you have?" "None." "Then, you may begin."

After thirty-five minutes, one girl turned in the CIRI. A few minutes later, the rest followed. At first, I thought that the CIRI was too easy. But I knew that the questions were appropriate for their grade level, so I thought that maybe they were all just gifted. As soon as the last girl settled back into her chair, she said, "May we study for our next exam now, Miss Lauron?" It then struck me that this was finals week for the girls. All the girls leaned forward—anxiously waiting for my response. I smiled at them and said, "Yes, you may study for your next exam."

After class, I walked with Mr. Lau down the stairs. He apologized for not informing me sooner that this was exam week. It apparently slipped his mind since he administered his exam early. I told him that we all forget sometimes but I was glad that I was later made aware of it. I knew that I would have to take it into account when reviewing the inventory.

Content IRI Profile Analysis

The first Content IRI Profile shows the raw scores of each student with respect to the different aspects of the CIRI. Partial credit was allotted to the students who answered the questions with the concept in mind but

Content IRI Profile

Student ID No.	Part I			Part II		
	Vocabulary 4 out of 4	Fact 2 out of 3	Inference 2 out of 3	Part of Text 80%	Graphics 100%	Symbols & Formulas 90%
1) 90-1	3	2.5	2	60%	100%	87.5%
2) 90-2	4	1.5	1	60%	100%	93.75%
3) 90-3	4	2	0	80%	60%	81.25%
4) 90-4	4	3	1	25%	100%	93.75%
5) 90-5	4	3	3	60%	80%	100%

could not express the answer in proper form. The need for the students to study for an exam was taken into consideration as a major reason for this failure.

Part I of the CIRI was graded on the basis of the number of questions answered correctly. The grades given in Part II of the CIRI were based on the percentage of correct answers given. Each blank was given equal consideration compared to the total number of blanks. Thus, Percentage = [(Number of Correct Responses)/(Total Number of Possible Correct Responses)] × 100.

The second Content IRI Profile shows the mastery skill of each student with regard to their raw scores in each aspect of the CIRI. The raw scores accumulated in the first Content IRI Profile were not rounded to the nearest whole number. Instead, these scores were taken at face value and compared to the criteria stated. This comparison lead to the allotment of gold stars to students who attained the criteria goals.

The most right column states the individual needs of each student based on their overall performance on the CIRI. Students who received at least one star in the areas of symbols & formulas and/or graphics were rated as needing "Some" assistance. Students who attained four stars overall were rated as needing "No" assistance. Students who have special individual needs were rated with "Yes." There were the students who

Content IRI Profile

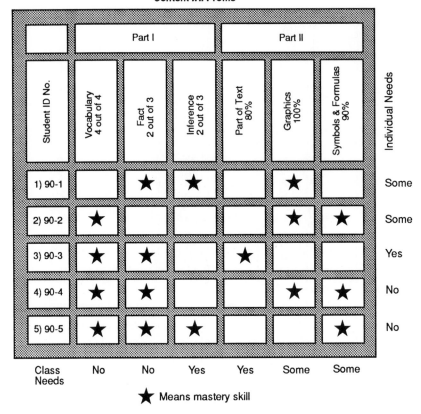

Student ID No.	Part I			Part II			Individual Needs
	Vocabulary 4 out of 4	Fact 2 out of 3	Inference 2 out of 3	Part of Text 80%	Graphics 100%	Symbols & Formulas 90%	
1) 90-1		★	★		★		Some
2) 90-2	★				★	★	Some
3) 90-3	★	★		★			Yes
4) 90-4	★	★			★	★	No
5) 90-5	★	★	★			★	No
Class Needs	No	No	Yes	Yes	Some	Some	

★ Means mastery skill

successfully completed all sections except symbols & formulas and graphics. Clearly, the symbols & formulas and graphics sections were the most important since they would determine success in this class.

The last row gives the overall class' needs in each of the CIRI sections. Four stars in any column were rated as "No"; meaning no dire need for assistance. Three stars were rated as having "Some" need for assistance while two stars or less were rated as "Yes." The inference and parts of text sections appear to be the most difficult sections for the students. Overall, however, the class needs "Some" assistance to succeed in this course.

The last two diagrams are bar graphs of each part of the CIRI. These graphs are an additional aid in seeing the standing of one student to the overall standing of the class in each corresponding section of the two parts.

Content IRI Profile

Overall Performance on Part I

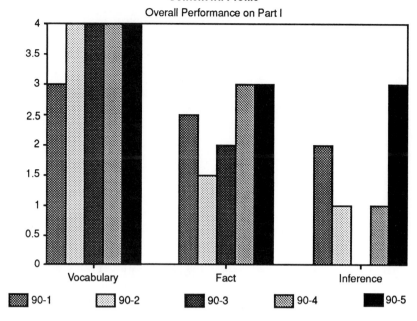

Content IRI Profile

Overall Performance on Part II

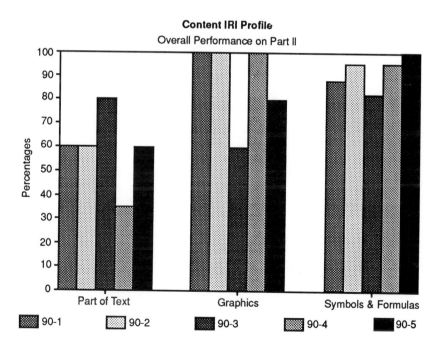

Appendix 4
Checklist for Developing Instructional Materials or Tests for Reading Rate Adaptability*
*Marian J. Tonjes

There is ample evidence of the need for developing instructional materials and tests that reflect the principles consistent with the concept of reading adaptability. The following is proposed as a guideline for teachers and curriculum specialists when selecting or developing reading rate adaptability materials.

> **I SET**

____ A. *PRACTICE:*   Is practice provided initially in reading similar material and answering similar questions? (warmups)

____ B. *PURPOSE:*   Is the purpose clearly stated? (e.g., main ideas, details)

OR

Are a variety of purposes proposed, allowing the reader to select?

Do readers accept and hold on to the purpose?

____ C. *STRATEGIES:*   Are strategies suggested based on the purpose selected? (the degree of effectiveness needed)

____ D. *TIME:*   Are readers asked to estimate the amount of time needed in terms of WPM (words per minute); time per page or time per selection?

____ E. *LENGTH:*   Are selections long enough to approximate actual reading tasks? (2,000+ words)

> **II MATERIAL READABILITY**

____ A. *SEQUENCE:*   Are the selections sequenced from easy to difficult in terms of reading levels as determined by readability formulas?

____ B. *CONCEPT LOAD:*   Has the material been selected with an eye to the density of concepts or their abstractness?

*These organizations have materials available for teaching about religion in the public school curriculum.

442

	C. *TYPOGRAPHICAL FEATURES:*	Has good use been made of such structuring devices as introductory previews, summaries, subheadings, and graphics?
	D. *MODES OF DIS-COURSE:*	Is a range of modes of discourse included, such as the personal essay, report, explanation?
	E. *INTEREST:*	In practice materials may students select the material which appears to be of most interest?
	F. *BACKGROUND EXPERIENCE:*	Is some connection made between reader's prior knowledge of the subject or topic and the comprehension score attained? (Do students check before reading whether the subject is known well, slightly, or not at all?)

III CONTENT ORIENTATION

	A. *SIMILARITY:*	Is material similar to actual textual demands of readers?
	B. *VARIETY:*	Is there a variety of content subjects from which to choose? (science, home economics, poetry, etc.)

IV RATES

Do materials include articles conducive to using one or a combination of the following rates?

	A. *SCANNING:*	For particular clues to answer specific questions
	B. *SKIMMING:*	Combining scanning and rapid reading to preview, get an overview, or gist
	C. *RAPID READING:*	To gain a general understanding, or main ideas using continuous contact with the text
	D. *PERSONAL READING:*	For enjoyment, relaxation, or general information
	E. *ANALYTICAL-EVALUATIVE READING:*	Detailed, intensive examination of content, critically analyzing and using higher-level reasoning
	F. *STUDY READING:*	Using a planned attack, a combination of techniques such as found in the study systems SQ3R or PQRST

V COMPREHENSION CHECK

____ A. Are questions at the lower, literal level? (Higher-order questions are important, too.)

____ B. Is provision made for responding without looking back as well as allowing readers to reread for answers?

____ C. Is the value of rereading stressed by such exercises as having readers skim first for the gist and then reread for details?

____ D. In lieu of responding to questions is there ever an option of asking readers to summarize the main points?

____ E. Is there provision for the reader to note after reading the external environmental conditions (noise, heat, etc.) and their level of anxiety or need?

VI ADAPTABILITY

____ A. Is internal adaptability (variety of rate within a selection) recognized in some manner? This can be accomplished by:

—asking students (after practice) to mark where they are in their reading at intervals of every 15 seconds,

—asking students to estimate how many times they slowed down to better comprehend or skimmed over a section.

____ B. Is negative adaptability (going against normal expectations) accounted for by asking if readers ever sped up for study reading or slowed down for personal reading when their purposes did not require it?

From Tonjes, Marian J., "Adaptable Rates and Strategies for Efficient Comprehension: The Effective Reader" in *The Reading Connection,* Gwen Bray and Anthony Pugh, eds. (London: Ward Lock Educational, 1980).

Appendix 5

The Language of Science:
Some Common Root Words and Affixes*

	Some Common Root Word and Affixes		
Root or Affix	**Meaning**	**Example**	**Write Your Word Here**
a-, an	without	anaerobic	
ab-	away from	abnormal	
ad-	to, toward	adhere	
aero-	air	aerobic	
ambi- amphi-	both	ambidextrous	
ante-	before	anterior	
anthropo-	man, human	anthropology	
anti-	against, opposite	antigen	
aqua-	water	aquatic	
astro-, aster-	star	astronomy	
auto-	self	automatic	
avi-	bird	aviary	
baro-	pressure	barometer	
bene-, bon-	good	benefit	
bi-	two, twice	biped	
bio-	life	biology	
capit, cephalo-	head	decapitate	
cardio-	heart	cardiogram	
carni-, caro-	flesh	carnivorous	
chlor	green	chloroplast	
chrom-	color	chromatin	
chrono-	time	chronology	
circum-	around	circumference	
com-, con-, co	together, with	combine	
contra, contro-	against	contraception	
corpus	body	corpse	
cyclo-	circular	cyclotron	
cyto-	cell, hollow	cytoplasm	
dermato-, derm	skin	epidermis	
di-, dis-	two	dissect	
dorsi-, dorso-	back	dorsal	
entomo-	insect	entomology	
epi-	upon, outer	epidermis	
erg-	work	energy	
ex-	out, from	excrete	
eu-	good	euphoria	
frater	brother	fraternal	

*These organizations have materials available for teaching about religion in the public school curriculum.

Root or Affix	Meaning	Example	Write Your Word Here
gen-	race, kind		
	born, produce	generation	
geo-	earth	geology	
germ-	sprout	germinate	
graph	write, record	graphite	
gyneco-, gyn	female	gynecology	
helio-	sun	heliograph	
hemi-	half	hemisphere	
hemo-	blood	hemoglobin	
herb	plant	herbivorous	
hetero-	mixed	heterogeneous	
hexa-	six	hexagon	
homo-	same, alike	homogeneous	
hydr(o)-	water	dehydrate	
hyper-	over, excess	hyperactive	
hypo-	under, less	hypodermic	
ichthyo-	fish	ichthyology	
in-	not	insomnia	
in-, en-	into	inbreed	
inter-	between	intercellular	
intra-	within	intramuscular	
iso-	equal	isometric	
-itis	inflammation	tonsillitis	
junct	join	junction	
kine-	movement	kinetic	
lact(o)-	milk	lactic	
-logy	science, study of	biology	
lunar	moon	lunarian	
-lysis,-lyze	break up	analysis	
macro-	large	macroscopic	
magni-	great, large	magnitude	
meta	change, beyond	metaphase	
-meter	measure	altimeter	
micro-	small	microscope	
mono-	one, single	monocyte	
morpho-	form	metamorphosis	
mortal, morti-	death	mortality	
multi-	many	multicellular	
natal	birth	postnatal	
nebul	cloudy	nebulous	
neuro-	nerve	neuron	
non-	not	nonnitrogenous	
octo-	eight	octopus	
oculo-, ophthalmo	eye	oculist	
omni-	all	omnivorous	
ornitho-	bird	ornithology	
ortho-	straight	orthopterous	
osteo-	bone	osteopath	
patho-	disease, feeling	pathology	
pedi-, pod	foot, footed	anthropod	

Some Common Root Word and Affixes

Root or Affix	Meaning	Example	Write Your Word Here
per-	through	permeate	
phono-	sound, voice	phonograph	
photo-	light	photosynthesis	
physio-	organic	physiology	
poly-	many, much	polyembryony	
pos, pon	place, put	position	
post-	after	postnatal	
pre-	before	prediagnosis	
pseudo-	false	pseudopod	
psycho-	mind	psychology	
pro-	for, forward	procreate	
pteron	winged	lepidoptera	
quad	four	quadruped	
retro-	backward	retroactive	
rhodo	rose, red	rhodolite	
-scope	view, examine	microscope	
sect	part, divide	dissect	
som(a)	body	chromosome	
somn	sleep	insomnia	
son(i)	sound	supersonic	
sphere	round, globe	spherical	
sub-	under	subconscious	
syn-	together, with	synthesis	
tele-	far, distant	telescope	
ten-	to hold	tenaculum	
thermo-	heat	thermometer	
trans-	across	transmutation	
un-	not	undeveloped	
under-	below	underactive	
vita-	life	vitamin	
-vor(e)	eat	herbivorous	
zoo-	animal	zoology	

*From Piercey, Dorothy, *Reading Activities in Content Areas: An Ideabook for Middle and Secondary Schools* (Boston: Allyn and Bacon, 1976), pp. 26–29. Used with permission.

APPENDIX 6

Directed Reading-Thinking Activity Lesson Plan (DRTA)
by Carolyn L. Lauron, P.O. Box 9615, Tamuning, Guam 96911

Directed Reading-Thinking Activity Lesson Plan

Topic: Optics
Class: 4th Period Physics
Seniors/Honors

Objectives:

1. to improve ray tracing/geometric skills
2. to stimulate interest in reflective devices
3. to encourage interaction
4. to provide insight into ray tracing theory

Time	Student	Teacher	Materials
10 min	Respond	I. Prereading (Preparation/Motivation) — Has anyone looked into a mirror lately? When? — How many of you have been fishing? What was it like? Share some experiences with us. — How many have been to the "Fun House" at the Carnival or Amusement Park? What was it like? What did it feel like when you saw multiple images of yourself? Or a distorted image?	Mirrors, other reflective objects
5 min	Listen/Respond	All these topics are related to OPTICS (write term on board). What do you think this term means? (List answers on board.)	
10 min	Respond	— Where would you find the book's definition of optics? — Which chapters are related to optics? — Where would you find the answers to the problems at the end of each section? — Where would you find the value of the speed of light constant (c)?	

10 min	Read	II. Directed Silent Reading

II. Directed Silent Reading
Purpose Statement: While reading, think of how optics relates to geometry. Try and recall the experiences you have had with mirrors or other reflecting objects and how these relate to the study of optics.
Carefully analyze the diagrams provided.
What questions do you have?

pp. 337 (Fig. 18.8)
pp. 338 (18.12)
pp. 346 (Fig. 18.17)
pp. 347 (18.23)

15 min — Group Work

III. Post reading (Follow-up/ Enrichment)
Form in pairs. With the materials provided, experiment with the different set-ups of optical devices in your book. Using the formula $1/P + 1/Q = 1/F$, measure P (distance from object to mirror/lens), Q (distance from image to mirror/ lens), and calculate F (focus) and the Radius of Curvature. Share observations with your classmates. Feel free to call our attention to your discoveries.
Do these observations coincide with what is presented in the book?
Use the sheet of paper I am passing out to list your observations. Be sure to CLEARLY PRINT YOUR NAME IN THE TOP RIGHT HAND CORNER.

Yardsticks
Concave Mirror
Converging Lens
Candle/Matches
Rulers
White Screen

(Extra Time)

Help your partner in solving the following problem: If the radius of curvature of a concave mirror is 5 cm, and an object is placed 10 cm from the vertex of the mirror, calculate the distance of the image from the vertex and the focal point.
  Answer: $q = 10/3$ $f = 5/2$

What other questions on optics and optical instruments would you like me to touch on?

DRTA Report

Date Administered: Wednesday, 25 April 1990
Academy of Our Lady of Guam
Agana, Guam
4th Period
Physics (Honors class for Seniors)
Mr. Wai Chi Lau, Instructor
Subject: Optics

I was very excited about going back to Academy and teaching the girls about optics. I woke up so early in the morning to once again test the optical instruments before bringing them into the classroom. I was having so much fun playing with them that I was a few minutes late for my 9:00 A.M. class.

When I arrived at Academy, it was 10:45 A.M. I had given myself enough time to see Mr. Lau and to answer any questions he had for me. Honestly speaking, I was also hoping for some verbal support from him.

As I entered the classroom, I received the same puzzled looks that greeted me more than a month ago. The girls were intrigued by the stranger wearing civilian clothing. I continued to smile at them as they stared on. Mr. Lau was glad to see me. He wanted to see exactly what I was planning for his class. I showed him my detailed lesson plan and answered the two questions he had. Just as we finished, the bell rang.

Two girls entered the classroom, smiled at me, and sat down. As Mr. Lau approached the front of the room, one girl whispered something to him. He looked a little surprised. He then approached me and told me that three girls were absent and my class would be composed of two students. I was startled at first but as I thought about it, I realized it would be easier for the two who were present to be more personal and open with me.

After a brief introduction by Mr. Lau, I started teaching. I could see the smile on the girls' faces when I tried to get them motivated. For a while, the classroom was filled with funny stories of "The Fun House" mirrors, fishing around Guam, and the habit Academy girls have of looking in the mirror. It was great hearing them participate and share. I really felt a bonding among us—as if we now had a special relationship.

Everything went as planned according to my DRTA. I could tell that the girls were quite interested in the formation of images by a concave mirror and a magnifying glass. They started getting a little noisy but that was expected. I did not expect for one girl to say she was going to show her little brother when she got home. Apparently, her brother was a "whiz" at science, and she wanted to tease his mind with the combination of optical lenses and mirrors.

When the girls completed the group work, we had 10 minutes left. Luckily, I had planned an extra activity for them to enjoy. They were to help each other solve a problem in optics and to explain it if they wanted. They were quite fast in solving the college level problem. I was very surprised that these girls were functioning at such a high level.

After one girl explained how she arrived at her answer, I answered some questions they had for me. We were talking about all sorts of optical instruments: microscopes, film projectors, telescopes. We were in the classroom talking until five minutes into their lunch hour. It was truly a great experience for me and a fulfilling one for the girls.

Mr. Lau and I walked down to our cars in the parking lot. He invited me back to teach the other three girls who missed the class. I agreed and told him I would be happy to return. He said I did a nice job and motivated the girls quite well.

I left Academy at about 12:00 noon with a smile on my face, a strong sense of relief, and a feeling of accomplishment.

Appendix 7
A Method for Learning How to Write Research Papers in Any Content Area*
*Enid E Haag, Education Librarian, Western Washington University

MODULE 1 Systematic Approach to Using Library Resources
Objective
To introduce pertinent reference sources in the subject area.
Activity
After an explanation of how to do a systematic search is given, students should be shown the location of the references in the subject field along with a brief explanation of what may be found in each reference. Working from a special subject bibliography, students will begin a systematic search of the literature, starting with a general encyclopedia and working into the special encyclopedia available in the subject field (i.e., on the topic of volcanoes, *Encyclopedia of Science and Technology* to *The Planet We Live On, An Illustrated Encyclopedia*). As students go through these references, they will develop a list of synonyms for their topic, a list of broad topics under which their topic falls, and a list of related topics. In certain content areas, technical terms will be included.
Assessment
Students will keep a running log or diary of their search strategy. This will include date, name of reference, and topic researched. Running log or diary should be kept on a 4 × 6 card. (The log or diary is useful when students must retrace steps to locate information not taken down on note cards, etc. See figures A7.1 and A7.2.)

MODULE 2 Using the CD-ROM
Objective
To introduce the CD-ROM data bases available in the school media center.
Activity
Still using the list of synonyms developed in Module 1, have students complete the worksheet for the CD-ROM (see figure A7.3). After the worksheet is complete, students will run their searches on available CD-ROM data bases.
Assessment
Teachers work individually with all students to see that they have identified main concepts within the problem being researched. Each student should run a copy of the search strategy from the CD-ROM data base and include it with their diary or log.

*These organizations have materials available for teaching about religion in the public school curriculum.

Figure A7.1

Example of diary or log of search on the topic of volcanoes.

Date	Reference	Vol. Page	Topic
10/1/80	World Book Encyclopedia, Vol. 20, pp. 342-347		Volcano
10/1/80	McGraw-Hill Encyclop. of Science & Tech. Vol. 14, p404		Volcanic Mud flow
		Vol. 7, p.17	Volcanic rocks
		Vol. 4, p384	Volcanic soil
		Vol. 10, p. 493, 494	Volcanic vent
10/2/80	Van Nostrand's Scientific Encyclop. pp. 2303-2304		Volcano
10/2/80	McGraw-Hill Science Yearbook 1977 p.171		Volcanic dust
	" " " " 1979 p.269,		Volcano
		p.302, pp. 244-6	
10/3/80	The Planet We Live On, An Illustrated Encyclopedia of Earth Science	p.462	Volcanic chimney
		p.463	Volcanic Eruption
		p.465	Volcanic neck
		p.467	Volcano

Figure A7.2

Example of bibliographic card (numbered 14) and of a note card (14a) from the magazine, *Science News*.

14   Science News Goes to the Mountain; Volcano! the right to research. SCIENCE NEWS, 118:51, pp. 58-63. July 26, 1980.

> 14a   *Science News*, July 26, 1980; p.58
> all Ring of Fire volcanoes have the same geological origin.

Figure A7.3
Search strategy worksheet for CD-ROM data bases.

Search Strategy Worksheet for CD-ROM
Before using the CD-ROM, think
through your question carefully.
This worksheet will help you.

What is the problem or question you are researching?

If you were looking up information on this problem or question in a periodical index, what topic would you look under? Write the topic after ''1'' below. Imagine yourself looking down the list of titles in the periodical index under this topic. What word or words would you try to spot in the titles that would tell you to search out that particular magazine article? Write those words after ''2'' below. You have just identified the *Main Concepts* within your problem or question. Beneath the word you wrote after ''1,'' write synonyms either from your list or those located by using a thesaurus. Do the same for ''2.'' Check your words carefully. Nouns will work much better than adjectives as terms to enter into the CD-ROM data base. Now go to your CD-ROM data base and conduct your search using the words (terms) from this sheet.

1. _____   2. _____
   _____   _____
   _____   _____

MODULE 3 Analysis

Objective

To have students use different resources to develop skills in critical reading of written material.

Activity

Students will read about their individual topic where they located it the previous day in three or four different reference sources (encyclopedia, special encyclopedia, yearbook, handbook, etc.) checking carefully in the indexes under each topic written on their list. Students will look for (and add to their diary or log):

1. What are the commonly accepted facts or data on the topic?
2. What discrepancies in facts or data are in the reference?
3. What dates, names, and events are repeated in each reference?
4. List questions you have about the topic after reading in each reference.

Assessment

If the search has been thorough and honest, most students will have a better understanding of their topic and will be eager to locate further information on one or two aspects of the topic. In other words, they will have narrowed their topic from volcanoes in general to volcanoes in the United States, as an example.

MODULE 4 Using the Periodical Index
Objective
To introduce the periodical index to locate current or updated information on the topic.
Activity
Still using the list of synonyms, technical, broad, and related terms developed in Module 1, students consult the *Reader's Guide to Periodical Literature* under the various terms or topics. Students locate ten possible articles. The articles are located and read. Articles that are not useful or informative are replaced by others so that a total of ten articles are read and notes taken for use in the writing of the paper. Notes are taken on 4 X 6 cards with the correct bibliographic entry placed on a card by itself. One statement or fact is written on each card with a notation of the name and page of the magazine.
Assessment
The teacher returns the cards on the ten periodical articles with comments and suggestions.

MODULE 5 Location of Available Books
Objective
To have students use the card catalog to locate books cited in the resources that they have already read and to locate books that are on the topic.
Activity
Using the list of broad topics, related topics, and synonyms developed in Module 1, students look up each subject, carefully noting which books are available. Students skim the books once they are located, reading at length only those sections that give them additional information for their paper. Notes are taken as with the magazines. Students should also be encouraged to use their local public or academic libraries.
Assessment
The teacher continues to check the student's "diary" or "log" of references read, as well as to take note of the bibliographic cards being accumulated.

MODULE 6 Collection of Data and Information for the Paper
Objective
To have students locate needed information or data and take notes for a comprehensive research paper.
Activity
This module will take several days. Students should reread all the notes that they have taken. Notes should answer the following:
1. Biographical information about all important people dealing with topic.
2. Meanings of all new words that are encountered, including technical terms.

3. All questions that came to mind after doing Module 2 on analysis should be answered.
4. All cross-references should be checked.
5. All discrepancies in facts or data noted in sources should be explained or settled.

If the above questions are not answered, students consult their subject bibliography for possible sources of information that will assist them in the location of the answers. They continue to take notes and read on their topic.

Assessment
The teacher works individually with all students assisting them in deciding the gaps in their literature that must be filled in so that all necessary information and data will be collected prior to beginning their writing.

MODULE 7 Preparing an Outline
Objective
To have students develop an outline for writing the research paper.
Activity
Students will consider carefully the data collected on the topic and organize the information in a logical fashion so that the paper will present the information in a clear, concise, and logical manner. Usually students do this by shuffling their cards into subject piles.
Assessment
A proposed outline of the paper will be handed in for the teacher to grade and make suggestions.

MODULE 8 Developing a Rough Draft
Objective
To have students write the first draft of the paper from the outline developed using the note cards.
Activity
Students write the paper, introduction, body, and conclusion—paragraph by paragraph—working from the piles of note cards they have.
Assessment
The teacher checks the progress of all students as they are developing their rough drafts, giving suggestions as the work progresses.

MODULE 9 The Bibliography and Footnoting of the Paper
Objective
To have students develop the bibliography and the footnotes for the paper.
Activity
Students go through their rough draft with their note cards, putting in the footnotes as instructed by the teacher. The students' main bibliography cards are put in alphabetical order so that they are ready to be typed or written up for the bibliography.

Assessment

The teacher returns the rough drafts (which have complete bibliographical notes) with suggestions and corrections.

MODULE 10 Editing the Final Paper
Objective

To have students rewrite the paper using the suggestions and corrections given by the teacher so that a good research paper is produced.

Activity

Students rewrite as directed. Students also check and recheck all footnotes and bibliographic information.

Assessment

The teacher evaluates the overall progress that students have made through each of the modules. The final papers are graded.

Appendix 8
Assessment of Inservice Needs in Reading

SECTION ONE
Please complete the following:
1. Present position (check most appropriate)
   _____ A. Classroom teacher
   _____ B. Administrator or supervisor
   _____ C. Other. Explain:
2. Course or content area in which most teaching time is spent: _____
   _____ .
3. Grade with which you spend most of your teaching time: _____ .
4. Years of teaching experience: _____ .
5. Number of courses in: Developmental reading _____ .
   Corrective or remedial reading _____ .
6. Number of inservice programs in reading you have attended: _____ .
7. Please rate each of the following types of inservice on this scale:
   1—preferred, 2—acceptable, 3—unacceptable.

   a. Lecture   _____   f. Teacher centers   _____
   b. Illustrated lecture   _____   g. Visitations to other
   c. Demonstrations   _____   programs   _____
   d. Workshops   _____   h. Supervision from
   e. Simulation   _____   local reading re-
      activities   source personnel   _____

8. On the following time-place matrix, please indicate your willingness to attend reading inservice programs. Fill in each square using this scale:
   1—almost always, 2—usually, 3—sometimes, 4—seldom, 5—rarely

	Inservice in our school or neighboring school	Inservice anywhere within district or within 30 miles	Inservice outside district beyond 30 miles
After school	a	b	c
Saturdays	d	e	f
Professional days	g	h	i
Released time	j	k	l

From Sheila M. Allen and Robert D. Chester, "A Needs Assessment Instrument for Secondary Reading Inservice," *Journal of Reading* 21 (March 1978): 489–492.

Directions for Sections Two and Three

Column I. (Important Practices) Please rate each of the items in both Sections Two and Three as to how essential they are to your teaching. Use the scale below and place your responses in Column I.

1—essential	4—of little importance
2—important	5—of no importance
3—of moderate importance	6—lack of familiarity

Column II. (Present Practices) A variety of circumstances (e.g., lack of time, resources, training) may interfere with the use of skills and techniques which are considered important. What teachers consider important may not be what they can practice. To help us understand present classroom practices, please go through the items in both Sections Two and Three in terms of your present classroom practices and rate them on the frequency scale below. Place your responses in Column II.

A—almost always	D—rarely
B—often	E—never
C—sometimes	F—not applicable

Column III. (Priority of Need) Finally, to indicate your priorities for Reading Inservice, please rate each item in both Sections Two and Three on a scale of 1–5 using the classifications below. Place your responses in Column III.

1—high priority	4—not very important
2—important	5—of no importance
3—of moderate importance	

SECTION TWO Techniques and Strategies	I Important Practices	II Present Practices	III Priority of Needs
1. Determination of the reading levels of material			
2. Identification and selection of appropriate instructional materials			
3. Identification and selection of appropriate supplementary materials			
4. Identification, use, and interpretation of standardized tests for **assessing** and **interpreting** of standardized tests for assessing student potential			

SECTION TWO—*Cont.* Techniques and Strategies	I Important Practices	II Present Practices	III Priority of Needs
5. Identification and use of informal techniques for assessing student potential			
6. Determination of students' reading interests and attitudes			
7. Determination of strategies for dealing with disabled readers			
8. Determination of strategies for dealing with superior students			
9. Determination of strategies for dealing with divergent interests and attitudes			
10. Provision for individualizing instruction (e.g., small groups)			
11. Determination and development of appropriate reading objectives			
12. Utilization of various questioning techniques			
13. Development of motivational strategies for the classroom			
14. Identification of strategies for teaching specific subject skills related to reading (e.g., graphs, maps, diagrams)			

SECTION THREE Skill Development	I Important Practices	II Present Practices	III Priority of Needs
1. Provision for vocabulary skills development			
2. Provision for comprehension skills development			
3. Provision for the development of critical reading			

SECTION THREE
Skill Development

	I Important Practices	II Present Practices	III Priority of Needs
4. Instruction in study skills			
5. Instruction in research and reference skills			
6. Provision for the development of rate and flexibility			
7. Provision for the development of word recognition skills			

Appendix 9
United Nations Plan for Social Studies

Objectives: The students will demonstrate:

    a. increased writing skills;
    b. increased knowledge of current affairs of other places;
    c. appreciation for parliamentary/democratic skills;
    d. ability to make friends with foreigners;
    e. appreciation for cultural diversity.

Materials needed:
    a. Large modern wall maps of the continents
    b. Collection of maps suitably sized for xeroxing so that as particular areas are studied each student has a pertinent map
    c. Individual folders, one per student, to keep notes in.

Method:
    a. Begin term by briefing students on U.N., its history and purpose (keeping the peace), its units such as Security Council, General Assembly, Court, Secretary-General, World Bank.

S
T
E
P
    b. Assign a country to each student to represent at a classroom U.N. It is the job of each student to write to their country in order to get as much information as possible to present to the class. Teacher should assist with letter format, obtaining of addresses.

\#
    c. Assign students to various parts of the U.N. according to their countries. For example: France, China, U.K., U.S.A., U.S.S.R. are Security Council and others are General Assembly.

1
    d. Countries' delegates vote to select Secretary-General.
    e. Teacher briefs Secretary-General on organizing for smoothness.
    f. Teacher videotapes proceedings.

a. Pick a topic such as the Ethiopian Famine and have the students study with news magazines, newspapers, encyclopedias, TV news shows, etc. Using class time, prepare the students for discussion of this issue in the classroom U.N.

b. Take two days and hit the issue hard. First day various countries will express opinions. (Ideally, of course, students assigned one of the subject countries will have a reply to their letter and will be able to address the U.N. as an expert.) On the second day the Secretary-General should direct the Security Council to move for a vote from the General Assembly as to what should be done. Perhaps the countries will direct the Security Council to put the World Bank on the matter. The range of options is exceedingly wide.

c. Teacher videotapes proceedings.

These exercises are meant to be an ongoing exercise in Current Affairs. Every week the U.N. should meet. Doing this for two days weekly the students will be encouraged frequently to watch the news, study the paper, etc., so as to be able to choose for themselves what to work at.

It is imperative to switch membership from time to time on the Security Council and of the Secretary-General. Widest participation of students is the goal.

As responses from the foreign countries come in, those "authors" will report to the U.N.

As noted above, the teacher videotapes all proceedings. After an issue has been addressed, the videotape is played back for the students. It should serve to sharpen them for the next issue to be addressed, and it also should prove to be a fine method of closure to a busy week's agenda. Students enjoy watching themselves too.

Note. At a Middle School in Guam, proceedings were kept in the form of notes. While the students are issued folders for this it may become cumbersome without teacher-originated note facilitators.

Bibliography

Part I

Related
Monographs
Published by the
International
Reading
Association,
Newark, Delaware

Asheim, Lester; Baker, Philip; and Mathews, Virginia H.; eds. *Reading and Successful Living: The Family School Partnership.* 1983.

Cheyney, Arnold B. *Teaching Reading Skills Through the Newspaper.* 1984

Ciani, Alfred J., ed. *Motivating Reluctant Readers.* 1981.

Cowen, John E. *Teaching Reading Through the Arts.* 1983.

Dupuis, Mary M., ed. *Reading in the Content Areas: Research for Teachers.* 1983.

Earle, Richard. *Teaching Reading and Mathematics.* 1976.

Farr, Roger, and Carey, Robert F. *Reading: What Can Be Measured.* 1986.

Flood, James, ed. *Promoting Reading Comprehension.* 1984.

Flood, James, ed. *Understanding Reading Comprehension: Cognition Language and the Structure of Prose.* 1984.

Gentile, Lance M. *Using Sports and Physical Education to Strengthen Reading Skills.* 1980.

Graham, Kenneth G., and Robinson, H. Alan. *Study Skills Handbook: A Guide for All Teachers.* 1984.

Harker, W. John. *Classroom Strategies for Secondary Reading.* 2d ed. 1985.

Irwin, Judith W. *Understanding and Teaching Cohesion Comprehension.* 1986.

Labuda, Michael, ed. *Creative Reading for Gifted Learners: A Design for Excellence.* 1985.

Langer, Judith A., and Smith-Burke, M. Trika, ed. *Reader Meets Author—Bridging the Gap.* 1982.

Lundstrum, John, and Taylor, Bob. *Teaching Reading in the Social Studies.* 1978.

Mason, George E.; Blanchard, Jay S.; and Daniel, Danny B. *Computer Applications in Reading.* 2d ed. 1983.

Moore, David W.; Readence, John E.; and Rickelman, Robert J. *Prereading Activities for Content Area Reading and Learning.* 2d ed. 1989.

Nagy, William E. *Teaching Vocabulary to Improve Reading Comprehension.* (with the National Council of Teachers of English) 1988.

Page, Glenda; Elkins, John; and O'Connor, Barrie; eds. *Diverse Needs: Creative Approaches.* 1979.

Reed, A. *Comics to Classics: A Parent's Guide to Books for Teens and PreTeens.* 1988.

Samuels, S. Jay, and Pearson, P. David. *Changing School Reading Programs.* 1988.

Thelen, Judy. *Improving Reading in Science.* 2d ed. 1984.

Glossary

accountability   The responsibility of educators to do their jobs well and to provide measurable results to show the success of the educational endeavor.

acronyms   Words formed from the first letters of several words, e.g., NATO, WASP.

adaptability   Determining appropriate rate and changing it to meet different situations and purposes.

adolescence   The period of life from puberty to maturity terminating legally at the state of majority.

advance organizers   Introductory material written at a higher level of abstraction than the reading assignment. Advance organizers may be used with unfamiliar, new material in some perspective or may relate new material to previously learned ideas.

affect   A measure of a person's emotional response to any situation (feelings, interests, attitudes already learned). As contrasted to *cognition* (knowing and understanding), *affect* measures personal responses to whatever is read.

affective domain   Those human interactions that are measured by feelings, emotions, values, interests, attitudes. The affective domain includes students' enthusiasm or boredom, involvement, or noninvolvement in everyday teaching activity.

affixes   Prefixes and suffixes attached to root words.

alliteration   Repetition of the beginning consonant.

amelioration   Words that used to have a negative meaning and now have a positive one.

anaphora   The use of a word as a substitute for a preceding word or group of words.

assonance   Repetition of the same vowel sound.

bibliotherapy   The use of selected books for their therapeutic effect on students who have personal problems.

bottom-up processing   A sequence of events, commencing with the sensation of print on the retina, detecting and combining these into words, organizing syntactically into phrases, associating, reasoning, and storing meaning.

brain growth spurts   Specific age spans when the brain develops very rapidly.

chunking   Forming groups of words into discrete syntactical units, enabling readers to read ideas instead of individual words.

cinquain   Five-line poem with specific limitations, used here as a summary technique.

cloze   A measure of ability to restore omitted words in a message by carefully reading the remaining text.

cognition   Knowing; gaining knowledge through either firsthand or vicarious experience.

cognitive domain   All the learning that has to do with acquiring the academic content of the curriculum.

cognitive map   A diagram that gives students a visual overview of the structure of a chapter or unit. The purpose is to help clarify relationships among words that represent key concepts. It provides a framework to which new information or concepts can be added or subsumed.

collateral reading   Reading material related to the main topic or theme being studied which supports, broadens, or enriches the experience of the reader.

context clue   Identification of a new word in context by anticipation of its meaning from the other words and ideas adjacent to it.

criterion   A standard by which a test may be judged; a set of scores, ratings, etc. (Plural form is *criteria.*)

developmental tasks   A term used to indicate the specific responsibility that an individual faces at certain life stages in order to be a well-adjusted individual. Developmental tasks evolve as physical, social, and motivational maturity takes place within the individual.

diagnosis   Procedures for determining student characteristics and problems to facilitate planning a course of study.

discourse analysis   A study of the function and structure of language units. This includes passages longer than a sentence and relationships between sentences.

divergent thinking   Requesting, accepting, and encouraging the forming of many different solutions to a given problem. (How many different uses can you think of for the bricks we use for building?)

etymology   The study of word origins.

euphemism   A pleasant term for something considered unpleasant.

expository   Found in texts, a type of writing that sets forth meaning or intent, explaining and defining information.

extrinsic motivation   Behaviors directed toward achievement in anticipation of an overt reward.

figurative language   Figures of speech (simile, metaphor, irony, hyperbole, personification, synecdoche, oxymoron, metonymy) that create vivid mental pictures.

functionally illiterate   One who is unable to read at a fourth-grade level or above.

glossing   The technique of using marginal notes of explanation to improve comprehension, directing the reader's attention to both content and process.

grade equivalent   The grade level for which a given score is the estimated value: a 5.7 is the seventh month of fifth grade.

individualized educational program (IEP)   A lesson plan for any student that includes objectives, methodology, specific curriculum changes, and any classroom adjustments. IEPs are required by P.L. 94–142 for all exceptional students.

individualized reading   A method of teaching reading based on self-seeking, self-selection, and self-pacing in which teachers plan individual conferences with each student. Records of testing, diagnosing, and teaching are kept.

informal diagnosis   Any nonstandardized measure teachers administer to students to judge or evaluate their ability to handle text material.

intrinsic motivation   Behaviors directed toward achievement based on a personal, internal drive or wish to succeed.

inquiry   Similar to the scientific method, it is an inductive process where students actively develop generalizations about phenomena.

learning center   An area within a classroom with materials provided for following preset directions for meeting predefined objectives. Such centers provide for different ability levels and student self-checking.

lexical complexity   Vocabulary level of difficulty.

mainstreaming   Provision in Public Law 94–142 for the education of the handicapped, that all students who can profit from doing so must be accommodated in a regular classroom for some part of the school day.

mature reader   One who has mastered the basic "how to read" skills and has developed higher-level skills, attitudes, and behavior in reading.

metaphor   A figure of speech in which a comparison is implied by analogy but is not stated, as, *He has a heart of stone.*

morpheme   The smallest unit of meaning in words.

motivation   The forces that work within us to arouse and direct behavior. The inner force that causes us to do the things we do.

nonverbal communication   Messages sent by means other than the use of words: smiling, voice tones, distance, eye contact, body posture.

norm-referenced test   A standardized test in which a given student's performance is compared with the performance of others of similar age and educational achievement.

norms   Typical or average performances for students at given ages or grade levels on any predefined skills. Individuals perform below, at, or above the norm for their age or grade.

onomatopoeia   Words that imitate sounds; setting a mood through sound.

oxymoron   A figure of speech where words of almost opposite meaning are used together for effect.

pejoration   Words that once had a positive meaning now have a negative connotation.

percentile   A point on a scale of scores in a distribution below which a given percent of scores occur; 38 percent of the scores are below the thirty-eighth percentile, for example.

phoneme   The smallest speech sound unit.

prefix   A syllable before the root word that usually changes the meaning, as in *im*possible.

proposition level   Comprehending longer discourse, as opposed to word level comprehension.

proxemics   The way individuals use personal space.

Public Law 94–142   A federal law passed in 1975 that mandates that all handicapped learners must have optimum educational opportunity.

rate adaptability   The ability to adjust rate of reading according to the purpose for reading and the difficulty of the text material.

readability   The level of difficulty of a book or article as measured by formulas or checklists; the difficulty or ease with which material is read.

root   A basic word from which new words are developed by the addition of suffixes or prefixes.

scanning   A rapid search for specific details.

schemata   A series of ideas or concepts in a structure or framework into which information can be assimilated or categorized. (Singular form is *schema*.)

schematic organizers   A type of advance organizer that takes the form of a diagram, flowchart, table, or map.

schwa   An unaccented vowel. Written as an upside down *e;* has the sound of "uh" as in *a*bout.

semantics   The study of meanings, especially in language. Semantics studies meanings of words as opposed to etymology, which studies origin of words.

sentence combining   A technique whereby basic sentences can be syntactically manipulated or combined into lengthier, more complex sentences.

simile   Direct comparison using *like* or *as*.

simulation   Represents artificially a real experience, putting together a contrived series of activities to approximate a situation or process as closely as possible.

skimming   A very rapid form of overviewing a selection to get the gist, skipping over unneeded information.

standardized test   A test normed on a stratified sample of the population so that performance scores can be compared with all others who took the same test.

stanine   One of the steps in a nine-point scale of normalized standard scores with a mean of five and a standard deviation of two.

story grammar   A grammar that delineates relationships between episodes in stories and makes possible the setting of rules for generating new stories.

structural analysis   Analysis of words by affixes or roots.

structured overview   A visual or verbal representation of key vocabulary and concepts, similar to an advance organizer in that it helps to relate pertinent new information to existing knowledge in a hierarchical form. It differs in that students participate in its construction.

study guide   A series of problems, directions, or thought-provoking questions given to students to encourage efficient study habits and mastery of subject matter.

suffixes   Affixes attached to the ends of words.

survival literacy   Ability to perform reading tasks necessary for daily living.

syllabication   Division of words into syllables to assist in word identification.

synonym A word that has the same, or nearly the same, meaning as another word.

syntactic complexity The difficulty level of sentence structure or writing style.

syntax The grammar of the language, that is, the rules by which sentence structure is regulated.

synthesis The process of putting together information from various sources in a new, creative way, a higher level of comprehension.

taxonomy A classification in a hierarchy of an area of study or body of knowledge specifying its components and their relationships.

three-level guide A study guide prepared at three differentiated levels of difficulty to guide students through the study of a lesson or unit.

top-down processing Using abstract knowledge structure to direct attention to print in a selective way. (Going from *whole* to *parts*.)

transescence The stage in youth beginning prior to the onset of puberty and extending through the early stages of adolescence.

verbalism Word calling without comprehending the meaning of the words.

word attack Analyzing a new word into known elements for the purpose of identifying it and discovering meaning.

Author Index

Subject Index

Effect/cause, 391
Effective rate, 110–11
    reading rates, 123
Encyclopedias, 357–58
English, 385, 399–401
English debate, 332
Enumeration of steps in a process,
    391
ERIC CD-Rom, 356–57
Ethics, values, cultural heritage, 10
Etymology, 152
Euphemism, 157
Explanation of a concept, 390
Expository paragraphs, 207

Facets of language, 150
Fairy tales and folklore
    bibliographies, 373
Flexible grouping, 329
Following directions, 392
Forcast, 76
Foreign country bibliographies, 374
Foreign languages, 288, 385, 401
Formats for teaching, 280–90
Four D's, 18
Fry readability graph, 70–72
Functional illiteracy, 4

Gates-MacGinitie test, 88, 91
Generalizations, 393
Gifted, 277–78, 374
Glossing, 325–26
Grade equivalent scores, 89
Graphics, 241
Greek combining forms, 384
Group retellings, 289
Grouping, 280–84, 289
Guided writing procedure (GWP),
    331–32

Handicapped bibliographies, 375
Health, 375, 385, 401
Home economics, 386, 390,
    391–95, 401
Hypothesis-testing, 318–19

Indexes, 348–50, 351, 367
Individualized/personalized
    learning, 284
Industrial Arts, 361, 386, 391,
    396–97, 401
IEP, 279–80
Informal diagnosis, 88

Information-centered texts, 396
Inquiry, 310, 313
Interests, 40, 103–5
Interpreting
    graphic information, 241–54
    special symbols, 395
Iowa silent reading test, 88, 91

Kernel Distance Theory, 68
KWL strategy, 332–33

Language Experience Approach,
    284–85
Latin combining forms, 384
Learning centers, 285–88
Learning principles, 301–2
Lexical complexity, 68
Limited English Proficiency (LEP),
    46–48
Listening, 227–31
Literary terms, 158
Locating information, 223–27

Mainstreaming, 278
Mapping, 240–41
Marshall's readability checklist, 78
Mathematics, 375, 386, 399, 401
Mature reader, 15–16
Maze, 321
Mechanical rate devices, 135–36
Memory, 258
Metacognition, 191
Metaphors, 156
Motivation, 33–38
Multiple meanings, 387
Music, 361, 390, 401
"My Father's Hands," 6

NAEP, 14
Narrative writing, 208
Nonverbal communication, 54–56
Notes facilitator, 267–68
Notetaking, 235–40
Nouns of multitude, 177
Numerical word elements, 164

OPIN, 171
Organizational patterns study
    guide, 323–24
Organizing, 227–41
    information, 227–41
    materials, 275–76
    space, 274–75
    time, 274–75

Outlining, 231–35
Oxymoron, 157

PARS, 266
Patterns of writing, 388–96
Pejoration, 155
Percentiles, 89
Periodicals, 346–48, 359
Phonics, 164–66
Physical education, 361, 379, 385,
    389, 401
Pivotal words, 160
Poetry and rhymes bibliographies,
    377
Post reading, 304, 327–34
PQRST, 265
Practice rate strategies, 133–34
Prereading, 302, 304–22
Primary practices, 413–15
Problem solving, 290, 394
Process-centered texts, 396, 399
Public law 94–142, 278–80

Questions, 310–13, 314–18
    types, 312

Rate adaptability, 110
    factors affecting, 126, 130
    increasing effectiveness, 130–34
Rauding scale of prose difficulty,
    79–80
Raygor's readability estimator, 76
Readability definition, 67
    format/print factor, 68
    historical, 69
    personal factors, 67
    shorter passages, 74–75
    stylistic age, 81
    textual factors, 67
Reader response, 56–58
Reading
    insights, 15
    process definition, 412
REAP, 266–67
Recreation, 385, 401
Reference sources, 345–46
Reluctant readers bibliographies,
    378
ReQuest, 320
Retention, 259

San Diego Quick Assessment,
    92–93
Scanning, 131–32
Schema/Schemata, 17

Schematic organizers, 308
Science, 360, 379, 386, 388, 391,
    395–96, 399, 401
Search-insert-verify, 172
Search strategy, 357, 360–62
Similes, 156
Simulation/role play, 331
Singletree-Doubletree
    Anachronism, 408–11
Skimming, 131
Slicing, 320–21
SMOG formula, 70, 72
Social/emotional dimensions,
    53–56
Social studies, 360, 379–80, 386,
    389, 391, 393–94, 396, 401
SQRQCQ, 265
SQ3R, 265–66
Standardized tests, 88–91
    grade equivalent, 89
    misuses, 91
    percentiles, 89
    reliability, 88
    stanines, 90
    validity, 88

Stanines, 90
STEP, 88, 91
Storytelling bibliographies, 381
Structural analysis, 163–64
Structured comprehension, 318
Structured overview, 308–10
Study habits, 254
Study skills, 15
Study strategies, 265–68
Survival literacy, 4
Syllabication, 165, 384
Synonym clustering, 172
Syntactic complexity, 68

Talk-through, 169
Taxonomies, 196
Testing, 261–64
Textbooks, 340–41
Text structure, 210
Thesaurus, 168–69
Thinking, 211–14
    skills, 14–15
    types, 313

Three-level study guide, 322
Time schedules, 256–58
Tonjes interest inventory (TII), 104
Transescence, 48
Typographic clues, 324–25

Values, 10, 41–46
Verbalism, 387
Vocabulary
    levels, 159
    problems, 151
    receptive/expressive, 151

Word-for-the-day, 170
Wordmanship, 175
W.R.A.T., 92
Writing, 205–6, 208, 211–14
WPM, 110

Yearbooks, 358